A Complete Guide to the Buddhist Path

A Complete Guide
TO THE BUDDHIST PATH

by *Khenchen Konchog Gyaltshen*

edited by Khenmo Trinlay Chödron

SNOW LION PUBLICATIONS
ITHACA, NEW YORK

Snow Lion Publications
P.O. Box 6483
Ithaca, New York 14851 USA
607-273-8519
www.snowlionpub.com

ISBN 978-1-55939-342-3

Library of Congress Cataloging-in-Publication Data:

Konchog Gyaltsen, Khenchen.
A complete guide to the Buddhist path / by Khenchen Konchog Gyaltshen ;
edited by Khenmo Trinlay Chödron.
    p. cm.
Includes bibliographical references and index.
ISBN-13: 978-1-55939-342-3 (alk. paper)
ISBN-10: 1-55939-342-4 (alk. paper)
 1. Don-grub-chos-rgyal, 'Bri-guṅ Skyabs-mgon. Bslab bya nor bu'i baṅ
mdzod sñiṅ gtam brgya pa raṅ la bskul ba'i gros 'debs. 2. Spiritual life—Buddhism.
I. Emmerich, Delia. II. Don-grub-chos-rgyal, 'Bri-guṅ Skyabs-mgon.
Bslab bya nor bu'i baṅ mdzod sñiṅ gtam brgya pa raṅ la bskul ba'i gros 'debs.
English. III. Title.
 BQ5660.D6733K66 2010
 294.3—dc22

Designed and typeset by Gopa & Ted2, Inc.

: Table of Contents

DRIKUNG KYABGON CHETSANG

I AM DELIGHTED to know that Khenchen Konchog Gyaltshen has written *A Complete Guide to the Buddhist Path*, and that fortunately it is now coming into the light of publication. The text is a commentary on *The Jewel Treasury of Advice*, which was composed by Drikung Bhande Dharmaradza (1704–1754), the reincarnation of Drikung Dharmakirti. I am very happy that English readers will be able to benefit from it, since the commentary is written in English. Furthermore, because it is written in a manner that is easy to understand, it will reach far and wide.

This book contains the complete teachings of Buddhism, from the very basic, up to the very profound trainings of the Mahayana and Vajrayana systems, including the Six Yogas of Naropa. The text is based on the ground of the Six Perfections, which are generosity, ethical discipline, patience, perseverance, meditative concentration, and wisdom mind. From that ground, the tree of the Vajrayana blossoms with the flowers of the Six Yogas of Naropa: the practices of tummo, clear light, dream yoga, the illusory body, phowa, and bardo. The practice of all these teachings, step by step, will lead us one day to bear the fruit of complete enlightenment.

No matter how much confusion we suffer from, there are infinite opportunities for all of us to practice the teachings of the great realized Lamas of Tibet. Since we are all born as human beings our power of intellectual capacity is much greater than that of other sentient beings. We have the great opportunity to cultivate the field of our heart, and grow all kinds of good qualities that ripen into a meaningful life. Everything lies in our hands, so don't miss your chance.

I therefore thank Khenchen Rinpoche and welcome his light of commentary to illuminate the teachings of our great Lamas, making them available to all.

May it benefit countless sentient beings.

With my prayers,
Drikung Kyabgon Chetsang

⁝ Editor's Preface

T HE *JEWEL TREASURY OF ADVICE, One Hundred Teachings from the Heart,* the root text on which this commentary is based, is commonly known as the *Hundred Verses of Advice,* even though it actually contains 103 numbered verses and twenty-eight introductory and preliminary verses. The first lines of the "Hundred Verses" are indexed toward the back of the book.

We have styled this book to match the root text verse by verse, with a separate, more or less stand-alone commentary following each stanza. Within each commentary, we have italicized words or phrases echoed from the relevant verse the first time they are mentioned. This was done in order to more clearly correlate the commentary with the verse.

We anticipated that readers might choose to read one or two verses at a time and then stop to contemplate them. So that each commentary is understandable as a complete thought, there is necessarily some repetition that would not have been included if this were a continuous narrative. In addition, some points were repeated in the original verses for emphasis or because the same subject is presented from different angles.

To aid readers who might be unfamiliar with Tibetan Buddhism, we included a glossary that contains short definitions of specialized terms and identifies the persons mentioned in the book. As a quick reference, there is also a glossary of the many enumerated lists that are so typical of Buddhist writings. Brief biographies of both authors—Drigung Bhande Dharmaradza, who wrote the root verses, and Khenchen Konchog Gyaltshen, who wrote the commentary— were added to inspire confidence and devotion in the reader. Finally, there is an annotated bibliography of the writings mentioned that you may find useful as you pursue further study.

Thank you for your interest in the holy Dharma and this text. May it resolve your doubts and inspire you to attain complete enlightenment for the benefit of all!

Khenmo Trinlay Chödron

: Introduction

BUDDHISM, or the sublime Dharma, was born in India about 2,500 years ago. The founder of Buddhism, the prince Siddhartha, was born the son of King Shuddhodana, who was a learned and powerful ruler in Northern India. Until he was twenty-nine years old, Prince Siddhartha enjoyed the best that palace life had to offer and was well schooled in every aspect of learning. Since he was the king's only son, the king had high expectations that the prince would live out his life in the kingdom and rule the country after his enthronement.

But the prince was deeply stirred by the suffering he saw, the suffering shared by all sentient beings. Unable to enjoy the power and luxury of the kingdom any longer, he began to investigate whether beings could be freed from their sufferings. With great courage, he renounced the kingdom and assumed responsibility to seek the highest truth.

For six years, he traveled from place to place and met many different teachers and meditators. Not satisfied with that, he continued to thoroughly investigate and contemplate suffering and its cause using his own critical insight. He achieved a very profound samadhi, an all-pervading state, and thought he had attained enlightenment. But the buddhas of the ten directions appeared to him and said, "This state is not the final realization nor is it complete enlightenment." So, he proceeded to Bodh Gaya and meditated under the Bodhi Tree.

At early dawn on Vesak Day, he achieved complete and perfect enlightenment at the age of thirty-five. From then on, he was known as "the Buddha," the fully awakened one. At that time he declared, "I have found the stainless ambrosia of sublime Dharma that is profound; complete peace; free from elaboration; luminous; the uncompounded essence. This is the universal truth that is free from all confusion and all suffering."

The Buddha taught this Dharma for forty-five years, sharing his wisdom with hundreds and thousands of human and non-human beings. These trainees themselves achieved the various stages of enlightenment. Thus, he taught the complete Dharma teachings comprising both the sutra and tantra systems of practice as was suitable for the disciples. Over the following centuries, these teachings spread throughout India and many other countries. Among these, Buddhism arrived in Tibet in the seventh century.

Many great translators traveled from Tibet to India, where they learned from great masters. Over time, they translated the complete body of the Buddha's teachings, and many great scholars and realized masters were produced. So it continues until the present time. Currently, there are four great lineages: Nyingma, Kagyu, Sakya and Gelug. This presentation encompasses the teachings of the various traditions that comprise the Kagyu lineage.

Lord Gampopa, Milarepa's chief disciple and a particularly revered Kagyu lineage master, is respected by masters of all the lineages because he was highly learned and accomplished in meditation practices. He studied and perfectly practiced the teachings from three lineages in combination:

- ▸ the Profound Madhyamaka View lineage, as well as the special bodhicitta practice, passed down from the Buddha to Manjushri to Nagarjuna, and so forth
- ▸ the Vast Action lineage of the gradual training of the mind through bodhicitta, and the Madhyamaka system transmitted by Buddha Maitreya to Asanga and so forth
- ▸ the Vajrayana system of tantric study and practice, with the special Mahamudra teachings and Six Yogas of Naropa that originated with the Buddha's dharmakaya form, Vajradhara, and passed down successively through Tilopa, Naropa, Marpa, and Milarepa

Thus, Lord Gampopa thoroughly studied and practiced all aspects of knowledge passed down through Atisha's Kadampa lineage as well as Milarepa's lineage. In a single lifetime, he was established in the enlightened state—the perfection of view, meditation, and action—and passed all these teachings to the Kagyu lineages. Lord Jigten Sumgön incorporated them into the Drigung Kagyu tradition and explained them in his texts *One Thought* (Tib.: *Gong Chig*), *Heart Essence of the Mahayana Teachings* (Tib.: *Ten Nying*), and many others. The author of *The Jewel Treasury of Advice* was one of Jigten Sumgön's spiritual successors.

When our most meaningful and precious possessions are collected together in a jewel treasury, we cherish it above all other wealth and never tire of looking at it. Like a jewel treasury, this text contains a collection of the most valuable essence of the Dharma teachings, beneficial both for those with a general interest in Buddhism and for serious practitioners. Jewels of Dharma have been gathered together here as pieces of advice for daily life and, especially, for the spiritual journey toward enlightenment. Even though *The Jewel Treasury of Advice* is a small text, it maps out the complete teachings of Buddhism from beginning to end, from the four foundations to the perfection of buddhahood. This essence of the authentic teachings is called "pith instruction"—the essential points of both sutra and tantra, as well as their commentaries. Those who want to study and practice Buddhism sincerely will find this an indispensable guide that they can read over and over again.

The present text is simple and goes right to the point, providing clear instruction on the practical meaning of Dharma and on meditation practice. Our reason to study and practice Buddhism is to free our mind from delusions. Advice like this prevents us from getting lost in illusions in the name of the study and practice of Buddhism. In the world of samsara, all sentient beings, including humans, must suffer from the afflictions (Skt.: *klesha*) such as greed, pride, hatred, and so forth. These different types of afflictions follow us through limitless lifetimes and always cause suffering. Everyone's instinctive nature is to want happiness and peace, but these afflictions don't allow it. Rather, they bring one suffering after another without end. These afflictions cannot be healed by taking medicines or by living a luxurious life. They will not age or get sick; they always stay as fresh and young as they are now. The most powerful laboratory cannot pinpoint these afflictions; only Dharma can precisely identify their nature and provide us with a method to purify them. Modern technology, machinery, and science cannot eliminate or purify the afflictions. The only way to weaken their power and eventually uproot them is through the study and practice of the precious Buddhadharma.

The root text is organized into two parts. The first part contains general advice for daily life—how to relate to others peacefully, how to associate within groups harmoniously, how to be honest and kind, how to be supportive of each other, and how to be sincere Dharma practitioners. The second part, which contains the hundred verses of advice, is more specifically for practitioners, particularly those practitioners who are very serious about studying and practicing and want to attain enlightenment or buddhahood. Realistically, if we want to attain enlightenment without facing any obstacles, we have to know what to do and how to do it. *The Jewel Treasury of Advice: One Hundred Teachings from the Heart* outlines what to expect and gives us very valuable counsel from the author's own experience of the reality of samsara and nirvana.

The teachings were given from the author's heart, the mandala of perfect wisdom and compassion, and are not just intellectual musings. They were written sincerely so that practitioners could understand what Dharma is about and how to practice it. We should, therefore, take this advice into our heart sincerely and implement it wholeheartedly in order to free ourselves from obscurations and from the suffering that we face.

Acknowledgments

The production of this book took a long time. Initially, I gave oral commentary on *The Jewel Treasury of Advice, One Hundred Teachings from the Heart* in many different places. Khenmo Trinlay Chödron took great pains to transcribe these talks and consolidate them into the form of a book. Ani Jampa, Ani Wangmo, Ani Pelmo, Ani Dadron, Eileen Feldman, and David Griffin provided sincere help as critical readers. Victoria Huckenpahler provided expert editorial assistance. Terry Barrett aided this effort by helping to translate the quotations from the *Heart Essence of the Mahayana Teachings* (Tib.: *Ten Nying*) and *Wish-granting Jewel* (Tib.: *Tsin-dha Mani*). I am especially grateful to my long-time friend and fellow translator, Rick Finney, who not only helped me translate the root verses, but who then went through this text thoroughly and contributed many insightful comments.

This book has materialized due to the interest in Dharma of our many affiliated Dharma centers, groups, and friends. I am grateful for all the support I have received while finishing this major project. I hope that this small contribution to human society will be of benefit to readers generally, and especially to serious practitioners.

Khenchen Konchog Gyaltshen
June 2007

The Jewel Treasury of Advice,
One Hundred Teachings from the Heart

by Drigung Bhande Dharmaradza

Introductory Verses

I give this advice as a reminder to myself.

THE AUTHOR, Drigung Bhande Dharmaradza (1704–1754), is known as the second Drigung Kyabgon Chungtsang. The first Chungtsang Rinpoche was called the Great Drigung Dharmakirti. Because he was enlightened, a mahasiddha, and a great scholar who was expert in many different types of knowledge, he was widely recognized as an incarnation of Saraha. In one of his vajra songs, Drigung Dharmakirti mentions, "There is not a single doubt that once I was the great Brahmin Saraha, forefather of all the eighty-four mahasiddhas." He was a contemporary of the fifth Dalai Lama, who respected him highly for his scholarship and accomplishment in meditation practice. Drigung Dharmakirti wrote commentaries on many different subjects, most notably on the *One Thought* and the *Heart Essence of the Mahayana Teachings*, which are the texts that contain the most profound teachings of Lord Jigten Sumgön. Many other great teachers also wrote commentaries on these texts. His complete writings have been collected into about fifteen large volumes.

Drigung Bhande Dharmaradza was Drigung Dharmakirti's reincarnation and was also a great teacher and scholar. A brief account of his life is included in this book. What Dharmaradza wrote here is a concise abridgment of the essence of the *One Thought*, the *Heart Essence of the Mahayana Teachings*, and *The Jewel Ornament of Liberation*.

The author starts the text as a reminder to himself to reduce his ego. This shows that he is modest, just a simple, grounded practitioner. It also indicates that he wrote as a meditation practice. This reminds us that as we study books, we also have to practice. In this way, we will be able to engage in meditation practices properly because we understand the meaning of the Dharma. The actual understanding of Dharma will only come from experience based in practice.

With one-pointed mind, I supplicate the supreme,
  victorious Ratna Shri
and the one who holds the name Bhadra,
the embodiment of all refuges.
Please grant your blessings so that I may actualize
  the life of the lama.

THE AUTHOR first pays homage to the lineage and his root lama in order to receive their blessings and dispel obstacles. *Ratna Shri* (Tib.: *Rinchen Pal*, Glory of the Precious One) refers to Lord Jigten Sumgön, who founded the Drigung Kagyu lineage in Tibet in the twelfth century. This precious lord was himself a buddha who came in human form to teach sentient beings. If we carefully read the histories of great masters, we can discover that there was no greater assembly of disciples than that of Jigten Sumgön. These disciples were not ordinary people who just heard teachings and left. They received the teachings and then fully dedicated their lives to retreat. It is said that during his lifetime and afterward, the mountains were covered with thousands of Drigung retreatants. Such a great teacher! He wrote many important books that are studied to this day, notably the *One Thought* and the *Heart Essence of the Mahayana Teachings*. His *Inner Teachings* were collected by his realized disciples into five volumes. All together, his teachings comprise approximately fifteen volumes, called the *Outer and Inner Teachings*. His disciple Sherab Jungne praised his teachings, saying:

> Pristine, pure virtue is like a snow-covered mountain.
> May it cause Ratna Shri's teachings to flourish in the ten
>   directions!
> May it fully dispel the darkness of ignorance of all beings
> and may they all attain the perfect primordial wisdom
>   of the Buddha!

Lord Jigten Sumgön was the reincarnation of Arya Nagarjuna, who lived in India in the second century C.E., about four hundred years after Lord Buddha attained parinirvana. Buddha Shakyamuni had prophesied his coming in many sutras, such as the *Lankavatara Sutra*. Nagarjuna was responsible for revitalizing Buddhism in general, but especially the Mahayana and Vajrayana. Some Buddhist schools say that the Mahayana teachings were not taught by Buddha, but rather by Nagarjuna. This is because he is the one who firmly re-established Mahayana Buddhism after it had nearly disappeared. As Nagarjuna's reincarnation, Lord Jigten Sumgön likewise firmly established Buddhism in Tibet—both in general and the Mahayana system in particular. His accomplishment was recognized by many great masters, such as Mipham, who said:

> You established, through the doors of study and practice,
> the methods of the Mahayana in this Land of Snows.
> The sun of your activities pervades the whole world.
> I bow down to you, Lord Jigten Sumgön.

Lord Jigten Sumgön has shown us a clear way to understand the reality of samsara and nirvana, so that we can have a clear mind about how to attain buddhahood and how to free ourselves from samsara. In an absolute way, he is the embodiment of the wisdom and compassion of all the buddhas. His life story has been briefly translated in the books *Prayer Flags*, *The Great Kagyu Masters*, and *Calling to the Lama from Afar*. It is important to read such biographies because they are not just stories but also contain profound Dharma teachings.

Bhadra refers to the author's root lama, Ratna Karma Bhadra, the second Drigung Kyabgon Chetsang. Saying that his root lama is the *embodiment of all the refuges* means that he attained perfect buddhahood and so embodies all three refuges—the Buddha, Dharma, and Sangha. His mind equals the Buddha's. Buddha taught the Dharma, so his speech is the embodiment of the Dharma. His body is that of the Sangha, those who practice successfully. Ratna Karma Bhadra perfected all the qualities of a buddha, so he is the embodiment of the Triple Gem. In this manner, the writer takes refuge.

To *actualize the life of the lama* means to become successful in the practice of the Dharma teachings and attain buddhahood. That is the life of the lama—to implement the practices in one's heart, to take the journey on the path to buddhahood successfully, to attain complete enlightenment, and to benefit all sentient beings.

I don't know much about the two ways of life
and have not studied the various classes of knowledge,
so I am not qualified to write these words of advice.
But because you, my close attendant, have asked me so
  persistently,
I will briefly set down whatever comes to mind.

WITH THIS VERSE, the author is again being modest by saying that he is not qualified to write these words of advice.

The *two ways of life* are religious and secular. Religious life is concerned with how to study and practice all these different methods taught in the Dharma. Secular life is about the day-to-day management of a society or a monastery.

The *various classes of knowledge* refers to all the things that are knowable, which are as countless as the stars in the sky. In brief, knowledge is categorized into ten well-known classes—five minor and five major.

The five minor classes of knowledge are

1. *performance*, meaning dance, story-telling, opera, historical plays, and so forth
2. *astrology*, the study of systems involving the stars and moon, including weather forecasting and horoscope calculations that reveal one's previous and next lives
3. *poetry*, understanding how to write with figures of speech—metaphors, similes, and so forth
4. *synonyms*, meaning the many names or labels used to describe the various aspects of phenomena. For example, there are more than thirty ways to refer to the sun, such as daybreak, friend of the lotus, jewel of the sky, and that which clears away the darkness. Earth can be called the holder of the jewel, basis for all, and so forth.
5. *composition*, the skill to write beautifully in verse and prose, to set words together in special ways.

The five major classes of knowledge are divided into four classes of knowledge that are common to all societies and religions, and a fifth class that is unique to Buddhist thought.

1. *Creative arts,* such as drawing and construction. This is a vast subject. All modern technologies are in this category. There are physical arts like painting, sculpture, architecture, computers, airplanes, trucks, buses, building, road construction, and driving. These are important bodies of knowledge and skill with which one can benefit many sentient beings. There are also verbal arts like melodious speech, and speaking true and constructive words. Mental arts include skill in meditation, keeping the mind in good shape, and putting it in the right place through training in meditation.

2. *Healing arts,* which include all the schools of medicine, both physical and mental. One studies how to make medicines from various materials like plants and rocks, as well as how to diagnose diseases and heal them. Through this knowledge, one can benefit many sentient beings, especially those who are sick physically or mentally.

3. *Linguistic arts,* which include knowing all the different kinds of languages and sounds. This is not limited only to human languages. Every sound has a meaning—even the noises of trees, rocks, water, and animals. By knowing these different languages, one can gain great skill in writing without mistakes in spelling or grammar. Great bodhisattvas can benefit all kinds of beings this way. For example, a vulture once flew over Lord Jigten Sumgön while he was meditating. He gave instructions to the flying vulture, who immediately landed and began meditating. There is also a famous account that tells of Milarepa establishing a deer and a dog in meditation practice.

4. *Logic or reasoning.* There is a reason for whatever exists. For example, if we do this, that will happen; this is happening because of that. Looking at the result, you will know the cause; looking at the cause, you will know the result. This skill is especially useful to dissolve confusion and misunderstanding. These days, sciences like subatomic physics and quantum theory would be included in this category. With these skills, one

can gain great insight into deeper meaning, so Buddhists value knowledge of reasoning.

5. *Metaphysics or inner meaning*, which is the study of mind. To understand the inner meaning of mind, we have to study the Buddhist teachings, where mind is the central topic. If we know mind well, this will give us a clear picture of how to free ourselves from unwanted suffering and create peace, happiness, wisdom, and compassion. If we are confused about its nature, mind is our worst enemy, bringing all suffering and delusion. Therefore, samsara and nirvana are a reflection, or manifestation, of mind. When mind is deluded and confused by the afflictions, the very nature of all-pervading emptiness wanders in the six realms of samsara. But when that delusion has been fully dissolved into primordial wisdom, everything is a buddha field, intrinsically pure and perfect.

Demonstrating his modesty a second time, Bhande Dharmaradza says that he is *not qualified to write these words of advice*. But actually, he is fully versed in all the different aspects of inner and outer knowledge, as we can see by what he writes in this text. He says this to demonstrate how to be modest, sincere, and down-to-earth.

Könchok Drakden was Bhande Dharmaradza's *close attendant*. He understood that Bhande Dharmaradza had great wisdom that could benefit himself and others, so he repeatedly requested the master to write this important pith instruction as advice for all sentient beings' benefit.

Whatever comes to mind. This shows that the author has such great wisdom and confidence that he writes spontaneously. When we write, we have to rewrite many times. First we make a draft, then a second one, then a third, and finally we check again to see if there are any more mistakes to correct. Here, Bhande Dharmaradza spontaneously writes down whatever comes to his mind, which means he expressed these teachings from his enlightened mind.

So in these two verses, the author has completed the requisite beginning of a text—paying homage and making a commitment to write the book. With the next verse, the body of the text begins.

General Advice

 A body endowed with leisure and fortune is the supreme basis,
*   which is difficult to find.*
You have entered into the precious teachings of the Buddha
and, especially, have heard the Vajrayana Dharma.
So don't waste your human life.
Cherish your practice.

THIS VERSE is concerned with one's precious human life, with the qualities of leisure and fortune, and how difficult it is to find them. *Leisure* means having time to study and practice the precious Dharma teachings. *Fortune* means having all the necessary conditions, like interest in the Dharma, texts to study, and access to teachers. These form the critical basis for freeing ourselves from delusion, the cause of suffering. They are the supreme basis for attaining enlightenment.

Directly or indirectly, we have a connection with the Buddhist path and have *entered into the precious teachings*. Something has caused us to become aware of the precious teachings of the Buddha. The teachings are precious because if we take them to heart and practice them sincerely, they will free us from all suffering; indeed, they are the *only* way to attain complete joy and happiness. In contrast, the deluded joy and happiness that we ordinarily strive for are temporary and don't last very long. Maybe we are happy today, but tomorrow we'll again experience suffering and confusion. Maybe we are balanced for a few moments, but then we go back to the same routine of samsara. The precious Dharma teachings give us an opportunity to uproot our delusions—all the afflictions—the very cause of our suffering. We cannot replace Dharma with other methods; therefore, the teachings are called *precious* and holy.

The word *Vajrayana*, the diamond-like vehicle, has become widely known in the world these days, but its corpus of translation and meditation practices are not complete everywhere. Until recently, they were barely known outside Tibet. Even when Buddhism existed in many other countries, the complete Vajrayana teachings, all four classes of tantra, were developed and taught only in Tibet. So it's quite rare to be able to hear and study these teachings. We who have contact with these teachings are so fortunate, but sometimes we take our good fortune for granted and don't pay much attention to them or appreciate them.

We cannot waste this life. Making a living is a part of survival for this life but not the most important part. We should regard Dharma practice as the most important part of life because it is the means, the complete method, to free ourselves from all suffering in this life and those yet to come. This is the reason why the author says to *cherish your practice*.

*According to the teachings of cause and example and so forth,
    leisure and fortune are difficult to find.*
*Even if one is born as a human, vast regions remain without
    the Dharma.*
Buddhas appear and teach the Dharma very rarely.
*In particular, it is barely possible to hear the teachings of secret
    mantra.*
Life doesn't stand still for even a moment.
*So think carefully, can you afford to waste this leisure and
    fortune?*

WE OFTEN HEAR that it is difficult to find a human body. Not just any human body, but a "precious" one that has contact with the Dharma teachings—that's what is difficult to obtain. There are descriptions of this in many books, such as *The Jewel Ornament of Liberation*. The Buddha himself gave this example:

> Suppose this entire world were an ocean. Beneath the ocean is a blind tortoise that comes up above the surface once every hundred years. On the water's surface is a yoke with one hole in the center being blown about by the winds, back and forth. It would be nearly impossible for the blind tortoise's head to meet with the hole in that piece of log. Yet that is easier—more likely—than to gain a precious human life.

It is common sense that everyone wishes to be free of all types of sufferings. So, if we utilize this life in the best way, it can give us total freedom from suffering. It can give us enlightenment—that's why it is so precious. In the world there are many different life forms such as animals and so forth. Some may be very clever, but if you tell them, "This is virtue and this is nonvirtue; avoid nonvirtue and practice virtue" or "This is samsara. One has to make effort to free oneself from it," they have no idea what you are talking about. But we human beings have a mind that can understand this, and that is very precious.

You can see how many beings there are in this world. Forget about hell realms and all that we don't see. Just think about human beings and animals, including all the birds, small bugs, and sea creatures. Among them, how many have the chance to study Dharma teachings? Among those of us who study and practice, who really look at the mind—how many are there, and how many are successfully practicing Dharma? Very few! This is the reason that meaningful human existence is said to be difficult to find.

Among all the practitioners, how many are enlightened? In this eon, one thousand buddhas are supposed to come, and it is said that four have already come. In our history, in more than 2,500 years, only Buddha Shakyamuni has appeared and taught. So the teachings that we study and practice now are extremely rare.

Why is this so? Basically, the cause for attaining a human body is moral ethics, such as the ten virtues. Briefly, these are

- three of the body: not taking life, not stealing, not engaging in sexual misconduct
- four of speech: not telling lies, not using divisive speech, not using harsh words, and not engaging in idle talk
- three of the mind: not coveting, not engaging in harmful thought, and not holding wrong views

Many texts mention that we must keep ethical discipline as the foundation for human existence. But as we know, it is not easy to practice the ten virtues. If we don't keep moral ethics, there is a strong possibility we will be born in the lower realms where there is no chance to study or practice the precious Dharma teachings. Not only that, there will be no peace even in this life. Since without ethical conduct it will not be easy to find a precious human life, bodhisattvas keep moral ethics purely so that in their next life they can again be born as humans where there are Dharma teachings.

In this life, ethical discipline refers to avoiding the ten nonvirtues and practicing the ten virtues. The ten virtues are the main cause for achieving human life. It is very important to understand them as the basis of *all* ethical discipline; all the other disciplines are built on this foundation. For example, on this basis, we practice the six paramitas and develop a pure aspiration to always meet with the precious Dharma teachings and attain enlightenment.

Look directly at yourself and see how much Dharma practice you are doing successfully. Be sincere. Watch the mind and see whether negative thoughts are diminishing every month or year, and whether positive thoughts are developing. It feels like the same thing year after year, doesn't it? That is why purifying our negative habits is said to be so difficult. With this precious human life we have every possibility, every opportunity, to free ourselves from all this if we make enough effort.

Secret mantra refers to the Vajrayana teachings. Because these teachings were not handed down through their own lineages, some Buddhists say that the Buddha did not teach them. They believe that Vajrayana is something Tibetans made up by mixing Hinduism and the Bön religion. However, at the time of Buddha Shakyamuni, only the exceptional, great disciples like Vajrapani received Vajrayana teachings; secret mantra was not taught in public. Therefore, we should not take the Vajrayana for granted. We are very fortunate to have accumulated enough positive karma from our many lifetimes so that we can hear these teachings. We should be inspired by their rarity, develop courage, and take responsibility to follow them sincerely.

Sometimes we may *hear* the secret mantra teaching, but do we *know* it? If we don't know it, then we haven't really heard it. This parable of the owl is instructive:

> Someone asked the owl, "Why is your head so flat?" He answered, "Because I have had so many empowerment vases put on my head." "Why do you have hair in your ears?" "Because I haven't heard even one word of Dharma."

This is called the paradoxical story of owls. The owl had received a lot of empowerments but didn't understand Dharma teachings. Like this, we also receive many empowerments, but our mind has still not matured and remains unaffected. This does not mean that we have not received blessings from the empowerment, just that our high expectations have not come to fruition.

Life doesn't stand still for even a moment; it passes by every second. Everything in our life is impermanent. We are born and we grow up; we are aging every day. One day we will go to the next life, but we don't know where we are going or when we will go. Just look at the mind. In one moment, we are inspired; in the second moment, our heart is broken. One moment we feel good; the next moment we feel bad. One moment we are so encouraged; the next moment we are completely crestfallen. All this continues constantly. Just as mind is fragile, life is also fragile.

This human life can create such powerful negative karma; no other life form can match it. On the other hand, if we utilize it in a positive way, this body can achieve much and can benefit many sentient beings; no other life form can do that. So, our human life is like an intersection: we can either to go to the hell realms or attain enlightenment. Both ways are very potent. Dharma teachings give us an introduction to how to use this life in the optimal way. At the same time, this human life is so impermanent, so very fragile. If our breath goes out and just once doesn't come back, our life is finished.

Think carefully. Please contemplate these things. There is no question that every sentient being desires happiness. It is also very clear that every sentient being wants to be free from suffering. It doesn't matter who they are, what kind of culture they were born into, or what kind of belief system they have. Even if they don't believe in any religion, still, they want to be free from suffering. But, you see, happiness doesn't come just by saying, "I want it." Suffering doesn't go away because you say you don't want it. This shows that happiness and suffering are results that must be caused. Because of that, everyone makes effort and works hard in their lives, whether spiritually or not, whether they study Dharma or technology. They look for something to bring them happiness, something to relieve suffering. Everyone keeps busy without becoming free from suffering.

Milarepa said, "Sentient beings—to be free from suffering, they create more suffering." We don't do this on purpose. So what happens? Our pattern of suffering is caused by delusion and ignorance. Dharma teachings show us the path, the real way to understand suffering and rid ourselves of its cause. That is very important and why we hold the Dharma in such high regard. We are working anyway, so why not make a little more effort in Dharma study and practice, which give us incisive wisdom to know the true cause of freedom from suffering? This is very logical.

All the past great masters worked hard to preserve the Dharma teachings, so that we have them today. Now we have the responsibility to study and practice this precious Dharma in order to maintain it for future generations. Take Marpa's life story as an example—how he sacrificed his life for the Dharma. He traveled to India on foot through hot, dense jungles filled with bandits and wild animals. There were no roads, no airplanes or trains, no air conditioning, not even electric fans. After he had received the great teachings, he said, "I have walked on such a long journey in the hot jungle where there are many wild beasts. Even though my mind was very stable, my body stumbled when I heard the tiger's roar and the snake's rustling." He had to carry everything on his back—food, clothes, money, books. He journeyed for months and months without even knowing where he might find the teachings. On his third trip to India, he didn't know where Naropa was, so he searched for many months saying prayers, meditating, supplicating, running here and there. Because he made that kind of sacrifice, we have this precious Dharma teaching today. So we too should shoulder the responsibility to perpetuate the Dharma teachings and not take them for granted.

Marpa received the teachings in the daytime and then practiced at night. Through this kind of effort, he became accomplished as a great master and translated many important Dharma texts from Sanskrit into Tibetan. That's how he could produce a great disciple like Milarepa. So we should not practice just for our own sake, thinking, "How can I become happy in samsara?" Rather, open your heart and build a big mind. Develop courage and work to establish the Dharma teachings. Every individual who is interested in the Dharma teachings has a responsibility to become free of suffering for the benefit of future generations, just as Marpa the great translator did.

Considering how rare a precious human life is and how difficult it is to create all the causes and conditions for enlightenment, now that we have one, can we afford to waste this precious opportunity?

*The root of the Buddha's teachings is the morality of
the Vinaya.
Without this, even if you are called a practitioner,
you are still a samsaric person.
Therefore, guard your discipline as you would your eyes.*

THE STUDY and practice of Dharma requires a clear mind. Discipline
is the foundation that makes a good and decent person. Without the
good foundation of discipline, our life is just chaos and confusion,
so the Buddha taught the *Vinaya* first. Vinaya is basically the monastic system, but it includes moral ethics for all four assemblies (lit.,
"gatherings") of practitioners:

- *bhikshu* (monk)
- *bhikshuni* (nun)
- *upasaka* (layman)
- *upasika* (laywoman)

Of these four, the first two constitute the monastic or ordained
community, and the second two are called the householders.

The moral trainings for householders are the five precepts:

- not taking life, especially that of human beings
- not stealing from others
- not telling lies, particularly spiritual lies
- not engaging in sexual misconduct
- not using intoxicants like alcohol or drugs

Those who are lay practitioners must keep these disciplines. *Brah-
macharya* practitioners keep five disciplines, including celibacy. In
addition to those five, *gomigenyens* hold the precepts of not eating
dinner, not using high or expensive thrones, and not using ornaments or perfumes. Monks and nuns must observe even more disciplines than these. These five basic precepts are taught in order to
create a mental environment of calm and clarity. From such a state

of mind, one has a great opportunity to practice Dharma successfully. Sometimes people get a negative feeling toward taking vows, thinking that they are a trap or a prison. It is not that way at all. The precepts form the line between causing more suffering and causing peace, joy, and harmony.

These disciplines are not only for the Buddhist world. Imagine if everyone kept these five disciplines! How harmonious and peaceful things would be! They make up the crucial method for becoming a better human being with less confusion and with more wisdom and compassion. They are the foundation, the starting point, for all levels of Dharma practice and for creating a peaceful environment in the world at large. Through them, we can eventually purify all obscurations and perfect all excellent qualities.

Whether you are a monk, nun, or lay person, unless you keep these disciplines well you are still a confused *samsaric person* and not a successful practitioner. You might be able to make a connection toward enlightenment with a few meditation sessions, but you cannot expect very much to result from just this. Moral ethics is a real practice that we do twenty-four hours a day. Therefore, *the root of Buddha's teachings is the morality of the Vinaya.*

All of us, but especially those who have taken monastic vows, have to protect our moral ethics with utmost care. The eyes are the most sensitive organ in our body. If someone hits you on the back, you still close your eyes. *Therefore, guard your discipline as you would your eyes.* This does not refer only to physical discipline but to mental discipline as well. When we protect our mental discipline, then our physical discipline will follow, and verbal discipline follows that. If mental discipline is not well established, then just tightening the physical and verbal disciplines is not enough. We cannot ignore physical discipline, but we should take more care of mental discipline so that the body, speech, and mind together are well equipped with the practice of Vinaya's moral ethics.

Desires are a hoard of nonvirtue.
Spirituality aside, even in ordinary, worldly life
there are many who have lost life, wealth, and power.
Therefore, regard desire as an enemy.

DESIRES HERE refers to attachment, sensual desire and greed, which cause mental suffering. Contact with sensual desire causes some to *lose their life*, and others to *lose their wealth* or their title. Strong attachment brings all different kinds of unfavorable conditions. This is where the Vinaya discipline becomes so necessary. We keep the various precepts to protect ourselves from confusion, from all these different sufferings. Negative thoughts are the ultimate enemies that destroy our inner peace and happiness.

Of course, Dharma teachings are based on this. If a person doesn't know Buddhism well, I say to them, "This is a Buddhist teaching." But when you know the teachings well, you understand that Dharma isn't limited to Buddhism, but rather is the law of peace and happiness for the entire world. If an individual were to practice this kind of discipline, people would respect him regardless of what beliefs he held. People would see how honest and sincere even an ordinary person is. In Dharma it is the same thing. We should eliminate, or at least minimize, strong attachment as much as we can.

The inveterate propensity toward attachment in all its forms—be it sexual desire, wealth, power, an idea, fame, or arrogance—is one of the most difficult defilements to purify. Even if we have practiced Dharma for years, we still find it very difficult to risk reducing our attachments, a barrage of desire. The following story about a scholar-monk who lost everything illustrates this point:

A monk went to a monastery to study Buddhist philosophy. After becoming well established as a scholar, he left the monastery and started giving teachings on his own. Because of his eloquence and scholarship, he gathered many disciples and patrons. But, unfortunately, he fell in love with one of his female patrons. The disciples felt that they could no longer trust him, so they left him as did all the other patrons. The monk was ashamed of himself and thought that he should move away, but the female patron pleaded with him to stay with her and be treated as a prince in her household. He accepted this offer, but in time he was cast aside and ended up as a servant in that house. After his death, he was reborn in the lower realms because of his misdeeds.

When we study and practice the Dharma, we must do so with complete sincerity. With great determination, we dedicate ourselves to the purification of all our afflictions—desire and so forth. With enough realization, these afflictions will not manifest again.

Sometimes, those who cannot fulfill their attachments with worldly activity practice Dharma to protect their attachment. They use spiritual methods to fulfill their desire or attachment. So, we should clearly understand that attachment in any form invites suffering. By having this insight, we will utilize Dharma to purify attachment at all costs, never to increase it.

Sometimes it is very painful to break this long-held habit; sometimes it brings fear. But if we understand samsara well, then we see how important it is to make an effort to cut attachment at the root. We should understand that if we make enough effort to purify this sticky habit, that great achievement would bring about the fearless state, and in this there is great inner joy. The song *Meaningful to Behold* quotes the great acharya Nagarjuna as saying:

> When propensities arise, the seeds of further propensities
>   are sown.
> Out of these accumulated propensities, samsara-sprouts
>   are grown.

It also quotes Jigten Sumgön this way:

> Although different traditions conclude that it is either the
> mind or the body that wanders in samsara, I don't take a

particular position on this. But I would say that causes and conditions give rise to conceptual thought. Because of that, embodied propensities wander [in samsara].

Attachment to wealth, either one's own or others', causes great suffering.

At the time of Buddha Shakyamuni, there was a scholarly monk to whom a patron offered a begging bowl. He lived simply, going to the village for daily alms, but he was tenaciously attached to that bowl. During his study and meditation, his attention was drawn to the bowl, polishing and cleaning it constantly. When he passed away the Buddha said, "All his wealth should be divided among the community of monks." The Buddha foresaw that the deceased monk would be reborn as a dangerous snake inside that begging bowl, so he told the monks not to touch the bowl before he could attend to it. The Buddha gave teachings to the snake, and asked him to leave without harming anyone. Then the Buddha explained the faults of attachment to the monks and instructed them to practice Dharma sincerely. Everyone present was moved and practiced meditation wholeheartedly.

Beer and the others in its group are a source of all harm.
Liquor, even if you boil it,
still possesses great faults.
Gradually, come to regard even beer as poison.

THESE FIRST FEW verses are about how to be a good and decent person. When you become intoxicated, you lose all your mindfulness and awareness. This affects your spiritual as well as worldly life. If you can't even drive properly when you are drunk, how could you expect to meditate? Clearly, without mindfulness you won't know how to practice Dharma. When someone is intoxicated, there is no harmony in their family. Instead of peace, there is a lot of hatred and confusion.

This advice refers to all different types of drinks and illegal drugs; any kind of intoxication is unhealthy for our mind and body. Some say alcohol is acceptable if it has been boiled because all the alcohol evaporates. But it still brings about some subtle side effects, so it is best to avoid alcohol completely. If you are already accustomed to drinking, then gradually abandon it. If you do not drink, that is excellent. When we practice, we can become truly wonderful people in every way.

Sometimes drinking is allowed in the Vajrayana system, but this depends on the individual. Some masters are highly accomplished and can actually transform alcohol into wisdom nectar, so it doesn't affect them. But we should be realistic about our abilities.

When one is intoxicated by alcohol or drugs, one loses mental clarity. In that state of mind, it is very difficult to have awareness of virtue and nonvirtue, so there is a greater risk of engaging in violence, stealing, sexual misconduct, lying, and so forth. Intoxication makes a person stupid and, in that way, becomes a source of nonvirtue and negative karma. Then a lot of confusion and suffering arise in both this life and the next. Those who are excessive drinkers or drug users become unhealthy.

So if one studies and practices Dharma free from nonvirtuous thoughts, and moistens one's mind with loving-kindness, compassion, and bodhicitta, there will be peace, joy, and stability in one's mind and life. If one makes an effort to achieve these good qualities, there will be no need to drink or take drugs. Drink a nice cup of tea or have some fruit juice instead. Drink the beer of kindness and become intoxicated with compassion. This advice is both for common people and for Dharma practitioners.

Also, wandering distractedly, giving in to vanity and frivolity,
and watching others dance and sing and so forth
are like the sounds that lure wild animals to their death.
These increase desire and the deceptiveness of samsara.
Therefore, avoid them.

AS PRACTITIONERS, we must always have mindfulness. *Wandering,* *vanity, frivolity,* and so forth are great obstacles because they disturb our mindfulness. If we have strong mindfulness, then it doesn't matter where we are. Even if we are in the midst of singing and dancing, we will not lose our mindfulness and our Dharma practice will remain firm. Our mind will not be disturbed or polluted by such conditions; we can keep our minds pure and clear, unstained by these influences. But until we have this quality, it is good to protect ourselves from conditions that disturb and distract our mind.

Sounds that lure wild animals to their death—some hunters play beautiful music on a flute or other instrument to attract deer. When the animals come in closer to hear better, the hunters kill them with their bows and arrows. We should not allow ourselves to be deceived by apparent pleasure and happiness. Deep down, they create suffering and the cause of suffering. The more we see of them, the more we want to see. As a side effect, depression and all kinds of negative thoughts come, and our Dharma practice falls apart. Even lay people who are not involved in Dharma practice are affected in this way.

Through wearing robes, one cultivates a virtuous mind.
Wearing lay dress and weapons is a cause of the mind of
nonvirtue.
In particular, religious dress inspires and reminds one
of renunciation.
It is a sign of the glory of the Victor's teachings.
Therefore, abandon meaningless dress.
Be an ornament to inspire those who have devotion.

THIS VERSE contains advice for the ordained. When you become a monk or nun, wearing robes becomes a special method to support your mindfulness. The thought, "I am supposed to practice and study more than other people," is a kind of protection. If, after becoming a monk or nun, you go back to wearing lay dress and no longer think you are different from others, your mindfulness can decrease. Wear this robe first for your own *renunciation*—reminding yourself that you wear this robe in order to be free from samsara and to attain enlightenment—and secondly *to inspire* others.

Just wearing the robes is not miraculous or magical. It is very important that you practice more than other people. It is necessary that you wear the robes mentally just as you wear them physically. Try to exhibit all the good qualities of mind when you wear robes. Of course, you won't have this right at the beginning. But you start to practice and progress through each step, one day at a time. That will inspire others and will become a cause for their respect.

If you wear robes as a means to encourage other people to serve you in a way not available in your ordinary life, then this becomes a cause of delusion and suffering for yourself and others. Instead of inspiring others, you will cause people to resent you. They will say, "Those who wear robes are the troublemakers. Instead of building the sangha, they are the ones destroying the sangha." We have to be very careful. Monks and nuns are the ones who have formally started their study and practice of the teachings, who have accepted the responsibility to become a good example, a source of wisdom, peace, and harmony—not a source of confusion and delusion.

Why *abandon meaningless dress*? If you wear neat and clean robes with discipline, you can be an ornament, an example to inspire devotion. If it happens that a monk or nun acts badly, this brings great negative karma for themselves and for others. Those who say negative things about them will create negative karma, and those who wear robes will create negative karma, too, because the two are interdependent. So, as I said, wearing robes is not magic. It is not something to create expectations. Rather, it creates the responsibility to purify negative thoughts and actions, to develop the good qualities of inner wisdom and compassion, and to free ourselves from samsara. Knowing how important this is, the author mentions it here.

On the first day you put on robes, you will not be perfect. Ordination is just the beginning of your commitment to the Dharma journey to become free from samsara and achieve enlightenment. Wearing Dharma robes is a sign of nonattachment and commitment to practice Dharma for enlightenment or buddhahood, and thus becomes an ornament to inspire those who have devotion. These days in the West, the ordained sangha community is growing. This life is not easy because modern monks and nuns don't have support from others as they did in the past. So it is very important for individuals to have courage, the strength to sustain their commitment, and to face adversity in a positive way. They need very strong bodhicitta to do these things. If we can do this, the ordained sangha community will grow and be more respected by future generations and, because of this, support will increase and Buddhism can be firmly established in many places.

Meaningless diversions and idle tales
are a cause of wasting one's life
and of obstructing the mind of Dharma and so forth.
You should develop as much virtue as you can.

A LOT of our talk is meaningless—stories that just waste our time and energy and cause us to waste our lives. They are mostly related to our attachments and aversions and do not contain much meaning. Our lives are so short. If we live one hundred years, it is nothing. Even if we live for two hundred years, we will still die anyway. Life is not long or stable. This is taught not to create fear but to help us understand that we can utilize our time in a better way.

Sometimes we have to sacrifice a little bit. In the midst of anger, desire, hatred, and so on, can we have a successful Dharma practice? No, clearly it is not possible for us to enjoy all the pleasures of samsaric life and be successful in Dharma practice. So we have to sacrifice some temporary things and develop enlightenment for the long run. *The mind of Dharma* means mindfulness in Dharma practice. Being attentive to Dharma makes the mind astute, as can be seen from this story:

> There once was a king called Geö Dzepa, who was quite handsome and was very skilled in training his subjects. When the king saw the suffering of sentient beings, he prayed to the Buddha, Dharma, and Sangha for guidance on how to help them. Every day, he made immense offerings. One day a voice from the sky said, "All sentient beings are attached to samsara. If one wants to achieve perfect primordial wisdom without any contradiction between the words and the meaning, take the sky as an example. There is nothing more to express or describe." When the king and his subjects heard this, they all achieved the non-returning state.

This means that they realized the ultimate meaning of nonattachment, the realization of Mahamudra. The cause for this accomplishment came from a previous lifetime. The king had formerly been born as a householder who abstained from idle talk and conducted a pure life. Because of that, he was born as a king in this life. Due to the purity of his previous life, he received the pure teachings and actualized the ultimate meaning.

All wealth is like the honey of the bees.
It binds one to samsara and is freely taken by others.
Much is lost and wasted to no purpose.
Therefore, it is important to take wealth's essence by using it
  for the Dharma
  and by practicing generosity.

WE DEVOTE so much energy to the accumulation of wealth. We plan
many projects and endure hardship, even risk our lives, to accumulate wealth. Once we gather some wealth, we then expend a lot of
effort to protect it. But you can see that most of the wealth you collect is used by others; you don't get to keep much of it yourself. We
work so hard to make money, and then at one time or another, we
lose most of it. In this short life, we don't have much opportunity to
use our wealth in a positive way.

This is illustrated by a story about one of the Buddha's previous
lives.

> There were once thousands of honey bees, whose queen
> bee was a bodhisattva. All those thousands of honey bees
> collected a huge amount of honey, and after some time a
> honey-hunter came to their hive and took the honey away.
> The bees suffered so much! "We worked hard for many
> years, but now we can't enjoy the result. What should we
> do?" They moved to another place and produced honey for
> several more years, suffering in the heat and rain. Again,
> after some time, a person came and took all the honey
> away. Finally the queen of the honey bees said, "Just listen
> to a few words. I have something to say. Repeatedly, we
> collect pollen from all the different plants and flowers and
> work so very hard. But someone always takes it away. This
> is the nature of samsara. Even now, no matter how much
> effort we make to collect pollen and produce honey, the

same thing will happen. There is not a single day in this life when we will have only happiness and peace. What we should do from now on is take refuge in the Buddha, Dharma, and Sangha, renounce samsara, and practice the precious Dharma teachings. This is the only way to really bring peace and happiness." All the honey bees followed the queen bee and released their attachment to the production of honey. They sincerely practiced Dharma, and that was the beginning of peace and joy in their lives.

This doesn't mean that we shouldn't have any wealth. It means that we should cut our attachment to wealth, develop contentment, and use the wealth that we have in a better way for ourselves and others. This way, it won't become a source of suffering.

So use *the essence of your wealth* for Dharma. For example, when you have something extra, you can support those who sincerely want to practice but don't have the resources to go into retreat. Many stories from the time of the Buddha tell of great people who supported monks and nuns, built monasteries, and established places for the study and practice of Dharma in order to preserve and propagate these precious teachings. Here is one such story:

> Once there was a householder named Dawa Sangpo who had a big family and a very prominent position. One day a monk, a bhikshu, asked for alms at his house. The family made offerings to the monk and then asked whether he knew of any methods to bring wealth. The monk gave them an image of Dzambhala, and told them to put it in their treasure room and make offerings. He assured them that they would increase their wealth this way. The householder Dawa Sangpo made offerings according to the instruction, and the image grew bigger and bigger. Later, they found many precious objects—gold, silver, and so forth—in the house.
>
> The karma that caused all these results was this: in his previous life, Dawa Sangpo had been born into a family where the father was a professional thief. Then, when the child grew up, the father tried to teach him to steal, rob,

and so forth, but the boy wouldn't cooperate. Because of that, the father became angry and expelled him from the house. The boy went to a teacher, took a vow never to steal, and abided by that vow sincerely. Later, when he was born as the householder Dawa Sangpo, he encountered the same teacher, now incarnated as the monk who gave him the Dzambhala statue and instructions.

This book is another good example. Preparing it and printing it involved some expense. But through others' generosity, we now have it and can read and study it to gain wisdom. It provides an opportunity for others to practice and develop wisdom. Seeing the nature of cause and result, we should be inspired to receive the precept against stealing, abstain from theft and, further, practice generosity. We ourselves will benefit, not anyone else.

Ceaseless chatter is a source of faults
and is despised by others,
but if we are completely silent we cannot point the way.
Therefore, it is important to know when to speak.

WHEN WE SPEAK, we should have some subject in mind. Otherwise, there is no reason to talk. Ceaseless chatter shows that there are so many things going on in our mind that there is no space to contain them all. In this circumstance, there is no peace or calm, let alone joy. In the mind of such a person, there is no quality of meditation.

Chatter involves so many useless topics. This brings attachment and resentment and leaves no place for the mind to relax. Often, it gives rise to different stories about others who have made mistakes. When we talk about other people, we are perceived as untrustworthy. People dislike those who have this habit of chattering, and avoid their presence. These days, those who are engaged in this not only waste time and energy but also run up a big phone bill. In this way, we waste important time. In contrast, great Dharma practitioners go to the mountains by themselves and stay in retreat for years. Instead of chattering, they contemplate the meaning of the precious Dharma teachings and calm their minds. They develop compassion, utilizing their short time and resources for enlightenment.

On the other hand, if we don't talk at all, there is no communication, and people wonder what we are thinking about. Without at least some talking, discussion, and conversation, we cannot communicate clearly. We need to explain experiences in a clear and precise way so that others get the point of what we need to say. We should use our wisdom to make things clear, and then use the rest of our time for the study and practice of the precious Dharma. This advice is given to help us become better human beings, ones possessing greater peace and clearer minds.

Due to the degeneration of the times, many of those friends whom we have
   aided will arise as enemies.
   Provoked by advice, confidences, and so forth,
   many will become argumentative and resentful.
   There are many who mistake our help for harm.
   Therefore, whatever benefit you provide through the giving
      of wealth and so forth,
   do it without expectation and with a noble mind.
   The fruit of this will ripen without a doubt.
   It is important to know when to offer heartfelt words.

THIS VERSE provides general advice. These days, the afflicting emotions are coarser than ever. Ignorance, anger, and attachment are all much stronger. These negative thoughts give us little opportunity for happiness. They enslave us and destroy our peace and joy. We are left empty-handed, and we suffer helplessly. We must realize that these negative thoughts are our real enemies. The most effective weapon against them is bodhicitta, so we should make every effort to cultivate altruistic thought on the basis of wisdom and compassion.

There is a traditional story that can help us remember that friends are not always reliable. We have to trust ourselves and build up our own abilities.

Once, a monkey and turtle somehow became close friends. The monkey, of course, lived in the forest and the turtle lived in the ocean. Still, they made a vow not to be evil to each other and, especially, never to harm one another. Time passed, and one day the king of the nagas fell ill. His doctor told him that a monkey's heart was essential for his recovery. Without one, he would surely die. The naga-king declared that a great reward would be given to anyone who brought a monkey heart to him.

The turtle saw this as a great opportunity. He went to the forest to see his friend and suggested that they go together to his place by the ocean. This was appealing to the monkey since there are a lot of interesting things to see and eat there, so they went. Then when they arrived, the turtle said, "Our naga-king is sick and he needs a monkey's heart to make him well. My friend, can you give him your heart?" Monkey immediately understood the evil thoughts of the turtle, and agreed to donate his heart, but not here. "I will have to climb up on top of a tree and only from there can I take my heart and give it to you. Let's go back to the forest so I can give you my heart."

Once they were back in the forest, the monkey climbed up a tree and called out, "Now I will throw you my heart. Open your mouth as wide as possible." The monkey climbed up in the tree and threw his excrement into the waiting mouth of the turtle, saying, "A bad friend is the source of all evils. For no reason, you took me to the ocean and I almost lost my life there. If you want this monkey's heart, you can eat this!" The turtle left, disappointed and embarrassed.

The turtle had often spent the night in a cave with the monkey, so sometime later he went to the cave thinking that the monkey might be there. Without the monkey's knowledge, the turtle hid in a corner. The monkey eventually climbed down from the tree and approached the cave but suspected that the turtle might be there. Then the monkey yelled, "Oh, cave!" The turtle thought that if he responded, the monkey might come in so he called out, "Hello!" Thinking that a talking cave was a bad sign, the monkey didn't stay and returned to his tree.

While we are keeping our bodhisattva vow, we must be careful not to create any kind of negativity around us. But things can happen unexpectedly. Even at the time of the Buddha, some people were resentful and argued with him. There are accounts like this in Milarepa's life story as well. Every individual has a different personality, a different state of mind. A piece of advice may be very helpful to one person but harmful to another, so you have to be skillful and know when to use helpful words. Sometimes we sincerely try to help others, but the other person may perceive our help as harm. At first, you become good friends, but later you become enemies. If you give sincere advice, they are provoked. Even if you say meaningful things, they argue with you, saying, "You are saying bad things about me." If you say, "Don't do this," they become resentful.

When you give wealth, advice, or instructions, do so *without expectation*. This is a very important policy for all our practices. Whether you get something back or not, whether it's successful or not, whether it's appreciated or not, when you give something, just give it so that the other person can have happiness and be free from suffering. Do it this way, rather than thinking, "How will this person return my favor?" That attitude may bring disappointment.

If you give things or advice, do it with a *noble mind*, a mind motivated by compassion. If you act in this way, you will truly do virtuous deeds. Results will come even if you are not expecting them. The results may not come directly from that person, but sometime— maybe in this life, maybe in the next—you will receive them. Of this there is no doubt.

Abandon that which harms yourself and doesn't benefit others.
If you expect too much from your good deeds,
you will often be let down.
Keep this in your heart.

THIS REFERS to actions based in hatred or attachment, things like telling lies or using harsh words. When we act under their influence, it always brings us harm. For example, out of our delusion, harsh words may come. They don't help us, and they don't help the other person either. There are many cases like this.

I once heard a news story about a woman whose daughter had been murdered by a man who was sentenced to life in prison as a result. For a long time, she hated that man very much and repeatedly told everyone she met that she wished he would be executed. Her hatred consumed her; she felt no peace and her health began to deteriorate. But eventually, she came to see that her hatred and harsh words had no good effect—they would not make her daughter live again and they would not affect the prisoner in any way. Even if he were executed, it would not bring her daughter back to life. She realized that she was harming only herself. So she went to the prison and forgave the murderer for what he had done, and actively sought his release. Once she released her hatred and resentment, her health also improved. I don't think she was a Buddhist, but that is real Dharma practice!

We should help others as much as we can. But at the same time, if we try to do too much without being asked, they won't appreciate it or accept our help. So, they won't get any benefit, and we will be hurt and discouraged. So *abandon that which harms yourself and doesn't benefit others.*

This is useful not only for Dharma practitioners, but for everyone in the world. This is particularly good advice for those who work in a group or in an office. High expectations lead to big disappointments. So it is very important to act out of compassion and skill. Just sincerely try to help others, but without expectation.

gifts, and brought it all to Nyima. "I deeply regret what I did, and apologize. Please accept these gifts and help bring back my sons." Nyima said, "Even though the sand turned back into gold, your sons cannot become human again." Dawa wept and insisted very strongly, so Nyima eventually gave him back his sons.

So, when you practice Dharma or make a friend, do so out of sincerity and honesty, with love, compassion, and respect, and without many expectations. Then, as time passes, the result will be genuine.

Another example from Buddhist history also demonstrates this point:

> Shantideva was a great scholar at Nalanda University who was also highly accomplished in meditation practice. First, he studied Buddhist philosophy and other subjects with great contemporary masters. He was particularly moved by the Madhyamaka and bodhicitta teachings, which led him to completely focus on meditation practice—so much so that he neglected the necessities of life. As a result, the other monks at Nalanda perceived him as being indifferent about everything except eating, sleeping, and using the toilet. They thought he was a disgrace to the monastic community because they didn't see him doing much of anything. They decided to humiliate him by asking him to give a public teaching in the hope that he would leave the community of his own accord. On the appointed day, it was the group of monks who were embarrassed. Shantideva gave an extensive, profound, and beautiful teaching. That teaching is still revered and studied to this day as the famous *Bodhicaryavatara*. His compatriots' minds were completely changed, and they developed admiration and profound devotion for him.

As you can see, the wise do not judge others by appearances or superficial behavior.

If, with like or dislike, you overreact to small amounts of
  benefit or harm,
in the long run you won't know who will help or harm you.
It is good to respond without much anger or delight.
Have noble thoughts.
Be even, like the strings of a guitar.

WHEN, IN ORDINARY samsaric life, we react with strong *like or dislike*, this makes for a very colorful life. It's exciting when we like something and are overjoyed or when we dislike something so much that we get upset and depressed—even suicidal. This emotional display makes life dramatic, and we come to regard an even disposition as boring. But in the long run, to experience genuine peace and joy, it is best to control our emotions.

We should not overreact to small things. This supports good Dharma practice as well as a peaceful family and society. Reacting too much, either positively or negatively, makes an individual unstable and reveals how fragile the mind is. If you encounter something you dislike, transform the way you perceive it. You should see that its nature is impermanence, or even illusory, and use it to enhance your practices of wisdom and compassion. If you like something, do not become attached to it. As a Dharma practitioner, see everything as a display. Keep your mind gentle, peaceful, compassionate, and filled with bodhicitta.

Sometimes the one who harms you will actually help you the most, even more than someone who likes you. So, without expectation, reduce your anger toward the disliked actions, and reduce your attachment for actions that you like. When we play *a guitar*, the strings have to be at just the right tension, not too tight and not too loose. Similarly, it is important to maintain an *even, noble* mind at all times.

If someone speaks harsh words, try to see if they are true.
Many are deceived, like the rabbit who heard "chal."
If someone depends on you from their heart,
it is important to treat them like yourself.
If you betray them, you will experience that result.
So be careful.

IF SOMEONE speaks harshly to you, do not just hear the sound of anger but look at the meaning of the words to see whether the criticism makes sense. If it doesn't make any sense, then of course there is no need to listen. Some people, out of love and respect, want you to be hard-working, so they scold you from their loving-kindness, as a mother does her child. But if it does make sense, investigate further to see if what they say is true. Look at yourself to see whether you have made a mistake. If you did, admit it and accept the criticism as a teaching, and change your inveterate propensities.

There is no need to react to every sound you hear. Look carefully before you respond. The following story illustrates this idea:

> There was once a rabbit in the forest who went to a pond to drink some water. While he was drinking, a big tree branch fell in the water and made the sound *chal*. The rabbit was very scared. He thought there was a wild beast coming to kill him and, without checking, he ran away. He ran so fast that each animal who saw him thought that something terrible must be happening. When they asked him what the matter was, he said, "There is a monster coming, and he makes the sound *chal*! I am frightened and running from him." So one after another, they all followed him. After some time, a big crowd came to be running with the rabbit. Eventually they met a lion, who asked, "What is going on here?" They replied that a monster was coming, and was calling out *chal*. "Just wait a minute," said

the lion, "Let me get to the bottom of this." Finally, the lion got to the rabbit, who explained his story. The lion said, "Let's go back and see what this monster looks like." They all went back and found that the frightening sound was only a tree branch that had fallen in the water. They berated the rabbit, saying how stupid he was and how he had unnecessarily made much trouble for them all.

The moral of this story is that we should examine all words that come to us. We don't have to follow everything we hear. Mostly, our chattering doesn't make too much sense. After all, it just wastes our time and energy without having much meaning. So don't create such a big phone bill! Reflect on mindfulness instead.

If someone depends on you, sincerely do whatever you can. For myself, I understand that my happiness and peace are my own responsibility and depend completely on how I act. If I practice Dharma sincerely and keep my mind in the right place, then I feel that I am taking my responsibilities in the right direction. If I destroy my virtue and good qualities through negative actions, then I am not taking responsibility for myself. Likewise, if someone else sincerely depends on me, I have to do the best I can. Maybe there are a lot of things I can't do, but I should try as sincerely for them as I would for myself. This is very important. This is how to be a good person.

Just going around taking advantage of others will only lead you to create negative karma. If you betray others, you actually betray yourself. When we do good things for others, we are doing good things for ourselves. When we say bad things about others, we are creating bad circumstances for ourselves. We experience the world that we create, as in the saying, "What goes around, comes around." Therefore, the way that we support each other is important because it provides a sincere sense of community. Be careful what you do. This verse gives us wisdom to really understand what Dharma means, what Dharma is about—how to live our lives on a day-to-day basis in a clear way without delusion or fantasy.

Knowing the various aspects of ritual, dance, melody, and so
       forth is a source of upliftment.
   It is important to make effort in this.
   But if you are bound by jealousy and pride, the result of your
       practice will be birth in lower realms.
   Therefore, establish the true meaning of this and future lives
       by having noble thought and by generating loving-kindness.

As was mentioned in the beginning verse, there are ten aspects of knowledge. Great scholars who accomplish them are uplifted by them. There are those who know how to chant melodiously, who have different skills like torma-making or thangka painting, and who can perform sacred dance and so forth. In sacred dance, each deity has a characteristic physical movement; the wrathful and peaceful have a distinctive way of gesturing. Through these performances, the audience gets a chance to glimpse the enlightened deities, which plants a seed for them to awaken to full enlightenment. A bodhisattva can skillfully use different aspects of knowledge, as well as modern technological skills, to benefit others. So, if we have time, it is good to increase our effort in these subjects.

Thinking "I know this and others don't" can build *pride*, and if someone else knows more than we do, *jealousy* can arise. These negative karmas are unnecessary. If we don't understand the purpose of knowledge, it just becomes a cause of suffering. Therefore when you have special knowledge or skill, use it in a way that helps others. To benefit this life, use these skills to help individuals, help monasteries, or help society. For the sake of your future lives, act without jealousy or pride whether others respect you for it or not.

But as beginning practitioners, we should know how to prioritize our efforts by understanding that these things are not the most important. For Dharma practitioners, especially those who do retreat practice, these things are not a priority. When you are in retreat, all your time should be spent developing stabilization and clarity. Paying too much attention to other things may become a distraction.

As Dharma Lord Gampopa says, if we don't practice Dharma properly, Dharma may cause rebirth in a lower realm. This doesn't mean Dharma itself was the cause of rebirth in a lower realm, but if we misuse or don't know how to employ Dharma practice, *that* becomes a cause of lower rebirth. Gaining skills and knowledge along with bodhicitta brings a better condition in this lifetime and in the future. It makes us better human beings. The author repeatedly mentions *noble thought*. This is very important. Noble thought refers to love and compassion, to bodhicitta. There is no greater or higher "thought" than this.

Whatever we do, whatever skill we have, we should act with altruistic thought and compassion. Even if we just clean the shrine, we should do it with respect in order to purify our mind. This way, everything we do can become part of our Dharma practice. Practice is not necessarily only sitting in one place and chanting mantras. When you drive a car, travel in a bus or taxi, or cook, just watch your mind and think, "I am doing this to benefit others. By my doing this, may other beings be free of suffering. May they have peace and happiness." In this way, everything can become part of a wonderful Dharma practice.

You may think that small actions of virtue and nonvirtue may not help or harm.
But small karma gives rise to great results.
So be careful even in little things.

THERE ARE MANY stories about small karmas bringing great results. Some are mentioned in the books *In Search of the Stainless Ambrosia* and *Transformation of Suffering*. One such story is about someone who once said to a monk, "You are like a dog," and was himself reborn as a dog for five hundred lifetimes. In another story, a family went to a cemetery to deliver a relative's body and came upon a monk. Their child said, "Look—that monk looks like a raven!" A great teacher heard this and saw that the child would be reborn as a raven for five hundred lifetimes. The family protested and said that the child was innocent; he didn't really mean what he said; there was no anger or hatred in his remark. The master replied that if there had been, the child would have been reborn in a hell realm. Actions we take in this life, good or bad, can also ripen in this life, as shown in the following story:

> Once when the Buddha was staying in Kapalivastu, a Brahmin couple gave birth to a son and daughter. The daughter was named Da Wö, Moonlight. After the children were grown, the father passed away and the mother and son wandered to different places. The daughter Moonlight became a servant for the king, Shakya Mingjin. It was her habit to take her meals in the garden, where she often collected flowers and made garlands. One day, she caught sight of the Buddha as he was going around for alms and immediately developed strong devotion for him. She lamented, "I am such an unfortunate person. Such a noble object of refuge is right here and I don't have an opportunity to make offerings. If only I could, I would

surely make offerings." The Buddha read her mind and, with great compassion, approached her and said, "If you have any offerings, place them here in this bowl." Moonlight was thrilled, completely filled the bowl with alms, and devotedly prostrated at the Buddha's feet. Then she said this dedication prayer, "Due to whatever virtue I have created from this, may I never be a servant again."

After time passed, a friend of her father's, a Brahmin who could read signs, noticed the garland girl and asked where she was from. She said she came from the countryside and explained, "I am a servant in this house." "Where is your father?" She replied, "My father passed away some time ago." "Where are your mother and brother?" She said, "I don't know. They are wandering somewhere." The sign-reader said, "Show me your hand." He found significant signs on her palm; in fact, her face and entire body held beautiful signs. He told her, "Don't worry, you won't be a servant much longer. You will become a queen instead."

Later, a king came from Kosala to hunt. His horse stopped near that garden, and the king saw the girl from a distance. He noticed all the significant signs and her gentleness. "Who are you?" he called out. She replied, "I am a servant of the king Shakya Mingjin." "You can't be a servant," he said, "you must be his daughter!" King Shakya Mingjin saw the king from Kosala, invited him into his palace, and arranged a luxurious banquet. The Kosala king asked King Shakya Mingjin, "Where did this garland girl come from?" Upon hearing again that she was a servant, he protested, "This is no servant, but your daughter. Please give her to me." King Shakya Mingjin protested, "But there are many other beautiful daughters in our kingdom. You could have any of them. Why do you want this one?" The king insisted, "I want her." So they made arrangements, and Moonlight became his queen and lived happily and peacefully.

The ripening of karma can also be understood by analogy. When you plant one kernel of corn, you can see that the result is two or three ears of corn, each with many, many kernels. If you plant a single grape seed, it produces hundreds of grapes. It is the same with positive and negative actions. A sutra says, "Don't perform any kind of nonvirtue. Perform all forms of virtue. Thoroughly tame your mind. This is the Buddha's teaching."

When we practice, we can glimpse cause and result, but a detailed understanding is very subtle and difficult to achieve. However, we can gain a partial appreciation of karma through some examples:

> ▸ If someone uses nice words, this is a cause. When the other person responds in a nice way, this is the result.
> ▸ If you plant the seed of a poisonous plant, poison will grow.
> ▸ If you plant the seed of a medicinal plant, medicine will grow.

Even great arhats cannot always perceive the full range of karma.

> At the time of the Buddha, a farmer went to Shariputra and asked for ordination as a monk. Shariputra examined him but found no seed, no cause, to attain arhatship in that lifetime, so he said, "No, I cannot accept you as a monk." The farmer was very disappointed and cried, "People who have created terrible negative karma are allowed to be monks. Why not me? I haven't done anything bad in my whole life." After some time had passed, the Buddha came along and asked, "What happened here? What has upset you?" The farmer described the situation. With a great, compassionate mind, the Buddha took his hand and said, "I will give you ordination. You do have a seed to attain arhatship." Then Shariputra asked, "What kind of potential did you see that I couldn't perceive?"
>
> The Buddha explained, "Thousands and thousands of kalpas ago, this man was born as a fly. He was sitting on a pile of cow dung when a sudden rush of water caught the cow dung, along with the fly, and sent them into the river. Downstream, someone had placed a prayer wheel in the water, and that cow dung and fly swirled around and around it. Because of that circumambulation, this man now has a seed to attain arhatship in this lifetime."

Cause and result are so subtle that only omniscient wisdom can perceive every detail. That is why we must be very careful that our actions are truly beneficial.

Reciting just one mantra, protecting the life of even one small bug, giving a small thing—we should not ignore such actions by saying, "This is nothing; it makes no difference if I do it or not." Many small actions will gather and swell like the ocean. These are not merely Buddhist beliefs; these are the causes that create our world no matter who we are. Our study and practice give us the opportunity to understand this and to be sincere with ourselves even in small things.

Saying or doing whatever comes to mind is the storehouse
  of all nonvirtue.
Investigate before you act.
Until you gain the fruit of what you do, it is important
  to continue.

DON'T SAY or do everything that comes to mind. Most of the time what comes into our mind are negative thoughts related to pride, jealousy, hatred, and attachment. There are not so many positive thoughts. Negative thoughts arise effortlessly, like a running stream, because we are so used to that pattern. Virtuous thoughts are more rare because they require a lot of effort and mindfulness. So when thoughts arise, examine them. Investigate very carefully before you say anything or act. Look at your motivation. If your thoughts are negative, purify them and implement other practices. When a strong negative thought arises, it tends to push you into action. Then, after some time, you experience regret. So, it is better to wait. This is not to say that we should suppress our anger. Rather, this is a way to practice and to see our limitations, a way to purify our thoughts and develop good qualities.

Whatever you do, the primary activity is watching your mind. Take a deep breath for a few seconds. That is mindfulness. When the telephone rings, let it ring three times. With the first ring, develop noble thought and think, "This is a sign of impermanence." Let your mind rest on the second ring. After the third ring, pick up the telephone and say "hello." When you drive, you may tend to rush a little. Instead, just get in the car and take a deep breath. Watch your mind and drive with peaceful thoughts. This way, anything can become a meditation practice.

We have so many methods and practices. There are methods that help negative thoughts not to arise. Then, if they do arise, there is a way to purify them or transform them without suppression.

Suppressing anger is not good. Instead, look at the face of your anger. Does it do you any good? Does it do others any good? Investigate until you see the true nature of anger. Even if you have a good reason to be angry, acting on it still brings you suffering. There is a saying, "Do you want to be right, or do you want to be happy?" If you hold onto reasons to be angry, you will never be happy. Even if there is justification for your anger, purify the anger; this is the best way.

Often, we begin a project and then abandon it. We begin another project and then abandon it. We gain nothing for ourselves this way, and we have nothing to show others. Once we investigate and decide that something is the right thing to do—that it is definitely helpful for ourselves and for others—we should pursue it until it is finished. This is the sign of a noble person, a sign of strength. People will trust such a person.

If you cannot finish something, it would be better not to accept the task. If, out of pride, you say that you will do something, people will rely on you. But if you can't actually complete it, people will lose trust. Once we are committed, once we accept responsibility to do something, we should do it no matter what it takes. If you cannot do it, say so. This is the kind of thing the author is talking about.

Sometimes people think that all these details are a little boring, but they are very, very important. This is how we establish our Dharma practice—with the details. Even in the highest view of Mahamudra and Dzogchen we need to understand these details. Mahamudra is not separate from them. As the *Heart Sutra* says, "Emptiness is form, form is also emptiness. Form is none other than emptiness, and emptiness is also none other than form." We cannot find a higher, more respected view apart from these teachings. When we possess these detailed understandings, especially about maintaining our discipline, our realization of Mahamudra will be very effective.

If you are too direct, you will make enemies.
Improper behavior ripens heavy karma.
Getting along with everyone is superficial.
Not getting along with anyone is worse.
Therefore, it is important to be skillful in various methods
and to be free from deceit, cunning, and nonvirtuous mind.

THIS VERSE shows us how to be skillful. If you are too direct, it doesn't matter whether you are right or wrong because you will make a lot of enemies and no one will listen to you. To counteract this, first understand that no one is perfect; people make a lot of mistakes. Everyone has some good knowledge and good qualities, but they also have some shortcomings. If you turn all imperfect people into enemies there won't be anyone left. You will only create negative karma as you argue back and forth and harm each other.

Unless we avoid responsibility and don't do anything at all, we can't get along with everyone. If we try, the result will be superficial, as we can see from this story.

> In a small village there was an older gentleman who wanted to live alone and not be involved with anything or associate with anyone. The head of the village wanted to include him in the village affairs, so he went to the old man and said, "Since we have to live together harmoniously and help support each other, come have a picnic with us." The man said, "I don't want to go. I just want to stay by myself. I don't want anyone around me." The village chief persisted, so the man went to the judge and said, "These people won't leave me alone. I just want to live in peace and quiet. Judge, please give me permission to do this." The judge said, "Yes, you are right." Then the head of the village went to the judge and said, "We want to help this man when he has a problem. We want to be his friend and

support him; we want to include him in our association. Judge, please give us permission to do this." The judge said, "Yes, that is very good." The judge's assistant heard this and said to the judge, "These decisions cannot both be right." The judge said, "Yes, you are right, too." Thus no one's problem was solved.

Especially when we are working, some people will act properly and some won't. We can't go along with something that will make things worse; we have to do the right thing. Even the Buddha could not get along with everyone. For example, his cousin Devadatta was always criticizing the Buddha. There was another monk who studied with the Buddha for twelve years, and then said, "We are equals. I don't agree with you." So even the Buddha could not please everyone, but he did what was right.

We cannot go along if someone is creating negative karma. We need to rely on our own wisdom and skill. If others follow us, that's wonderful. If someone disagrees with us, what can we do? Not so much. Be skillful—know when to talk, when to discuss things, when to follow others. We cannot take responsibility for other people's minds, but we can at least take responsibility for our own minds. When we study these precious Dharma teachings, especially those about bodhicitta, we can gain the skills that will help us know how to act. Our minds should always be free from cunning and deceit. These things are not good for us, and they are obviously not good for others. It is important to keep these small details in our awareness.

Bodhicitta is the source of all bodhisattvas,
and all Dharma is only for the benefit of others.
Especially on the path of attaining buddhahood in one life,
it is essential to practice the teachings
of arising and completion of secret mantra.

BUDDHADHARMA IS a precious and holy teaching because of bodhi-citta. Bodhicitta is the backbone, the center, of the Buddhadharma. Without it, the Buddhadharma is nothing special. Bodhicitta is the universal mind, the attitude that we develop so that every sentient being, regardless of who they are, can attain buddhahood, the com-pletely awakened mind. This is the single most important thing to keep in mind. It is the consummate practice of Buddhadharma.

Bodhicitta is composed of two factors—great compassion and wisdom. The projection of the compassionate mind is the desire to take responsibility to free all sentient beings from suffering. The pro-jection of the wisdom mind is complete enlightenment. The wisdom mind has great discernment, through which critical insight mani-fests. Buddhahood is freedom from suffering and all causes of suf-fering without exception. So, for all sentient beings to be completely free from suffering, they have to attain complete enlightenment.

Bodhicitta is the source of all bodhisattvas of the past, present, and future. The *Bodhicaryavatara* says, "The moment you cultivate bodhicitta, even in the midst of negative afflictions, you become a bodhisattva and are an object of refuge for all sentient beings." Even in the midst of samsara with all its predispositions, the very moment you cultivate bodhicitta, your body transforms into a bodhisattva's body. This is such great alchemy! Ordinary alchemy might turn iron into gold, but bodhicitta can turn an ordinary human being into the gold of a bodhisattva, a precious object for all sentient beings.

Look at the life story of Milarepa. In the first part of his life, he used black magic to harm many people. But later, after he culti-vated bodhicitta, he became so precious. He attained buddhahood and became a source of peace and happiness for all sentient beings because of this practice of bodhicitta.

The Buddha did not give all these Dharma teachings for his own benefit, or to become famous and rich. The Buddha is fully perfected, free from all suffering, so he doesn't need anything from sentient beings. He taught only *for the benefit of others*. Therefore, we too must study and practice these teachings for others' benefit. First, it is most important that we begin our practice; second, that we implement our practice; and third, that we perfect our practice. The Buddha became awakened through the perfection of bodhicitta. All the other practices are methods to perfect bodhicitta. In the Vajrayana, all visualizations, mantra recitations, and "inner practices" of chakras and channels are nothing other than methods to perfect bodhicitta.

The Buddha taught Dharma for others' benefit, meaning that we, too, can receive this benefit ourselves. Unless we ourselves benefit from the Dharma, we cannot give this benefit to others. It would not be possible at all. We have to implement the practice, not just have intellectual knowledge. Intellectual knowledge is an important first step, but it is even more important to accomplish what we have learned. Cultivating bodhicitta means putting Dharma into practice in order to attain buddhahood. Thus, bodhicitta is indispensable to the attainment of buddhahood. With the support of bodhicitta, buddhahood can be achieved in just one or two lifetimes.

We suffer in samsara because of our delusions and negative thoughts. There is nothing other than bodhicitta and the precious Dharma teachings that can definitively free us from all this suffering. No matter what modern technologies we use or how powerful our scientific investigations may be, there is no way they can permanently free us from suffering.

Bodhicitta is such a great and reliable friend! An ordinary friend cannot give us the kind of comfort and fearlessness that bodhicitta can. As soon as one cultivates bodhicitta and practices this precious mind, one is freed from all fears. No matter what we do in samsara, we always encounter fear. We build a beautiful and expensive house with lots of protection and insurance. We buy beautiful and expensive cars for enjoyment, but then we have to pay insurance to protect them because of fear. But when we make a friend of bodhicitta, all fears are transformed—not only for this life, but also for the future. So build the house of bodhicitta and drive the car of bodhicitta. Eventually, bodhicitta will provide us with the incomparable opportunity to become a buddha. Therefore, we should make a friend of bodhicitta. Milarepa used to say, "If you eat, eat the food of bodhicitta. If you drink, drink the water of bodhicitta. If you travel, travel with your friend, bodhicitta."

We respect and pay homage to Buddha and great bodhisattvas as a source of peace. They are reliable; we can take refuge in them. This is because of bodhicitta. Bodhicitta is the best wealth we can have in our life. Other wealth can be lost or stolen; anything can happen to it. But if we have bodhicitta, this one wealth provides all comforts. One who possesses bodhicitta owns the wealth of the universe.

Great bodhisattvas have indomitable courage because of their practice of bodhicitta. When we have bodhicitta, we will be happy if we are rich; we will be happy if we are poor. We will be happy when we are successful in our career; we will be happy when we are not successful. Bodhicitta will give us the opportunity to live in an even way.

If we don't have bodhicitta, our egos will always undermine our work in one way or another. All other practices are superficial without bodhicitta; sometimes they are not even Buddhist practices. Without bodhicitta, even if we practice Mahamudra or Dzogchen it won't bring the expected result. But if we have bodhicitta, we will attain buddhahood even if we don't expect it. Without bodhicitta, even if we practice highest yoga tantra or the chakras and channels, these practices will not bring the result of the perfection of enlightenment.

Arising and completion refer to Vajrayana, also called tantra or deity yoga, which are advanced practices. Vajrayana practice is a special method to purify the imprint of the most subtle obscurations to buddhahood. This practice directly reveals the complete buddha nature, which is itself buddhahood. So the Vajrayana includes vast and profound skillful means. In order to digest this method, one has to be gifted, have courage, and have great renunciation of samsara. To enter the Vajrayana, one has to have understood the basic teachings and meditation practices, such as the Four Noble Truths, preliminary bodhicitta, and the meaning of emptiness.

The arising stage takes place when you visualize the form of the meditational deity, or yidam—either as yourself or in front of you—as the inseparability of appearance and emptiness. Its appearance arises from emptiness and is a reflection of its unceasing quality. In that state, we practice completion, where all physical, mental, and verbal obscurations are purified. There are two types of completion stage practice: with signs and without. In completion with signs, all physical, mental, and verbal phenomena are purified by visualization, by chanting mantras, and by practicing with the chakras and channels. Completion without signs is the practice of Mahamudra, which reveals the very mode of abiding of all phenomena, the pure nature of awareness without boundary. When we practice with the motivation of bodhicitta, the practice becomes so powerful that we have an opportunity to achieve buddhahood even in a single lifetime.

In this degenerate time, many rely on ghosts.
The worship of te rang *as deities is like death at the edge*
  of a knife.
It creates mischief and takes one's life for no purpose.
Therefore, to the unfailing Three Jewels,
go for refuge from the bottom of your heart.

TE RANG are mischievous spirits that are sometimes involved with gambling. When I was a child in Tibet, I heard that when you gambled, the one-legged *te rang* would come. Perhaps you don't have this kind of superstition in the West. People make these things important because they want to win at gambling or business. These are people with samsarically motivated interests, focused only on this life and on themselves, so they rely on ghosts. If we perceive the Buddha as distant, then such local spirits may seem useful. Small-minded people become involved in such things, but sometimes it makes their problems worse, causing quarreling and fighting in which they die *at the edge of a knife.*

If we take refuge in the Buddha, Dharma, and Sangha, we find they are unfailing now and in the future. There are no negative side effects. Dharma always teaches us how to be better human beings. It doesn't involve any type of negative thought, but the *te rang* and other types of local deities do. So, it is important to know how to take refuge.

Even though we are Buddhists, many of us do not have a good understanding of taking refuge in the Buddha, Dharma, and Sangha. When we go to the temple, we see that Buddha's image is in the center. We remember that he is great, the one who taught the Dharma—we pay that much homage. Maybe we even make an incense offering or light a candle. Then in the corner of the temple or under a tree or rock, we see some local deity's image and our heart is drawn to that one. We hear how powerful and magical it is; how it can give you wealth and this and that. "Please dispel all my obstacles!" we ask them. "Do favors for me!" We end up by taking refuge in this local deity. We think that the Buddha does not have so much power to help us, but that the local deity has power to do anything. This kind of confusion or misunderstanding brings about many problems.

The Buddha is the one who attained enlightenment, who perfected all positive qualities, wisdom, and compassion. But when we come to the Buddha, we don't pay attention. This means we are not practicing properly. The Buddha should be first. The Dharma protectors should protect Dharma practitioners and all sentient beings at large, but we should pay attention to our Dharma practice more than to the Dharma protectors.

Ghosts, local deities, and other powerful beings are not free from samsara. They are confused, and if we rely on them we will also become confused. Most local deities are hungry ghosts. We are human beings. So why would a higher being take refuge in a lower one? Therefore, we should take refuge in the unfailing Three Jewels, the Buddha, Dharma, and Sangha.

The Buddha is the nature of dharmakaya, the uncreated state of total peace, and the nature of clarity. He is fully perfected with spontaneously created qualities. Buddhas attain buddhahood by dispelling delusions and by realizing their own buddha nature. Thus, the Buddha has the quality of omniscience, the great wisdom that knows everything. Along with that wisdom, he has nonobjectified compassion. If the Buddha had great wisdom without compassion, he would not be anything special. So why do we respect the Buddha so much? Because out of his great compassion, the Buddha takes responsibility for every sentient being. His compassion is impartial, unyielding, unfailing, and unconditional. This is how sentient beings and the Buddha are connected.

The Dharma is the Buddha's teaching, given to sentient beings so that they can recognize the nature of samsara, follow the method to free themselves from it, and attain complete enlightenment. The Noble Sangha consists of the successful practitioners who have actualized higher levels of realization and who have undivided devotion, confidence, and courage regarding buddhahood. They are examples of perfect Dharma practitioners. Therefore, take refuge in these Three Jewels from the bottom of your heart if you want to be free from suffering and attain enlightenment. It is the unmistaken path.

Some do not fully trust the benefits
of the Buddha's speech, the holy Dharma.
Instead, they put their faith in mo *and* bön.
This kind of wrong view is a cause for rebirth in the hells.
The results of obscurations of wealth and mistaken behavior
  and so forth
may not appear immediately, but will ripen without a doubt.
So fully trust.

THE BUDDHA explained that we should avoid all the different types
of nonvirtue as they are the root cause of all the different types of
suffering. He also taught that we should engage in and develop the
various types of virtue in order to experience relative and definite
goodness. So in the Dharma there is not much emphasis on things
like divination and superstition. If we follow the path sincerely and
fully, we will achieve whatever peace and happiness we desire. If we
avoid nonvirtue, all suffering will disappear; there is no doubt of
this. But instead of taking these teachings to heart, we sometimes
misuse them to get some temporary benefit in this life. Instead of
practicing Dharma sincerely, we look for magic and power. This is
not the best way to solve our confusion and problems, so the author
advises against it.

Mo is a divination system. Some people rely wholly on *mo* to
achieve good fortune. But we don't need *mo* to tell us whether or
not we should practice Dharma. Suppose you ask a fortune teller
whether you should go into three-year retreat. If the *mo* says you
should not go, it becomes an obstacle to your Dharma practice and
doesn't help you. *Mo* is sometimes useful for business people and
travelers, but, then again, we have no control over whether the most
important days of our lives, our birth and our death, will fall on an
auspicious day or not.

Here, the word *bön* refers to a particular type of ritual, not the
Tibetan belief system named Bön. *Bön* involves ritualized deity

practices performed in order to obtain protection from curses, dispel the obstacles of evil spirits, or gain some other benefit. To dispel obstacles in this life, we sometimes become involved in these things and then develop a wrong view of karma that is contrary to what the Buddha explained so clearly in his teachings.

Instead of becoming involved in these activities, it would be better to fully rely on the Buddha's speech and wholeheartedly follow his teachings without distraction. In the face of adversity, implement the Dharma in order to dispel obstacles and undesirable conditions. There is a saying: "By seeing the condition of this life, you will know what you did in the past. By looking at your own mental condition, you will know what will be in the future." Thus, we don't have to depend on *mo* and the rituals of *bön*.

If we purify our negative karma and develop good karma, it is clear that the result will be good sooner or later. We should rely on the precious Dharma and practice it sincerely. Even if the whole world collapses, if we personally have positive karma we will not be harmed. If we have the karma to experience negative things, then no matter how well we are protected, these things will happen. This shows the importance of Dharma, that it is not just some superficial concept. If one has wrong view, doesn't follow what Dharma says about virtue and nonvirtue, and gets fully involved in things like *mo* and *bön*, one can be reborn in a hell realm.

Instead of superstitious activities, the most beneficial path is to practice bodhicitta and direct all our good or bad experiences toward enlightenment. When you face obstacles or get sick, you can use that as a special opportunity to purify negative karma and loosen the hold of the afflicting emotions. Meditate with compassion and discernment: "By this effort, may I purify the afflictions of every sentient being." If you experience joy and happiness, think, "May joy and happiness entirely pervade samsara. May everyone achieve complete peace, happiness, and buddhahood."

The root of attainment is the vajra master.
Developing faith in all his activities,
holding his instructions as valid,
and respectfully serving and attending him without hypocrisy
is the root of all Dharma.
But those who think that samaya is like an egg deceive
  themselves.
This is my heart's advice.

ATTAINMENT refers to the complete attainment of buddhahood, enlightenment, freedom from all suffering. To be a *vajra master*, one must first have the qualities described in the Vinaya as well as in the Mahayana, which are outlined in the third chapter of *The Jewel Ornament of Liberation*. Buddha Maitreya also describes the qualities of a spiritual master in *The Ornament of the Mahayana Sutra* (Skt.: *Mahayanasutralankara*). A spiritual master must

- ▸ have mastered the three trainings: moral ethics, meditative concentration, and critical insight wisdom
- ▸ have strong renunciation of samsara with little concern for his own life and be able to dispel the confusion of others
- ▸ be well versed in the sutra teachings
- ▸ have actualized special insight
- ▸ possess skill to articulate the teachings
- ▸ have a compassionate nature
- ▸ be free from discouragement

These seven qualities are essential, but there are also several others. In the Vajrayana system a vajra master must have wisdom and understanding of the various tantra systems, and especially must have done meditation practices and kept samaya well. Above all, the experience of bodhicitta is essential. Therefore, merely bearing the title "lama" does not necessarily indicate that one is a qualified vajra master. Every Dharma student should carefully investigate the qualities of their lama—not with a limited, emotional judgment, but with one based on the Buddha's teachings. Lord Jigten Sumgön said, "The vajra master must have at least three qualities: incisive wisdom through which he can show the path without mistake; great compassion so that he can bear the suffering of trainees; and no concern or attachment for himself."

If a vajra master is truly qualified, the disciple must develop faith in his or her activities, since a qualified master's activities are performed only for the benefit of others. Those who recognize this will rejoice, and because of their connection, confidence and devotion will grow. This is not a cultural tradition. Rather, it is a method of connecting our mind to the spiritual path so that, step by step, we can progress and become free of our delusions.

We may not find a perfect vajra master like the Buddha. And even if a vajra master were perfect, we might not be able to perceive it. Our confused and bewildered mind will always find faults. But, instead of projecting that the vajra master is "mistaken," we should purify our impure view of the master. For us, the vajra master is more important than the Buddha himself because he or she represents the Buddha in this degenerate time when we have no opportunity to see the Buddha. We don't even know right from wrong. But we can see the vajra master in ordinary form and receive teachings on how to follow the Dharma step by step. Through the light of these teachings, we have the opportunity to dispel our own darkness and see the real qualities of the Buddha, Dharma, and Sangha. Thus, we gain the inspiration and courage to attain buddhahood. For all these reasons, we need to show gratitude and respect to the vajra master.

Even if the master's qualities are not fully perfected, we should still receive his or her teachings and take them to heart. We can attain enlightenment only through study and practice, and these depend on the instructions of the spiritual master. Examine carefully whether the master has the necessary qualities and whether his or her teachings are taught on the basis of sutras or the commentary of great masters, and then accept them if they are valid and reliable. Then, if we sincerely implement what is taught, this becomes a special cause to free us from all of our delusions. If we say "I am a good practitioner," but our actions show that we are not so good, this is called "hypocrisy." We have to be sincere.

Our actualization of the Dharma depends on taking the teachings to heart and serving the spiritual master in whatever way is needed. This allows us to purify all our negative thoughts and tendencies toward nonvirtue. This is the responsibility of the student. The best way to show respect for a master is to be a sincere and decent practitioner. In addition, the disciple must possess his or her own qualities. Aryadeva describes a good student as

- being honest and stable
- having the mental power of discernment that understands the teachings
- having sincere inspiration to follow the path.

To illustrate the keeping of samaya, the example is given of *an egg* that has two sides. To keep the egg from breaking, both sides have to be protected. But if even one side of the egg is broken, it is finished. Usually it is said that the disciple and vajra master each have responsibility for their own side of the samaya-egg. But here, the author is emphasizing that we as practitioners must take responsibility to maintain it for our own benefit and spiritual growth.

Ordinary people can't keep the discipline of the shravakas,
yet many think that the vows of secret mantra, the discipline
of maha-aryas, are easier to keep.
Even though the activities of union and liberating and so forth
are stated in the tantras,
these are the deeds only of those on pure bhumis.
In the name of secret mantra, some take women, drink, wear
strange clothes, and act like madmen and so forth.
If in this way one deceives oneself, one will become stuck in
the mud of samsara and then fall to the depths of hell.

ORDINARY PEOPLE refers to samsaric, unenlightened persons who are under the control of ignorance. For people like this, any type of discipline explained in the Dharma teachings will be difficult to keep. The *shravakas' discipline* refers to the basic Vinaya practices of observing monks', nuns', and lay precepts, as described earlier on page 26. Sometimes people think that these earlier vows are harder to keep, that Mahayana vows are easier, and that Vajrayana vows are easier still. Actually, it is the other way around. The Vinaya is easier because one refrains from harming others only for oneself. Mahayana vows are kept both for yourself and for the benefit of all other sentient beings, and the Vajrayana vows are kept in the pure view of the nature of buddhahood. Thus, they become progressively harder and more numerous.

Vows of secret mantra refers to the tantric vows, called *samaya*. It is not easy for ordinary people to keep these. In Sanskrit, *maha* means great, and *arya* means noble ones, the highly accomplished practitioners who have attained the eighth bodhisattva's level (*bhumi*) or above, whose afflicting emotions are under control, and who possess great realization of critical insight. Since they have such great mental strength, they can keep these higher vows. If we more ordinary people cannot keep the basic ones, how can we even think about keeping the higher ones!

In the Vajrayana, each and every symbol has a profound meaning. Male and female figures shown in union symbolize the inseparability of appearance and emptiness, or compassion and unafflicted wisdom. The male symbolizes appearance, and the female represents emptiness. One has to realize appearance and emptiness as indivisible, which is a profound and powerful method to directly uproot sexual desire. So the figures in union do not depict samsaric sexual activity.

Some deities appear in a fierce, wrathful form. This does not mean that the deity has the nature of anger. Rather, it shows that the delusion of anger has been forcefully destroyed and uprooted. The deity's bone ornaments symbolize impermanence and the renunciation of samsara. Likewise, when you see a deity with a five-pointed crown, this indicates that you should aspire to actualize what the crown signifies: the five buddha families, the embodiment of the five wisdoms that result from purifying the five types of afflicting emotions.

A deity's other ornaments also have meaning. The two earrings symbolize the two truths, relative and ultimate. The three necklaces represent the three bodies of a buddha. The bracelets, arm bands, rings, and ankle bracelets represent the six perfections. Furthermore, the deities' seats have significance. The jeweled throne symbolizes the jewel of all the excellent qualities. The lion symbolizes fearlessness. The lotus symbolizes the pure nature of wisdom and compassion that is unstained by the mud of obscuration. The sun disc symbolizes the clear nature of wisdom that dispels the darkness of delusion. The moon disc symbolizes the coolness of the compassionate mind, free of the heat of attachment and aversion. Sitting in the vajra position shows that the deity is not abiding in samsara or nirvana. All together, the images depict the complete, perfect qualities of a buddha. We should exert effort to experience and actualize the qualities they represent

Liberating, or putting others to death through curses and black magic, is also mentioned in the tantras. This type of liberating does not harm others' lives, but rather it frees them from samsaric delusion, causing them to attain enlightenment. But this can only be done by highly realized bodhisattvas who are accomplished in their meditation practice and who have attained the eighth or higher bhumis, called the "pure bhumis." The great Indian master Tilopa is an example of such a bodhisattva. He was nicknamed "Fisherman" because he fished all the time and then ate the fish. However, he was not fishing out of delusion or a craving for fish, but out of great compassion and intuitive insight. Those fish were all liberated; they no longer had to wander in samsara. However, going through the motions of such practices does not necessarily indicate a legitimate and genuine practice. You must be your own sincere witness to determine whether you have the realization to do this.

From beginning to end, all Dharma teachings and practices are designed to purify the gross and subtle mental obscurations. Sometimes, because of their mental delusions, practitioners don't understand the complete meaning of such things as union and liberating. Instead of being purified by Dharma practice, their minds become more gross, more coarse with negative thoughts. This is a serious issue. Because we don't fully understand Dharma, we can deceive ourselves about whether our mind is becoming more clear. It is important to know how to be careful and honest with ourselves.

As long as we have negative thoughts like attachment or anger, that itself is a cause of suffering. We should never create negativity, especially in the name of the Dharma. There is enough confusion in samsara already; there is no need to use the Dharma to make more. It is very important to keep the Dharma as pure as possible. If we cannot practice Dharma well, we should just say, "I cannot do it." That doesn't damage or water down the Dharma. Respect the Dharma; it is the only way to purify our negative thoughts and actions.

What do we have to do in order to achieve pure vision? First, we should avoid all nonvirtues, and then develop all virtues. Right from the beginning this will start to make our mind pure. By purifying our mind, we will achieve pure vision. Then, in the Mahayana, there are detailed teachings about loving-kindness, compassion, and bodhicitta. Purifying negative thoughts by using these methods is the root of achieving pure vision for all sentient beings. On the basis of these practices, the Vajrayana provides the opportunity to see all beings as deities. Without having a pure and sincere sense of loving-kindness and compassion, how could we visualize our enemy as a deity or Buddha? When we can see everyone as a deity, how could anger and attachment possibly arise? When attachment and anger are purified, then there is pure vision. That step-by-step development is what our practice is all about.

One cannot accomplish buddhahood without holding
all three vows.
If you observe purely the discipline of the Vinaya, bind all
you do to bodhicitta,
and practice the arising and completion stages of secret
mantra,
it will not be difficult to gain the fruit of the three kayas.

THIS VERSE CLARIFIES and expands on the last verse. As mentioned before, the *three vows* are (1) Vinaya vows, (2) Bodhisattva vows, and (3) Vajrayana vows.

We have to hold all three types of vows in order to attain buddhahood in one lifetime. We should keep the Vinaya discipline and abstain from all nonvirtuous actions, which are the cause of suffering. Then, with this as a foundation, on the bodhisattva's path we practice Dharma for others' benefit: develop loving-kindness, compassion, and bodhicitta; practice generosity, patience, perseverance, samadhi, and wisdom; benefit sentient beings; do all those things that bring peace, temporary happiness, and finally enlightenment. In this way, we exercise these practices fully and train the mind to be as firm as a mountain. Then, in order to accomplish these practices quickly and effectively, we must practice the Vajrayana and arise as a fully enlightened deity who represents inseparable appearance and emptiness in the enlightened state. When we arise as a deity we purify all ordinary vision, ordinary thoughts, and appearance. That is the purpose of deity, or yidam, practice. After we have attained this pure vision, we can practice ultimate wisdom. These are the methods that reveal buddha nature, the original mind that is perfect and complete.

At first, the Buddha taught in very simple way, and then progressively his teachings became more profound. Taking refuge is like going to kindergarten. Then, keeping the monastic vows is like elementary school. Bodhisattva practice is like going to secondary school. After that, we can go to college and study the Vajrayana. When we get a Ph.D., we still have all the qualities that were gained from kindergarten on up. In this way the teachings build upon one another. Nothing is wasted; nothing is contradictory. Rather, each level supports the others.

A single action can involve all three categories of vows. For example, a basic vow from the Vinaya says not to take life, not to kill people. We keep that vow for our own sake because we don't want to experience the consequences of creating negative karma and suffering. The bodhisattva's vow teaches us not to kill because we understand that all sentient beings desire peace and happiness and want to be free from suffering just as we do. In another bodhisattva practice, we regard all beings as our mother, a close relative, or a friend whom we couldn't possibly kill. In the Vajrayana, we don't kill others because we understand that their nature is that of a deity, of buddhahood. How could you dare to kill a buddha? Thus, that one action of not taking life can involve all three vows.

Take another example—drinking alcohol. In the Vajrayana, drinking is permitted and yet the Vinaya teachings say that drinking is not allowed. Some see a contradiction in this. In the Vajrayana you are allowed to drink *if* you can perceive the alcohol as nectar. If you can actually do this, you are drinking nectar, so in that case it's not contrary to the Vinaya. But if you drink alcohol as alcohol without having realized it as nectar, you are violating both the Vajrayana and Vinaya vows. When you have the ability to definitely perceive alcohol as nectar, the alcohol can no longer make you drunk, so drinking it does not violate any of the three vows. Therefore, these vows do not contradict each other; rather they support each other. If we can practice all three vows in this way without contradiction, it will not be difficult to gain buddhahood within one lifetime.

When we practice these three types of vows, we should not expect that the vows will do something for us, like bring us enlightenment. Instead, we should take full responsibility to do this ourselves by implementing these practices. The three vows are the instrument or tool that helps us to know what Dharma practice is about. For example, some people say that if you do Chenrezig practice, everything will be fine: Chenrezig will take care of everything and solve all your problems. With this idea, they proceed with high expectations.

Then, if things don't go well, they wonder what went wrong: "Chenrezig is not helping me enough" or "Maybe Chenrezig doesn't have the ability to help me." In this manner, doubt and hesitation mix with the meditation. In such cases, we should know that the Chenrezig meditation is a special tool to use for purifying mental obscurations. It has the ability to purify every one of our obscurations without exception. We ourselves have the responsibility to take up that tool and use it to dissolve our mental obscurations and purify the mind.

Take another example: if we have a sharp and powerful chainsaw that we want to use to cut a tree, leaning it up against the tree trunk will not get the job done. We have to actually apply the saw to the tree trunk. Likewise, we should utilize the powerful tool of the Dharma to uproot the tree of obscurations.

When one practices the Dharma by keeping the three types of vows, attaining the *three kayas* is not difficult. The three kayas are nirmanakaya, the emanation body; sambhogakaya, the complete enjoyment body; and dharmakaya, the perfect wisdom body. Vinaya practice purifies the gross obscurations, which becomes a cause to perceive and accomplish the nirmanakaya. Bodhicitta practice purifies the more subtle obscurations, which becomes a cause to perceive and accomplish the sambhogakaya. Vajrayana practice purifies the most subtle obscurations, which becomes the cause to perceive and accomplish the dharmakaya. But, of course, each vow is a tool to actualize all three kayas. Therefore, all Dharma practitioners who wish to be free from samsara and to attain complete buddhahood should practice all three categories of vows together.

Thus, I have briefly presented this general advice.
Now, for those who wish to practice the holy Dharma
from the depths of their heart,
I will explain these things by means of analogy.

THIS ENDS the first part of the text, the advice for both spiritual practitioners and ordinary people that relates to Dharma study and to daily life. If you carefully go through these verses, you will come to understand how to implement this universal advice. If you practice them well you will be respected by all cultures, whether spiritual or not, for they are the very foundation of Dharma that leads to the achievement of enlightenment. Up to this point, the text presented general advice from which anyone can benefit. From here on, Bhande Dharmaradza's hundred verses of heart-advice are concerned more with Dharma practice.

There are 84,000 types of afflicting emotions in an individual's mind that cause us to wander in samsara. Therefore, the Buddha taught 84,000 categories of Dharma as the antidote or remedy to purify these afflictions. Those who have a strong renunciation of samsara see that samsara holds no absolute peace and happiness, and that the only way to achieve undefiled peace and unafflicted joy is through complete enlightenment. For such practitioners, the following hundred pieces of advice are taught in a concise, precise, and complete form. So it is very important to go through them step by step, contemplating and meditating on their meaning, and putting them into practice.

Advice for Meditation Practitioners

FROM THIS POINT on, Bhande Dharmaradza ends each stanza with *This is my heart's advice*. He is giving this advice from his heart, completely for the benefit of others. So we should sincerely take it into our heart.

 Impermanence and death are like the spreading shadow
*   of sunset at the mouth of a pass.*
It approaches without stopping for even an instant.
Apart from Dharma, nothing will help.
This is my heart's advice.

This verse is about *impermanence*, the momentary nature of all phenomena. The following four contemplations apply to all the phenomena that exist in this world and demonstrate the nature of impermanence:

▸ The end of meeting is separation. All the people we meet in life, whether friend or enemy—in the end we are separated from them without choice. Consider a big meeting in a hall where thousands of people gather together and after some time disperse, each in his or her own way. This is a sign of impermanence. Even our dear family—husband, wife, children—we stay together for many years. Still, one day we have to separate without choice through the power of impermanence. On that day, we can only get comfort from our Dharma practice.

▸ The wealth we accumulate is also subject to dissipation. Some people collect so much, but in one instant everything can be lost. Some people are very rich and in one moment can become desperately poor. This also is a sign of impermanence.

▸ Everything that is constructed—buildings, roads, towers, airplanes—in the end they all fall to pieces.

▸ Those who are born in this world have to face death. From the day we are born, our journey toward death does not pause for even one second. In the past, many politically and spiritually powerful people were born, but all have passed away. Only their histories are left. Even if one were to stay for hundreds or thousands of years, still one's life would end one day.

The spreading shadow of sunset is used here as a metaphor for inevitability. From daybreak in the east to sunset in the west, the sun moves without stopping for even one second. No one has any doubt about this, do they? Likewise, from the moment of our birth, we are making a journey toward death with every moment. We aren't aware of it, but each day we are rushing to see the face of the Lord of Death, as though we were running a marathon. We think we are alive, but basically our nature is that of death. This body is nothing but an animated corpse. No matter how powerful our technology, no one can stop the sun from setting. Death is like that. No one can refuse to die. Death is inevitable.

At the time of death, it is obvious that nothing can help. No matter how powerful a person may be, even if he is the world's most powerful ruler, that power cannot help him prevent his own death. A person may have many friends and relatives, but they will be completely unable to help at the time of death. A person may have accumulated vast wealth, but at the time of death this, too, is useless. The best physician, who knows everything about medicine and disease: he or she is also impotent in the face of death. Even if the Buddha himself appeared before you, he could do nothing for you unless you had a connection to the Dharma. At the time of death, all the sophisticated machines and technology in the world are powerless. These days, you can see people dying in the hospital surrounded by machines. At that time, Dharma is the only way to help individuals who are experiencing death.

Dharma is the only possible help—*if* we have experience in practice. Someone can tell us, "Be peaceful, be mindful," but unless we practice this, these are just words. Intellectual understanding is not enough. No matter how well versed we may be or how many books we have read, without practice—without having experienced the real meaning of Dharma in our minds—mere knowledge is of no use. This is why it is emphasized that everyone has to take the individual responsibility to study and practice.

We don't have much time for this. Life passes by with each moment, so practice Dharma sincerely. When the time comes, the Lord of Death will not give us permission to live longer because of our excuses. We can't negotiate with the Lord of Death, either. So, we must apply our minds to practice while we have the opportunity. If we had no opportunity to practice, what could we do? But since our circumstances allow it—since we have interest, time, and opportunity—we should practice from the moment our interest arises. This story illustrates the importance of taking advantage of the opportunities we have:

> One day a man was walking along a hazardous trail bounded by a cliff face on one side and a steep drop-off to the ocean on the other. Through inattention, he stepped in the wrong place and tumbled over the edge. As he was falling, he grabbed at anything that passed by as best he could. Midway down, his hand found a clump of grass and he held fast to it. He also found a little support for his feet there, so he rested safely for a while. He soon discovered a honey-filled bee hive within reach, which he came to enjoy very much. The honey was quite delicious; every time he tasted the honey he became more and more attached to it.
>
> He was visited by two mice, one white and one black, who each day alternately ate one blade of the grass he was holding on to. He was very concerned that one day all the grass would be consumed by these two mice. Looking down, he could see three animal dwellings on the ground below—one for a pig, a bird, and a snake. Beyond that was the ocean being fed by a raging river. When he looked up, he could see magnificent palaces in the distance. There was one in particular that was especially beautiful, so neat and fresh, that was being enjoyed by some heavenly beings.
>
> He was frightened by the thought of falling, and had a strong desire to climb up to those palaces. There were

people above who were ready to help him up if only he would ask. He thought, "I really must do that one day. It would be wonderful to live there." At the same time, he was so attached to that honey that he could not give it up. He looked at the diminishing grass and thought, "I must get out of here soon," but the honey always held him back. Finally, having done none of the things he had thought about, he fell to his death.

In this parable the palaces symbolize the human and god realms and, above that, the state of enlightenment. The pig sty represents the animal realm, the bird's nest is the hungry ghost realm, and the snake hole is the hell realm. The water is the endless ocean of samsara. The honey depicts our samsaric enjoyments. Even though we have the seed of enlightenment, beginningless buddha nature, we wander along the trail of samsara with our delusions. The clump of grass is our life span. Instead of using that human life to practice Dharma, we just waste it enjoying the five senses. The white mouse represents daytime and signifies the passing of time. The black mouse is night time and also shows the march of time, our ever-shortening lifespan. If we asked for help by taking refuge in the Buddha, Dharma, and Sangha, we could get help and be freed from falling into the lower realms or even from the entirety of samsara itself. But instead, we don't apply ourselves to sincere Dharma practice and end up consuming our life without creating much benefit. Consider this carefully, and make every effort to practice the Dharma.

The purpose of saying this is not to create fear. Death will come whether we are afraid of it or not. But the awareness of death provides critical inspiration for serious study and practice, the purification of all our mental delusions and afflictions. Otherwise, we may waste a lot of time and opportunity indulging in our fantasies and illusions. Milarepa said, "I escaped to the mountains because of my fear of death. Once I got to the mountains, I practiced persistently by meditating on the uncertain time of death. Thus, I captured the fortress of the unchanging nature of mind. Now I am free from the fear of death." Because we have such methods, teachings, and instructions that overcome our fear of death, and help us to realize the nature of death as an illusion, it is important to apply ourselves as much as we can. If we had no methods to overcome our fear of death, it would be useless to talk about death. There would be no solution, no remedy for it. But since we have those methods, practice is very important.

When we die, we don't know where we will go. We will be bewildered and wander in blind darkness. Beings have so much anxiety and fear about this. Where are we going? What will become of us? But good Dharma practice is like a map. Because of Dharma, we will be well prepared, and know where to go and what is supposed to happen. This is what Dharma practice is for. Do you see how precious it is? This is why the Buddha gave all these precious teachings. If we apply Dharma successfully, we can die without fear. We can die joyfully, or at least we can die without regret. Therefore, reflecting repeatedly on the impermanence of all phenomena is crucial in order to overcome laziness and to practice the Dharma effectively.

Take a moment. If you are depressed, reflect on impermanence. Everything is transitory, like the blowing of the wind. If you are suffering from attachment, reflect on impermanence. Everything is momentary, like the fading of a beautiful flower. If you are suffering from resentment or rage, reflect on impermanence. The object of your anger will die one day without control. In this way, we should make an effort to reduce these sufferings and encourage ourselves to develop more wisdom and strength for clarity of mind. The past is past; it is not here now. The future has not yet arrived. This present moment passes in an instant, like a flash of light.

The joy and happiness of this life are like dreams and illusions.
We are left with nothing at the time of death.
Practice the holy Dharma without distraction.
This is my heart's advice.

THE JEWEL ORNAMENT OF LIBERATION mentions that we should contemplate impermanence in order to free ourselves from attachment to this life. But of course, we do have attachment to this life, so this practice is not easy. We should be mindful and practice to familiarize ourselves with impermanence. It takes a lot of energy and courage to do this, and we don't like it because our attachment to this life is great.

But consider this: At the time of our death, how much of what we were so attached to actually brought any benefit? Was any of it meaningful? No. It was just like a dream. Suppose that in a dream we go to a beautiful place, make wonderful friends, and experience heavenly enjoyments. Then, in the middle of the dream, we happen to wake up. Now where are all those beautiful mountains? Where are all the people? Nowhere! This is so mysterious. If you really think about it, it is inexpressible. Did that dream have any essence? Did it bring any benefit? As soon as we wake up, it all disappears. A magic show is also like this. In a magic trick, when the magician does his conjuring, one can see elephants, horses, rabbits, and birds. But as soon as the trick is over, they all disappear; they are nonexistent.

Suppose that we had a wonderful time yesterday. We went someplace with dear friends and had such a good time—one that we think we will never forget. Today, though, it is just like a dream. Even if you lived for a hundred years and enjoyed wonderful things, see if those hundred years of joy brings any benefit at the time of death. What benefit was created through attachment to that happiness? None! It is like a dream, an illusion. Look at a rainbow—how beautiful it is, so vivid, so precise, and so clear. But it's really nothing. We ourselves are like that "nothing" at the time of death. Not only that, but this "nothing" brings more suffering at the time of death—more pain and more predicaments.

In the daytime, our experiences seem so real. For example, you might have a strong, painful headache for a while but then it passes. While you have the headache, the pain is so real that you can't eat or sleep. But when it disappears, you say, "Now I am free from the headache." Where has it gone? Has it dissolved into the air? If you investigate carefully, you can understand the headache was illusory. This is what life is like. We are left with nothing at the time of death. We work so hard for this life, sacrificing everything to create something tangible. Then, when we need it most, it is not there.

This does not mean that we shouldn't work for a living. We do need things. But don't become attached to them. Don't be distracted by the happiness of this life. Instead, put the Dharma into practice. If you can do that, there is a possibility that you can die joyfully, peacefully, and happily. You could also live peacefully. How wonderful that would be! For this reason, we need to develop a keen awareness of our own impermanence.

During our lifetime, we have the opportunity to do many things. When we die, these opportunities are gone. Because the Dharma is holy, you become holy if you practice Dharma sincerely according to its meaning. Dharma is the teaching on how to achieve inner peace and clarity. How precious that is!

Take a brief moment and meditate how everything is like a dream. For instance, suppose a man finds a most precious object in a dream and is very happy about it. Then after some time, he loses it; he is very sad and suffers tremendously from his loss. Then when he wakes up, there is nothing found or lost. Regard all things in this way. See them as a reflection or a dream. This practice gives us a priceless opportunity to reduce our mental burden.

The eight worldly concerns are like a snare.
Exhausted by meaningless effort, we end our lives in dissatisfaction.
Meditate well on renunciation.
This is my heart's advice.

AS TAUGHT BY Nagarjuna, the *eight worldly concerns* are

- gain and loss
- pleasure and pain
- praise and blame
- fame and disgrace

In samsara, we involve ourselves with these notions. As a matter of fact, these are the concerns that we spend most of our energy on in this life. We make great effort to gain things, experience pleasure, win praise, and become famous, and then we have to protect what we have. We also make great effort to avoid loss, pain, blame, and disgrace. This is not just a Buddhist view of things—the entire world is driven by these eight concerns, and so we suffer here helplessly. We are trapped in the *snare* of these eight worldly concerns.

Even if we achieve some success in our endeavors, still we are not satisfied. Again and again, we need something else. Some people in the world are dying without food or clothes. Others have everything they could possibly want but still suffer. All of us are suffering from *dissatisfaction*. We are not satisfied with what we achieve or with what we have.

If you become famous, you will encounter more obstacles. When you have little fame, you are free. When you have a lot of fame, then you have to work to protect it. So try not to become attached to your fame, likewise to your praise, pleasure, or gain. Just work sincerely. If you have no attachment to these things, they will not become a cause of suffering. Likewise, if you have no aversion to loss, pain, blame and disgrace, these will not become a cause of suffering. The more aversion we have for them, the more they become a cause of suffering.

Renunciation means giving up attachment and aversion toward these eight worldly concerns and all other mental delusions that are the root cause of suffering. Sometimes people think that this means giving up life, having nothing, not eating, or going without clothes. That is one kind of renunciation, but here renunciation means nonattachment. With this kind of renunciation, you can be famous but you remain unattached to your fame. If you gain something, you have no attachment to it. Great bodhisattvas can have many things but are not attached to them. They are like a lotus that is born from the mud. A lotus blooms fresh and pure above the water, not stained by the mud at all. Similarly, even if you are famous or possess many things, they will not cause you suffering if you have no attachment.

Take a deep breath and meditate well on renunciation. Look at the mind—what causes you to suffer? Your mental state. Therefore, apply yourself to purifying nonvirtuous thoughts. Renounce ignorance and delusion, the causes of suffering. Appreciate what you have and rejoice in your good qualities. Develop great compassion and wisdom for those who indulge in these eight worldly concerns.

The appearance of happiness is like burning ash.
Unaware of this, we cannot reach the final goal.
Make effort to generate revulsion.
This is my heart's advice.

WHEN A FIRE has burned down and all the wood is gone, some coals will remain in the fireplace. They look cool on the surface, but underneath the ash they are still burning. If you step on one, it will definitely burn you. If you know this, you will naturally avoid that ash. In the same way, pleasures may appear to bring joy, but we can't be sure of what lies below the surface. Underneath, they may bring a lot of suffering.

Sometimes, when you look at other people, their success seems quite admirable. Also, we can be swept away when we have achieved some happiness, but we don't know what will come afterward or what the side effects will be. Not recognizing it as burning ash, we can become engrossed in momentary pleasure, which keeps us from reaching the final goal, enlightenment. For this reason, we should make effort to generate *revulsion*. Here, revulsion and renunciation have the same meaning: nonattachment.

This verse is about the suffering of change. In samsara you first want to become rich. You may think, "When I am rich, I will be so happy. All my problems will go away; my life will be perfect." Then, when you become rich, you begin to worry about how to maintain your wealth. So, wealth apparently causes happiness, but deep down suffering is still present. When we experience attachment to the *appearance of happiness*, we should know it as a source of suffering, the basic nature of samsara.

There is a story that illustrates this point:

There was once a king who was praised by all his subjects. People said, "You are so wise and compassionate. You take good care of your people," and so forth. One day a man praised him, saying, "You are the happiest man in the world. You live in such a rich palace. You eat the most delicious and expensive cuisine. You sit on a golden throne." The king replied, "Thank you for your compliments. I'd like to invite you to come here tonight and sleep in my golden bed." Of course, the man was overjoyed to do this.

When the man arrived, he was served an ambrosia-like meal. Then the king took him to the bedchamber where he had hung a very sharp sword from the ceiling directly over the bed. The king said, "This sword may fall at any moment, but this is my order to you: sleep one night in this bed." The man tried, but he could not sleep at all. All night, he was afraid that the sword would fall down and kill him at any moment.

The next morning, the king returned and asked, "Did you enjoy my golden bed?" The man said, "No. I could not." The king said, "This is how it is for me, too. You thought I was very happy eating good food and enjoying luxuries. But I take the full responsibility on my shoulders for the country's welfare. I worry about how to protect it and how to protect my people. I experience no peace whatsoever."

Of course, some material possessions are very useful, but we should check to see whether they are the real root of happiness. For example, I may not have a car, so I want a car. Then I think, "I could travel freely and go anywhere without depending on anyone else." As soon as I get a car, though, I have to worry about insurance and gasoline. And if the car gets a scratch, I won't like it. We start with one suffering, a car, and that immediately starts building up many other sufferings. This doesn't mean that we shouldn't own a car, but as long as we are in samsara, dissatisfaction is unavoidable.

Because we are unaware of the danger of attachment, we do a lot of things to protect our comfort. Then we end up spending our entire lives protecting one thing after another but, in the end, nothing is left. No matter how much insurance we have, when the time of death comes, we die. So practice nonattachment and the precious Dharma, and earn the infinite wealth of enlightened qualities.

*Activities done only for this life are like a moth drawn into
   a flame.*
Deceiving oneself in this way is only a cause of suffering.
Abandon attachment to samsara.
This is my heart's advice.

A MOTH SEES the light of a candle as a magnificent palace and thinks, "If I could only get into that beautiful palace, I would be so happy." No matter how much you try to protect it, the moth just flies in. Likewise, in our daily, samsaric life we are attracted to accumulating possessions and to becoming famous due to our attachment to this life. Even if one practiced Dharma, one could not be called a true practitioner as long as this attachment remained. We never think of the next life, yet we make all this misguided effort to invite suffering into it. No one else could deceive us like this, but we deceive ourselves very successfully. If someone else had deceived us, we would have someone to blame, but when we deceive ourselves there is no one else to blame and we suffer helplessly. Therefore, abandon this habit of attachment, and thereby develop true compassion for yourself and others.

Some people don't understand this and might think you are crazy when you talk this way. You don't work for this life? You don't make every effort for your livelihood? They think this will destroy your life. Actually, this is the way to protect your life because, this way, you won't continue to create the causes of suffering. If one has attachment to samsaric pleasure, one has no renunciation. Afflicted virtuous actions done for samsaric achievement do not establish a basis for freedom from samsara. If you could do virtuous action for the next life, not only for this one, then you would have a deeper understanding of life and be called "far-sighted."

In this section, the author explains how to uproot the causes of suffering by saying, "Don't do this, don't do that." By saying this, he is looking out for our own best interest. If we have these attachments, we cannot practice loving-kindness and compassion. Nor can we practice deity yoga. We cannot even properly take refuge in the Buddha, Dharma, and Sangha, not to mention achieve enlightenment.

Take a moment and think about the moth mentioned earlier. Without any doubt or fear and with full confidence, he flies straight into the fire due to his ignorance. Because of attachment, his life ends right there to no good purpose. Likewise, there are so many people in this world who rush after suffering for no good purpose.

The activities of samsara are like ripples of water.
Before they cease, our lives come to an end.
Quickly give up concern for them.
This is my heart's advice.

UNTIL THE OCEAN dries up, its *ripples of water* will endlessly come one after another. In the same way, as long as samsara remains, our *activities* will never be finished. Throughout this life, there are limitless activities. Parents often say, "When my children are older, I will rest and enjoy life." But when they're grown up, there are other things to do like looking after their grandchildren. We say, "If I just finish this one thing, then I will practice Dharma." When we finish one thing, another important thing comes along. And when we finish that, another one comes. Then, before all our important things are completed, our lives come to an end. What kind of benefit will you get then by having been so busy your whole life?

We sacrifice today for tomorrow's peace and happiness. We sacrifice this year for next year's peace and happiness. So, using the same reasoning, why don't we sacrifice this life's pleasure for enlightenment? This story illustrates how to use this life to gain freedom from suffering:

> Once a hunter accidentally met Milarepa in his meditation cave. Through the power of Milarepa's skill, wisdom, and compassion, the hunter's negative thoughts were completely removed. He was inspired by Milarepa's way of life and said, "I want to study and practice under your guidance, but first I have to go home and give some instructions to my family. I will come back in a week." Milarepa replied, "Of course, it's your choice whether you want to meditate or not. If you really want to practice, stay. You will not starve here. There is plenty to eat." Again the hunter said, "I definitely want to receive your teachings, but first I have

to go home and take care of things." Milarepa replied, "Of course, if you want to go, you can go. But I may not be here when you return. If you have really decided to practice Dharma, stay here in the cave." So the hunter stayed and became a great practitioner. If he had gone back home, who knows what would have happened. Perhaps he would have changed his mind, or he might have put off returning and eventually lost his opportunity.

We should pray and contemplate: "From now until this time tomorrow, I will perform virtuous deeds with body, speech, and mind." This is the mental attitude that we should adopt. "From now until this time tomorrow" means that for the next few hours, you will make every effort to avoid negative karma. You will make every effort to develop positive thought. In this way you can continue your work, but your motivation is changed. Then the next day, you say the prayer again. You continue to renew that commitment each day. This is real practice. This is so beautiful!

When the ocean is exhausted, there are no more ripples. *Giving up concern* means giving up attachment to our unending plans only for this life. We still do what is necessary, but are not completely enslaved. We give up the causes of misery, the causes of suffering, and do something useful instead. We do things that are helpful for ourselves and others. We do something good for our next life and for the planet. Just as we need peace and happiness in this life, we will need the same things in the next life. Why should we jeopardize the next life for this one? Make the effort to free yourself from this delusion.

Do a short contemplation by looking at a running river. The ripples in the water flow endlessly without pause until the river dries up. Likewise, there is no end to the flow of our activity until the end of life. Reflecting on this, make some time to practice the precious Dharma and bring peace into the mind.

Relatives and friends can be like prison guards.
There are many who obstruct those who wish to practice
   the holy Dharma from the depths of their hearts.
Cut the mental bonds of clinging.
This is my heart's advice.

THIS VERSE is easily misunderstood, so we should be careful here. The author is not saying that we should hate or disrespect our family and friends. He is simply saying that the bonds of clinging bring no real benefit. There is a difference between clinging to loved ones and truly benefiting them. We can benefit our relatives and friends greatly with kindness, compassion, and skill. To do this, we need to study and practice Dharma, and then we can help to free them from delusion and show them the path of wisdom and compassion. Being confused by attachment to them won't do much good. Attachment to relatives doesn't allow us to do great things; in fact, it may create obstacles. Those of us who want to practice Dharma sincerely and successfully must sacrifice some small things for this greater purpose. This is the way of wisdom and skill.

Take Buddha Shakyamuni's life story as an example. His father was so attached to his son, Siddhartha, that he didn't want him to abandon the kingdom and tried in many ways to prevent him from leaving. But finally Siddhartha saw that there would be no ultimate benefit if he stayed. If he were attached to the kingdom, he could not help the people in the palace, much less in the whole country. He understood the deeper meaning of the suffering of aging, sickness, and death, and he understood that he had no ability to help anyone overcome those conditions. So out of great compassion and wisdom, he renounced limited love and compassion. To achieve what is immeasurable, he renounced his father's attachment to him. That's what this verse refers to. It was not that Siddhartha hated his father or family; rather, he saw that he could really help them only through greater wisdom and compassion.

After he attained buddhahood, Buddha Shakyamuni went with a great gathering of his sangha to see his father. He gave extensive teachings that freed all the people in the kingdom from samsara. His father finally realized what his son had been doing, and he developed great admiration for the Buddha, declaring, "You are not merely a king of human beings; you have become the king of all sentient beings, including even the gods!"

In the same way, we must allow an open mind and create great mental space in order to bring about real benefit for ourselves and all beings, including our family. We need courage to do this, courage based on wisdom and compassion. Without the precious Dharma it wouldn't matter what we did. We can always take samsaric action. But since we have the Dharma, we should cut the mental bonds of clinging and narrow-mindedness. This does not mean that we should ignore our friends and relatives but that we should help them sincerely and with compassion by cutting our own attachment.

Sweethearts can be like butchers holding knives.
Even if we benefit them, they respond to our kindness with harm.
Abandon attachment to everyone.
This is my heart's advice.

THIS IS MUCH like the last verse. People close to you can cut your
heart and bring you to the hell realms. Then you will have nothing—no samsaric achievement, no Dharma achievement. Many of
us suffer greatly from this. Regard those to whom you are attracted
as having the nature of illusion, like a rainbow. When you look
at them, they appear so beautiful and vivid. But you cannot wear
a rainbow or use it for any purpose. You can look at it and say,
"There's a rainbow. How beautiful it is!" but you don't try to hold
on to one. If we could see everything this way, our mind would
really achieve freedom.

Otherwise, these situations are painful and difficult to give up.
Samsara is just like that sticky glue that catches mice on paper.
There is no way to escape. You free your leg, and then your arm
gets caught. Your house is OK, and then your car goes bad. This is
why the text says to *abandon attachment to everyone,* not to just a
few things.

Again, this does not mean that you should not love, respect, and
care for your family. Care for them and do everything you can to
bring benefit to their lives. When we are free from attachment,
though, we can benefit our loved ones through bodhicitta just as
the Buddha, Milarepa, and other great teachers did. This is why it
is said that when a bodhisattva is born in the world he or she is like
a lotus, completely pure and fresh, not stained at all by the mud of
samsara. When we practice Dharma, we are trying to develop that
same quality. Of course, this is not easy. There is a lot of work to do,
but it's worthwhile work. When you finally experience an achievement after all your sacrifice, you will appreciate this path. You will
rejoice in what you did.

The activities of this degenerate age are like a madman's
      performance of dance.
   No matter what we do, there is no way to please others.
   Think about what is essential.
   This is my heart's advice.

IN ANY GROUP of people, there is always some misunderstanding. You cannot satisfy everyone, no matter what you do. The *Bodhicaryavatara* says that every individual has a different way of thinking. Thus, it is very difficult to please everyone. Even the Buddha could not do it, so how can we? Instead of trying to please others, please yourself by applying yourself fully to bodhicitta.

Investigate your situation carefully, according to the Dharma. For us, it is more important to know what is best than to know how to please everyone. Know what is right, and on the basis of your own wisdom and skill, just do it. Don't expect that other people will be pleased with you or that they will be happy about what you do. Rather, do what's best, what's helpful for yourself and for others. If they are happy about it, that's fine. If they are not happy, what can you do?

Most of the time we enjoy a lot of activities but we don't really analyze what we are doing. We plan what we will do next year, discussing and describing a lot of plans, but in reality we don't know what will happen tomorrow. This is the behavior of a *madman*. We try to please others, but it is very difficult. So think about *what is essential*—that is, work with your own mind to free yourself from delusions and negative thoughts. Once you purify your delusions, there will be a chance to make others happy. Until then, it will not be possible.

Almost all speech is like the startling sound of "chal."
It has no essence and results in many deceptions.
Investigate carefully.
This is my heart's advice.

IN THIS degenerate time, because of their unruly minds, many people are involved in idle talk, gossiping about the world. This may include divisive speech that separates friends, families, or groups. It may include harsh words and lies. Harsh words can cut another's heart into pieces and create karma with negative results for the future. The story about the *sound of* "chal" is on page 50.

Most conversations do not have much meaning and are only a waste of time. When you engage in conversation, use pleasant words and spend the right amount of time expressing yourself. Communicate the point precisely and say things with a kind heart to benefit others. When you look at other beings, gaze with loving-kindness and compassion Think, "Whether these are positive or negative circumstances, by depending on these sentient beings, I have a great opportunity to develop my bodhisattva qualities. They are helping me purify all my negative, childish obscurations and quickly attain enlightenment." We have to investigate things carefully. If you have studied Dharma well, you will have the skill to distinguish between what is right and what is wrong. Otherwise, you may be easily deceived. So pay no attention to what people say about you, good or bad. Protect your mind by practicing Dharma. This is very important.

All desires are like poisonous food.
They are the cause of nonvirtue and cut the root of liberation.
Apply vigilance without distraction.
This is my heart's advice.

THIS VERSE describes samsaric desire—greed and sensual desire—
not the desire for enlightenment! All samsaric desires are causes
of nonvirtue. When we have a strong attachment to something,
whatever we do based on that attachment will always create problems. There will arise many types of obstacles that we don't like.
Then pride and jealousy arise from our attachment, and that in turn
encourages aversion and hatred to arise. Thus, we create heavy negative karma. Without desire, there is no reason for anger or hatred to
arise. Without ignorance, there is no reason to have desire or attachment. So, you can see that they are closely interconnected. Attachment, hatred, pride, and jealousy—these are the real obstacles that
keep us from enlightenment, from attaining liberation. Not only
do they obstruct liberation, but they prevent us from experiencing
peace and happiness even in samsara.

This verse is especially directed to serious and sincere Dharma
practitioners. While you are in samsara, use your wisdom carefully.
Apply vigilance means to use your wisdom awareness to discern
what kind of essence there really is in samsara. Be vigilant about
every action you perform, and don't let poisonous, samsaric desires
distract you. Recognize both the real root cause of suffering and the
real root cause of liberation.

This verse also concerns the suffering of change. At first, *poison-*
ous food may be delicious, but after some time you feel the poison;
it may even kill you. All sensual desires are like this. It may seem that
they bring pleasure, happiness, and joy, but they steal away the life
of unafflicted happiness and peace. Instead of being attached to temporary happiness and joy, practice Dharma in order to achieve absolute happiness and joy. Anger is the suffering of suffering because as

soon as anger arises in our heart, it destroys happiness and gives rise to suffering. Ignorance is the suffering of conditions because as long as ignorance exists, suffering is ready to manifest. Milarepa said,

> When you first look at samsara, it's very attractive.
> Then in the middle, it is very deceptive.
> In the end, one is doomed to suffer.
> Therefore, I renounced samsara.

Take a moment to contemplate this verse. At first, things are very attractive, desirable and beautiful. One longs for them. But in the end, that attraction invites undesirable conditions, and we suffer helplessly. So meditate on how moderation is important, and appreciate the opportunity to study and practice this precious Dharma teaching.

The results of virtue and nonvirtue are like the shadows
of flying birds.
We may not see them now, but they will appear at the
time of death.
Make effort to abandon nonvirtue and to accomplish
wholesome deeds.
This is my heart's advice.

THIS VERSE describes the inexorable law of cause and result that we must all pay attention to. Some develop doubt about karma when they see people who are ruthless, are involved in many negative acts, or create a lot of negative karma but who are still very successful. Other people are so religious, warm-hearted, and kind, but continually face misfortune and obstacles. How can this be?

When a bird takes off, we can see its shadow. As the bird flies far up in the sky, the shadow disappears. But as soon as the bird lands again, the shadow returns. Virtue and nonvirtue are like that. When we first perform an act, we know what we did and whether it was virtuous or nonvirtuous. But after some time, we forget. This doesn't mean that the karma we created disappeared. When causes and conditions come together, we will experience the results. This is irreversible. We may not see these results now, but they will appear at the time of death or after. Even if at the time of death, we experience regret, by then it's too late. This is why the Dharma emphasizes the different kinds of suffering. Sometimes it is depressing to hear about suffering all the time. But by reflecting on suffering, one gains an opportunity to awaken.

Sufferings do not manifest without cause or through an unrelated cause. Each has a precise cause. The Dharma uncovers our intuitive wisdom to perceive this precisely. Because of this, these teachings can give us inspiration and strength. Dharma practice prepares us to face suffering in a positive way without blaming anyone. With Dharma practice, we get an opportunity to awaken from suffering;

we can search for solutions. Using suffering in this way leads us to develop wisdom. Therefore, we should make every effort to purify nonvirtue and to accomplish good qualities.

Sometimes we may do something good and then encounter some misfortune soon afterward. We may even think, "Maybe this misfortune is a result of my good deeds. I shouldn't do any more." When we encounter these conditions, we shouldn't doubt at all. All the good that we have done—dedicate it to complete enlightenment, to freedom from samsara. If misfortune arises, understand that this is the result of the ripening of some other, negative karma—not of this virtue. Always trust in the unyielding nature of karma, both positive and negative. Even the Buddha experienced the results of negative karma.

> When the Buddha was in India, he held a three-month summer retreat each year. Each retreat had a sponsor, usually either the king or an important merchant. One year, the king of a country close to Shravasti promised to be the sponsor for the Buddha and five hundred monks, and he proclaimed to his people that no one else was allowed to make any offerings to the Buddha and his disciples during those three months. He didn't mention that he himself was going to arrange everything, but only told them that they were not allowed to make offerings for that time.
>
> That night, the king dreamt that his kingdom was surrounded by intestines. This was an unprecedented omen, so the next day he consulted a famous Brahmin about its meaning. The Brahmin told him, "This is a terrible sign; your life is in danger. You must go into retreat for three months, starting today." The king became very frightened and immediately left for retreat, telling the people that for the next three months no one was allowed to come see him or talk to him.
>
> The next day, the Buddha and his disciples came to do their summer retreat. Shariputra was sick and Maudgalyayana was caring for him, so it happened that they could not attend the retreat and went instead to the God Realm of the Thirty-three. The king was gone, and no one in the

kingdom dared to offer anything because the king had for-
bidden it, so there was no one to sponsor the retreat. Word
of this went around. A merchant from another place had
some horse fodder, some of which was rotten. "If it pleases
the Buddha, I have this much to offer," he said, and the
Buddha accepted it happily.

Ananda watched these things with tears in his eyes. He
thought, "This Buddha practiced for three limitless kalpas,
attained buddhahood, the state of perfection, and still he
has to eat such things. How could this happen?" The Buddha said, "Don't be upset. Everything is fine." A grain of
what the Buddha was eating fell from his mouth, and the
Buddha told Ananda to taste it. Ananda experienced it as
being utterly delicious, with a hundred different undefiled
flavors. The Buddha said, "Whether it is good or bad for
you, I experience all food and drink like this."

In other kingdoms, people heard that the Buddha was
without food. Kings like Bimbisara tried to bring food, but
a torrential rain arose and they could not pass through
the flooded roads. None of the horses could make the trip
through the rain. So in this way they passed the entire
three months. When the king came out of his retreat and
heard what had happened, he apologized to Ananda for
his poor planning. The king also went to the Buddha and
apologized profusely for his mistake.

The Buddha said, "You don't have to apologize. It was
not your mistake; it happened because of my karma. Limitless kalpas ago, there was a buddha with many monks.
One day a rich, powerful king invited them all to a very
special, nectar-like meal. At that time there was a Brahmin
with five hundred followers who was very jealous of the
Buddha. He said, 'They do not deserve to have such a delicious meal. They should be eating rotten food instead.' All
but two of his followers rejoiced in what he said. These
two said, 'No, they should enjoy what is offered to them.'
So this is the result of that karma. I was the Brahmin who
led those five hundred monks, and we have now all experienced this result except for Shariputra and Maudgalyayana.

They did not rejoice in what the Brahmin said, and so they spent this time in the god realm and for three months ate nectar instead of rotten horse feed."

Thus, we should trust in what the Buddha taught about the inexorable nature of cause and result, and how it manifests. When we face misfortune, trouble, or obstacles—any negative condition—we should simply contemplate that this is the result of negative karma and is a great opportunity for purification. Then, when good things happen, we should rejoice in the virtuous karma we have created and, without attachment, continue to create even better karma—not just for the benefit of samsaric life, but rather to attain enlightenment for others' benefit.

Virtue and nonvirtue, positive karma and negative karma are not just a system of belief. They are the law of the universe. Whatever we do becomes a cause that manifests a result. If, for example, someone tells a lie, whether it is spiritual or not, others will not appreciate it and will not respect the liar. On the other hand, if you always speak the truth, everyone will appreciate and respect your words. This is a universal truth. *Meaningful to Behold,* a life story of Lord Jigten Sumgön, quotes that precious lord as saying:

> The nature of virtue and nonvirtue is that they cannot be exchanged." The noble, great acharya Nagarjuna said, "If one acts with attachment, aggression, or ignorance, that is nonvirtue. If one acts with nonattachment, nonaggression, and unobstructed mind, that is virtue.

So reflect on the ten virtues and become inspired to live your life in that way and be free of the ten nonvirtues. In this life, we are studying and practicing the Dharma sincerely. But if we feel we cannot accomplish all these practices in this one lifetime, we'll need to obtain another human life in the future. Therefore, we need to recall the causes of a precious human life and perform virtuous activities.

First, it is most important to keep moral ethics. Then, in order to practice and study the Dharma in the next life, we will again need food and clothes, so practice generosity during this life. Whatever you can share, give it. When you give something away, it is not wasted at all. Just practice generosity without expectation and, without much effort, you will have ensured the conditions to study and practice the Dharma in the next life. The six paramitas are designed distinctly and decisively for just this purpose.

However, if one practices generosity, but without moral ethics, there may be unexpected results. Occasionally we see dogs and cats that live with rich people. They are treated much better than some human beings. Because these animals practiced generosity in the past, they are treated very well, but because they lacked moral ethics, they were born as animals. All these results come without fail, so make every effort to develop virtue in a complete form.

13 *The accumulation of wealth is like bees gathering honey.*
We are bound by it, and it is freely taken by others.
Therefore, accumulate merit through the practice of generosity.
This is my heart's advice.

ACCUMULATING WEALTH out of attachment to becoming rich for this life is like *bees gathering honey.* That wealth *binds us to samsara* and is easily *taken by others* by many means, including stealing and so forth. That becomes a source of suffering, so this verse explains the practice of generosity. While we are accumulating wealth, we should also accumulate merit by practicing generosity. Generosity results in real wealth that can be used in this life and in future lives. This wealth can be used to attain enlightenment. Such wonderful wealth!

In *The Jewel Ornament of Liberation*, Lord Gampopa explains generosity using a quotation from the *Sutra Requested by House-holder Drakshulchen:*

> A thing that is given is yours; things left in the house are not. A thing that is given has essence; things left in the house have no essence. A thing that has been given need not be protected; things kept in the house must be protected. A thing that is given is free from fear; things kept in the house are kept with fear. A thing that is given is closer to enlightenment; things left in the house go in the direction of the maras. The practice of generosity will lead to vast wealth; things left in the house do not bring much wealth. A thing that is given will bring inexhaustible wealth; things kept in the house are exhaustible.

Milarepa said, "Wealth—our first impression is that it is like a wish-fulfilling jewel. Later, at the second step, we cannot live without it. Finally, it becomes a hook that draws in thieves and bandits."

Once Milarepa was going from one place to another and the local village people said, "Don't go that way; it is very dangerous." He asked, "What kind of danger is there?" They told him that there were a lot of thieves and bandits on that road. Milarepa just laughed. "But I have no wealth to steal!" He was so free.

On another occasion, Milarepa was meditating at night in a cave. A thief sneaked into his cave, searching in every corner for something to steal. Milarepa began to laugh. The thief asked why he was laughing, and Milarepa said, "If you find anything in the night that I myself cannot find in the daytime, please take it freely." The thief also laughed and left.

So having wealth and being rich will not necessarily result in a good life or happiness. A donkey with a load of gold on his back has a lot of gold, but it does not make him happy, since he doesn't know the meaning of wealth or how to experience it. Whether one is rich or not, knowing how to be content and to appreciate what one has is what brings happiness. We really only need enough to live on if we appreciate what we have and are content.

Take a moment to contemplate the honey bees who work day after day, regardless of the weather, to accumulate honey. The bees get very little chance to enjoy their honey since most of it is taken freely by others. Likewise, there are many of us who work without taking time to eat properly or rest in order to accumulate a little wealth. This approach creates suffering for oneself and others, with little to show for it. So practice generosity as long as you have wealth.

Much of what we hope for and rely on is like a mirage.
It will deceive and upset you when you need it most.
Therefore, direct your mind toward the Dharma.
This is my heart's advice.

IN THIS LIFE, we keep busy with many things because we hope for a reward or payback. But in reality, all of this *is like a mirage.* In the desert there are animals that don't get water for many days; they are so thirsty. When they see a mirage, they think they see a running river in the distance and chase after that mirage with high expectations. But there is no river so they become exhausted, and sometimes they die.

So it is in our life. Day after day we work, and then when we need it most, the result is just a mirage. We don't get what we expected, and it breaks our heart. We feel disappointed and miserable. We have a lot of dreams and so many plans: "If I do this, it will be wonderful." This is all a mirage. We are like wild beasts chasing around after nothing. This is not to say that life is negative, but we need an accurate perspective. At the end, there is no essence left. All samsaric deeds become just a memory. When we discover this, it upsets and depresses us, especially when we are old and near the end of our life. Suppose you have been a very powerful person in politics or business where everyone respected you. But when you retire and have no authority left, you then feel your life has no meaning. All your accomplishments are gone, like a mirage.

The only thing you can trust is the Dharma. Dharma is such an illumination; it dispels the darkness of ignorance as no other light can. Dharma is such a great friend, a trustworthy friend that we can follow life after life unlike any other friend. Dharma is such a splendid jewel, one that satisfies our desire for happiness as no other jewel can. When we are depressed, when we are suffering, Dharma is there to support us and give us wisdom if we practice. What more do we need? Dharma is such a great gift. When we give our friends the gift of Dharma, it frees them from their delusions as no other gift can. If we make a friend of Dharma, we have the wealth of Dharma in our hand. If we have the light of Dharma, then all the great masters and buddhas will be pleased. That's why we need to direct our heart and mind toward Dharma study and practice.

Dharma practice means avoiding nonvirtue and developing virtuous thoughts and actions. Reciting mantras is not necessarily Dharma practice. Prayers are not necessarily Dharma practice. It depends on our inner motivation. Wearing a mala around your neck does not necessarily mean you are a spiritual person. These are important ideas to investigate to determine whether they are true or not—not just for Buddhists, but out in the world. Such investigation gives us confidence and mental strength. Based on just emotion, one might say, "I like this practice. I want to buy a mala and chant this mantra." But then, after some years, the mind remains the same. Such a person might look at how many mantras he had recited and wonder, "What did I get out of this? I recited so many prayers, but nothing happened. What's the use? I don't want to do this any more." Even though there was some benefit, a lot of time can be wasted this way.

Basically we have to know the nature of samsara. Then on that basis, we learn how to develop our mental attitude. Dharma has nothing to do with culture. Rather, it is about building the proper motivation in our mind, purifying neuroses, and developing mental qualities. When approached in that manner, Dharma practices become very useful. We will be able to appreciate them as we understand their benefit and pursue our study and practice on the basis of reason and wisdom.

Take a moment to reflect on this analogy of the mirage. In the hot desert, wild animals see the mirage as a river. Because they are so thirsty, they chase the mirage without achieving relief from their thirst. Likewise, in samsara, many chase after the mirage of worldly concerns and their lives are consumed by them without much benefit. Dedicate yourself: "From today, I will practice Dharma."

Even this cherished body is like an autumn flower.
In an instant, it is destroyed by the frost of impermanence.
Therefore, without wasting time, contemplate death.
This is my heart's advice.

SUMMER FLOWERS are fragile, but autumn flowers are even more so. Especially in the high altitudes, their presence is fleeting. In the morning, the flowers are fresh and beautiful; but if a frost happens to come that night, the next day the flowers are all gone. People bring flowers to the temple as beautiful offerings; they pay a lot of money for them. But after a few days, we have to throw them in the trash. We cherish this body so much, eating the most delicious food we can, wearing expensive and beautiful clothes, sleeping in the most comfortable bed we can find, but in reality all this is like an autumn flower. We expect happiness from cherishing and pleasing our body, but the body is impermanent! When you get a powerful sickness, in one day everything is completely changed. Think about when you develop a bad headache; observe your face—it looks awful. All that you cherished for months and years is destroyed in one hour.

Now, this doesn't mean that the body is useless, that we should destroy it or not care about it. But the purpose of having this body is to make Dharma study and practice possible, not to encourage attachment. Utilize this body as a bridge to cross the ocean of samsara. Consider this body as a ship that can sail from samsara to nirvana. We need to eat, wear clothes, and take care of this body. If we take care of it, we can utilize it in a better way. Like a ship, we must protect it from damage and take care of it so that we can cross the ocean. Likewise, we eat and so forth while we use this body to free ourselves from the ocean of samsara.

In the past, there were some great practitioners in Tibet who remained strictly in retreat and meditated. Sometimes their meditation was very good and they would say, "Today my body was very useful. I will give it a nice meal." Of course, in Tibet, even a nice meal isn't so much—just tsampa, dried cheese, and butter. On other days their meditation was not as good, so they would say, "Today this body didn't do well. I won't give it good meal." This is a simple method they used to remind themselves of their practice of utilizing this human life in the best possible way.

We will die one day, so there is no time to waste in attachment to this body. We must use our limited time wisely, to study and practice Dharma. *Contemplate death* means more than just thinking about death. We know that death will come. We must release our attachment to this body and learn to die peacefully and joyfully, like returning to our own home, by bringing Dharma into our heart. When death comes, the four elements stop functioning one after another until the breath ceases and the heart stops beating. Then the subtle signs of death follow.

After these experiences, the consciousness leaves the body and wanders in the bardo. We can wander up to 49 days, going through different experiences and then finally connecting to the next life. Then we are born in one of the six realms, depending on our karma. In this way we wander endlessly in samsara. In *The Song That Clarifies Recollection,* Lord Jigten Sumgön said:

> When you see the growth and decline of the four elements
>   of the body,
> the illusion of strength and ability is also untrustworthy.
> The autumn flower of youth—
> Think! Can you put your trust in it?

Contemplate this nature. Implement the Dharma in order to awaken from this delusion. No matter how much we are attached to this life, one day, without choice, we must face death and leave the body behind. If we develop nonattachment to this body and practice Dharma sincerely, then greater joy can be experienced. Great bodhisattvas don't hesitate to go even into the hell realms to help others. They can do this joyfully because they have no attachment to the body. In contrast, we can't bear it if someone just pinches us.

Take a moment to look at a beautiful, fresh flower. It is so beautiful that it captures your attention. You smell it—so full of fragrance! But in a few hours, it fades and is no longer the object of your attention. Soon you will just throw it in the trash. Likewise, everything is temporary. Protect your mind with meditation, and balance it with harmony.

Sense objects are like filthy muck.
They have no essence, not even in their smallest part.
Therefore, you should generate revulsion and contentment.
This is my heart's advice.

THERE ARE FIVE objects of the senses: forms that we see; sounds that we hear; aromas that we smell; flavors that we taste; and materials that we touch. In this world, we all are involved with these objects. We constantly chase after these sensual experiences and endure great hardship trying to capture them. But in the end, *like filthy muck*, they only bring suffering.

Consider these analogies and how we risk our lives for nothing:

- Attachment to sights is like a moth who sees a candle flame. Drawn by his attachment to the beautiful flame, he dies.
- Attachment to sound is like a wild animal lured to its death by sound. In some places, hunters lure deer and other animals with a flute-like instrument. When the animals follow their attraction, they pay with their lives.
- Attachment to smell is like a bee trapped in a flower. Bees are attracted to the smell of the flowers, but then the flower closes in on them and they lose their lives.
- Attachment to taste is like a fish caught on a baited hook. They pay for that worm with their lives.
- Attachment to touch is like an elephant stuck in the mud. When it's hot, elephants enjoy water and mud, but then they get stuck because they are so heavy.

As in these examples, we also become attached to sense objects and are entrapped by them. Contemplate this and analyze what benefits are really there. Even in their smallest part, sense objects have no lasting meaning.

Sense objects are actually reflections of our mental activity; they all depend on our state of mind. For instance, when we meet a friend, that new friend seems like such a wonderful person and we become quite attached to him. After some time, we may disagree and fight, and then we perceive that friend as an enemy. All this is momentary and subject to change. So practice nonattachment and rejoice in what you have.

Revulsion means nonattachment; *contentment* means a simple appreciation that is free from grasping or clinging for what you already possess. Rejoice in what you have; you can't own the whole world. As Dharma practitioners, when we see nice things we can mentally offer them to all the buddhas and bodhisattvas in the ten directions as a way to accumulate great merit and wisdom. When you drive and come upon a place of beautiful flowers, say, "I offer all this to the enlightened beings." When you hear a beautiful sound, make that an offering to all the enlightened beings. Do the same with smell, taste, and touch. If you go in the supermarket, watch your mind and bring all the desirable items into your heart. Offer them to the enlightened masters. In this way, not only do you derive benefit from having made an offering, but the owners of these things do as well. Then, when we encounter these sense objects, they no longer entrap us in samsara but become a cause of enlightenment. This is a special method of Dharma practice.

Take a deep breath and consider the fly. The fly is attracted to filthy places. For him, the greater the filth, the greater the enjoyment. No matter how often we chase it away, the fly continues to risk its life for the sake of that filth. In the same way, there are many who suffer helplessly because of their attachments. So meditate: "What essence is there?" If you find yourself with too much attachment, investigate carefully to find the essence of the object of your attraction. If you don't find anything meaningful there, practice nonattachment step by step, and draw your mind back from that object. Place your mind where it is calm and peaceful. Generate kindness and deep compassion.

Birth, old age, sickness, and death are like fish struggling
    on hot sand.
    Their fierce torment and suffering are intolerable.
    Apart from Dharma, nothing will help.
    This is my heart's advice.

THIS PRECIOUS human life is wonderful. There are many opportunities for us, but best of all it allows us to practice and study Dharma. But life is also very difficult. No one wants the sufferings of birth, old age, sickness, and death, but whether we are educated or uneducated, rich or poor, ordinary or powerful, everyone has to experience them.

Birth is the beginning of our life. We are born in great suffering but don't remember it because the suffering was so intense. It was so agonizing that it also obstructs our memory of our previous life. Then, every year thereafter we age. When we are in our teens or twenties, we don't pay much attention to how things will be in the future. But when we become forty or fifty, we have more responsibility but less ability, and wish we were in our twenties again.

There was once a great lama in his sixties. He had many disciples and gave very precious teachings. Some of his disciples asked him repeatedly to tell them about his life. "How did you start your Dharma practice?" and so forth. He always answered, "I don't have anything special to say. I am just old now." They pressed him repeatedly, so he answered, "Until I reached my twenties, I didn't think of any Dharma practice. Life just passed while I played here and there. During the next twenty years, I thought I should make some effort to study and practice Dharma. But without actually starting, I just passed my time being busy with this life. Now I am sixty years old. Look how I've wasted my life. I still haven't done any Dharma practice. That is my story. I very much regret how I wasted my time." Reflect on these words and remember that we are aging moment by moment.

A man once made friends with the Lord of Death. He asked, "Will you please warn me some years before I die so I can prepare for death?" Heedless of the passing time, the man grew old with grey hair and a bent body. One day the Lord of Death appeared and said, "Tomorrow you will die." The man was very upset because he had had no time to prepare for the journey of death. "You are very cruel," he said. "I asked you to warn me." The Lord of Death replied, "But I did warn you. Just look at your body, hair, and face." "You are right," the man admitted. "I was mindless and too attached to this life's affairs."

In old age it is difficult to see, to digest our food, to stand up or sit down. Our hair turns gray, our faces become wrinkled, and we lose our teeth. Every human being in the world suffers when they get old. We become limited physically and mentally. It seems that here in the West we suffer even more. When we grow old here, there is nothing much to do. We retire from the world. If we have a nice family, our children try to take care of us, but they also have to work to take care of their own lives. Then they send us to a nursing home if we have enough money. No one listens to what we say and we feel so lonely. So much suffering; we feel life is not worth living. What can we do?

When I was in Tibet in 1998 and 1999, I noticed the old people circumambulating the temples, stupas, and monasteries, and constantly chanting mantras with great devotion. Even though they have seen terrible calamity in their lives, still many of them reflect on the preciousness of Dharma. They don't feel lonely or feel that life has no meaning. I think this is really wonderful. Even if nobody looks after them, each morning they do what they can, maybe making their way to a temple with a walking stick. If in one day they can recite a thousand mantras or so, they feel so joyful. This is how to bring meaning to our lives. We need something like that here, too, instead of allowing the elderly to feel lonely, neglected, useless, and depressed.

Aging is a sickness that cannot be cured by any medicine. Many people try to fight it and stay young by taking pills and undergoing cosmetic surgery. But they age anyway. In addition, aging attracts other sicknesses, and we easily succumb to them. So life ends as it began—with suffering.

As we age, friends or family may help us cook or clean. When we are sick, we can also get some help from doctors and medicines. But nothing helps at the time of death. Even if all our best friends surround us, we leave alone and take nothing with us. Like a hair drawn through butter, we leave everything behind.

Hook a fish that is swimming nicely in the water and suddenly throw it on the hot sand. What does that fish feel? It struggles help-lessly as if it were in a hell realm. Once I saw a restaurant on televi-sion where a fish was pulled from a tank. The chef cut open the fish's stomach, cleaned out the organs, and threw it in the hot oil—all while the fish was still alive. After the fish sizzled in the oil for few seconds, it jumped from the pan. Imagine that kind of suffering! This is the kind of helpless suffering we experience in birth, old age, sickness, and death. In *The Song That Clarifies Recollection*, Lord Jigten Sumgön says:

> When you see the suffering of birth and death,
> the happiness of the assemblies of gods and men is unreliable.
> The joy and suffering of the wheel of samsara—
> think! Can you put your trust in them?

These teachings introduce us to the reality of samsara. Each one of us has to go through these things. To face these experiences posi-tively, we have to have Dharma teachings. Without Dharma, we will find it impossible to face them positively. With the Dharma, it doesn't matter if we get old or sick or whether we die; we will always have confidence. Pay precise attention to the nature of suf-fering and deepen your Dharma practice. Knowing about suffering helps prepare us for it. When we talk about these things, it can seem very depressing because we are so deeply entrenched in the culture of denial. We try to hide suffering behind a screen. If we could avoid suffering, then there would be no need to make ourselves miserable learning about it. But we have to face it, so we should prepare our-selves. Then when we experience suffering, we will really appreciate these teachings about transforming our thoughts and looking at the positive side.

This story gives us an example of how to conquer the sufferings of birth, old age, sickness, and death:

In central India, there was once a king named Dawa Sangpo, whose son, the prince, was called Daway Ö, Light of the Moon. When the son grew up, the father said, "Now it is your time to rule the kingdom." The son replied, "I don't want to be king and rule the country." The father objected, saying, "But it is a prince's duty to be enthroned as the king and then subjugate all the enemies of the country." His son said, "I cannot do this task. We already have a powerful foe who is very difficult to confront, and I am more afraid of that enemy than all the other enemies of our country. First, we have to get that one under control."

The king-father asked, "What kind of enemy are you talking about?" The prince replied, "The general of that enemy's army is self-grasping, and its soldiers are birth, aging, sickness, and death. That mighty force is armed with the five poisons. Because we haven't defeated that enemy yet, it will be more difficult to subdue in the future."

Then King Dawa Sangpo asked, "Where is this enemy?" His son answered, "All the appearances of the king are the fixations and self-grasping of the great afflictions, the ministers of the five poisons. You are surrounded by the armies of birth, aging, sickness, and death. They wear the armor of the ten nonvirtues and wield the weapons of conceptual thought."

The father asked, "How can we defeat such an enemy?" And the son replied, "We have to ask the Buddha." So they went together to Shravasti, where the Buddha was staying, and requested him to teach them the methods for defeating these enemies. Buddha said, "If you, King, want to defeat these enemies, give up attachment to the bonds of wealth and practice generosity. Wear the armor of patience and ride the horse of perseverance. Build a palace on the field of devotion, and within its hall of meditative concentration, bear the weapon of discriminating wisdom. Fight this enemy with the ten virtues."

Both father and son practiced rigorously, as the Buddha instructed. After some time, their mental obscurations were fully purified, which freed them from the sufferings of birth, aging, sickness, and death. Even though they aged, got sick and died, they did not experience any suffering related to these events. Because of their achievement of such great realization, gods proclaimed this verse from the sky:

> The commander of samsara's impermanence
> waged a Dharma-war on the forces of birth, aging,
>   sickness, and death.
> Fully equipped and well prepared, he won a complete
>   victory.
> What a wonderful war this was!

In the same way, if we want release from the four great rivers of suffering, we must practice Dharma sincerely and diligently from our heart while we have the opportunity and ability.

There is no support for us either at the beginning or end of life unless we have realization. Of course we will age. But if we practice Dharma, especially bodhicitta and Mahamudra, these sufferings will be illusory. Milarepa said, "If you have not realized birth, old age, sickness, and death to be illusion, then the suffering they bring is intolerable." As long as aging, sickness, and death are real to us, all the pain that we experience in life will be real. When we actually face these conditions, Dharma will surely help. There is not as much suffering for Dharma practitioners as there is for those who don't have these practices. Therefore, we must practice the precious Dharma now, before we encounter these sufferings.

Take a moment to visualize a *fish struggling on the hot sand* at a beach. Helplessly, it dies there without any support. There are many people in the world; some are rich, famous, or educated, and some are not. But all face the suffering of aging, sickness, and death. Develop great compassion and pray that you can accept these sufferings. Make a commitment to achieve buddhahood and help all sentient beings.

One's consciousness in the bardo is like a feather blown
   by the wind.
   Powerless, it is blown by the wind of karma and led
      by the Lord of Death.
   Apart from the Three Jewels, there is no refuge.
   This is my heart's advice.

GENERALLY, those who die slowly, step by step, in their beds, will experience many different stages during the death process. Our bodies are composed of the four elements: earth, water, fire, and wind. When the earth element stops functioning, it dissolves into water, and the dying person feels like he is sinking into the ground. Then the water element dissolves into fire, and the dying person feels like he is being swept away in a great flood. When the fire element dissolves into the wind element, the dying person feels like he is burning in a fire. When the wind element dissolves into consciousness, the dying person feels like he is being taken by a tornado.

The corresponding physical changes are quite clear. When the water element dissolves, the mouth becomes dry. When the fire element dissolves, the body becomes cold. As heat draws into the heart, the extremities become cold. When the wind element dissolves, it becomes difficult to breathe. After that, the breath stops. The consciousness has not yet left at this point. What is called the *inner breath* is still there. Then the dying person experiences light white as a clear, full moon at the stage called *white appearance*. The mind becomes more subtle as gross thoughts dissolve. After that comes the stage called *red increase*, an experience of bright, deep, red light, and the mind becomes even more subtle. After that, the dying person feels that he is in a deep sleep, like a clear night without a moon. Then the dying person becomes unconscious for a period at the stage called *darkness near attainment*. This is followed by luminosity, that is called *clear light*. Whether they are Dharma practitioners or not, everyone goes through these stages. Ordinary people experience them without awareness, as in sleep. If one has a great and stable realization of Mahamudra, though, there is an opportunity to be aware of these experiences, to free oneself from samsara, and attain enlightenment.

The duration of the dying process varies from a moment to several hours, or as much as two or three days, depending on the individual. Toward the end, the mind becomes more gross, and retraces the steps from dark to red and back to white appearance. When the person is fully conscious, he feels a strong urge to leave: "I am in a rotten house. I can't live here. The roof is falling and the floor is no good. I must leave now." Then the consciousness leaves the body, and the person is fully dead.

Although there is no longer a flesh-and-bone body, the dead person has a mental body, in the state of *bardo,* the period between death and rebirth. This mental body runs back and forth due to karmic habits. When the east karmic wind comes, it is blown toward the west. When the southern karmic wind comes, it is blown toward the north, back and forth. Like *a feather in the wind*, we have no control over which direction it will take. Right now, even though our mind is very active, our physical body cannot move quickly because it is gross. To go somewhere, we need a car or airplane. But with only a mental body in the bardo we can go to another country in a mere second just by thinking of it. Faster than light! Because the mental body is so unstable, though, we experience more suffering. We are powerless and experience a lot of fear, as is described in the *Tibetan Book of the Dead*. This is what the author is referring to when he uses the metaphor *blown by the wind of karma*.

You stay in this bardo state a maximum of forty-nine days. Each week you experience a short death and then, depending on your karma, you are reborn in one of the six realms. During this time between death and rebirth, there is no refuge apart from the Three Jewels. There is not one moment you can take refuge in some powerful person, your relatives, or best friends. The only solace is to think of the Buddha, Dharma, and Sangha.

If you have good meditation, you can abide in your practice without being blown in all directions. If you take refuge in the Three

Jewels during this life and practice well, then, at the time of your death, they will be your true protectors. That's why taking refuge is important.

The Jewel Ornament of Liberation describes a contemplation on impermanence and death this way: "My life ends, this breath ceases, this body becomes a corpse, and this mind has to wander in different places." Without Dharma practice, we are helpless. Just look at our situation right now. We have little power to control our minds because we don't have enough experience with stabilization. We want to meditate, but the mind won't follow. We want to cultivate loving-kindness, but anger is so powerful that it takes our mind away in the opposite direction. Even while we are alive, have teachings, and can practice, we are powerless. Our cumulative habits, the karma we have created, will take us without choice. We plan so much, but we really don't know what will happen because our own karma takes the decision out of our hands.

We talk about the objects of refuge, the Three Jewels of Buddha, Dharma, and Sangha, as being external to ourselves. But the subject here is our own practice. Relying fully on the Buddha and practicing the Dharma teachings is the true refuge. A sense of clarity in the mind, confidence in bodhicitta, purifying negative thoughts—if we do Dharma practice in such a state of mind, that is the true refuge we can really count on. Without it, no matter how smart or clever we may be, we cannot escape samsara.

Pause a moment and look at the mind, so flittery, like a feather in the wind. The mind is taken to and fro by its own projections and has no stability. It cannot calmly abide. The different types of mental suffering are created from this busyness. Stop and take a deep breath and try to ease the mind. Rest like a stable mountain. This will bring inner peace and real joy. Make a commitment: "I will practice the Dharma for the rest of my life."

The three lower realms are like an iron house with no door.
There, one is tormented by suffering and has no chance for lib-
    eration.
Therefore, attend closely to cause and result.
This is my heart's advice.

THE *THREE LOWER REALMS* are the hell, hungry ghost, and animal realms. Each has a distinctive type of suffering. For example, there are eight hot hell realms. A sandalwood fire is said to be seven times hotter than a regular wood fire, and the first hot hell realm is seven times hotter than that. As one descends, each hell realm is seven times hotter than the one above it, and there is more intense suffering. There are also eight cold hell realms. When beings are born there, the body and ice are indistinguishable, cracking into many pieces. Then the neighboring and occasional hells make the total number of hell realms eighteen.

Hungry ghosts suffer from unimaginable hunger and thirst. This story describes the experiences of a hungry ghost who suffered from outer obscurations:

> Once, at a time when the Buddha was staying in Rajgir, Maudgalyayana and Shariputra generated bodhicitta and practiced it very sincerely. In order to demonstrate this teaching, they went to the lower realms to benefit the sentient beings there. They met a hungry ghost, an old woman whose belly was large as a valley and whose mouth was small as the eye of a needle. Hair covered her entire body and fire blazed from her mouth. She was suffering terribly, moaning and crying in anguish. Food and drink appeared to her as pus and blood. She did not have the good fortune to be able to eat or drink at all, not even the excrement and urine that she perceived. Maudgalyayana and Shariputra asked her, "What kind of karma did you create that led you

to endure this terrible suffering?" She replied, "Please ask the Buddha that question." They went to the Buddha and asked about what they had seen, and he told this story.

"In the past, many lifetimes earlier, there was a rich merchant in Rajgir who owned a big sugar cane factory. In a nearby forest lived a solitary realizer (Skt.: *pratyeka-buddha*) with very few possessions. He suffered from an unquenchable thirst, so he asked a doctor for treatment. The doctor recommended that he drink sugar cane juice. So, the solitary realizer went to the factory owner and asked for some juice. The merchant agreed to give it to him but had to rush to attend to an important business matter, so he asked his maid to offer the juice. The servant was very stingy, even with another's wealth, and she thought, 'If I give him enough juice now, then he will come back again and again.' To avoid that, she disrespectfully filled the begging bowl with goat's urine. On the surface she put some bubbles of sugar cane juice and gave it to the solitary realizer. That noble one understood her nature and threw it on the ground. This act is what caused her rebirth as a hungry ghost with terrible suffering. Considering this story, we should purify our mental stinginess and greed, and come to regard wealth—our own or another's—without attachment.

Some hungry ghosts suffer from inner obscurations, as illustrated by this account:

Once when Maudgalyayana and Shariputra went to the countryside, they met a female hungry ghost whose face was covered with burns. She suffered terribly: water and rivers dried up when she looked at them; when rain fell, it turned into sparks; whatever she ate turned to iron metal inside her stomach. They asked her, "What kind of karma did you create that led you to endure this terrible suffering?" She replied, "Please ask the Buddha that question."

They went to the Buddha and asked about what they had seen. The Buddha told this story. In the past, there was a young woman who was carrying a big pot of water to her house. On the way, she met a monk who was thirsty and asked her for water. He said, 'If you give me water, you will accumulate virtue.' She said, 'Even if you were dying of thirst, I would not give you any water.' Because she was stingy with that water, she was reborn in this condition and suffers inconceivably. Seeing this, we should purify all our obscurations of stinginess and attachment, and practice generosity, even with a little water.

Animals suffer being killed and eaten. They are generally extremely stupid, and have no opportunity to comprehend virtue and avoid nonvirtue. They have no comprehension of the benefits of mantras. So they also have no chance for liberation. This is like being trapped in an *iron house* with thick walls and no door.

In the lower realms, beings may possess some clarity of mind with which to understand virtue and nonvirtue, but because of their negative karma those beings can only suffer torment. These three lower realms are described in detail in *The Jewel Ornament of Liberation* and *Transformation of Suffering*. The purpose of these teachings is not to depress people. These teachings are a most important foundation for the higher teachings. They inspire you to avoid rebirth in these conditions, and to cultivate an appreciation for this precious human existence. They become a firm foundation for the practice of great compassion. The more we contemplate these teachings, the more compassion we generate, especially toward those who are helpless, like animals.

We have to look closely at the causes of the lower realms and turn away from them. The worst result of engaging in the ten nonvirtues is to be reborn in the hell realms. The middling result leads to rebirth as a hungry ghost. At the least, the ten nonvirtuous acts will cause you to be reborn as an animal. Practice of the ten virtues causes you to be reborn in the three higher realms. That is why avoiding the ten nonvirtues and protecting the ten virtues are so important for our Dharma practice. There is no possibility to encounter the precious Dharma in the lower realms, let alone to study or practice. So cherish this opportunity of a precious human rebirth and protect the ten virtues.

As was mentioned earlier, reflecting on our precious human life frees us from depression. It uplifts our mind. Human birth means we can solve our problems, open our hearts, and develop all good qualities. It is very important to have positive, uplifting thoughts. If you look at the nature of samsara with a positive mind, especially if you contemplate the three lower realms and understand the cause of that suffering, then you will happily avoid all nonvirtues and will joyfully apply yourself to virtuous practices. When the Buddha taught the Four Noble Truths, he said, "This is the Truth of Suffering." We contemplate suffering because there is a way to be free from suffering.

The Hinayana system emphasizes precious human life and how difficult it is to gain, but only for the sake of attaining individual liberation. On the bodhisattva path, precious human life is yet more important because having it means that we can cultivate bodhicitta, the great thought that leads to complete buddhahood. This is the mind that can bring benefit to all sentient beings. In the Vajrayana, human life is even more precious because, with it, one can meditate on the nature of the Buddha; the five skandhas, or aggregates, can be seen as the five buddhas; and enlightenment can be attained in one lifetime. As you progress through these different stages of the Buddha's teaching, human life becomes more and more precious.

Take a moment to think of a jail built with iron walls and no door. The prisoners inside have no chance to leave. Likewise, those in samsara have little opportunity to free themselves and attain enlightenment. So contemplate this and inspire yourself by saying, "I will free myself from samsara and attain buddhahood, and help guide all sentient beings to freedom from the cycle of samsara."

The bliss of higher realms is like poisonous food.
It has the appearance of happiness but is only a cause
   of suffering.
Samsara has no essence.
This is my heart's advice.

HIGHER REALMS refers to the human realm and, especially, to the god realms. The metaphor of *poisonous food* has the same meaning that it does in verse 11. This poisoned food looks delicious, very colorful and tempting. Innocently, we think, "If I eat this, I will be happy. It will bring me joy and satisfaction." But then, after eating it, we end up in a lot of pain and suffering. Likewise, we are attracted by the bliss and happiness of samsara. We throw ourselves into samsara and are completely taken by its power. But in the end, there is no lasting happiness or peace. This describes the suffering of change or fickle pleasure; it is fugitive bliss.

Suppose you are having an important dinner party, and have invited your friends and some influential people. You have to dress in your most expensive things. When you drink tea, you have to be very careful so that not even a drop is spilled on your clothes. If a drop of tea falls, you feel embarrassed and immediately take out a napkin and clean it up. This is real suffering. You have to behave so well, be so careful about how you walk, how you sit, how you talk. All your freedom is lost! Your table has to be perfect, with all the dishes arranged in the right place. Everything is artificial, superficial. What ultimate essence is there in this? What lasting benefit does it bring? This does not mean, of course, that we should be careless in society.

This teaching doesn't change samsara into something negative, but rather it introduces us to samsara's true nature. All of samsara is without lasting happiness or peace. Even after sacrificing all our peace, time, and energy, we find no real happiness. So why not sacrifice some small happiness for the study of Dharma, and then practice to achieve ultimate happiness?

Thus, the suffering of samsara is like a prison.
There is no chance for happiness or freedom there.
Therefore, generate pity and revulsion.
This is my heart's advice.

THIS VERSE SUMMARIZES the different types of suffering described above. Briefly, from the god realms to the hell realms, all samsara is *like a prison*. No matter where we are born within the six realms, there is no chance of real happiness or freedom. Suffering is with us as long as we remain in the state of samsara. Suffering is usually classified as three types:

- the suffering of suffering
- the suffering of change
- the all-pervasive suffering, or the suffering of condition

The first is the most obvious. It refers to physical and mental pain, which was discussed earlier in connection with the suffering of the lower realms, and in the birth, old age, sickness, and death of the human realm. In addition, we suffer in relationships with other people and while building wealth. We don't get what we want, and we do get what we don't want. Once we gain wealth, it is difficult to protect. Whether we are spiritual or not, whether we believe in a religion or don't believe in anything, we all try to free ourselves from physical suffering and have some happiness. Not only human beings but animals also are skilled in freeing themselves from this first kind of suffering. For instance, they build protected nests or find special places that shield them from danger.

The second type of suffering is called the suffering of change. Animals have little opportunity to recognize temporary happiness as a type of suffering. Many human beings and spiritual practitioners are aware of this suffering, though, and try to free themselves from it through various behaviors and meditation practices. All our happiness, peace, joy, and pleasure in samsara are subject to change. Yet even though these happinesses are temporary, people continue to grasp at them until they are exhausted.

We have to understand this clearly. Take a delicious meal as an example. We are so attracted to it, especially when we are really hungry. But if that meal were truly a cause of pleasure, we should get more and more enjoyment the more we eat. However, when we eat too much, we develop stomach problems. That which we thought was pleasurable changes into a cause of suffering. This is called the suffering of change. It is better to choose a policy of moderation, or the middle way, in everything.

The third suffering is called the all-pervasive suffering, or the suffering of condition. As long as we are conditioned by ignorance, we exist in the state of suffering. No matter where we move, no matter which country we might live in, we cannot find a place without suffering. This points to the true nature of our life, of samsara, and leads us to yearn for liberation from this suffering state. One needs a special wisdom or insight to comprehend this suffering; coming to know its nature will cause us to be free from samsara. The Buddha taught this so that we could eventually perceive the suffering of condition as suffering through critical insight. The Dharma is so profound; it allows us to penetrate the absolute reality of samsara and to attain enlightenment by crossing the ocean of samsara. In order to do this, we need to generate *pity and revulsion*. When we know how to generate pity and revulsion, we will truly be inspired to practice Dharma wholeheartedly.

We do experience happiness, joy, and peace, but this is called *afflicted* happiness because it is experienced by a mind that is not yet free from afflicting emotions and ignorance. This is not to say that there is no peace or happiness, but rather that our experience is not the ultimate peace and happiness. That's why we shouldn't be attached to temporary joys. We should fully renounce samsara and cultivate the mind that aspires to complete enlightenment. These subtle distinctions are very important. They define the line between samsara and nirvana.

So, reflecting on suffering reminds us of many positive qualities. The *Bodhicaryavatara* reminds us:

Being disheartened by it, haughtiness is dispelled.
Compassion arises for sentient beings in samsara.
Nonvirtue is abandoned, and joy is found in virtue.
These are the benefits of reflecting on suffering.

Offering-wealth, meat, and the wealth of sinful persons are like burning ash.
They carry heavy sin and obstruction and obscure all one's virtuous qualities.
Therefore, make effort in purifying meditation and recitation.
This is my heart's advice.

WHEN PEOPLE OFFER wealth to the Buddha, Dharma and Sangha, they do so with devotion and high expectations. They work hard to generate wealth for themselves and offer the results to monks and nuns with great respect. For example, at a Dharma center, the monies that are collected from teachings and different programs must be handled sensitively—not wasted without purpose or benefit, or used to enrich individuals. These resources should be strictly used to increase Dharma activities, establish facilities, and print texts. If we are not aware that offered wealth is unlike other wealth and misuse it, heavy negative karma will result.

There are many stories that illustrate this point. Here is one of them:

> Once there was a monk who was the manager of a monastery and responsible for taking care of the offerings. But he misused them by inviting his friends and lay people to enjoy them, and also by hoarding some for himself. When they died, the manager was reborn in the form of a tree, and all the people who selfishly took advantage of the offerings were reborn as locusts eating that tree. The tree-creature made a horrible sound as it experienced the constant agony of being eaten.

From this we can see that our attachments cause us great harm. Their appearance is wonderful, but underneath, the *hot ash* burns our virtue.

All people, especially those who are not ordained, are discouraged from using wealth that has been offered. The misuse of offerings makes the mind dull and unclear. Doing purifying meditation such as Vajrasattva practice will make our mind sharper, and then we will be able to gain insight and awareness.

Concerning meat: every sentient being cherishes and protects its own life. If you merely threaten or just look down on someone, they will not appreciate it. When innocent animals are executed and eaten, their suffering is immeasurable but they cannot express it. For this reason, we have to respect each other's lives and practice pure love and compassion. When this kind of relationship is built, we can gain uncontrived peace and joy within our society and in the world at large. But if we take another's life in order to secure our own life or for enjoyment, it brings a negative influence to the environment. Because we eat many different types of beings, lots of different diseases manifest, many of which weren't heard of in earlier times. So for health reasons and to be free from negative influences, it is advisable to abstain from eating meat.

Not wasting what is offered is also very important. Many of us have some bad habits in this regard. Of course we have to use what we need, but sometimes we are unnecessarily wasteful. Lord Jigten Sumgön is a good example for us to follow. He received mountains of offerings from the kings of the gods, humans, and nagas, but never wasted a penny. Everything was used for his hundreds and thousands of monks and nuns in the Sangha community, and for other Dharma purposes. This teaches us not to risk this precious opportunity for small things. In the midst of the many important things we can do in this world, Dharma is the most important for one who has renunciation and the mind to abandon negativities.

If we have created negative karma in this life or in the distant past, it is most important to purify it. The way to do this is to use the four powers (see verse 34). Motivated by a wish to be released from the results of this negative karma, use the techniques of bodhicitta or of any deity yoga. Visualize a deity, like Chenrezig, either as yourself or as seated above the crown of your head, then chant the mantra with full confidence and devotion. At the end, do the dissolution and say dedication prayers. Finally, make a commitment not to repeat the negative action.

If wealth offered to the sangha is not used in a proper way, there are grave consequences. The following is a story that illustrates this:

> During the time of Buddha Shakyamuni, there was a big, filthy swamp near where he was staying in Shravasti. A strange creature lived there; it had the head of a man, but its entire body was covered with millions of biting insects. The creature was suffering dreadfully, of course, so much so that the pain caused it to run back and forth in the muddy swamp. News of this spectacle went around, and many people went to see the strange being. The Buddha also heard the news. With his compassionate wisdom, he knew that it was time to help that being and to benefit many other sentient beings as well. So he proceeded to the swamp with a large retinue of monks and other religious teachers. The monks prepared a special seat for the Buddha next to the swamp. The Buddha sat in meditation posture and asked, "Are you the one known as 'Master of the Tripitaka'?" The creature replied, "Yes, I am." The Buddha then asked, "Who caused you to be here, suffering so terribly?" The creature replied, "None but myself." The Buddha continued, "Are you suffering this way because of nonvirtuous acts you committed with body, speech, and mind?" The creature admitted, "Yes, I am."
>
> The assembled monks and lay people were full of curiosity about what had happened to cause this situation, so Ananda asked the Buddha to explain the karma of this creature. The Buddha responded: "Limitless kalpas in the past, Buddha Omniscient walked the earth. A certain householder understood the nature of samsara and was inspired to become a monk. He had been rich, but he offered all his wealth to Buddha Omniscient and was ordained. With full attention, he studied vigorously and became quite a scholar. He was well versed in all aspects of knowledge, but particularly in the Tripitaka, so he was called Master of the Tripitaka. He became well known as a teacher and was widely respected.

"In the vicinity of Black Hill, there were monks who had achieved different stages of realization: the training path, the path of no more learning, and so forth. In total, 70,000 monks made the commitment to do a summer retreat there. They requested Master of the Tripitaka to be their manager, and he accepted. During the retreat, a group of five hundred merchants returned from a successful ocean voyage. They temporarily settled near that place and noticed many monks in retreat. They were pleased and developed great devotion. They went to the manager and said, 'We have offerings for these monks who are doing retreat. If you can accept gold and silver coins, please do so. Otherwise, we will arrange to offer something else.' After the manager had received all these offerings, his attachment to this wealth grew and instead of using it to support the retreatants, he kept the gold and silver for himself and supplied very poor food to the monks.

"After some time, the monks complained to the manager, 'We can't live on this meager food. Can you try to get something a little better for us?' The manager replied angrily, 'I'm giving you what I have. If you are not satisfied, go begging in the village and manage the retreat yourselves.' Some of these monks saw the nearby merchants and asked them for donations for the retreat. The merchants sent them away, saying, 'We have already offered you enough gold and silver for the whole retreat.' Suspicious, the merchants went to the manager and asked, 'What happened to the wealth we offered? Why are you giving the monks such poor food?' Master of the Tripitaka was embarrassed and upset. He told the monks, 'You are trying to humiliate me! Instead of serving you monks, I would better off sinking in a swamp of human waste.' At this, the monks remained quiet. Later, Master of the Tripitaka regretted what he had done and apologized.

"This creature in the swamp is the rebirth of that monk who was so knowledgeable in the Tripitaka. He was born this way because of his resentment and harsh words toward the 70,000 monks who were well disciplined and had achieved the non-returning state. He has been born like this for many lifetimes. In each life, he lived in a filthy swamp like this. In the future, after one thousand buddhas have appeared on this earth, Buddha Appearance will come. Because of his connection with Buddha Omniscient, Master of the Tripitaka will become a monk under that buddha and will achieve arhatship."

Then the Buddha taught extensively about the infallible nature of causality and the nature of samsara. The monks and lay people were deeply moved and took refuge in the Buddha, Dharma, and Sangha. They went on to take precepts and sincerely practiced the Dharma. Many achieved different stages of enlightenment.

Reflecting on this story, we should all be aware of the consequences of karma and keep our precepts well. We must practice Dharma sincerely and purify our negative thoughts for our own and others' benefit. It is not enough just to know some Dharma. It is very important to experience the meaning of the teachings in our heart and make our mind very pure.

Heartfelt recollection of the Dharma is like one's hair
  caught on fire.
  Nothing is as important as that.
  Therefore, don't be lazy or attached to pleasure.
  This is my heart's advice.

RECALL WITH SINCERITY the teachings that were mentioned earlier: samsara has no essence; it is like a burning ash or poisonous food. It is nothing but endless suffering. Recollect the nature of samsara: precious human life, infallible cause and result, the sufferings of the six realms, the impermanence of all phenomena, and delusion. Then practice sincerely. Lord Jigten Sumgön said, "Recollect the nature of enlightenment—the practices of loving-kindness, compassion, and bodhicitta." He also said, "Uninterrupted mindfulness is the highway of the buddhas."

When we begin to recognize how precious the Dharma is, we want to practice sincerely. We feel that there is no substitute for the Dharma, and we happily commit to practice with a feeling of fortune and joy. Dharma is the greatest thing that one could want to do. That is *heartfelt recollection*—not merely an intellectual exercise, but a genuine feeling in the heart. This is the way to be free from samsara. But the temptation of samsara is so strong and our propensities are overwhelming when we lose our recollection.

If your hair were on fire, what would you do? You would want to douse the fire immediately, no matter what it took to do it. Even if you were cooking a very special meal for important guests, you would stop and take care of the fire. In the *Letter to a Friend,* Nagarjuna said, "Let your hair be caught by the fire. Continue practicing the Dharma because there is absolutely nothing more important than this." Here in this text, the author is also advising us to have this attitude toward the Dharma, so that we do not miss even one moment's opportunity for practice. If you burn your hair, it will grow back again. But if you do not practice while you have time, you will have no end of suffering. You can't get that time back. It's gone forever.

We must have very powerful recollection or mindfulness. Whenever negative thoughts such as attachment, anger, pride, and jealousy arise in the mind, immediately recollect the suffering that will surely result from them. Remember that they are the cause of samsara. Pause whatever you are doing at that moment, and recall your Dharma practice. This is the indispensable antidote for the three types of laziness: attachment to pleasure, attachment to worldly activities, and listlessness and procrastination.

There is a story from the Buddha's time that illustrates this:

> There once was a king who did not follow the Buddha but whose wife was a very devout Buddhist. One day, they arranged an extravagant ceremony. The husband invited all his important teachers, and the wife asked permission to invite her teacher too. She sent a message to the Buddha inviting him to come to the ceremony or send those of his disciples who would be most beneficial. The Buddha sent his disciple Katyayana.
>
> The celebration was arranged magnificently with dance, food, and drink. At the end of the day, the king asked all his ministers and important guests how they had enjoyed the festivities. Everyone replied, "This was magnificent! Wonderful!" When he came to the Buddhist monk, he asked the same question. The monk replied, "I had no chance to enjoy it." Shocked, the king exclaimed, "How can you say such a thing? This magnificent display was provided for your enjoyment right in front of you!" The monk answered, "I understand your confusion. It must not be easy to comprehend my reaction. May I request you to do something that will help you understand what I mean?" The king agreed. "Tomorrow, please repeat the same music and performances. Bring a prisoner who has been sentenced to death and provide two guards—one in front and one in back. Give him a bowl filled to the brim with liquid and tell him to walk around the grounds and enjoy the festivities. But also tell him that if he spills even a

single drop from the bowl, he will be executed on the spot, and that if he does not spill anything, he will be released from prison." The king agreed.

Everything was done just as the monk suggested. The prisoner went around the grounds and did not spill even a drop. At the end of the day, the monk requested the king to ask the prisoner whether he had enjoyed the beautiful songs and displays. The prisoner said, "I did not see or hear anything. My mind was entirely concentrated on this bowl. If I had spilled a drop I would have been killed." The monk said, "This is my witness. In the same way, I have no time for enjoyments. I understand impermanence and see everything as illusion. If I can maintain my meditative concentration, I too will be released from the prison of samsara." The king was quite impressed. "How wonderful! This monk is fully mindful of the suffering of the six realms and of impermanence." At that moment, the king took refuge in the Buddha, Dharma, and Sangha, and thereafter sincerely followed the teachings.

Nothing is more important than Dharma. *Therefore, don't be lazy or attached to pleasure.* We must overcome our laziness by thinking of the precious nature of the Dharma teachings.

Reflect for a moment. When someone's hair is on fire, he will stop whatever he is doing and put out the fire because of the risk to his life. Likewise, there are so many things to accomplish in our lives, but the most important is Dharma practice. If we don't attend to it wholeheartedly, we will lose this opportunity to gain a life of inner peace and eventual freedom from samsara.

*Renunciation and the mind that abandons negativity are like
  a captain piloting a ship.
Freedom from samsara depends upon them.
Therefore, always think about this without distraction.
This is my heart's advice.*

OUR FIRST STEP is to renounce samsara, especially negative thoughts. At the very least, we can make a commitment to renounce such things as ignorance, attachment, anger, hatred, pride, jealousy, and so forth. They are the root cause of suffering. On the basis of strong renunciation, any kind of Dharma practice, even a very simple one, can be a cause to attain enlightenment. On the other hand, without such renunciation, even very high tantra or any other profound Dharma practice will not lead us to freedom from samsara. The passengers in a ship and the captain all have to share a strong feeling that they want to get to the other shore. Without this, they wouldn't be interested in being on the ship in the first place. By having this attitude of renunciation, we will be free from the ten nonvirtues.

For example, consider the pilot of an airplane flying across the ocean with many passengers. Until the pilot arrives at the airport, no matter how long this may take, he has to be vigilant each minute. Likewise, to cross the ocean of samsara, we need powerful renunciation. If the mind is distracted and drawn away by samsaric activities, we will face many obstacles, and freedom from samsara and the achievement of enlightenment will not be possible.

Abandon negativity means to give up all the mental and physical nonvirtuous actions that are the root cause of suffering.

No matter how profound our practices are, they all begin with these critical teachings. These preliminaries or foundations are considered much more important than what we usually call the higher teachings. Always contemplate this, because without the root and trunk, there can be no leaves, flowers, or fruit.

Obtaining a life of leisure and endowments is like arriving at an island of jewels.
Whether we attain liberation or not is up to us.
Be sure, therefore, not to leave empty-handed.
This is my heart's advice.

THIS VERSE again addresses precious human life. Leisure means being free from eight unfavorable conditions; that is, not being born

- in the three lower realms: the hell, hungry ghost, and animal realms
- as a barbarian with no sense of virtue or nonvirtue
- as a long-life god, where all the senses are shut off, or where the gods are distracted by temporary pleasures and have no time to contemplate Dharma
- without full faculties
- holding wrong views of causality
- at a time when no buddha has appeared.

When we are free from these unfavorable conditions, we have the possibility to contemplate the precious Dharma.

Endowment, or fortune, consists of ten essential conditions, divided into two parts. Five are related to oneself:

- being a human being
- living in a place where the Dharma is taught
- possessing all the faculties
- being free of heavy negative karma
- having devotion for the Triple Gem and acknowledging Vinaya as the foundation for all spiritual practice

And five are the excellent conditions that must appear or be encountered:

- ▸ a buddha must have appeared in the world
- ▸ a buddha must have taught the Dharma
- ▸ the Dharma that he taught continues
- ▸ sangha members practice Dharma and follow masters
- ▸ there is compassionate support

When one possesses all ten endowments or attributes, one has the ability, opportunity, and conditions needed to study and practice the Dharma.

Possessing these eighteen favorable qualities is like arriving at a *jewel island* where wish-fulfilling jewels can be found. If someone had such an opportunity and returned empty-handed, the whole world would consider that person foolish or even crazy. Likewise, one who arrives at the gateway of enlightenment and doesn't enter but turns back to the prison of samsara is most unfortunate.

Now we have obtained a precious human life, we have heard the teachings, and we have time to practice. Whether we become free from samsara or not *is up to us*. We have the full responsibility. If, when we die, we have gained no benefit from the Dharma, this is much more foolish than failing to bring jewels back from a jewel island. Wish-fulfilling jewels may give us wealth for this life, but a precious human life can free us from samsara forever.

Milarepa was such a successful Dharma practitioner. He attained buddhahood in a single lifetime because he had strong renunciation of samsara. He looked at his precious human life and recognized what a great opportunity it provided. But he also saw how impermanent it was—how fragile. He meditated on the nature of samsara. For him, samsara was the worst prison, a place where there was no chance for any peace. The nature of cause and effect became so vivid, so clear to him, that his mind became thoroughly infused with the Dharma. For him there was no doubt, not even the smallest hesitation to sacrifice his life for the Dharma. It was for these reasons that he became such a successful Dharma practitioner.

Just reflect. If, for example, you found a very precious and expensive jewel, how overjoyed you would feel. You would consider carefully how to use that windfall skillfully. Likewise, we should recognize the precious human life as a most precious jewel. It provides us with every ability to attain buddhahood. So make a determination to use this life in the best possible way, to free yourself and others from samsara. For this, you should rejoice.

Knowingly doing wrong is like a madman taking his own life.
One only destroys oneself in this way.
Remember this again and again.
This is my heart's advice.

FIRST, it is important to have an idea of what is right and what is wrong. When you have been introduced to and understand the Four Noble Truths—the various forms of suffering, the origin of suffering, the cessation of suffering, and the path to cessation—then you will no longer be interested in repeatedly creating negative karma. Consider the examples of sickness, the cause of sickness, freedom from sickness, and the taking of medicine to cure the sickness. First, one should identify the sickness. Then, one should understand and abandon the cause of the sickness. One should then have a strong desire to be cured, and then one should take the appropriate medicine. In the same way, you should make every effort to avoid negative actions and perform virtuous actions because you cherish your own happiness. One who consciously creates negative karma in spite of this knowledge is like a *madman*. He is committing spiritual suicide. It is bad enough to be mad, but taking one's own life in addition to that is worse. Likewise, it is bad enough just being in samsara. Creating more negative karma on top of that is disastrous.

In this world there is no one who does not sincerely look after himself, not even an animal or insect. In fact, some will sacrifice anything for the sake of their own happiness and joy. Of course, this only creates a mass of nonvirtue and destroys root virtue, which results in yet more suffering. This is all due to delusion, a sort of mental blindness. Shantideva said, "Everyone desires happiness, but out of ignorance, they destroy it as if it were an enemy. Even though they wish to be free from suffering, they chase after it."

The suffering we experience comes from our own negative action. No one can give us suffering. No force can throw us into a hell realm except our own negative actions. We sacrifice so many things and make a lot of effort to bring a little happiness into our lives. But trying to create happiness through negative actions can only destroy our happiness. For example, if you take another's life, you may think you are destroying the cause of your suffering, but in reality you are only destroying yourself. You yourself are the true victim, and you will suffer for many lifetimes. When one is overpowered by anger and pride, the wisdom eye is blinded. Therefore, look carefully at karmic causes and remember the example of the madman for your own benefit and that of others.

The following story gives an example of a being destroyed by his anger:

> Once there was a lion that killed one animal from his territory every day for food. One day, it was the rabbit's turn to be eaten. The rabbit was terrified, and considered how to avoid this untimely death. Anxiously pacing around, he happened to find a well nearby. When he looked down into it, he saw his reflection. He shook his head and the reflection did the same. He bared his teeth and the reflection did likewise. This gave him an idea.
>
> After a while, he presented himself to the lion, who was very angry and demanded to know why the rabbit was late for lunch. The rabbit said, "I am late because on the way here I met a fierce creature who has come to challenge you." The lion became very upset and demanded, "Who could that be? Show him to me!" The rabbit took him to the well and said, "Look down. There, you can see him clearly." The lion looked into the well and, of course, saw his own reflection. When he shook his head the well-creature did too and when he showed his fangs, the stranger did the same. The lion became furious, lunged at the stranger, and jumped to his death in the well.

In the same way, we should understand the disadvantages of being angry. It destroys our environment and causes everyone to arise as our enemy. Therefore, we have to examine anger and its faults very carefully and purify them with Dharma practice.

The spiritual master is like a guide on the path.
He protects one from the lower realms and leads one
  to liberation.
Attend him respectfully with body, speech, and mind.
This is my heart's advice.

IT IS very important that a *spiritual master* have all the required qualities (see page 70) A spiritual master with all the required qualities, especially one who has bodhicitta, will help you on the path toward enlightenment. When you travel to an unknown area, a guide can show you exactly where to go. Similarly, a spiritual master will guide you on the right path by explaining how to avoid negative karma, the cause for rebirth in the lower realms, and how to practice the path toward enlightenment. When one follows the spiritual master's instructions properly, that is how he or she *protects one from the lower realms and leads one to liberation.*

Attending a spiritual master means to listen to his or her teachings carefully and then sincerely put them into practice. One is *respectful* because the spiritual master represents the teachings, the beacon of light that kindles our wisdom mind. How precious it is to find the way to become free from all suffering, the way to achieve all peace and happiness! One should perceive an authentic spiritual master as a buddha. That master's teachings are the Buddha's teachings. Also, it is important to perceive the spiritual master as a buddha, because then we will receive the complete blessings. The important point is not what the spiritual master gives, but rather how much of the Buddha's qualities we experience.

If you read stories about the Buddha's enlightenment, you will find that he studied for three limitless kalpas before becoming a buddha. As his teachings are profound and infinite, so, too, are his life stories. Here is one of them:

> The future buddha was once born as a king. He approached
> a master in the jungle, did prostrations, offered a priceless

jeweled mala, and asked for teachings. The master thought that the king might take the mala back, so he said, "First, jump from this cliff down into the valley." The bodhisattva king replied, "But if I die before receiving the teachings, what will happen? Please give me the teachings first, and then I will jump." The master gave teachings about the ten virtues. When he had finished he said, "Now jump." The king was fully satisfied and felt so happy and fortunate that he jumped without any fear or hesitation. Fortunately, he had no karma to die that day and he survived the fall. This is an example of how the Buddha attended a spiritual master and practiced the teachings, even at the risk of his own life.

One should also see the spiritual master as a doctor. Whatever the doctor says to do, the patient should do. It is the same with the study and practice of Dharma. The spiritual master should be seen as a dear friend or as a very kind and responsible parent.

*The holy Dharma that he teaches is like the nectar
    of immortality.
It dispels all faults and possesses all good qualities
    without exception.
Make offerings to him of the three ways of pleasing.
This is my heart's advice.*

THE PURE, *holy Dharma* teachings given by the spiritual master are
like nectar, a stainless ambrosia that transforms all our negativities
into something positive and transforms all poison into nectar. If we
take these teachings to heart, they purify all our negative thoughts
and karma. Dharma has all the techniques needed to transform
our negativity if we make enough effort. We shouldn't expect to
be perfect at the beginning. If we were perfect right at the start, we
wouldn't have to study and practice. Since we have these negative
thoughts and obscurations, we make mistakes. But then through
Dharma practice we can recognize mistakes and manifest good
qualities instead.

If we know how to practice, all our negative thoughts can be utilized as Dharma practice. Take a flower as an example. The flower
that is so beautiful today fades after a while, and we throw it in the
trash. But what we throw in the trash can become good fertilizer that
will bring more beautiful flowers when it's put on the fields. In the
same way, our negative thoughts are the basis from which we can
develop great wisdom and compassion. Without negative thoughts
like hatred, anger, attachment, and ignorance, there is no way to
uncover enlightenment. But we must know how to utilize them.
Otherwise they are just trash, a cause of suffering. A mind without
negative thoughts can grow nothing; it's like a dry desert. A mind
with a lot of ego attachment—there the Dharma can grow so beautifully when we practice because it has a lot of fertilizer. That's why
we should encourage ourselves to know how to utilize negativity.

We shouldn't feel bad when we have a lot of anger and attachment.

Rather, we should acknowledge it and learn how to use these feelings instead of following them. This technique is explained in the *lo jong*, or mind training, practices. Rather than being enslaved by anger or attachment, we learn to utilize them to develop great wisdom and compassion. In this way, the more anger we have, the more firmly we become committed to continuing our practice.

Since we obtain the precious qualities of the buddhas from the Dharma teacher, we *make offerings in three ways*: by providing necessities, by being of service, and especially, by doing Dharma practice.

It is not that the spiritual master needs our wealth or service. Rather, we carry out the practice of making offerings in order to purify our own stinginess and attachment. In order to be free from arrogance and laziness, we practice being of service. These things are done for our own benefit, to reinforce our devotion to the Dharma teachings.

Even if we can't reach the heights that Milarepa did, we can learn from his example. His renunciation was so powerful, and his yearning for the Dharma teachings was so strong, that he served Marpa by pleasing him in the three ways even at the risk of his own life. After he received the teachings, how he practiced! This is the true meaning of *making offerings of the three ways of pleasing*.

When Atisha was in Tibet, one of his Tibetan disciples was called Drom Tonpa. He offered completely devoted service to Atisha. When Atisha crossed the Himalayas through the snow, he couldn't travel as fast as the native Tibetans and had to rest along the way. Drom Tonpa carried a bag of dry dust on his back all the way from the lowlands. When Atisha needed to rest on the snow mountain, Drom Tonpa threw the dust on the snow and asked Atisha to sit there so he wouldn't be so cold. This kind of practitioner becomes very successful in Dharma practice. But it is important to remember that the master has to have all the necessary qualities. Otherwise, we are just slaves for no good reason.

The third way of pleasing the teacher, practicing Dharma, is the most important. Whatever teachings you receive, practice them with heartfelt sincerity. Dharma practice means developing our mental qualities, not counting how many mantras we chant. One may chant many mantras, but if there is no growth in one's qualities of compassion, openness, tolerance, courage, and so forth, then the effort didn't do any good. We have to develop good qualities along with reciting mantras and meditating. One may achieve good sama-dhi, but if our negative thoughts are not uprooted by critical insight, they will still come back.

Pause and contemplate for a while. Suppose you are very hun-gry; you haven't had a meal in several days. How happy you will be when you get a delicious meal! Without wavering at all, with full enjoyment, you will eat that food. Likewise, for many lifetimes we have had no opportunity to study and practice the Dharma. Because of this, we are still suffering in samsara. Now, our meeting this Dharma is like a hungry person meeting with food. Without any doubt or fear, make full use of this opportunity to practice the Dharma, the precious teachings.

*Not taking the teachings to heart through practice is like
   the sound of an echo.
   It is empty and without meaning.
   Therefore, apply your mind to the Dharma.
   This is my heart's advice.*

FIRST, WE MUST recognize suffering and its causes. Then, to free ourselves from this state, we must see that Dharma is the only answer.
Find the courage to take a moment to reflect. Watch the silence and
quiet of the mind. How peaceful and beautiful is its nature! In this
same way, we can come to understand how precious the Dharma
is, that it is the method to uproot our delusions. We begin to see
the absolute peace and happiness that we can realize. On this basis,
we can take the Dharma into our hearts and practice it. If instead
we take Dharma as merely another type of knowledge, like art or
mathematics, it is like *an echo*. An echo has no meaning, no essence;
it's just a reflection. You can hear its sound when you go to a rocky
mountain, but it is meaningless. You just hear it and let it go. So if
you hear the teachings and don't follow them, you turn them into
echoes—a waste of time for both the spiritual master and yourself.

Even if you hear just one hour of Dharma teaching, pay full attention. Make every effort to apply it instead of merely being argumentative. Dharma is the way to achieve peace, harmony, tranquility,
and a mind of gentleness. Bring that into your heart by contemplating, "I want to achieve these qualities by receiving these teachings."
This is the purpose of receiving teachings—not just to intellectual-
ize, not to become an expert in philosophy, but rather to learn how
to practice and to mix your mind with the teachings. This is what it
means to *apply your mind to the Dharma*.

For example, we persistently try to bring loving-kindness and compassion into our hearts. It's not easy. In fact, it's quite hard because
our mind is so habituated to negativity. We may think, "Maybe I
will lose my identity, and then who will protect me?" Our mind just

automatically goes in that direction. Sometimes we think, "Is there any hope? I have practiced so many years, and my mind is running in the same direction all the time." Still, we have no choice. We have to continue to practice. Purifying all the disturbing emotions is our most crucial activity, so put all of your effort into mixing your mind with Dharma.

The spiritual master explains instructions on how to train and purify the mind according to the teachings of the Buddha. When we listen to these teachings, there are three faults to avoid:

Not studying: First, not receiving the teachings with your whole heart is like a bowl turned upside down. No matter what kinds of delicious things you pour in, they won't go into the bowl. Your body may be present, but your two ears are closed. Sometimes your mind wanders—the body is present but the mind goes out or is sleeping during the teaching.

Not contemplating: Second, not remembering the teachings that you do hear and not contemplating them is like a bowl with a hole. Even though the bowl is upright and open, no matter how much you pour in, it all drains out. Likewise, you may receive teachings and say they are wonderful and precious, but as soon as you leave the cushion, the teachings stay behind. Only an empty mind remains.

Not meditating: Third, listening to and contemplating the teachings with an impure motivation is like a poisoned bowl. When food is put inside such a bowl, it is ruined and no longer of any use. Likewise, if you don't have a pure motivation (i.e., the thought of bodhicitta) to purify your mind, to help all sentient beings, and to attain enlightenment, and instead are confused by pride, jealousy, attachment, or anger when you receive these teachings, the teachings become "poisoned." They are no longer useful for purification. Instead they support our arrogance and jealousy. The pure, pristine, clear water of precious Dharma is thus sullied by the mind of impure motivation and is no longer drinkable.

The Buddhadharma—especially the Mahayana and Vajrayana teachings—explains the different levels of the mind in great detail: how to understand outer phenomena, and how to maintain and purify the inner mind. This is such precious wisdom! There are so many types of knowledge in the world, but none can fully explain our mind. Mind is the root of samsara and of nirvana, or in other words, the root cause of our suffering and our enlightenment. The Buddha himself thoroughly revealed the absolute mode of abiding, the nature of mind, and taught it to his followers out of all-pervasive, intrinsic wisdom and great compassion for all sentient beings. He treated each sentient being as he did his own mother or son.

Therefore, take the Dharma deeply into your heart. When we practice Dharma, it is crucial to build strength in our motivation rather than feeling physically and mentally fragile. When we receive Dharma teachings and then become mentally fragile, this shows we do not have clear understanding. We should learn how to face our problems, how to dispel our obstacles with our mental strength, how to accept suffering and overcome it with the practice of meditation. If we are taught in this way, then obstacles don't matter, suffering doesn't matter. Whether it is physical suffering or mental suffering, we can handle it. The Dharma contains all possibilities—that's why I say it is so precious.

We need such strength to overcome mental conflicts and obstacles, to uproot confusion and to reveal the fundamental nature of our being. With mental strength, one will be unafraid to face obstacles. Moreover, through wisdom and experience, suffering and obstacles provide an opportunity for the purification of negative karma because they reinforce the thought of enlightenment. This makes Dharma indispensable.

Take a moment to reflect. On a rocky mountain, an echo has no essence or meaning. Likewise, life without the precious Dharma is empty and meaningless.

The four preliminaries are like the foundation of a building.
Without them, nothing can be perfected.
Therefore, cherish persistent recollection.
This is my heart's advice.

WHEN WE CONSTRUCT a building of a hundred stories, it must have a good foundation. Without a stable foundation, the building could collapse at any time. It is like building a castle on sand or ice. So the foundation is as important as the structure itself. *The four preliminaries* are the foundation for our spiritual palace. Without them, there is no basis from which to start our spiritual practice or study. There is no foundation from which to develop our experience. Our meditation practices cannot advance; nothing can improve or be perfected. There is no way to free ourselves from samsara. These four preliminaries are very important; we must recollect them repeatedly and cherish them in order to enhance our Dharma practice. Without these reminders, we would become lazy practitioners. Being attached to samsara but unaware of it, we would simply pass meaninglessly through our lives. This is why the four preliminaries are so precious.

The four preliminaries are the recollections of

- ▸ the precious human life, the basis of working toward buddhahood
- ▸ the impermanence of all phenomena
- ▸ the suffering nature of samsara
- ▸ the cause and result of all our actions.

These four form the essential foundation for productive meditation. Often, when we advise people in the West to "meditate," they think that something is wrong with their mind, that they are not "normal" people. They meditate to free themselves from that difficulty. Actually, one needs to have a very good, well prepared, astute mind for meditation, one that is very precise yet relaxed. Without a clear, relaxed mind, one cannot meditate. Even if one did do some meditation, it would be superficial, not a productive meditation. For example, when the ground in a garden is well plowed and the soil is soft and fertilized, any seed we sow will grow. Otherwise, we cannot expect a good result no matter how good a seed is planted.

Some people think these preliminaries are unimportant. They point to Highest Yoga Tantra practice or Mahamudra and say, "Now, *those* practices are profound." Thinking that the foundations are not important is a sure sign of an unsuccessful practice. No doubt, these other practices are high and profound, yet to become successful as a practitioner, you have to build a good foundation. With just an emotional feeling of "Oh, how good this is!" and high expectations, our interest won't last long. In other words, we have to have good preparation, a good mind.

In order to really know these things, we have to have a precious human life connected to the Dharma. Dharma provides every opportunity to overcome suffering and the causes of suffering, every opportunity to become free from samsara and to attain enlightenment. So precious! Interest in the Dharma cannot be purchased anywhere. We can only develop it within the mind. This interest gives us great wisdom, which is the key to dispelling ignorance and delusion. Through this interest, we can establish bodhicitta, the mind of enlightenment. Take a moment to rejoice and feel fortunate about yourself, about your precious human life, and your meeting the holy Dharma. Such a precious human life is rare and difficult to find.

All phenomena, including our own lives, are subject to change. This precious human life is as fragile as dew on a blade of grass. We think that we are healthy, but we never know for sure. Especially in these modern times, life goes faster than ever before. In addition to natural death, there are accidents with cars, buses, and airplanes. Life is so fragile. It is like a car; if one tiny wire is missing, the whole car is unusable. In our body, if one tiny nerve system fails, the whole body is gone. Impermanence is not something we Buddhists made up. This is the true nature of all phenomena, of all that is composite.

The nature of samsara is suffering. This doesn't mean we are miserable all the time, but suffering is bound to arise. No matter what we do, suffering is waiting there. Even if we get what we want, we still are not free from suffering. It is important to recognize this. All sufferings are the manifestation of causes that we ourselves created. We can see this very clearly in the nature of samsara. This leaves us no choice other than Dharma study and practice.

Without this good foundation, and with high expectations for our practice, we cannot rest the mind in meditation. Thinking such things as, "Maybe during this session I will get such and such realization. During this retreat, I will get the highest result," distracts us. Then we press the mind, which makes it worse. We need our minds to be relaxed and clear with the knowledge that when thoughts occur, there is nothing to be achieved outside of the mind. When thoughts pass this way, there is nothing to get. If they go that way— nothing to get there either. We need the discerning awareness that there is no place for the mind to go. You don't suppress thoughts, but seeing that there is nothing to achieve besides the mind, you can simply meditate and purify your thoughts. This kind of wisdom is achieved through these four most important foundations.

Without this kind of skill and awareness, we won't feel the need to take refuge in the Buddha, Dharma, and Sangha. When we know that samsara is suffering, that suffering is caused by our negative thoughts and confusion, and that we don't know how to free ourselves from suffering, then we have a reason to take refuge. We come to know what Buddha is, come to know what Dharma is, come to know what Sangha is, and to rely on them.

The second most important thing is that, through the *recollection* of these four foundations, we enhance and make progress in our practice. These four foundations are very important in order to sustain a life in retreat. If we are not convinced about these four preliminaries, especially about impermanence and the suffering of samsara, even though we may go into retreat on a mountain, our minds are still wandering in samsara, hunting for something. Not only that; if you push yourself and go into retreat with only temporary, emotional enthusiasm instead of a foundation of reason, you may lose your interest after a few weeks. On the basis of the four foundations, you can practice Refuge, Vajrasattva, Guru Yoga, Bodhicitta, any deity yoga or Mahamudra—anything you like—and you will enjoy your practice.

Of final importance is emptiness. Which things are empty? The

Heart Sutra says, "Form is emptiness, emptiness is also form; form is no other than emptiness, and emptiness is also no other than form." The very nature of these four foundations is emptiness. There is not any emptiness that exists elsewhere. That is why they are called "foundations." We cannot ignore them at all. If we think they are unnecessary, this is a sign of becoming an unsuccessful Dharma practitioner.

The five skandhas, or aggregates, are form, feeling, perception, mental formation, and consciousness. They are the basis of all composite phenomena, including the four foundations, samsara and nirvana. Even the precious human life depends on these five conditions. They are naturally impermanent, the basis of our suffering, of the karma we create, and the results we experience. Having understood this well, we take refuge in the Buddha, Dharma, and Sangha. We cultivate bodhicitta with the five skandhas. We transform into the deity state with them. Without these five, nothing can be purified. We practice Mahamudra with this five-skandha body. We practice emptiness with these five skandhas. This is how we ground our practice. In reality, nothing exists outside of these skandhas.

The four great seals of Dharma, which outline the general teaching of the Buddha, are

1. All afflicted phenomena have the nature of suffering.
2. All compounded phenomena have the nature of
    impermanence.
3. All phenomena are empty by nature.
4. Nirvana is complete peace.

The supreme place of solitude is like a well-guarded fort.
The eight worldly concerns are the cause of wandering mind.
Therefore, keep to the mountains and retreat.
This is my heart's advice.

WITH A GOOD understanding of the four foundations, a pure sense of renunciation will manifest. Because of that, attachment to samsara weakens, and you look for a *place of solitude* to practice meditation. When you have sincere nonattachment to samsara, wherever you find yourself can be a supreme place of solitude.

Solitude is usually found in the mountains or in any place that is well protected from distractions. This place should be like a *well-guarded fort*, where no harm can come to your body or mind. When your mind is free from activities, any place is solitude. Your apartment could be solitude. On the other hand, being in solitude is not a guarantee that you are in good shape. If your mind is not protected, then your retreat place may be just another samsara. Your body may be on the mountain, but your mind will still be in the bazaar.

Although being in solitude is one of the best methods to accomplish mental quiescence, this does not mean that those who don't have this opportunity should not practice. We must practice whenever we can. We have to remind ourselves constantly to bring Dharma into the heart and to establish the practices of calm abiding and pristine wisdom. So it is important to find a place of solitude, without which it may not be possible to firmly establish these practices.

People often ask why we don't hear about very many enlightened masters these days. Mostly it is because we are all so busy that there is no time to establish ourselves in meditation. If you really want to establish the spiritual qualities that are mentioned in the life stories from previous times, you have to decide to keep to a mountain retreat for many years. A three-year retreat is just a start. Some very gifted people can have great accomplishments in such a short time, but more commonly people have to stay in retreat for fifteen, twenty, thirty years, or even a lifetime. Once a person is well established in mind training practice and has achieved the realization of certainty, then they can help others more effectively.

A clear, stable mind is essential to meditation, but the *eight worldly concerns* don't allow the mind to settle in the right place. These eight—the gaining and losing of wealth and so forth—are the root cause of a wandering mind. So we can see that a busy life does not support a successful meditation practice. To calm the busy "monkey" mind, serious practitioners must go into a retreat with a peaceful environment and other good conditions.

When the mind is in full calm abiding, the resulting acuity fosters effective reflection on the four foundations and bodhicitta. On the basis of repeated meditation on the four foundations, a thorough conviction in their truth arises, and true renunciation results. Then the meditator is ready to do retreat in solitude, where the realization of complete enlightenment can be achieved. Once you decide to pursue serious practice, what teachings are there to support this endeavor? What practices should you do? In the next section of the text, the author begins to explain this.

*The precious teachings of the Drigung Kagyu, which are like
   the treasury of a king,
lack nothing of the holy Dharma.
There is no need to depend on anything else.
This is my heart's advice.*

A UNIVERSAL MONARCH'S treasury lacks nothing; it contains every wealth that exists in the world. Likewise, the Drigung Kagyu lineage holds all the Dharma teachings that Buddha taught for those who want to attain complete enlightenment. Shortly before his parinirvana, Dharma Lord Gampopa gathered all his disciples together. He told the assembly that his Dharma-heir, Phagmo Drupa Dorje Gyalpo, was the one among them who was most accomplished in the understanding of Buddhist philosophy and in meditation practice. Lord Gampopa said, "He and I—there is not one single difference in our spiritual achievement. If any of you has doubts or questions about Dharma, go to him and receive teachings."

Phagmo Drupa established his own monastery at Phagdru. There he gathered 80,000 disciples, among whom 500 were highly accomplished in their realizations. Within that elite group, Lord Jigten Sumgön became his throne-holder, meaning that his and Phagmo Drupa's realizations were equal. In particular, Lord Jigten Sumgön was one who fully perfected the Fivefold Path of Mahamudra, the heart essence of Phagmo Drupa's teachings that encompass all the sutras and tantras of the Buddha.

After rigorous study and arduous retreat, Lord Jigten Sumgön attained buddhahood when he was thirty-five years old and founded his monastery at Drigung Thil when he was thirty-seven. There he gathered thousands of disciples, both human and non-human, and gave vast and profound teachings to them for forty years. Many of his disciples attained complete buddhahood by following these five paths, while others attained realization on the bhumis. Even the least of them actualized the full nature of the mind. Accounts of

Lord Jigten Sumgön's life and liberation have been published under such titles as *Calling to the Lama from Afar*, *The Great Kagyu Masters*, and others.

Since that time, the Drigung Kagyu lineage has preserved and practiced the Fivefold Mahamudra teaching. This teaching includes everything an individual needs to achieve complete buddhahood. Because it contains all the necessary factors and components, it *lacks nothing of the holy Dharma*. When you fully understand this, you won't have to look for teachings in so many different places. Life is short and there isn't much time. Therefore, fully focus and dedicate your life to Dharma study and practice.

There is a saying, "Mahamudra is like a snow lion, but without the Fivefold Path it is blind." The Fivefold Path of Mahamudra consists of these five aspects:

1. Bodhicitta cultivation, which includes the study of all the sutra systems—the four foundations, refuge, loving-kindness, compassion, bodhicitta, the three trainings, the six paramitas, and all the stages of the bodhisattva's path to buddhahood.

2. Yidam practice, where one studies all the stages of kriya, carya, yoga, and anuttara yoga, the types of empowerment, and the arising and completion stages, including the Six Yogas of Naropa.

3. Guru Yoga. Here, the ultimate guru is the Buddha. "Yoga" means a method to unify one's own mind with the Buddha's mind—the ultimate uncontrived, intrinsic awareness, the original mind. In this study and practice, the four kayas (forms) of the Buddha are the *nirmanakaya*, a physical form that a buddha manifests whenever needed in any of the six realms; the *sambhogakaya*, a subtle form that a buddha manifests for great, highly accomplished bodhisattvas; the *dharmakaya*, the complete buddhahood that is comprehended by a buddha alone; and the *svabhavikakaya*, the unified nature of all buddhas' forms.

4. Mahamudra, the Great Seal. Here, one studies all the manifestations of mind: samsara—contrived and fabricated out of confusion—and enlightenment, the uncontrived perfection of mind. On this path, there is a progression of practices beginning

with *samadhi* (Tib.: *samten*, meditative concentration). There are four stages of samadhi in the form realm and four in the formless realm. The meditator must continue until he is well established in and habituated to this meditation so that less and less effort is needed. That becomes a good foundation for Mahamudra realization. The Four Yogas of Mahamudra identify and introduce the nature of mind with special insight (Tib.: *lhag thong*). This teaching explains how to stabilize the nature of mind and how to progress through stages until the dharma-kaya is actualized. Briefly, the Four Yogas of Mahamudra are as follows:

▸ *Yoga of one-pointedness.* A vajra-like stabilization is required for Mahamudra realization. In order to taste Mahamudra, the meditator needs an unwavering mind that is undisturbed by any obstructions.

▸ *Yoga free from elaboration.* Through incisive special insight, the meditator directly perceives the inseparable union of effulgence and emptiness.

▸ *Yoga of one taste.* After practicing what he has realized on the path and familiarizing himself with what he experienced through special insight, the meditator will experience the one taste of the single, essential nature of samsara and nirvana, the inseparable nature of interdependence and emptiness.

▸ *Yoga of non-meditation.* Purifying all the subtle or left-over obscurations completely reveals the uncreated original mind, which is primordial awareness. When there is no gap between meditation and non-meditation, and everything is effortless, non-meditation has been accomplished, the full enlightenment.

5. Dedication. Whenever one is involved in any kind of project or work, at the end there is a result to enjoy for oneself or share with others. It is the same with study and meditation practice. Whatever accumulations one has gathered—virtue, merit, or wisdom—all are dedicated to the achievement of buddhahood, which brings the result of ultimate peace and joy for oneself and others.

Thus, we can see that the complete teachings of the Buddha are contained within this system.

The Fivefold Path of Mahamudra is the heart essence of the sutras, tantras, and commentaries, a key to open the door of all the buddhas' teachings. It contains the quintessential point of all classes of tantra and is the heart treasure of the root and lineage lamas. It contains the three pitakas, or divisions of the canonical writings, and four tantras that an individual needs to achieve enlightenment. This path is complete; without it, buddhahood would not be possible. Directly or indirectly, one has to practice each of these five methods to attain buddhahood.

If you learn these teachings and practice them well, you may understand how to free yourself from samsara and how to help other sentient beings. Don't think that these five paths are too difficult to practice. One moment of practice can contain all five teachings. If one possesses the instructions and knows how to practice, one can accomplish them within a single lifetime. For example, when you eat a meal, first cultivate bodhicitta and then transform your whole being into bodhicitta, which manifests as a yidam deity. Then, in the heart or throat, visualize your lama. In nonduality free from attachment or aversion, enjoy the meal. Finally, dedicate the merit to enlightenment. In this way, one can carry out all five of these practices at one time.

Lord Jigten Sumgön's spoken advice on this was recorded in the *Wish-granting Jewel* this way:

> Speaking of the virtues in the beginning, middle, and end
> that are taught again and again by the buddhas of the past,
> present, and future, the sublime lama told me:
>
>> The virtues of bodhicitta, yidam deity [practice],
>> devotion for the sublime lama,
>> the key points of the ultimate Mahamudra, and
>> dedication of the virtues collected in the three times
>>   and the innate—
>> there is no sublime Dharma other than these.
>> Practice them until you attain perfect enlightenment!
>
> Thus he spoke.

The Three Jewels are like the sphere of the sun.
Their compassion is impartial and unfailing.
Take refuge from the bottom of your heart.
This is my heart's advice.

THE *THREE JEWELS* are the Buddha, Dharma, and Sangha. In Sanskrit, they are called *ratna*, the precious jewels that bring joy. *Sphere of the sun* is a metaphor for something that is complete, all-pervading and unfailing, that dispels darkness and shines impartially on all. The Buddha, Dharma, and Sangha have complete and perfect qualities and possess every ability to dispel suffering and bestow blessings on sentient beings.

Buddha means one who is fully enlightened. In other words, a buddha has fully awakened from the sleep of delusion. He is free from all obscurations, both gross and subtle, and has revealed the two intrinsic wisdom awarenesses. Buddhahood is the spontaneously established, uncompounded nature that does not depend on any other conditions. A buddha has perfect wisdom, has perfectly accomplished the nature of compassion, and has every ability to manifest all excellent activities. There are many buddhas in the past, present, and future. In fact, there are as many buddhas as there are particles of dust. Basically, the term *buddha* refers to anyone whose mind is fully awakened and who is free from all suffering and its causes. When we point to Buddha Shakyamuni as a buddha, he is an example of this. A buddha has four forms, all of which emanate from the dharmakaya:

1. *Nirmanakaya* is a buddha who has emanated in a physical form. A nirmanakaya can emanate anywhere as anything animate or inanimate—as a human being, an animal, or even a bridge, if necessary. For example, we see in Asanga's life story that Buddha Maitreya emanated as a dog covered with maggots in order to create the conditions through which Asanga

might gain an opportunity to see him. In reality, a buddha's manifestations cannot be measured, as they are infinite.

2. *Sambhogakaya* is the expression of the complete, perfect manifestation of the Buddha's excellent, infinite qualities, called the enjoyment body—splendid and glorious. All the buddhas appear and manifest in the limitless buddha fields in this form. They are not crowded there, nor are they smaller. The sambhogakaya is inconceivable and beyond ordinary thought or measurement. Yet, the great bodhisattvas who are highly accomplished in their realization can perceive this form. The sambhogakaya has limitless speech that is harmonious and melodious and suits the minds of all sentient beings. The nirmanakaya and sambhogakaya manifest to benefit all sentient beings through undefiled, all-pervading compassion.

3. *Dharmakaya* is one's own perfection, fully free from all delusion and suffering. It is infinite and transcends all boundaries. We cannot see it with physical eyes or touch it with the hand. Yet it is the basis of all excellent, infinite qualities—boundless, immeasurable wisdom, primordial awareness, and compassion. It is the basis for the manifestation of peace, harmony, and virtue, even in the relative state. All the various forms, or bodies, of a buddha emanate from the dharmakaya.

4. *Svabhavikakaya* is the indivisible nature of the other three forms. In other words, the emptiness nature of the body is dharmakaya. From that, the unceasing manifestation of all form is nirmanakaya, and the inseparability of these two is sambhogakaya. The nirmanakaya and sambhogakaya together are known as the *rupakaya*. The rupakaya and dharmakaya are inseparable and are contained within the svabhavikakaya. For example, Buddha Shakyamuni's wisdom mind is dharmakaya, his speech is sambhogakaya, his body is nirmanakaya, and their inseparable nature is svabhavikakaya.

Dharma means the method to protect the mind from the *kleshas*, the mental afflictions. Dharma teachings are related to absolute and relative truth, first presented by Buddha Shakyamuni as the Four Noble Truths:

- the Truth of Suffering
- the Truth of the Origin of Suffering
- the Truth of the Cessation of Suffering
- the Truth of the Path to Achieve Cessation

These four comprise the two truths—the first, second and fourth are included under relative truth, and the third is absolute truth. The relative truth is a bridge for ordinary beings to use to actualize the absolute truth. Relative truth is also called the "Truth of the Path," meaning that it is a method to purify gross and subtle obscurations. The path reveals all the perfect qualities of the Buddha, including great compassion and intrinsic wisdom. The path is the ultimate antidote to all mental afflictions without exception. Absolute truth is inconceivable, meaning that it cannot be conceptualized by the afflicted mind. Nonduality cannot be perceived by the duality-mind. Our busy minds cannot conceptualize the ultimate meaning yet they are inseparable by nature—without relative truth, there is no absolute truth.

We study Dharma teachings and practice the relative truth in order to experience and realize the absolute truth, enlightenment. Everything that we study and practice is related to the two truths: right from the beginning when we start to read the alphabet and count, then later when we recognize the ten virtues and begin to avoid the ten nonvirtues. We then progress step by step and traverse the Five Paths. The first four paths (the path of accumulation, the path of preparation, the path of incisive insight, and the path of meditation) are related to relative truth. The absolute truth (the path of no more learning or path of perfection) is realized when we achieve buddhahood.

We follow these paths with the support of the three trainings: *shila* (morality), *samadhi* (equipoise meditation), and *prajña* (critical insight awareness). When we build a house, we need the materials to make pillars, walls, and ceilings. By combining these conditions, we can build a beautiful house. Likewise, to build the house of enlightenment, these three trainings are the crucial raw materials. If one of these is missing, the mansion of enlightenment cannot be built. So all Dharma practitioners must take care of each of them equally. Cherish them in your heart.

Sangha refers to the community of those who are committed to studying and practicing the Dharma. There are many classifications of Sangha: Shravakas (Hearers), Pratyekabuddhas (Solitary Realizers), and the bodhisattvas who have achieved various stages such as the different paths or the ten bhumis. They all have different qualities, depending on their accomplishments in the spiritual path. Lay sangha practitioners keep the five precepts and have unshakable confidence in the Buddha, Dharma, and Sangha. The sanghas of monks and nuns are practitioners who take the precepts of ordination and commit their lives to Dharma study and practice. These sanghas are great examples of successful practitioners who are following in the footsteps of the Buddha. They are objects of respect, devotion, and inspiration. They are fully dedicated to purifying mental delusions and negative thoughts and to embracing the enlightened attitude. We can take refuge in the Sangha that has actualized the Third Path and above, those who have achieved incisive, critical insight. In particular, we take refuge in the Sangha consisting of those who are highly accomplished in their realization of the two types of wisdom and are free from samsara. Thus, these three refuges—the Buddha, Dharma, and Sangha—are precious and the source of all benefit in the world.

A wish-granting jewel has these qualities:

- it is very rare to find in the world
- it is pure by its nature
- it has the ability to fulfill the wishes of human beings in its vicinity
- it is the peerless ornament of a country
- it is the supreme wealth among all types of wealth
- it has a nature that never changes

Likewise, the Buddha, Dharma, and Sangha possess qualities similar to those of a wish-granting jewel:

- they are rare in samsara
- they have fully purified all the gross and subtle obscurations
- they have every ability to bring about temporary and absolute peace and all excellent qualities

- they are the supreme ornaments of the world that can create absolute harmony
- they are foremost among sentient beings
- they never waver in benefiting sentient beings through their wisdom, compassion, and activities

On the basis of the four foundations, understand that these three—Buddha, Dharma and Sangha—are the unfailing and compassionate refuge. So from the bottom of your heart, take refuge in them. In particular, the Buddha has unconditional compassion for all sentient beings. The Buddha's compassion and wisdom reach every sentient being without exception. In the Buddha's mind, there is no discrimination at all, not even between human beings and nonhuman beings. He cultivated loving-kindness impartially. The Buddha's blessings are not greater for high lamas, and are no less for ordinary beings, even for small insects. We may hear that such and such a lama has had a vision of the Buddha, so we may think that the Buddha is closer to them and farther away from us. This is not true. We should feel complete confidence that the Buddha is impartial and unfailing. The sun shines impartially on the high mountain and in the narrow valley. The sun can be reflected in thousands of pools without exception. In the same ways, the blessings of the Three Jewels reach all sentient beings equally.

If we make an effort, the Buddha's support is always there. The Buddha's impartial nature is real for all sentient beings. This explains why Dharma is not reserved just for monks and nuns, but can be practiced by any ordinary being. Dharma teaches us how to be free from universal suffering. Wherever there is a chance to help, the Buddha is unfailingly there. When we are in hot weather and are touched by a cool breeze, we can feel that this is the Buddha's refreshing blessing. When it's cold and we feel a touch of heat-giving sunshine, that also is the Buddha's unfailing blessing-activity. The blessings of the Buddha, Dharma, and Sangha are coemergent with our inspiration to be free from suffering and to take refuge. Both are necessary for the perfect result.

We know that samsara is confusion and suffering and we want to be free of that state, but we don't know how. Thus, we need a guide who can give us a complete method, who can show us the way to become totally free from all our delusions. For this, we turn to refuge in the Buddha, Dharma, and Sangha. These are the benefits of taking refuge:

- One becomes a Buddhist and gains every opportunity to study and practice the precious Dharma.
- Refuge becomes the foundation to receive all other vows and illuminates the path of liberation.
- Refuge purifies and dispels all obscurations without exception, in the same way that water washes away impurity.
- Harm from human and nonhuman beings becomes powerless.
- Refuge is not merely intellectual; rather, refuge involves one's whole being.
- Buddha is the body of purification of all the obscurations, Dharma is the method to purify obscurations, Sangha is the company in which one practices Dharma. So when one takes refuge in the Three Jewels and practices the Dharma, obscurations cannot function, just as darkness fades when the sun rises.
- One accomplishes all that one desires. For example, one can accomplish the perfection of the intrinsic, pure nature of wisdom. One can effortlessly manifest peace, happiness, fame, and wealth and can ultimately attain buddhahood. Meanwhile, one will be reborn in the god and human realms.
- Through taking refuge, all the qualities of wisdom and compassion will infinitely increase.
- By taking refuge in the Three Jewels, one quickly attains buddhahood. The study and practice of Dharma, step by step, purifies all obscurations without exception and eventually leads to the final goal.
- When we practice properly and sincerely, we will not be reborn in the lower realms.

The following story illustrates this point:

> Norbu was a powerful divinity, a leader among the gods. He played in the garden of the God Realm of the Thirty-three, where he was surrounded by many sons and daughters of other gods. A pleasant fragrance radiated from his body

and his ornaments were always fresh. The others couldn't bear to be parted from him. They were so absorbed in their pleasure that one hundred years passed by in a short moment.

Unexpectedly, bad omens began to appear on Norbu's body. His flowers and ornaments faded, and a foul smell arose from his body. He became displeased with his seat. The gods' sons and daughters noticed this and abandoned him. Norbu reflected and wondered, "What is happening to me?" Since the gods have partial clairvoyance, he looked at the situation and discovered that all the virtues and good karma that he had created in the past had been consumed and exhausted. Busy with enjoyments, he had accumulated no new merit in his lifetime. Then he looked for where he would be reborn after death and saw that he would be conceived as a pig in a huge mud puddle. His anticipation of this fate caused him intolerable suffering.

Norbu went to Indra, king of the gods, and asked for protection from that awful rebirth. But Indra said, "I have no ability to assist you. You should go to the Buddha for help." In a flash, Norbu appeared in front of the Buddha and made his request in a sincere and desperate way. Prostrating, he asked for protection from rebirth in the lower realms. The Buddha advised, "Take refuge in the Buddha, Dharma, and Sangha," and gave him refuge ordination and instruction in meditation. Norbu practiced sincerely with a one-pointed mind. Immediately after death, Norbu was reborn as the king of the Brahma realm.

Indra began to wonder where that son of the gods had been reborn, so he asked the Buddha. The Buddha told him to search in the Brahma realm because Norbu had been born there as a king. When Indra saw that this was true, he was astonished at the extraordinary power of taking refuge and he sang this praise:

The one who took refuge in the Buddha, Dharma, and
    Sangha—
though he was destined to be reborn in a lower realm,

he was born in another god realm instead
because he took refuge while here in a god realm.
How magnificent, how wonderful, are the power and
    blessing of refuge!

Further, if we take refuge in the Three Jewels and follow the path, there are benefits for future lives:

- ▸ We will meet face to face with buddhas adorned with the major and minor marks, or with great vajra masters.
- ▸ We will never be separated from hearing the Dharma teachings in life after life.
- ▸ We will join the assembly of the sangha.

Take a few moments to relax. Take a deep breath. In the space before you, visualize the Buddha, the embodiment of wisdom and compassion; the Dharma, the perfect teaching; and the Sangha, the great bodhisattvas and arhats. Arouse strong devotion and yearning to be free from samsara. Take refuge sincerely and say this prayer twenty-one times or more:

Namo Buddhaya.
Namo Dharmaya.
Namo Sanghaya.

After that, dissolve the visualization into light, which then dissolves into you. Meditate that you receive the blessings of wisdom and compassion that purify all your obscurations. Rest the mind in the natural state, which is the Buddha's mind, for some time. Finally, dedicate the merit.

The stain of bad deeds and obscurations is like mud covering
a jewel.
Even though the alaya is pure, it cannot manifest the qualities.
The confession of four powers is essential.
This is my heart's advice.

ALL SENTIENT BEINGS in the six realms are ruled by the afflicting emotions, by karma and result, yet the innate nature of each
and every one of us is pervaded by the perfect buddha nature. The
stain of bad deeds and obscurations refers to our negative thoughts,
obscurations, and all the different types of karma, especially the
deeply rooted inveterate propensities. These stains are like mud
covering the precious jewel of buddha nature. When a diamond is
covered with mud, is its quality lessened? No; a diamond is a diamond. But when it is encrusted with mud, we don't use it as an
ornament. When we realize that a diamond is underneath the mud,
we take it out and polish it. Similarly, the essence of our own mind
is no different from the Buddha's mind. When we realize this, we
can "uncover" the mind by purifying negative thoughts. When we
experience this directly, that is the Buddha's omniscient mind.

Before we can do anything, we have to recognize that a naturally
pure jewel is present in the mud. Once discovered, we first clean the
jewel with a rough cloth or salty water. After that, we clean it more
gently. Finally, we wash it gently with medicinal water and polish it
with a silk cloth. Through these efforts, the pure jewel is revealed.
We reveal our buddha nature in the same manner. First, we practice
the four foundations to remove the gross layer of mud. Then we
do the practice of *ngöndro*—the preliminary practices—to uncover
more subtle obscurations. After that, relative and ultimate bodhicitta will uncover the most subtle layer of mind, and out comes the
pure jewel of enlightened mind!

The word *alaya* has different meanings. Sometimes it refers to "storehouse" or "store consciousness" where all thoughts and karma are stored. Sometimes it refers to emptiness, the basis for both samsara and nirvana. When we are confused about the meaning of emptiness we wander in the six realms of samsara. When we directly penetrate emptiness, we achieve nirvana. In this case, *alaya* is used as a synonym for buddha nature, the basis of our meditation practices and the ground for enlightenment. If we don't understand the Dharma and create nonvirtue instead of practicing well, it is the basis for samsara. When we practice with understanding, confidence, courage, and devotion, we directly reveal the pure alaya, the buddha-mind.

Suppose a poor family is living in a dilapidated house not knowing that a vast treasure lies underneath their property. Then suppose a miner comes along and tells them that they have a great treasure under the ground. He instructs them in how to reveal the treasure, and they ceaselessly dig through one layer after another according to his instructions. They don't lose courage, even though the work is very hard and takes time and energy. Eventually they reveal the treasure and become rich. In reality, they had been rich all along because the treasure had always been with them.

Sentient beings wandering in the six realms of samsara are like that poor family. The treasure of all the excellent qualities of the Buddha is within them, but it is concealed by the mud of gross and subtle afflicting emotions. As a result, sentient beings feel poor and full of suffering. The Buddha, like the miner, came to this world and taught the Dharma. He demonstrated that we each have buddha nature, like an endless treasure, within us. Because of this, the Buddha doesn't have to create anything. He only has to show us how to actualize that reality. Thus, he taught all the different stages of Dharma as the complete method to reveal our buddha nature. We don't have to feel so miserable and suffer all the time. If we make an effort to reveal the treasure, we have every possibility for achieving ultimate happiness. We just need to clear the mud away, to purify the adventitious defilements that obscure this buddha nature.

The Buddha has given us many tools to use to reveal this seed of enlightenment. With confidence in the Dharma, we study and practice the four foundations, immeasurable loving-kindness and compassion, bodhicitta, the Vajrayana meditation practices, and the Fivefold Path of Mahamudra. By applying this complete set of tools, we will, without a doubt, be able to perceive enlightenment. From among these tools, application of the *four powers* is an essential technique to purify obscurations. The four powers are (1) remorse, (2) antidote, (3) resolution, and (4) refuge or reliance.

Remorse. We must recognize that the negative thoughts and karma we have created are of no genuine benefit. Looking at things in this way is called the power of remorse. Deluded by attachment, anger, and ignorance, we think that we are protecting ourselves or destroying our enemies, but actually we are only creating negativity. However, at the time of death we will see clearly just how little benefit there was in attachment to ourselves and our relatives. The negative karma we created will follow us like a shadow and be a source of suffering lifetime after lifetime. Our activities may have resulted in some superficial benefit, but the negative karma we created is so much greater in comparison.

Remorse is not guilt. Rather, it is a recognition of the delusion that has caused us to exert so much effort without bringing happiness. It is like becoming aware that you have fallen into a filthy swamp. You feel embarrassed and urgently wish to wash as soon as possible to be free of the dirt. These teachings are based on reason, not mere "say-so." So contemplate this well: despite the sacrifices we have made, we are left without much benefit in the long run.

Purification can be practiced through application of any one of the four powers, but it is more effective with all four together. But remorse is most important because, without it, the others are unlikely to arise. We should develop clear understanding that all deluded actions are unnecessary and are subject to purification, and that purification should be done as quickly as possible. For example, if someone has unwittingly taken poison, that individual will experience great remorse when he learns of his mistake. This will lead him to take urgent action to rid himself of the poison. Likewise, we should regard negative karma, even very small actions, as deadly poison.

Antidote. The power of antidote comes next. A feeling of remorse alone is not enough. Purification is incomplete if we only recognize the poison; we must act to get rid of it. This is like actually getting into the shower and washing the filth away. We must use all the methods we can to purify our obscurations—practice, meditation, and mantra recitation. What can we do? We can utilize many different Dharma practice techniques as an antidote to counteract the poison that causes suffering. For example, we can do Vajrasattva's practice, recite Chenrezig's mantra, or do Tara's practice. We can cultivate loving-kindness and compassion and practice bodhicitta and emptiness.

Resolve. Having applied these methods of purification, we then resolve never to repeat our negative thoughts and actions again. Once the poison has been removed, we must be cautious not to take it again. Similarly, we resolve to watch our step so that we do not fall into a swamp again. Now that we know these negative karmas are unnecessary and only bring suffering, we pledge, "Even at the risk of my life, I will never commit this fault again. In the past, I did this without awareness and meaninglessly. Now and in the future, I will not act this way again."

Reliance. The fourth power is reliance on the Buddha, Dharma, and Sangha. Reliance is taking refuge, relying on the enlightened beings and on bodhicitta. It is thinking, "Right now, I have no ability to free myself from all obscurations." So we have to rely on a good chef to prepare food that is not poisonous or on a dependable guide who will show us a path where we will not stumble. It is very important that we understand that every sentient being has buddha nature, for with this knowledge, we gain the confidence that "We, too, have the potential to attain buddhahood." We can say with conviction, "If I practice the Dharma, enlightenment is genuinely possible just as it was for the buddhas of the past." Once they were deluded beings like us, but they applied all their energy to studying and practicing the precious Dharma until they attained buddhahood which is free from suffering and its cause. So we too, can rely on the antidotes with complete confidence that purification, and eventually enlightenment, will take place. For example, a farmer cultivates the field to grow his crops. He plows the ground, makes the ground soft, applies the fertilizer, moistens the soil, plants the seed, and protects it well until it is fully harvested. In the same way, we should cultivate our Dharma practice.

The following story demonstrates the possibility of purification, even after many lifetimes of misdeeds:

> Once there was a family in which the wife was very devoted to the Dharma and delighted in the practice of generosity. A son was born into that family, and it soon became apparent that he had a miserly nature. He continually obstructed his mother's desire to give things away. The father passed away, so the son assumed responsibility for the household. The mother continued trying to give things to others, but the son always prevented her from doing so. One day the son said, "It looks like you don't want any wealth in our house, so stay out of our affairs. I will take care of the house by myself." The son did not allow his mother to have any authority in the house; he only gave her enough food each day to survive.
>
> But because of her generous nature the mother continued to give half of her meager food to others. The son was angered by this and said, "You are going to empty this house. I won't give you any more food." He kept her without food for six days, after which the mother begged for some food. He threw a handful of dust into a bowl of water and gave it to her. The mother drank it but soon died of starvation.
>
> As a result of this karma, the son was reborn in the Howling Hell for many kalpas, and then in the hungry ghost realm for many more kalpas. Even when he was born again as a human being, he held on to his miserliness, and ended up being reborn as a hungry ghost for still more lifetimes. Finally, he regained a human rebirth, but was born into circumstances where he was always hungry. Once, a pratyekabuddha passed by on his alms round. The man saw that the monk was receiving offerings, and this aroused jealousy and miserliness in his mind. He stole the monk's begging bowl and threw it on the ground. Because of that karma, he was repeatedly born in poor situations.
>
> After many such lifetimes, Buddha Kashyapa appeared on the earth and the man felt devotion for him. Because of

that connection, he was born as a human during Buddha Shakyamuni's time and had the opportunity to meet him. Understanding what the Buddha taught, he did everything he could to purify his negative thoughts and habitual tendencies. He succeeded in purifying his negative mental patterns and achieved a high level of realization.

We should be inspired by this story to purify all our negative thoughts and sincerely practice the Dharma.

The Buddha taught, or "turned the precious Dharma wheel," in three stages. In the first turning, the Buddha introduced the nature of samsara—why and how to renounce samsara—in order to inspire the wish for enlightenment. In the second turning, the Buddha gave instructions on how to follow the path step by step. In the third turning, he taught the purification of the subtle obscurations and the actualization of complete and perfect buddhahood. This heart advice on how to reveal the wish-granting jewel of our buddha nature—how wonderful it is!

Just as a jewel is primordially pure, our buddha nature is pristine luminosity. It is merely obscured by adventitious confusion. People often say, "You can drink this water because it has been purified." What does that mean? If the nature of water were to be polluted, we could not purify it. The nature of water is pure in itself, but pollution was added along the way. So when that pollution is removed, we call it "purified" to indicate that we have returned the water to its already-pure state. It is the same with our mind. The nature of mind is pure by itself. The delusion and confusion polluting it need to be removed. When these obscurations are fully removed, the luminous nature of mind freely manifests. Then we say the mind has been "purified" to indicate that the overlay of confusion, like mud, has been cleared away. This is the way to purify the mind.

Take a moment to cultivate compassion and bodhicitta for all suffering sentient beings. Then visualize Vajrasattva or Chenrezig as the embodiment of wisdom and compassion seated on a lotus and moon disc above the crown of your head. Chant the one-hundred-syllable or six-syllable mantra as light radiates from the deity to purify the six realms of sentient beings, including yourself. After this, the deity dissolves into you, bestows blessings, and purifies all your defilements. Then meditate on the inseparable nature of emptiness and appearance and rest the mind. At the end, dedicate the merit.

One who gathers the two accumulations is like a wise investor.
Though he enjoys his wealth, it is never exhausted.
Therefore, apply yourself to virtuous deeds.
This is my heart's advice.

THE *TWO ACCUMULATIONS* are the gathering of merit and wisdom. Merit is like fuel, and wisdom is like fire. The more merit-fuel we accumulate, the greater our wisdom-fire will be. Bringing these two together creates an opportunity to destroy all our obscurations. From among the six perfections, generosity, moral ethics, patience, perseverance, and meditative concentration constitute the accumulation of merit. Doing prostrations, chanting mantras, offering lamps, making offerings to monks and nuns or highly accomplished masters, visualizing enlightened deities, circumambulating temples, monasteries, or holy mountains, offering the mandala—these all are specific methods of accumulating merit. If these are done with the frame of mind of pure wisdom, through critical insight, then they also become the accumulation of wisdom. When, through these methods, a vast amount of merit has been collected, it is easier to kindle the fire of incisive wisdom. When all these conditions come together, the result (wisdom) manifests naturally. These methods can uproot the two types of obscurations and prepare us to experience the luminous nature of mind. For example, when there is a large collection of fuel, the fire will be big and long-lasting. Likewise, when we have gathered a great accumulation of merit it will consume all the obscurations and manifest in the accumulation of wisdom.

If a person invests his money in the bank, it gathers interest whether he is aware of it or not. While he is enjoying that interest, more interest accumulates. Similarly, when we invest ourselves well in Dharma practice, we create real peace in the mind. While enjoying that peace, we continue our practice unceasingly until we attain enlightenment. We need to be good spiritual businessmen and devote our lives to virtuous deeds.

When we do something good for another, how good we feel! That other person doesn't even have to give us anything, we just feel good when they say thank you. When you act negatively toward someone, and their face turns angry and they say negative things to you, how do you feel? The difference is obvious, isn't it? There is no need for special teachings on this. The benefit of doing virtuous things for others is clear. Apply this knowledge in your daily life—avoid all negative action, especially the ten nonvirtues, and engage in positive actions, including the ten virtues. When you know how to do this, your peace, harmony, joy, and happiness will increase without limit, especially if these noble acts are performed with the support of bodhicitta. These practices are also grounds for achieving enlightenment or buddhahood.

There is no need for any special reason; just do virtuous things for others. This means not causing harm and bringing peace. Peace is the absence of obscurations, negative thoughts, delusion, and distraction in the mind. Most people appreciate the good things that you do, but if someone doesn't understand, apply compassion.

Take a moment to visualize the whole universe containing tremendous excellent wealth and magnificent jewels. Without expectation, offer everything, including yourself, to enlightened beings. Rejoice and dedicate the merit. Whenever you walk in a park with many lovely trees and flowers or encounter a bright, beautiful sky, or a mountain with an attractive forest, flowers and grassland, or a great ocean, offer these to all enlightened beings and pray, "May I actualize loving-kindness, compassion, and bodhicitta. May each and every sentient being experience happiness free from suffering and quickly attain enlightenment." Then relax the mind.

Mahayana dedication is like a well-guarded treasure.
It bears fruit each day until enlightenment is won.
It accomplishes the benefit of oneself and others.
This is my heart's advice.

MAHAYANA DEDICATION means that we don't selfishly keep our virtue, good qualities, and merit for ourselves. With an altruistic mind, we share them so that all sentient beings benefit. From beginningless time, we have had many opportunities to accumulate virtue and merit. But we didn't have the wisdom to dedicate it for others, especially for their attainment of buddhahood, and because of this we haven't yet achieved liberation. There are four ways to exhaust virtue:

- ▸ The virtue was not dedicated to achievement of enlightenment.
- ▸ The virtue was dedicated to the wrong purpose, such as samsaric enjoyment.
- ▸ Virtuous deeds were proclaimed to others in order to gain praise.
- ▸ Virtue and merit that were created were later regretted before they could be dedicated.

If one becomes enraged at a great master, such as a bodhisattva or one's vajra master, that also causes the destruction of virtue. So whatever virtue you have accumulated, dedicate it without self-interest to attainment of complete enlightenment for all sentient beings.

Further, dedication does not have to be limited to our own immediate virtue. All the virtues of oneself and others that were accumulated in the three times, all virtue in samsara and nirvana, as well as the innate virtue, should be brought together within the sphere of the mind and dedicated. Understand that this is the way to accomplish dedication practice:

1. One dedicates with bodhicitta.
2. One dedicates in front of the Three Jewels and Three Roots as witnesses.
3. Dedicate with the support of sangha members.
4. Dedicate in the state of equipoise, free from the three spheres.
5. Dedicate again and again.

If we do the dedication practice in this manner, then dedication will seal our virtues so that they become a cause to manifest the result, buddhahood. Through this practice, we can purify our self-cherishing and expand the noble mind. In this way, we freely hand over to all beings a special cause of freedom from suffering and of the attainment of enlightenment. Instead of becoming attached to this prize and using it for our own peace and happiness, we share it with others.

A king's treasure that is *well guarded* will never be wasted or lost. Likewise, we won't have to worry about losing the treasure of our merit if we have sealed it by sharing it with all sentient beings. This is a very powerful practice. A mind that holds this great, noble thought has space without limit, room for all sentient beings. This Mahayana way of dedication is also a special means to attain dharmakaya for one's own benefit, to attain the form bodies for others' benefit, and to thereby effortlessly manifest activities for others.

If we plant the seed of a medicinal tree, it will sprout, grow, and eventually bear fruit. The fruit, leaves, branches, and even the bark can all be used as medicine. Each part is beneficial and can perpetually heal and benefit. In the same way, our merit and virtue will continue if we plant them firmly by dedicating them to the attainment of buddhahood for the benefit of all sentient beings. Each part will continue to bear fruit. We ourselves will be freed from suffering, confusion, and delusion. Then, because of our merit and virtue, we can help all beings to attain enlightenment.

When we study and practice the precious Dharma, it is crucial to possess the Three Excellences:

1. Pure bodhicitta motivation, which establishes the purpose of meditation as the attainment of enlightenment, not individual liberation or some samsaric goal

2. The actual meditation practice of deity yoga, guru yoga, or Mahamudra, the journey toward enlightenment and perfection of our motivation with full attention, without wandering or distraction during meditation
3. The dedication of all virtues for the benefit of sentient beings

Dedication is one of the most important practices that we can do. Happily, this powerful practice is very simple to do. We dedicate immediately after each practice. Maybe our practice was just a short session, but if we dedicate it, it becomes infinite. If we dedicate each time we study or practice, the results will continue to manifest until we attain complete buddhahood. It is important that we dedicate with a mind of bodhicitta and that we sincerely use our practice for the benefit of sentient beings rather than dedicating it to our own small benefit.

The dedication section of the *Wish-granting Jewel* says:

> In general, the Mahayana, the precious and unsurpassable vehicle, includes everything in the paramita- (or sutra-) yana and the vajrayana. The practice of this precious Dharma comprises three parts: preparation, actual practice, and conclusion. All practices of preparation and actual practice generate roots of virtue.
>
> [As for the practice of conclusion:] Every sutra and commentary of the Mahayana teaches that dedication is very important because to whatever the roots of virtue are dedicated, that is exactly what one will accomplish. The *Buddha Avatamsaka Sutra* has extensive teachings on the importance of dedication:
>
> > Dedicate to perfect enlightenment both the roots of virtue accumulated in the three times by oneself and all others and the innate root of virtue.
>
> The chapter of the *Buddha Avatamsaka Sutra* entitled "Vajra Victory Banner's Comprehensive Dedication" states:

May all states of goodness to which migrators dedicate
    their virtue—
that which they have and that which they have
    generated,
will generate, and are generating now—
be the states of goodness that they become.

Or, in other words, dedicate both the innate root of
virtue and the virtues accumulated in the three times by
yourself and all sentient beings as found in the *Buddha
Avatamsaka Sutra:*

By both the innate root of virtue
and the roots of virtue accumulated in the three times
by myself and all sentient beings,
may I and all sentient beings
quickly attain the precious, unsurpassable, authentic,
    perfected enlightenment.

Dedication can also become a cause for one to gather all the
excellent qualities of the Buddha's wisdom, compassion, activities,
and virtues, the merit of bodhisattvas and arhats, and also all the
good qualities, virtue, and merit of all sentient beings. Bring them
together with the power of bodhicitta into the mandala of your own
heart and dedicate them all to the attainment of complete buddhahood, to the purification of all obscurations, and to the attainment
of all excellent qualities. Perform this dedication while seeing the
emptiness of the three spheres—i.e., the act of dedicating, the virtues
being dedicated, and the goal to which they are dedicated. These are
all of "one taste," the illusory nature.

The pratimoksha vow is like the Holder of Jewels.
Without depending on this, there is no holy Dharma.
It is the foundation of everything.
This is my heart's advice.

THE NEXT THREE verses explain the importance of the *pratimoksha* vow. What is the meaning of pratimoksha? Pratimoksha is known as the vow of individual liberation through which each and every non-virtue is individually purified and each and every virtue is gathered for liberation. This is fully explained in the Vinaya. One achieves liberation and the omniscient state of buddhahood by Vinaya practice. Some scholars say that Vinaya is only for the practitioners of the Hinayana. Such assertions demonstrate only a partial understanding of Vinaya. Vinaya is the ground of meditation practice; it is the foundation for all Buddhist practices, and because of this, Mahayana and Vajrayana are practiced on its basis. In order to take the bodhisattva's vow and tantric samaya, one has to hold at least one of the pratimoksha precepts as a foundation.

Of course, the discipline of Vinaya is emphasized for monks and nuns, those who fully dedicate their lives to Dharma study and practice, but lay practitioners also hold pratimoksha vows in the form of the five precepts. These disciplines are crucial, as they form the foundation on which all other practices are based. Therefore, the author puts particular emphasis on them here.

The *Holder of Jewels* is a metaphor for the earth. All the different jewels and precious stones come from the earth, so it is called the "holder of jewels." Earth is the foundation and ground upon which human and nonhuman beings alike settle and move. Trees and crops are planted and grow in the earth. Without the earth we could not function, so we say it is the source of and the container for everything that is precious, all "jewels." Similarly, the ten virtues, six perfections, the good qualities of the relative state, and the qualities of buddhahood are based on moral ethics. Love, compassion, and bodhicitta are planted in and depend on the ground of moral ethics. Meditative concentration and critical insight are also based on personal discipline. The noble Nagarjuna wrote in the *Letter to a Friend*:

> Morality was declared to be the foundation for all virtue,
> just as the earth is for all things moving and still.

When we hold and observe the five lay precepts, or monks' and nuns' precepts, we can say that we are real Dharma practitioners. Without at least the five precepts, we are not counted among the sangha members.

Only one who is disciplined will be able to keep moral ethics. This is clear even in ordinary life. If a student has no discipline in school, he cannot learn well or get good grades. On the other hand, if he goes to school on time, concentrates on the homework, abides by the school's discipline, and is not much interested in parties or in wasting time, he becomes successful. Generally, those who are cautious about respecting others' lives and feelings, who abstain from stealing from others, who always use gentle words and speak the truth, and who use skillful words to bring others into harmony are well respected throughout the world. Such a person has the ability to bring about peace and benefit to others. In the same way, one who keeps moral ethics possesses the foundation to increase and perfect all the peerless qualities of a buddha. Therefore, we should keep moral ethics as we protect our eyes.

There are many more benefits of maintaining ethical discipline: By keeping the moral ethics of Vinaya, one purifies mental obscurations. The sponsors of those who keep their vows purely also accumulate great merit. As the wish-granting tree bears great fruit, pure moral ethics bring great fruits for oneself and others. Moral ethics is supreme among all ornaments.

One who keeps moral ethics well gains great dignity and glory. All the bodhisattvas are pleased with such an individual, and he or she is praised by distinguished and wise people. Even when such individuals grow old and weak, they are still respected by gods and humans and are an object of praise. Moral discipline will bring about all the temporary peace and happiness of gods and humans. Ultimately, it will lead to complete buddhahood.

At the time of death, those supreme practitioners who kept moral ethics purely will be reborn in a lotus in a buddha field. Those who were mediocre will be born at the time of a buddha and become ordained. Inferior practitioners who kept their vows sincerely will make a connection to ordination in successive lifetimes and will eventually attain enlightenment. Where there are more monks and nuns, there is greater opportunity to establish the Buddha's teachings and bring peace and harmony to the community. Keeping the moral ethics of Vinaya well is a special training of the mind that we can practice throughout our life. Everyone should encourage themselves and others to practice Vinaya.

38 *Pure morality is like a precious shrine, imbued with sacred*
     power.
     It is an object of prostrations for all beings, including the gods.
     One should guard the three trainings as one guards one's eyes.
     This is my heart's advice.

MORAL ETHICS do not comprise just one type of discipline. They consist of all the means of maintaining a pure life, one free from both physical and mental nonvirtuous actions. They are the foundation for freedom from samsara and for the attainment of enlightenment for shravakas, pratyekabuddhas, and bodhisattvas. Almost everyone in samsara respects those who keep pure moral ethics. Like *a precious shrine*, such people are honored with prostrations and devotion because their behavior is a source of serenity, integrity, and peace. Those who keep moral ethics purely, the lay people who keep five or eight precepts, and especially the monks and nuns with full ordination, are very precious.

After the time of the Buddha, many spiritual masters appeared. Nagarjuna was among those who gathered the largest numbers of disciples and wisely spread the Dharma. Many great teachers also appeared in Tibet. Among them, Dharma Lord Gampopa and Lord Jigten Sumgön were of the greatest significance. They benefited many sentient beings, gathered hundreds of thousands of disciples, and firmly established Buddhism in the world. All of these great beings emphasized the teachings of moral discipline and perfectly maintained it themselves.

Keeping the moral precepts is our best form of protection. This discipline protects us from delusion and the causes of suffering. It also gives us a clear perspective on how to deal with suffering. Truly, all peace and harmony for individuals and society at large arise from the purity of our morality.

The *three trainings*, called *trishiksha* in Sanskrit, are

- training in moral ethics, or *shila*
- training in meditative concentration, or *samadhi*
- training in wisdom awareness, or *prajña*

These three trainings are profoundly interconnected. If one is missing, the other two cannot be accomplished. Shila means maintaining virtue by avoiding all nonvirtuous thoughts. Maintaining discipline or moral ethics brings about the coolness of peace of mind, which itself becomes the foundation to actualize calm abiding and maintain samadhi. Samadhi, in turn, becomes the foundation for prajña, or special insight. Without being well established in meditative concentration, neither achievement of the incisive special insight nor realization of Mahamudra is possible. Without the critical insight that uproots all delusion, we cannot free ourselves from samsara. This kind of organized and powerful mind depends on calm abiding, the mental discipline of samadhi that is rooted in moral ethics, shila. When we have wisdom, we can see the necessity of meditative concentration and will continue to enhance that practice. Once we understand that samadhi is crucial for special insight, we will know that we must practice moral ethics as its foundation.

Many people associate the three trainings exclusively with the Hinayana. However, regardless of your selected path, these three must always work together if you want to free yourself from samsara. In the Mahayana, it is difficult to have bodhicitta without properly holding a pratimoksha vow. Unless you protect your mind from thoughts of attachment, hatred, anger, ignorance, resentment, and so forth, how can you hope to develop love and compassion? One can try, but at best it will only be superficial, afflicted compassion. Instead, one must first pacify attachment, anger, resentment, and hatred with the pratimoksha vows. Then, on that basis, one can develop love, compassion, and bodhicitta and belong to the Mahayana. On the basis of bodhicitta one has the great opportunity to see all sentient beings as deities or buddhas according to Vajrayana practice. So this Hinayana training is crucial for Mahayana development. First we must abstain from harming others. Then, based on that, we can help others.

These trainings associated with Vinaya and bodhicitta are especially important in the Vajrayana. Without physical and mental discipline, we cannot practice the arising or completion stages of practice. Without a stable visualization and meditation on the deity in the arising and completion stages, it will not be possible to accomplish Mahamudra or any other meditation practice. Without love, compassion, and bodhicitta, deity yoga practice is not effective and will not lead to freedom from samsara or to the attainment of complete enlightenment. In fact, deity yoga practice can be dangerous if done without proper bodhicitta. One could be reborn as a powerful ghost, for example, if one's practice is distorted by anger or resentment. This phenomenon is called "the deity arising as a demon." Instead, tame the mind to be as soft as cotton and as strong as a mountain. Develop the courage to face obstacles and suffering, making the mental afflictions powerless. Vajrayana meditation practices then become an unsurpassable means to bring about complete enlightenment.

Our eyes are among the most important parts of our body. Everyone cares about protecting their eyesight and making their eyes beautiful. People spend a lot of money to keep their eyes healthy. In the same way, we need to cultivate the "wisdom eye" to realize the nature of special insight. Without it, there is no way to attain enlightenment. So, we guard our moral ethics to protect the eye of wisdom, and practice samadhi to improve our vision. Through these supports, we will gain the penetrating wisdom that perceives the nature of samsara and enlightenment. Therefore, we should cherish these three: moral ethics, meditation, and wisdom. This is a story of someone who did so:

> Once there was a rich couple who, unfortunately, were childless. They prayed to the Buddha, Dharma, and Sangha for help, and after some time, the wife gave birth to a son. The couple raised him carefully, lovingly, and with compassion, and named him Padma Dokchen, Lotus-like, because he was very handsome. Because of their prominent position, the parents thought that they should arrange a marriage for their son. But when he was grown, the son said, "Listen, my good parents. Household life is like a swamp and I don't want to get stuck in it. Household life is like a poisonous stalk that I cannot eat. I want to renounce

samsara and become a monk. Please give me permission to do so." The parents gave their permission, and the son became a sincere monk who achieved realization through his meditation practice.

Time passed and according to tradition, the monk Padme Dokchen went out every morning to collect alms for his noon meal. On one occasion, he went to an unfamiliar area and came to a place where prostitutes gathered. There was one extremely beautiful prostitute who was struck with such attraction to him that it was as if an arrow had been shot into her heart. Without hesitation, she approached the monk directly and respectfully invited him into her house. Thinking that she was inviting him to lunch, he accepted the offered seat. She set out a lunch and asked him for Dharma teachings. But when he sat on the seat, she came close and asked him to sleep with her. The monk covered his nose and ran away, exclaiming, "For me, it would be better to die than do something like that!"

The prostitute was so completely overpowered by her desire that she hired a female magician to trick the monk into coming back. Upon being paid a great deal of gold, the magician cast a spell that brought the monk back to the brothel. The prostitute said to the monk, "You must either sleep with me or jump into this fire." The monk took off his robes and, looking at the magician, said, "Give this robe back to the monastery. For me, sleeping with a woman is out of the question, so I will jump into the fire." As he prepared to jump, the magician experienced profound regret and released the spell. She then prostrated at the monk's feet. The prostitute joined her, and they both requested Dharma teachings. With great compassion and care, he gave them deep teachings on the faults of attachment that were exactly the teachings they needed. They practiced sincerely and achieved the stream-enterer state.

Motivated by this account, we should practice Dharma sincerely and free our mind from all negative thoughts.

The Dharma should be kept in the center of our heart. This is a good way to undertake sincere study and practice. There are some who want to study Buddhism only intellectually. Such people don't need to take this advice personally. They don't have to take precepts or refuge if they choose not to. This text contains plenty of information to enhance their general knowledge and understanding. But for those who really want to follow the Dharma and practice it, these verses precisely define the way to take it into your heart and show the way to follow the path while making the inner journey toward enlightenment. Whether we do this or not is up to each of us individually. Sometimes, people have illusions or fantasies about the path and suppose that there is a magic potion that produces buddhahood. Sadly, this expectation causes people to waste their time and energy to little purpose.

Immorality's effects are unclean, like a corpse.
They arouse the concern of holy persons and destroy the root of
    virtue.
Those who violate morality become an object of scorn.
This is my heart's advice.

WHEN WE EXAMINE spiritual discipline in more detail, we find that three of the moral behaviors are associated with physical action— avoiding killing, stealing and cheating, and sexual misconduct.

Avoid killing. Instead, protect and respect others' lives, especially those of human beings. This is a story about a man who vowed not to take life:

> Once there was a childless couple who earnestly prayed for a baby. Finally, they conceived a child and bore an attractive son. The parents and all their relatives were very happy, so they arranged an elaborate celebration near the bank of a river. During the celebration, everyone wanted to touch the child and hold him. Unfortunately, as one woman held him while standing near the river, the child fell out of her arms and into the water. The child did not have the karma to die then, and because of this he sank into the water and was swallowed by a big fish, in which he remained alive.
>
> Not too far away there was another small village. A fisherman from this second village happened to be fishing in that same river and caught the big fish. When he cut it open, to his astonishment he found a live child. Another childless couple lived in that second village, so the fisherman brought the child to them. They kindly and tenderly raised the child as their own.
>
> News of the miraculous baby found in a fish traveled and eventually reached the first village, where the child's

real parents heard the news. The father went to the fisher-man's village and explained, "Not long ago, our child fell into the river. It appears that your child is really ours, so please give him back." But the second family didn't want to give him up and said, "Your child must have drowned in the river. Even if he had been swallowed by a fish, how could he be alive after that? In the past, we prayed and prayed for a child. This one is ours and we won't give him up." Because they could not settle this disagreement, they went to the king and asked him to settle their dispute.

The king listened carefully to all the information pre-sented to him, and then announced his decision: "This child should be raised by both sets of parents." The child was fortunate, then, to have four parents, two mothers and two fathers, who raised him in luxury. When the child was grown and could make decisions for himself, he told his four parents, "After my birth I fell into the river and was swallowed by a fish. Because of this, I have to suffer excru-ciating pain. I can endure this no longer; I must practice the Dharma. Please give me permission to go to a monas-tery since I want to free from samsara and achieve enlight-enment." The four parents gave permission, and thus he became a monk and successfully practiced Dharma.

The karma that brought about these results was this: In the child's previous life, he had offered a gold coin to a great master and vowed never to take life. Because of this act, his life was protected and he was raised in luxury by two sets of loving parents. Eventually, he achieved the arhat state.

When we encounter stories like this, we too will be inspired not to take life and, further, to protect others' lives.

Avoid stealing and cheating. Everyone cherishes their own health and wealth, so stealing from others is not right legally or morally. Instead, practice generosity.

Abstain from sexual misconduct. For householders, this means abstaining from harmful sexual activity and for the ordained, abstain-ing from sexual activity altogether. Many couples are divorced once or twice in their lives due to the results of sexual misconduct in this life or in previous ones.

There are four moral behaviors associated with speech: abstaining from lying, using divisive speech, using harsh words, and indulging in idle talk.

Abstain from lying. Avoid telling lies, especially spiritual lies. Instead, speak the truth. The following story shows us the results of abstaining from lying:

> There once was a king in Varanasi named Tsangjin. His queen give birth to a daughter, and they lavishly celebrated the birth. The girl grew up to be exquisitely beautiful and was called Beautiful Daughter Kashika. Her fame spread until it reached the surrounding six kingdoms. Each of those six kings wanted the girl to marry his son. King Tsangjin had a hard time deciding which one he should choose. "If I give her to one," he thought, "then all the others will become resentful."
>
> One day, all six princes arrived in Varanasi accompanied by great entourages and adorned with magnificent ornaments. King Tsangjin paced the roof in sorrow, pondering what he should do in this delicate situation. His daughter noticed his troubled mood and asked the reason. Her father explained, "I have no idea what to do or how to handle this situation. The fathers of all the princes I don't select as your husband will declare war and destroy my kingdom." She said, "Oh, this won't be difficult. Tell all six princes that they should come here on a particular day and I will choose my own husband." The king was happy and instructed the kings as she advised.
>
> On the appointed day, all six princes arrived with their glorious ornaments, spectacular entourages, golden thrones, and so forth. Each one thought that he would be the one chosen. The girl Kashika and her attendants went before the six princes unadorned by any ornaments. In a beautiful and melodious voice, she said, "Alas! All types of bodies are like a magician's display—impermanent. All forms are like a rainbow that will disappear without a

trace. Don't be attached to such things. This body is like an autumn flower that will fade easily and inevitably, so don't be attached to it. Why do you invest so much importance in a body? Your great arrogance ties you to the kingdom; this results in lower rebirth. Purifying arrogance gives rise to bliss. I have no interest in these samsaric activities. Being a householder in samsara is the primary cause of suffering. Don't attach yourselves to this. All accumulated wealth is illusory; don't hold to it as permanent. I have decided not to stay in this kingdom. Instead, I will devote myself to Dharma and meditate in solitude." After saying this, she left for the nunnery and became a nun.

Those six princes were so captivated by Kashika's beauty and melodious voice that they followed her. Under her influence, they also followed the Dharma. They practiced successfully and became free from all causes of suffering.

Her power to have such influence came from previous lives. Formerly, she had been born in a family where lying was practiced and encouraged. But as the wife in the family, she never told a lie and always spoke the truth. Because she had never told a lie in her previous life, her speech in this life had a powerfully magnetic quality, and the princes spontaneously followed whatever she said.

Avoid dividing a community. Especially avoid dividing the sangha. Instead, seek to harmonize others.

Avoid the use of harsh words. Instead, speak gently. This story provides us an example of the possible results of using harsh words:

Once, at the time of Buddha, there was a householder who gave birth to a monkey. Later, the monkey turned into a boy who, when he was an adult, saw the nature of samsara and wanted to become a monk. He made this request of the Buddha, and the Buddha gave him permission to be ordained. The young man sincerely studied and practiced Dharma and achieved the arhat state. He then asked the Buddha why he had been born as a monkey that had changed into a human boy.

> The Buddha said, "Many lifetimes ago, at the time of another Buddha, you were born as a boy who followed after a monk. You once took a journey together and came upon a channel of water. The monk leaped to the far bank and the boy said, 'You are like a monkey who can jump really well.' The monk reproached him, saying, 'Don't say such things! A monkey is an animal and you will create heavy negative karma by comparing me, an arhat, to a lower being." You, as the boy, felt great regret and apologized sincerely. Even though you didn't speak with anger or negativity, you were born as a monkey for five hundred lifetimes. Because you apologized, you turned back into a human being each time."

We should always watch our speech as well as the activities of our mind and body. We have to be very careful with each type of karma we create, whether it is big or small. The karma that we create, even if it was created one hundred kalpas ago, cannot be ignored because it will not disappear unless it is purified. When the time comes and conditions come together, that karma will surely manifest.

Avoid idle talk. Instead, speak meaningfully and to the point.

There are three moral behaviors associated with mental activity: avoiding covetousness, malicious thought, and wrong views.

Avoid covetousness. Instead, practice contentment. The nonvirtue of covetousness often leads to rebirth as a hungry ghost. This story concerns one who successfully abstained from this fault:

> A son was once born to a successful merchant. As soon as he was born, the family's wealth and prosperity increased; even crops in that region grew especially well. Because of these things, the boy was named Lekye, Well Born. After some time his father died, so the virtuous Lekye went into business to help support the family. While traveling, he rented a room in a country town and went to sleep there. The cunning landlord took a golden statue from his own house and hid it amidst the merchant's goods. His plan was to accuse the merchant of stealing the golden statue the next morning.

But during the night, Lekye's father appeared to him in a dream and warned, "This country is not a peaceful place. Be aware that the landlord has hidden a golden statue among your possessions. Take that statue out and hide it under the ground." After he awoke from the dream, Lekye became curious and began to look through his merchandise. To his surprise, there was indeed a golden statue among his things. He quickly hid it, as the dream had advised. In the morning, the landlord said, "You have stolen my statue." The merchant denied this, and the landlord demanded that they inspect his possessions. The entire household searched meticulously, but they never found it. Then Lekye packed all his wealth and returned to his own country where the local people were astonished by all that had happened to him.

The cause of these events came from his previous lives. Lekye had been born as the son of a merchant in former times, too. Although he was involved in business, he always abstained from covetousness, harmful thoughts, cunning, and deceit. He was always satisfied with what he received and content with whatever he had. Since he practiced in that way for many lifetimes, he always enjoyed prosperous and peaceful lives.

This story can inspire us to practice Dharma by freeing ourselves from covetous and harmful thoughts. We should always rejoice in and appreciate what we have.

Avoid malicious thought. Instead, practice love and compassion. Malice is one of the nonvirtues that most easily results in rebirth in a hell realm. This story concerns one who avoided such a rebirth:

Once there was a king named Lekjin who was faithfully supported by a gifted minister. After some time, the king and minister were divided through the cunning of some of the other ministers. The minister, who was actually gentle, mindful, and clear-minded, remained quiet and peaceful. But the king began to distrust the minister because some said that he was trying to overthrow the king. The king became so upset that he ordered the execution of that minister and sent him to the cemetery to be killed. The minister said, "Not only in this lifetime, but in many past lifetimes, I have never had a harmful thought—not toward anyone, and especially not toward the king. Because of this, even if the king tries to kill me, I won't die."

Thinking, "He's very talkative. Let's just see what happens," the king dispatched the executioner. When he raised his blade, it broke into pieces. The king then directed him to throw the minister into a river. As soon as he did so, the river completely dried up. Then the king imprisoned the minister in a demons' cave. The demons proclaimed to the king, "Look at the example of your own body and abandon harming others. Look how much you cherish your own life, and start cherishing others' lives in the same way. Listen to the Buddha's teachings and keep all the vows." Having said this, the ghosts and demons perceived the minister as the Buddha and circumambulated him out of respect. Thereafter, they abstained from harmful thoughts. After this, the king again trusted his minister and apologized sincerely.

The karma that caused all these results was this: In his previous life, the minister had a very harmful enemy who continually threatened his life. Nevertheless, he always guarded his mind from harmful thoughts. He sincerely and carefully practiced this, and never harbored even a single moment of harmful thought for another sentient being. For that reason, the minister was peaceful, harmonious, and kind in this life. The harmful enemy from his previous life was born as the king. Both eventually attained buddhahood after living in harmony for the rest of their lives.

Avoid wrong view. Instead, believe and understand the teachings on cause and result. Here is a story of one who was overpowered by ignorance:

Once there was a witless man who made his living by climbing trees to find fruit. One day he sat on a branch while sawing it. A man happened by and warned him, "Don't cut the branch that way. You and the branch will both fall to the ground, and you could die." The fruit-picker asked, "What happens when one dies?" The passerby replied, "Bleeding, an open mouth, and closed eyes," and left. The stupid man continued to cut the tree branch and, of course, in the end he and the branch both fell to the ground.

Although his arms and legs were badly wounded, he didn't die. But because of the bleeding and so forth he thought, "I must be dead now." The man went home and told his family, "Please take me to the cemetery because I am dead." They protested, but he insisted, "Look! I have been bleeding, my mouth was open, and I closed my eyes." Because of his persistence, the family took him to the cemetery. There he stayed with no food except for the flesh of the surrounding corpses. In time, the man's eyes turned yellow; his body turned blue because it was not protected by clothing or shelter. His hair grew long all over his body.

A teacher happened to pass through the cemetery, and remarked, "Your hair makes you look like a cat." The stupid man replied, "In that case, may I stay with you as your pet, master?" The master agreed, and he remained with that master for some time until one day a big gathering was held in a nearby town. The master instructed the man to go to town and see all the entertainments and sights there. The stupid man said, "But if I wander around in a big gathering, I may get lost." The master assured him, saying, "You will not get lost. Other people have different ornaments, earrings, necklaces, and so forth for identification. Put this thread around on your neck and you won't become lost. This will be your mark." So the man put on the thread and left for the gathering.

He saw many pleasant things and thoroughly enjoyed himself in the throng. But there, in the midst of all the people rushing back and forth, he lost his thread. He thought, "Now I am lost. What should I do?" He called out plaintively, "I am lost. Has anyone seen me?" The people said "You are you, as you've always been." He said, "No, I lost my thread, so I am lost." He looked all around, back and forth through the crowd, and eventually met a kind man who said, "You sit here. I will search and see if I can find you." Because he was exhausted, the fruit-picker fell asleep sitting there. The kind man found some thread, came back, and tied it around his neck. When he woke up, he saw the thread and cried out in joy, "I found me! I was here all along!" Whereupon he returned to his master and told him of his adventures.

This is a metaphor about ourselves. We have buddha nature, the seed of enlightenment, within. We already have every opportunity to free ourselves from delusion and achieve complete enlightenment. It is within our own mental capacity to dispel all ignorance, but we continue to look for a solution outside ourselves. Therefore, we must trust ourselves and have confidence in our ability to actualize all the excellent qualities of the buddhas and bodhisattvas through Dharma practice.

Those who maintain these ten practices are called "those with pure moral ethics."

This list of ten virtues and nonvirtues is referred to in many different texts. This present discussion is just a reminder for practitioners and readers. Of course, there are additional precepts for the ordained; they should study other texts and observe whatever vows they have taken. Those who break their vows and engage in these nonvirtuous actions are called immoral, whether they are lay people or ordained.

In this verse, *immorality* refers specifically to the breaking of vows. The effect of such actions destroys one's spirituality. Any practice that you had undertaken is dead, like a corpse. Those who cannot keep moral ethics are a source of confusion for others as well as for themselves. That is why they are said to be immoral and spiritually unclean, and are despised by others. Those who suffer mentally and physically, especially those who are depressed and despairing, may feel as if they are contaminated or tainted. Engagement in the nonvirtues causes this kind of suffering, so it is also said to be "unclean." These are not just Buddhist beliefs but are a universal reality. Those on the spiritual path, as well as the leaders of countries or communities, have a special responsibility whether they are Buddhists or not. They must maintain morality and remain steadfast in the face of human weakness.

Holy persons are those who sincerely practice Dharma, purely keep these moral ethics, and who are highly accomplished or on the way to accomplishment. Spiritual masters, who have impartial love and compassion, feel sadness at seeing practitioners who haven't been able to keep their vows. They know that these persons have destroyed their own virtue, the root of peace and happiness, and of their own enlightenment.

Most of us can perform one or two sessions of meditation practice each day without much trouble, but keeping moral ethics is not easy. We have to watch ourselves twenty-four hours a day, every week, every month, every year. One who does so is a *real* practitioner. Life is so hectic; there is less support for spiritual practice than ever before. Look at the monks and nuns who can keep their vows. There is no need for them to fly in the sky or display magic powers; just keeping vows in this day and age is a great miracle. Under these circumstances, lay practitioners should respect and have more regard for ordained ones. They are holding the victory banner of liberation.

Morality is the practical way of pure Dharma practice. It is a grounded way to become a good person, a good citizen. You become warmhearted with a good personality, trustworthy, and reliable. By practicing ethics, we are able to free ourselves from delusion and negative thoughts. Morality is not a prison or trap, or a way to limit your life. Rather, it is a special method to free you from negative thoughts and actions and the suffering that they cause. Take moral ethics as an ornament instead of as a heavy load.

The verses up to this point have presented the foundation teachings of all Buddhist schools. Therefore, it is crucial that Buddhists understand that we are all practicing the Buddha's teaching and have respect for one another. We are all followers of the same historical Buddha.

Advice for Mahayana Practitioners

 Loving-kindness is like a warrior victorious in battle.
In an instant, it annihilates all the hordes of maras without
*   exception.*
Meditate on all beings as your parents.
This is my heart's advice.

T HE BUDDHA SAID, "If you cannot help others, at least abstain from all harm." Thus, the essential meaning of the Buddhad-harma is rooted in an understanding of loving-kindness and com-passion. Although the four Immeasurable Thoughts are studied and practiced by all Buddhist schools, they form a particular foundation for Mahayana practice and the cultivation of bodhicitta. It is impor-tant for all Buddhists to understand their meaning and to practice the Four Immeasurables step by step as much as possible. These four are

- ► loving-kindness
- ► compassion
- ► joy
- ► equanimity

Loving-kindness is the mind that wants all sentient beings to have happiness and the causes of happiness. The causes of happiness are practicing the ten virtues and so forth. Loving-kindness is a pure mind that is free from attachment, not a partial, emotional mind. That kind of pure loving-kindness is like a *warrior* that fights all negative thoughts, particularly anger and hatred. In order to estab-lish the true meaning of compassion in one's heart, the practice of loving-kindness is indispensable.

We can escape from outer enemies and obstacles. If we have a bad time in one city we can move to another and feel much better there. But inner enemies move with you and constantly steal your wealth of harmony and peace. They always follow you no matter where you are, like a shadow. If you go to the mountains, they go along with you. If you go to the city or to the beach, they go with you and destroy your peace. In the battle with the inner enemies, delusion and ignorance, loving-kindness is one of the most effective weapons we can use.

Maras are devils or obstructers. Historically, you can see how the Buddha overcame them when he was a great bodhisattva on the path to buddhahood. He sat on the vajra seat at Bodh Gaya, and said to himself, "I will sit on this seat until I achieve buddhahood, no matter what happens. Even if my body crumbles and disintegrates, I am committed to attaining enlightenment." With this powerful motivation, he sat and meditated. During that time, hundreds and thousands of maras came to create obstacles to his meditation and enlightenment. Monsters surrounded him. Some brought huge mountains and threw them toward the Buddha while others hurled weapons. With one-pointed mind, the Buddha meditated on pure and all-pervading loving-kindness. His whole being, the complete nature of his mind, was pervaded by sincere love. Without artifice, he saw all those maras as his own mother and wanted them to have whatever happiness and peace they sought. Through the power of that mind, the scene completely changed. The mountains and weapons were transformed into flowers, and the maras became powerless. The spiritual warrior is victorious in battle not by means of hatred and weapons but through great love. Thus, both inner and outer maras are successfully defeated in this manner.

The practice of loving-kindness has great benefit. When you develop loving-kindness, first there is peace in your own mind that gradually brings greater peace to your family and to the surrounding society. It may take some time before genuine feeling arises. At first, you may feel the practice is artificial or merely intellectual. But recall how much benefit you get and how much benefit you can give to others, and continue step by step. As we transform our mind in this way, others will respect and protect us. This kind of pure thought is the best kind of gift. It puts a smile on your face and not only changes your mind, but also changes your physical appearance, making you a beautiful person. If we practice this successfully, poisons will change into medicine. We can achieve these qualities even before we are free from samsara; therefore, make great effort to practice this.

Why does the text say to meditate on all beings as *your parents*? This is given as an example because most people have a good connection with their parents. You can meditate on any good connection you have, be it with a friend, relative, or child. Practice seeing all beings as if they were the person closest to you.

One can contemplate the loving-kindness of one's parents in four ways:

- ▸ their kindness in giving you this precious human body, which serves as the basis of Dharma study and practice
- ▸ their kindness in giving you a life that is stable and strong, and possesses all the faculties
- ▸ their kindness in providing you with wealth
- ▸ their kindness in introducing you to the world and providing you with an education

These four supports are what distinguish you as a human being. They are of critical importance and cause you to reflect and to cultivate genuine loving-kindness for your parents to whom you owe everything. Your parents raised you with a pure motivation. Whether they were rich or poor, educated or uneducated, they wanted you to be successful and attractive. So you have a responsibility to repay their kindness by developing loving-kindness and by bringing them peace and happiness, whether in a general way or in a more spiritual sense.

You can practice loving-kindness meditation like this: First sit for a few moments. Take a deep breath and exhale all your tensions to quiet your mind. Reflect that you wish all good things—wealth, peace, and happiness—for your parents, or for the person who is closest to you. Contemplate how dearly you love that person. Then expand that thought to include your whole family in the same way, because they too desire happiness and prosperity. Then consider your neighbors, then your whole village or city, and finally even those people who are your enemies. Wholeheartedly wish them all happiness and benefit. Totally transcend your hatred and resent-ment for anyone. Then expand that to all the people in your state, your country, the whole world, and to animals, insects, and all the sentient beings of the six realms. Do this repeatedly every day. This meditation allows you to transform your environment into a pure land. Take all sentient beings as your friends, and take care of them just as you would your own child. When one has genuine loving-kindness, then joy and equanimity are naturally included. As in the other verses of this text, the great master Dharmaradza gives this advice from his heart, so we should take this practice into our own hearts.

Supreme compassion is like a skillful mother nurturing her child.
Abandoning comfort, it engages in the benefit of others.
Therefore, generate the courage of altruistic thought.
This is my heart's advice.

SUPREME COMPASSION—what is that? Each and every sentient being has some level of compassion. Even wolves and hawks, who constantly try to take others' lives, have compassion for their own offspring. In taking another's life, they are acting to protect their own family. Having a mind that wants to free others from their suffering is called "compassion." *Supreme* compassion extends to all sentient beings, including one's bitter enemies. It is more than just sympathy; it is a mind that is willing to exchange one's own happiness for another's suffering. When you practice loving-kindness, you wish for all sentient beings to have happiness, but in reality they have suffering and they create the causes of more suffering. Considering that they are victims of suffering, allow strong compassion to arise in you.

A *skillful mother* will raise her child well. Physically and mentally she will undergo a lot of hardship and will give up her own comfort to protect her child. Compassion is like that: looking at each sentient being as if he or she were your own child. When a child is in pain and crying at night, the mother will abandon her own comfort and sleep. If the child is swept away by water, she will jump in to save her. Whatever the circumstance, the mother will risk her life for her child's safety and happiness. In the same way, bodhisattvas possessing great compassion will sacrifice their lives for others' benefit. Where there is that kind of compassion, one has no fear or hesitation to sacrifice oneself for others, and one joyfully acts for others' benefit. This is the real *courage of altruistic thought*.

Before we act, though, we must develop this thought in our minds and practice it. That is what Milarepa did. He spent all his time in the mountains cultivating these qualities. Then, after he actualized them, he came back into the world and benefited sentient beings without any doubt or fear about doing so. He had such great skill! Thus, we too must come to understand what compassion is and then make the effort to actualize it within our minds before we put it into action for others.

To practice compassion, sit down and take a deep breath. Exhale all your tension and calm your mind. Look at your own suffering or that of one who is close to you. How you long to be free from that suffering! Develop such strong determination that no one can take it away from you! Next, expand this mind to include your loved ones. Cultivate enough compassion to free them all from suffering. Then encompass your town or city, even those enemies who destroy your happiness and bring you suffering. In your mind, cultivate sincere compassion, wishing that each person were free from suffering. Again, expand that mind to include people in your state, country, and the whole world. Eventually, extend yourself toward all sentient beings everywhere, not just human beings. This doesn't take much time; it costs nothing. It only requires your interest, mindfulness, and awareness. This heals the wounds in your mind and brings a smile to your face. This is the way to give rise to unfabricated peace and joy.

These are important and wonderful teachings. Deity yoga practices can be considered "high" and "exotic," but even those practices must be done with compassionate motivation. The practice of compassion is very profound and deep and can have many different levels, depending on the practitioner's spiritual development. The great master Chandrakirti explained this in terms of a threefold progression:

1. Compassion can be developed based on seeing the suffering of the six realms. Look at the physical and mental suffering of sentient beings. Contemplate their physical aging, sickness, death, hunger, thirst, and torture. Beings don't get what they want but do get what they don't want. Depressed and overcome by the afflicting emotions, they become discouraged and desperate. Whether they are your friends or enemies, everyone tries to

be free from these things. Also consider that the sufferings of the different types of animals and sea creatures are immense. Looking at this situation, develop compassion.

2. All these different types of suffering are created by the confused mind. Delusion and the afflicting emotions, the three poisons and their activities, repeat within us one after another without end, like a turning wheel. Contemplate this in order to understand its truth. On that basis, develop genuine compassion, the wish for all these sentient beings to be freed from these causes of suffering. Since each alone is limited, it is imperative that the practice of compassion be based on wisdom and that wisdom be based on compassion.

3. All phenomena are like a mirage, rainbow, or magician's show. They are illusory. But beings in samsara? Their minds are totally focused on delusion. They perceive everything as tangible, but gain little benefit no matter how much they sacrifice. Their egos are so strong, their arrogance so powerful. Because of that, the waves of their suffering are endless. Seeing this, the highly accomplished bodhisattva develops indomitable compassion, and his activities manifest without ceasing.

Among the four Immeasurable Thoughts, the third, joy, is not mentioned in the root text. Rejoice when someone else experiences some joy, peace, success, or happiness. Instead of becoming jealous, say to yourself, "I am so pleased that they are so happy. May their happiness last a long time."

Practicing the fourth Immeasurable Thought, equanimity, means seeing even your best friend and worst enemy as equal. Both have an equal right to experience peace and happiness. Purify your attachment to your friend and hatred for your enemy. This becomes a genuine source of peace and joy.

As we mentioned earlier, these four thoughts are practiced by all Buddhists and particularly by Mahayana practitioners. Bodhicitta arises from these powerful mental states. Mahayana and Vajrayana practitioners should not treat them with indifference, for they are the foundation for the generation of bodhicitta. They are the path for the perfection of bodhicitta. They are the fruition, buddhahood, from which enlightened activities endlessly manifest.

Dharmaradza's text is such a good guideline. Read one or two verses each morning and keep them in mind all day. When you come home again, read a few more verses. Even if you know the text well, it will continue to support you when you read it again and again.

The supreme mind of bodhicitta is like an unspoiled seed.
Without it, it is impossible to achieve perfect enlightenment.
Therefore, cherish the cultivation of the mind of Mahayana.
This is my heart's advice.

THIS VERSE points out the distinction between the Hinayana and the Mahayana. Those who do not have bodhicitta can still practice Buddhism. This is called the *Hinayana*, a Sanskrit word meaning "small vehicle." Hinayana practitioners are inspired by and interested in individual liberation or arhatship. Those who cultivate bodhicitta belong to the *Mahayana*, the "great vehicle." It is "great" because it consists of those who take responsibility for the welfare of all sentient beings. Regardless of the type of practice you do, what distinguishes one from the other is bodhicitta. If you possess bodhicitta, then even if you only sit and watch your breath to calm and purify the mind, that is a bodhisattva's practice. Without bodhicitta, you are not on the Mahayana path even if you perform the highest yogas and most complicated rituals.

Loving-kindness and compassion alone are not bodhicitta. These two constitute the critical foundation for bodhicitta but should not be mistaken for the mind of enlightenment itself. Some texts say that compassion is the same as bodhicitta, but this is not always so. There are many people who generate love and compassion, but they do not necessarily have bodhicitta. On the other hand, if you have bodhicitta, then compassion and loving-kindness are definitely also present, since they are its precursors.

It is critically important to identify exactly what bodhicitta means before we attempt to practice it. To generate bodhicitta (the mind of enlightenment), there are two indispensable factors: compassion and wisdom. Compassion concerns the suffering of all sentient beings, which means that one has a strong desire that all beings be free from suffering. Wisdom concerns the achievement of complete buddhahood, the state of total peace. Thus, in order to cultivate bodhicitta properly, it is essential to study and practice these two first. Plant the seed of bodhicitta in the well-plowed ground of a mind that has been fertilized with loving-kindness and moistened with compassion. Studying and practicing limitless loving-kindness and compassion are imperative causes for generating the infinite mind of enlightenment, bodhicitta.

On a farm, perfect, *unspoiled seed* is needed in order to produce a crop. If the seed is spoiled, no matter how good the soil is, how much fertilizer is used, how much sunlight there is, and despite the water you apply, nothing will grow because there is no primary cause. But when good seed joins with proper conditions, perfect crops will result. Likewise, bodhicitta is the *unspoiled seed* that causes all the qualities of a buddha to manifest.

When bodhicitta is present, enlightenment is in your hand. Without it, there is no possibility of buddhahood. There is no doubt that you need the universal mind that desires the attainment of buddhahood in order to become a buddha. Otherwise, even if you practiced the most profound view, there would be no way to attain buddhahood. There is a story told by Atisha of a person who diligently practiced Hevajra, a highest yoga tantra. But because he lacked bodhicitta, that yogi attained the arhat state instead of buddhahood.

Here, it is crucial to pinpoint what bodhicitta is. Talking about it without at least a rudimentary understanding is like shooting an arrow without a target. Bodhicitta is concerned with benefiting all sentient beings, regardless of who they are. It doesn't matter what beliefs they hold or what culture they are from. Even if they don't believe in anything at all, this mind does not exclude them or any other being in the six realms. Bodhicitta expands the mind to include everyone and reveals mind's total perfection.

We admire Buddhism not for its rituals, visualizations, or mantras but because it promises freedom from suffering and delusion. To accomplish these goals, bodhicitta is the most effective practice. Because the Buddha perfected bodhicitta, his compassion manifests unceasingly for sentient beings. Thus it is said that buddhahood is the perfection of bodhicitta. Therefore, understand the factors that make up bodhicitta and make every effort to cultivate it. *Cherish* this mind.

The five elements—the basis of all life—perform their function without expectation. In the same way, with harmony and clarity as the basis of your mind, benefit others without effort. One's bodhicitta should increase to its full potential like the waxing moon. Just as the sun dispels all darkness, bodhicitta dispels the darkness of confusion. And as the king of beasts roams his forest fearlessly, the bodhisattva practitioner travels fearlessly in samsara.

Bodhicitta is the backbone of Mahayana Buddhism. Bodhisattvas study and learn all aspects of knowledge to achieve omniscient wisdom and to benefit limitless sentient beings through limitless activities. In the sutras, the Buddha uses more than two hundred analogies to describe bodhicitta. The following are a few examples:

- Bodhicitta is like a light dispelling the darkness of ignorance.
- Bodhicitta is like a sword cutting the tree trunk of attachment.
- Bodhicitta is like a spear destroying the enemies—suffering and the afflicting emotions.
- Bodhicitta is like a wish-fulfilling jewel bestowing all excellent qualities.
- Bodhicitta is like a great shade tree under which all sentient beings can rest from the heat of samsara.
- Bodhicitta is like a bridge on which we can cross the ocean of samsara.
- Bodhicitta is like a parent who provides every comfort.
- Bodhicitta is like a seed producing the crops of enlightenment and buddhahood.
- Bodhicitta is like a stupa, an object of respect, devotion, and offerings. It makes one supreme among gods and humans. Even the dust from a bodhisattva's feet is a blessing.
- Bodhicitta is like gold under the ground, never stained by the rust of afflicting emotions.
- Bodhicitta is like the sun, ripening the fruit of enlightenment.
- Bodhicitta is like a great alchemy transforming the ordinary, leaden mind into the gold of enlightenment.
- Bodhicitta is like a conflagration consuming the dense forest of delusion.
- Bodhicitta is like a saw cutting the tree of ego.
- Bodhicitta is like protective armor shielding one from the armies of hatred.

▶ Bodhicitta is like a most powerful protector defending one against harm from nagas, gods, yakshas, humans, and non-humans.

Further analogies for the benefits of bodhicitta are derived from the seven articles of a universal monarch:

▶ Bodhicitta is like a golden wheel attracting all the excellent qualities within samsara and nirvana.
▶ Bodhicitta is like a steed racing to the country of enlightenment.
▶ Bodhicitta is like a minister accomplishing the wishes of all buddhas and bodhisattvas by performing effortless activities.
▶ Bodhicitta is like a general annihilating all enemies—the four maras—without exception.
▶ Bodhicitta is like an elephant impartially carrying anything and bearing the burden of sentient beings without becoming exhausted.
▶ Bodhicitta is like a queen bringing peace and joy to all sentient beings.
▶ Bodhicitta is like a jewel fulfilling the wishes of all beings in samsara and nirvana.

Moreover, just as a small amount of poison cannot pollute a vast ocean, a small number of negative thoughts cannot pollute vast bodhicitta. If one possesses bodhicitta, even a small amount of virtue becomes infinite. For example, if a bodhisattva gives a mouthful of food to an animal, the virtue of this act multiplies by as many times as there are sentient beings in the universe. This is called the skillful means of a bodhisattva.

One who possesses real bodhicitta will not be carried away by the torrent of samsara, will not be veiled by the darkness of ignorance, and will not be distracted by the wealth of the world. Suppose that all sentient beings became arhats, and that you made offerings to them of food, drink, clothes, medicine, and bedding. Establishing even one person in bodhicitta has far greater benefit than that produced by all those magnificent offerings. Knowing these infinite qualities, one should increase bodhicitta through the practice of the seven-limb offering:

1. Prostrate to all enlightened beings with your body, speech and mind.
2. Offer outer, inner and ultimate offerings.
3. Purify all obscurations.
4. Rejoice in all excellent qualities and virtues.
5. Request the turning of the wheel of precious Dharma.
6. Beseech the enlightened beings to perform activities and not pass into parinirvana.
7. Dedicate the merit.

These are special methods to accumulate great merit and wisdom in order to strengthen bodhicitta. Each action can become the activity of a bodhisattva. Always act in the interest of enlightenment. Energize your interest in bodhicitta. Have strong devotion to bodhicitta and always be vigilant and mindful while walking, sitting, eating, or drinking. Remain within the sphere of bodhicitta.

Each of us has the opportunity to cultivate this mind since bodhicitta makes no distinction between male and female, rich or poor, high or low. Anyone can be inspired to hold this pure, holy and precious mind in their heart and to put it into practice joyfully and diligently.

There are many different factors that might cause one to cultivate bodhicitta. For example, practicing great compassion and seeing the suffering of samsara will inspire some people to cultivate bodhicitta. They will be unable to bear the immense suffering of sentient beings and will realize that the only way to free them is to cultivate bodhicitta and attain buddhahood. Others will cultivate bodhicitta by seeing the perfect qualities of a buddha: ease, splendor, harmony, peace, and freedom from all delusions. Such persons understand that the only way to attain these qualities is through the cultivation of bodhicitta. Some are motivated to cultivate the mind of enlightenment through the inspiration of a spiritual master. The spiritual master explains to his or her disciples how important bodhicitta is, how important it is to be free from samsara and so forth, and this leads the disciples to cultivate the mind. Some are driven to cultivate bodhicitta by the force of their own great accumulation of merit and wisdom. These things are explained in detail in *The Jewel Ornament of Liberation* and *The Heart Essence of the Mahayana Teachings*.

The wonderfully inspirational book *Vast as the Heavens, Deep as the Sea* can now be read in English. In that text, Khunu Lama Rinpoche explains the importance of bodhicitta with beautiful metaphors and analogies, like the following:

- Bodhicitta is such a vast treasure! When it is possessed by a bodhisattva, no other wealth is needed. Such a precious thought!
- Bodhicitta is such a great medicine! It can heal the chronic disease of confusion, which no ordinary medicine can do.
- Bodhicitta is such a great bridge! Only bodhicitta can take us beyond all of samsara, which no ordinary bridge can do.
- Bodhicitta is such a great healer! It heals all negative thoughts and mental confusion, the roots of suffering, which no ordinary doctor can do.
- Bodhicitta is such an airplane! It takes us to the continent of enlightenment, to which no ordinary plane can fly.

Bodhicitta is everything. It is the consummate path to buddhahood. If we only make the effort to cultivate it, bodhicitta is like a wish-fulfilling jewel. It can fulfill all our wishes and free us from all suffering. If we were free from suffering, what else would we need? Each one of us has the opportunity to cultivate this mind, to maintain this mind, and to cherish this mind. No one is excluded. That is why it is so precious. Please keep this advice in your heart, and use it to heal the wounded mind.

People go on vacations to more peaceful environments, to see new things in other countries, or to spend time high in the mountains or at the beach. People do this to have different experiences, to gain some knowledge, or take a rest, but these things don't last very long. Wouldn't it be better to visit the island of bodhicitta for a vacation? To climb the mountain of bodhicitta? Or to swim at the beach of bodhicitta? To eat the delicate cuisine of bodhicitta? To enjoy the beer of bodhicitta? To rest on the hammock of bodhicitta? What a wonderful way to have a vacation from the misery of samsaric delusions! Take a moment and consider this.

Aspiration bodhicitta is like a traveler setting out on a journey.
Before long, he will arrive at buddhahood.
Therefore, make a pure aspiration.
This is my heart's advice.

THERE ARE TWO basic types of bodhicitta: *aspiration bodhicitta* and action bodhicitta. Here, aspiration bodhicitta is described.

A *traveler* first prepares to set out on a journey by forming the aspiration "I want to go to Hawaii." It's a good place for a vacation—a good place to rest, with swimming and good weather all year round. Seeing these good qualities, the traveler aspires to go there because it is a much better place than where he already is. But then he has to plan how to get there: by airplane, car, bus, or boat. He has to think about what he will need there and what he will need on the way. In the same way, if we want to attain enlightenment, we have to make good preparations, and have a pure aspiration. First, look at the nature of samsara and know well the suffering of sentient beings—not just your own but that of all sentient beings. Then look at the qualities of enlightenment, a state of great ease. Enlightenment is always free from the extremes of heat and cold, free from the clouds of conceptual thought. There we can see the deep blue of the all-pervading sky of dharmakaya and breathe the fresh air of love and compassion. By seeing these qualities, we are inspired to achieve that state. But we must know what to do and be sure to pack all the things we need to attain enlightenment.

A *pure aspiration* is an aspiration that is not mixed with samsaric thoughts. On our journey, we don't need negative thoughts, ignorance, attachment, hatred, and so forth, so we leave them behind. They're just garbage, aren't they? Sort out all these negative things and gather up all the good qualities you will need to reach enlightenment.

The cultivation of aspiration bodhicitta has many beneficial effects. Here are just a few:

‣ Just by cultivating this mind, one joins the Mahayana family. Without bodhicitta, one cannot attain buddhahood.

‣ Cultivating bodhicitta immediately becomes the foundation to practice the three moralities of a bodhisattva (see verse 46), so it is like the ground that supports all crops and fruits.

‣ Bodhicitta is the supreme antidote that purifies all nonvirtues and delusions without exception. It destroys them just as the fire at the end of a kalpa consumes the whole world.

‣ Bodhicitta is the root of enlightenment. When the seed of enlightenment takes root, then the tree of enlightenment can fully manifest and bear the fruit of all awakened qualities. That tree provides shade in which sentient beings take refuge from the heat of samsara.

‣ Cultivating bodhicitta accumulates immeasurable merit. There are many ways to accumulate merit and virtue, but bodhicitta is one of the supreme methods for gathering unlimited merit and wisdom. The Buddha said, "If the mind of bodhicitta had form, it would be vaster than space." If there were no bodhicitta, even if one accumulated great merit through many virtuous activities, it would not bring buddhahood.

‣ Bodhicitta is the complete way to please the buddhas because that mind promises to benefit all sentient beings without exception. The buddhas' activities manifest in order to free all sentient beings from suffering and purify all their obscurations, while bodhicitta promises to purify all faults, delusions, and obscurations. That is why bodhicitta is a special way to please all the buddhas. The Buddha said, "The buddhas will be more pleased if one pays homage to them by joining the hands with bodhicitta than by filling the whole world with jewels and offering it to them."

‣ Bodhicitta is the source of benefit for all sentient beings. There are many ordinary ways to benefit sentient beings—giving wealth, comforting them, and so forth. But bodhicitta is committed to uprooting *all* the causes of suffering. It is an endless source of peace and inspiration. It is practiced life after life for countless lifetimes until one attains buddhahood. Bodhicitta, like space, has no boundary or limit. Like the four elements, it constantly sustains life.

▸ When one possesses bodhicitta, one will attain buddhahood quickly, because bodhicitta is the special method to purify both the afflicting emotions and the subtle obscurations. It causes one to achieve all the excellent qualities of the Buddha. It is the mind that abides neither in samsara nor nirvana, so one attains nonabiding, unsurpassed, complete buddhahood. Everyone should be inspired to embrace it. This mind will reveal the complete purity of your own awareness, and will give you an opportunity to ease your exhausted mind.

Seeing these beneficial effects, one must have vigilant awareness so as not to lose or forget bodhicitta. Specifically, there are four nonvirtues that may arise:

1. Telling lies that deceive your root master, any other bodhisattvas, or those who are worthy of respect. The root master is the one from whom you receive Dharma teachings and instructions, especially the teachings on bodhicitta.
2. Damaging your bodhisattva vow by abusing other bodhisattvas, especially if this causes them to lose their own vow. This is even heavier negative karma than the five heinous acts.
3. Creating regret in others for the virtuous deeds they may have accomplished for the Dharma.
4. Deceiving others through an insincere motivation.

Avoid these four nonvirtues and engage in the four virtues as their antidote:

1. Respect the root master and never tell a lie to him or to those worthy of respect, even at the risk of your life.
2. Perceive all bodhisattvas as buddhas and praise them.
3. Rejoice in others' virtuous deeds and inspire them to perform more Dharma activities, especially Mahayana practices.
4. Perceive all sentient beings as your best friends or as being just like yourself and treat them kindly and with sincerity.

These few guidelines will help you to protect your aspiration bodhicitta. Perform these four wholesome deeds, rejoice in them, dedicate their merit, and increase them. If you experience a downfall, sincerely purify your nonvirtuous actions.

The bodhicitta of activity is like a well-built channel.
Through that, one can perfect the two accumulations
   without concern.
Merit will continuously arise.
This is my heart's advice.

THIS VERSE introduces action bodhicitta. When a *channel* is *well-built*, all its water is directed to the right place without effort or waste. Similarly, taking the vow of action bodhicitta channels all of one's virtuous actions toward attaining enlightenment. One can formally take this vow from a qualified master. Then, even if you recite only one mantra, perform one prostration, or speak one kind word, that small action becomes a cause to attain enlightenment.

Merit will arise continuously, just as interest accumulates on money deposited in a bank; it grows day and night without effort. If we deposit our good qualities in the bank of bodhicitta, the merit-interest will accumulate endlessly. When we hold the action bodhicitta vow, our virtue will increase whether we are awake or asleep until we arrive at buddhahood. It will continuously benefit sentient beings, both directly and indirectly, so bodhicitta is a great source of inspiration and courage to practice Dharma.

Understanding how beneficial this vow is, we must care for it and keep it as carefully as we do our eyes. If we were to break it, it would be as if we had taken a person's life. Thus, it is important to be aware of what might cause us to break the vow. The most important reasons are

1. Misunderstanding emptiness by believing that nothing, including causality, exists within emptiness
2. Becoming overwhelmed by the unending nature of samsara
3. Becoming overwhelmed by the infinite number of sentient beings
4. Abandoning vigilance

5. Becoming overwhelmed by the torrent of afflicting emotions

Guard against the four root downfalls that break the vow:

1. Abandoning Dharma teachings
2. Abandoning the bodhisattva's vow
3. Malicious stinginess
4 Raging, harmful thought

The Jewel Ornament of Liberation tells of eight different ways that strong afflicting emotions can cause us to break the vow of action bodhicitta according to Asanga's system:

1. Praising oneself through attachment to wealth and honor
2. Abusing others out of jealousy through attachment to wealth and honor
3. Not giving Dharma out of miserliness to those who have no guidance
4. Not giving wealth out of stinginess to those who are destitute (for those who have wealth to give)
5. Punishing others out of anger
6. Not accepting others' apology out of resentment
7. Abandoning the Mahayana teachings
8. Giving false teachings out of impure motivation

According to Shantideva's system, there are eighteen root downfalls and forty-six subsidiary downfalls. (These are listed at the end of this book in the Glossary of Enumerations.) These boundaries or distinctions are not set out to make outlaws out of Dharma practitioners. Rather, these guidelines are a skillful way to identify those actions to avoid and those to accept. Instead of looking at these downfalls as restrictions imposed from the outside, examine your mind and cherish the treasure of bodhicitta. Some may think that these vows are too difficult to keep, and that it would be better not to take them and have an easy life. But one cannot become free from suffering or attain buddhahood or benefit sentient beings by taking it easy. For example, one must take risks in business to be successful because without taking risks, one cannot succeed in one's work.

The *two accumulations*—merit and wisdom—were skillfully taught by the Buddha through his great compassion so that we would know how to purify the different types of suffering and establish ultimate joy. The more we gather the two accumulations, the more perfect our bodhicitta becomes. As bodhicitta grows more powerful, we can purify our negative thoughts more vigorously and successfully. If our bodhicitta is weak, the gross, negative emotions will be difficult to purify.

In order to keep and practice bodhicitta well, we should make effort to free ourselves from attachment to praise and honor, to wealth, and to the sense objects. If possible, we should maintain the mind, body, and speech in solitude. Renew and enhance your vow by repeatedly visualizing the buddhas and bodhisattvas in space before you and taking the vow again. These are the practices of bodhicitta. Say this prayer often:

> May all have happiness free from suffering and swiftly attain
> buddhahood.
> May I be useful to all sentient beings through my body,
> speech, and mind, just as the four elements are.

This bodhisattva's path has been set out in categories to make it easy for us to follow. For example, the two accumulations can be practiced as the six perfections, which are described in detail in the following verses. The practices of generosity, moral ethics, patience, perseverance, and meditative concentration comprise the accumulation of merit, and the cultivation of incisive awareness comprises the accumulation of wisdom.

To remind yourself of bodhicitta practice, you can say the following prayers, and reflect on their short commentary.

CULTIVATING ASPIRATION BODHICITTA

> All mother sentient beings—
> especially those enemies who hate me, obstructers who
> harm me,
> and those who create obstacles on my path to liberation
> and omniscience—
> may they experience happiness and be separated from
> suffering.

Swiftly will I establish them in the state of unsurpassed, perfect, complete, and precious buddhahood.

This is a special prayer to recite right at the beginning to cultivate
the right motivation. By specifically focusing on the obstructers
and enemies who create obstacles, we can directly cut through our
hatred and resentment. Saying "May *they* have all the happiness and
joy" is a genuine Dharma practice that brings peace to our mind.
This kind of prayer is a direct and powerful way to focus our mind.
It gives us the strength to persevere in our practice and not give in
to obstacles.

It is very easy to feel kindness and compassion toward those who
support us and our work and toward those who are suffering, but
in difficult times this practice will help us to feel kindness and compassion for those who do not support us. The problem is actually
within our own mind, but that is very difficult to accept. This prayer
helps bring the problem to the surface; otherwise our negativity
stays in hiding and we remain unaware of it. So, at the moment we
pray in this way, we are looking at our own mind and transforming
our own negative thoughts, rather than focusing on a troublesome
person and their anger and hatred. We can transcend and uproot
our negative feelings by praying for our enemies to achieve complete
enlightenment.

This practice is useful not just for daily life, or even this life, but
also for our future lives. What we go through in this life will one
day be just a dream. All our experiences will belong to the past.
However, this practice will remain with us life after life. This practice teaches us how to cultivate our mind and set it in the right
direction. It will show us the causes of suffering and the causes of
happiness. As we know, our habitual tendencies take us in one direction without allowing us a choice. We know what causes happiness,
but we are reluctant to follow that road because it may be painful.
This practice teaches us how to recognize these shortcomings and
allows us to change direction. It is worthwhile to sacrifice our delusion in order to achieve ultimate peace and happiness. This practice
provides a method to cultivate the universal mind and develop compassion toward every sentient being.

Sometimes when we meditate, we feel peaceful and may think,

"Oh! I must be enlightened now!" But then these other thoughts come along and drag us in all different directions. We say things like, "There's that terrible person who. . . ," and suffer so much. I'm saying this from my own experience. I feel this prayer is *real* Dharma practice. There is such profound meaning condensed into this short prayer. We should say this prayer sincerely and meditate on its meaning often.

CULTIVATING ACTION BODHICITTA

> Thus, until I achieve enlightenment, I perform virtuous
>   deeds with body, speech, and mind.
> Until death, I perform virtuous deeds with body, speech,
>   and mind.
> From now until this time tomorrow, I perform virtuous
>   deeds with body, speech, and mind.

We need to change our negative thoughts and establish new habits slowly and gently. This meditation practice is a process of discipline. Sitting in meditation for one hour does not constitute discipline; it must be a continuous and steady effort.

Until I attain enlightenment means until I have perfected this thought. Enlightenment can come in one lifetime or it can take many lifetimes, so we say "until I attain complete enlightenment," whenever that is. This is a big project, so we must use all of our physical, mental, and verbal resources. We must channel *all* our energy into performing virtuous deeds with our body, speech, and mind until our goal is reached.

Until death, I perform virtuous deeds with body, speech, and mind. This recitation recognizes that we have a precious human life and a rare opportunity to study and practice Dharma. Therefore, we must not waste it but rather engage in virtuous effort until we die. This life can be a bridge that crosses the ocean of samsara, so we must utilize it in that way as much as we can. When we talk about our precious human life, we recognize that every human being has a precious opportunity to study and practice the teachings and that when we do practice these teachings, our body, speech, and mind will develop virtuous qualities. These teachings represent the way to freedom from all confusions and suffering and show us how to achieve excellent qualities. In order to accomplish this, we must focus our time and effort toward that end. To see clearly, we must develop the necessary mental qualities and depth of mind that our precious human life makes possible. These excellent qualities of our precious human life provide us with a rare opportunity—the possibility of achieving enlightenment in this lifetime. Whether we take advantage of this is our own individual choice.

From now until this time tomorrow, I perform virtuous deeds with body, speech, and mind. This means that we have to start now. We remind ourselves every twenty-four hours to progress. When you read the life of Milarepa, you can see how much he sacrificed because he realized the rare opportunity granted to him. After studying the Dharma, he knew he could not waste one minute of his life. The time that we waste cannot be regained, no matter how much we try. Who knows when death will come—maybe tonight? Maybe tomorrow? The Buddha said, "We don't know which will come first—tomorrow or our next life." So we should prepare for our next life and not just for tomorrow.

Our life is transitory and fragile; it depends on just one short breath. Even though we have to cultivate our mind to achieve enlightenment, we still have to live one day at a time. The time to practice is now. When negative thoughts arise in the mind, that is the time to practice Dharma. No matter where we are—at home, at work, while driving, anywhere—if we practice this way, we will become better people and our minds will gradually become clearer. With this kind of motivation, we are ready to work toward enlightenment, not tomorrow or next week, but right now. This is what we call *action* bodhicitta.

Advice about the Six Perfections

45 *The giving of generosity, free from attachment, is like*
a farmer sowing seeds.
It accomplishes our wishes and intentions without waste.
Discover the essence of your wealth.
This is my heart's advice.

ONCE WE PROPERLY generate and cultivate bodhicitta, we
should by all means train the mind with full attention in order
to accomplish the beneficial effects that have been described. The
practice of the six perfections, or *paramitas,* is indispensable to perfecting bodhicitta and attaining complete enlightenment. When we
perfect our mind, we become free from all confusion. This very mind
that we have today, when perfected, is the fully awakened mind of
the Buddha.

Generosity is the first of the six perfections. It is placed first
because it is the easiest to practice.

The giving of generosity has a wide range of meanings. Giving
time, skills, directions, wisdom, fearlessness, love, medicine, compassion, moral support, wealth, food, drink, clothes, and even your
own body—all of these are called generosity. Basically, generosity is
a mind free from stinginess and attachment, an open heart that is
ready to help others. From giving very simple things to giving the
highest, complete enlightenment—all these activities are the practice of generosity. It is a way to cast aside our samsaric cocoon and
reveal the universal mind.

Like a farmer sowing seeds: a farmer sows seed freely, without
holding back. He must do this in the spring to get results in the fall.

It wouldn't make much sense for him to have attachment to the seeds and not plant them while still holding high expectations for a crop in the fall. But farmers know what they are doing and do it freely, because more will come of it. It is the same with our practice of generosity. If we freely sow this seed of generosity in the field of bodhicitta, the great harvest of enlightenment will surely result.

The principal purpose of the practice of generosity is to free our mind from the three poisons—ignorance, attachment, and hatred. This practice reduces our ego and self-cherishing and releases our grasping. If you give something and expect something in return, this is not true generosity; it is merely ordinary trade. Practicing generosity means giving to those who suffer physically and mentally, to those who have no friends, who have no leader or protector, who wander bewildered in the dense forest of confusion. They all depend on us to provide for their needs.

Giving to others in this way gives you great joy. When you do something good for another without expecting anything in return, that other person feels happy and relaxed, and with an open mind you share in their joy. If someone is suffering and you help them, you both feel such peace. That in itself is a great result; you don't need to look for anything more than that. If you expect something more, you may become disappointed and regret your act of giving.

According to the Mahayana, all sentient beings are regarded as equal because, in one lfetime or another over limitless time, they have all been our parents or friends. In the Vajrayana, they are all equal in possessing the nature of the deity. In the enlightened state, one realizes the all-pervading dharmakaya and sees that all sentient beings are buddha nature. Bodhicitta is beyond limit, so it reaches all sentient beings. Thus, even if you give a small amount, the results become limitless. The seeds that we plant are not wasted. They accomplish our wishes. When you attain enlightenment, you will have everything you desire. So instead of being stingy and attached to things, give them away with the motivation of bodhicitta and dedicate your action to the benefit of all sentient beings.

The primary result of generosity is the manifestation of wealth, but many other results can be achieved as well. For example, once while he was on the path to enlightenment, Shariputra offered a buddha a bolt of cloth, a knife, a needle, and a spool of thread, and he dedicated the merit of this act. Because of this action, his wisdom was incisive, sharp, and profound. When Ananda was on the path to enlightenment, he offered a bracelet, which led to his great accumulation of hearing wisdom and to his having a steady, unforgetful mind. Thus, generosity practice brings about many different kinds of result.

There are many moving stories of great bodhisattvas who have practiced generosity. When we hear them, they can inspire us to practice with a pure heart. As soon as a bodhisattva hears someone in need calling out, "Can you help me? Can you give me something?" they are overjoyed and think, "Now I have an opportunity to practice generosity. I have a way to perfect my bodhicitta. How wonderful!" We, too, should try to practice like this. If we exert the effort, we can achieve perfection step by step; everyone can. The following is one such story:

> Once there was a householder who was quite wealthy but who was miserly and lacking in compassion. He had a servant who was very old. The servant lived in great hardship because the wealthy householder provided her only with rags to wear and barely enough food to survive.
>
> One day she was sent to the river with a huge vase in order to fetch water for the house. When she arrived at the bank of the river, she cried out and lamented loudly. She felt she could no longer bear her conditions and wished to commit suicide. A monk named Katyayana happened by and asked why she was crying. She answered, "Noble One, I am old and have too much work to do. The food I eat barely sustains me. I want to kill myself." The monk asked, "Would you like to sell your poverty?" The servant scoffed, "Who would buy such a thing?" The monk nevertheless instructed her to bathe herself and to offer whatever she had. The servant objected, "What should I do? I don't have so much as a piece of cloth to give. Even this vase is not mine; it belongs to the owner of the house." The monk said, "You don't know how to practice giving. You can give even water or some wood. If you really have nothing, just fill my begging bowl with water and I will say

a dedication prayer for you." So the old woman offered a bowl of water to the monk. The monk dedicated the merit of her act and then gave her some teachings.

The monk then asked, "Do you have a place to sleep?" The old woman replied, "I sleep where I work, which is a very filthy place. Sometimes I sleep with the garbage." The monk said, "Just continue to do your work without resentment. Persevere in all the things that you were doing, but now always reflect on the Buddha, Dharma, and Sangha as you work." She went back to the house and did as the monk advised. One day she was given a bunch of dried grass to sit and sleep on, and she continued to think of nothing but the Buddha, Dharma, and Sangha. At dawn one day, she passed away and was reborn in the God Realm of the Thirty-three.

The owner of the house noticed that the old woman had died and hired someone to dispose of the corpse. A man came, tied a rope to her feet, and dragged the body to the cemetery. At the cemetery, many gods and goddesses rained down flowers and incense. Light radiated throughout the town and everyone was astonished at these events.

This story shows us how easily one can make a connection to the Dharma. Sometimes, we too may feel that we face difficult situations dealing with people or with our work. It is important to keep positive thoughts in our mind and to try to find good solutions to our predicaments. Think of the Buddha, Dharma, and Sangha and do good things for others. Results will happen according to the causes that we create. Instead of having expectations that can't be met, practice Dharma and free yourself from samsara.

In a similar story, a group of monks were out begging for their lunch and passed a female leper.

Along their way, people made offerings to the monks. The leper-woman felt strong devotion for them but was very poor, which caused her to lament, "I am so unfortunate. No one pays attention to me, and I have nothing to offer." In her hand she held only a bowl of rice broth.

Mahakashyapa walked by and noticed her. He perceived her intention and indicated that he would accept her offering. As she poured the broth into his bowl, her finger fell in. She picked out her finger and anxiously begged him not to eat the broth. But out of compassion, he accepted the offering and drank it. She was overjoyed. At her death, she was born in the Tushita god realm. So whatever we can offer—anything at all—we should offer joyfully and with the motivation of bodhicitta.

There is always some opportunity to practice generosity. Protecting someone from sickness, thieves, or robbers is a practice of generosity. Because of a bodhisattva's fearlessness and compassion, those around him or her will be attracted to that individual and feel no fear. That is the giving of fearlessness. If someone is depressed, saying a few kind words or even just smiling kindly are gifts that cost nothing. When we discuss Dharma teachings, or share Dharma with others according to their interest and the level of their mind, there is infinite benefit. That is the greatest gift. It floods our heart with joy and makes our lives meaningful.

The three kinds of morality are like a warrior's sword.
They cut the bonds of the obscuring emotions.
You should possess recollection, decorum, awareness,
  and consideration.
This is my heart's advice.

WHEN YOU ARE fully engaged in the practice of generosity, your mind will increasingly be inspired to be free from nonvirtuous thoughts and to engage in virtuous practices. Such a mind is said to be *like a warrior's sword.* The sword in a warrior's hand should be very sharp and powerful. With it, the warrior can easily overcome his enemies. In the same way, this practice of morality can *cut the bonds of the obscuring emotions* that tie us to the suffering of samsara. Morality, the second of the six paramitas, can sever the limbs of our delusions. With it, we will achieve real freedom.

A warrior's mind is alert in battle, looking in all directions to see whether an enemy is attacking. If an enemy appears, he acts quickly to protect himself from harm. Bodhisattvas who possess morality are like warriors in the battle of samsara. It is not easy to have such strong vigilance, determination, devotion, and mindfulness. But our enemies—ignorance, attachment, aversion, pride, and jealousy—are very powerful. In a moment, they can take the life of our peace and joy, and destroy the root of all virtues. As warrior-practitioners, we must not allow ourselves to be defeated by such enemies. We must carefully watch the mind with persistence, no matter how long it takes to overcome these enemies. In this way, our enemies will eventually be annihilated. Then we will attain the victory of buddhahood and effortlessly manifest enlightened activities without limit.

Of the *three kinds of morality* mentioned here, the first is the morality of abstaining from nonvirtuous actions. As described earlier, there are ten nonvirtues to be avoided because they are the root cause of samsara—the six realms with their different levels of suffering. Being motivated by bodhicitta, monks, nuns, bodhisattvas, and tantrikas should abstain from all nonvirtues. The following story of a couple who kept the precept of avoiding sexual misconduct is a good example of this:

> Once there were two couples who were very good friends with each other. They often talked about their plans for their children, saying that if sons were born to both families the boys would be good friends, too; the same would happen if two daughters were born. They agreed that if one family had a daughter and the other a son, the children should marry when they were grown. As it happened, one couple gave birth to a son and the other gave birth to a daughter. Both children were raised with kindness and skill and, as a result, were very healthy physically and mentally.
>
> When the daughter came of age, she told her parents that she wanted to receive ordination as a nun. The parents said, "You can't do that. A long time ago, we made a pledge for you to marry, so it's out of the question for you to go to the Dharma." But the daughter wouldn't listen to them and ran away to join a community of nuns. There, she successfully studied and practiced Dharma and achieved arhatship, which is freedom from samsara.
>
> In the other family, the son heard that the daughter had run away. Along with some close friends, he went to the temple where she was staying. They found the daughter meditating, wearing Dharma robes, and with a shaved head. The son pulled on her leg to get her attention, but because she had achieved arhatship she immediately flew up into the sky and proclaimed, "Samsaric life has no meaning. If you turn away from it and receive ordination, you will achieve liberation. The activities of samsara only cause suffering. I want no part of them. You, too, should renounce attachment to samsara, receive ordination, and pursue *real* peace and happiness." The son and his friends were inspired and deeply moved. As soon as he heard those words, he achieved the stream-enterer state, and then received ordination as a monk. Thereafter, he successfully meditated and also achieved arhatship.

These two were able to accomplish these things because of causes from their previous lives. Formerly, they were a married couple who took the precept from a master to abstain from sexual misconduct. Thereafter, they practiced Dharma sincerely and supported each other, saying aspiration prayers for each other to be freed from samsara. They dedicated these virtuous acts and meditations to the achievement of arhatship in their next life. The master who gave them ordination was the rebirth of the master who had witnessed their earlier dedication. Thus, when the cause matured, they both achieved arhatship because of the good example they had set for one another.

The second of the three kinds of morality is the discipline of studying and practicing Dharma teachings and gathering all wisdom. This is accomplished by engaging in the practice of the ten virtues and six perfections. These are the root cause of peace and happiness in samsara and are a bridge to the attainment of enlightenment. Until we attain complete buddhahood, we should always be inspired to practice Dharma, to study, and to gather the two accumulations of merit and wisdom.

The third type of morality is the morality of benefiting all sentient beings. When we are fully established in the Dharma and abide within the pure sphere of bodhicitta, then we can support, help, and inspire others to become free from samsara and attain enlightenment.

In order to *possess recollection, decorum,* and *awareness,* it is useful for trainees to follow guidelines concerning moral ethics. In general, we must

- ▸ receive the precepts of moral ethics
- ▸ abstain from all kinds of nonvirtue
- ▸ abide in a positive environment
- ▸ be alert to avoid even tiny nonvirtues
- ▸ perfectly keep moral ethics, which are the basis for all other training
- ▸ guard the sense-organs with persistent mindfulness

Respect your virtue by always equalizing the mind, calmly abiding, relaxing, and keeping the mind balanced.

Regarding eating: Do not eat while confused by conceptual thoughts or attachment, such as the desire to build pride or strength, or to make yourself beautiful. Rather, sustain your body with the pure motivation of eating only to dispel the sickness of hunger. Eat in order to keep the precepts and to dispel faults, confusion, and mistakes. Eat with the motivation of bodhicitta. Take food and drink as an offering to the yidam deity.

Regarding sleeping: In order to accomplish all excellent qualities, sleep with the motivation of bodhicitta. To take full advantage of this precious human life—the best condition to free oneself from samsara and attain enlightenment—practice Dharma before going to bed and early in the morning. Sleep with the motivation of bodhicitta.

Regarding daily life:

- Repeatedly recall the Dharma with joy.
- Maintain your precepts by being free from all downfalls.
- Keep your mind free from regret by not creating downfalls.
- Abandon strong attachment to any person or thing.
- Remain free from depression by appreciating the opportunity you have to understand and practice bodhicitta.

In these ways, we can be born in human form for life after life, can avoid falling into the three lower realms, can enjoy the precious Dharma, and can eventually maintain unafflicted moral ethics.

Having *consideration* means to be aware of what others will think and of what the Buddha will think. All buddhas have clear, incisive, unobstructed awareness of our behavior. Everything is obvious to them. We should be mindful that we are always in the presence of the buddhas. If we misbehave, the Buddha will perceive it and be dismayed. Especially among sangha members, always be considerate of others and guard your moral ethics through your speech and behavior. Carefully watch your mind. Not keeping our vows will cause us to be born in lower realms. Once there, we will find no opportunity to study or practice the precious Dharma, and we will have no means to create virtue and merit. Without these, there is no chance to create joy and happiness. Taking moral ethics as a precious and beautiful ornament, use them to adorn your body, speech, and mind. This is the path to enlightenment.

First, we must refrain from negative thoughts and actions. This makes our mind more peaceful and clear. Otherwise, it will not be possible for us to help others. Someone who is sinking in the mud of samsara cannot help others to get out of that same mud. We ourselves have to be free from that state first. Then, when we do try to help others, that help will be more effective. After taming our minds, we can study and practice further to build mental strength. Once we are well trained in these practices, we can more easily help sentient beings, regardless of who they are.

In the *Madhyamakavatara*, Chandrakirti compares the practitioner to a warrior. On a battlefield, you must protect yourself and defeat the enemy; up until the moment of loss, you have every opportunity to win. But once that enemy captures you, he can take away your weapons, confine you with chains and ropes, and throw you into a prison. You will have very little chance then to defeat your enemy. In the same way, now that you have a precious human life, have met the vajra master, and have received the precious teachings, this is the supreme opportunity to defeat the enemies of the afflictions and to free yourself from samsara. If, imprisoned by delusions, you are reborn in any of the lower realms, you will have little chance to escape samsara.

The following stories illustrate skillful ways in which one can benefit sentient beings. We must make every effort to train in these compassionate methods and then use them.

> Once when the Buddha was residing in Shravasti, he went walking with Ananda and came upon a monk who was terribly sick and racked with pain. The monk's clothes were filthy and stank. The Buddha, with great compassion, asked the monk to pass him his clothes so that he could wash them. As the Buddha began to take the clothes, Ananda said, "I will wash them." Then the Buddha said, "Good. I will pour the water." In this way, the Buddha and Ananda washed all the monk's clothes. The Buddha also gave the leftover food from his own bowl to the sick monk.

Soon the monk recovered, and he was moved to think that he had been served by the Buddha himself. "I cannot be lazy now," he thought. The monk built up his courage and enthusiasm, and persistently practiced Dharma day and night. Through this he quickly attained the arhat state.

The second story is of a woman whose only child died suddenly.

The mother of a child who died suddenly couldn't accept this unexpected death. She wandered from place to place, hoping that someone would bring her child back to life. At last, she met the Buddha. "I cannot accept my child's death," she lamented. "If no one can bring him back, my own life will be meaningless. I should die, too." Weeping, she begged the Buddha to revive her child. Seeing her agony, the Buddha gently said, "I completely understand your pain. Let us see what we can do."

He said, "I will watch the corpse. You go from door to door in this village, and bring back a handful of mustard seeds from any house where no one has died. If you can find such seeds, we can try to bring back your child's life." The mother was overjoyed and, expecting that she could find the required seeds, she set out. She spent the whole day going from door to door asking the same question, but could not find even one house where no one had ever died.

She became exceedingly frustrated by the end of the day but also began to gain some insight. She finally realized that her child was not the only one to have died. Everyone, young and old alike, eventually dies. Grief-stricken, the woman returned to the Buddha and said, "I could find no mustard seeds. What should I do now?" With compassion and wisdom, the Buddha instructed the grieving mother in the nature of impermanence, the transitory nature of all phenomena. "This is what you yourself have experienced today. Suppose your child's life were restored? He would still die again one day. It is the same with you and me. One day we too will die. The only way to be free from this suffering is to be free from samsara itself. The only way to experience true joy is to attain nirvana." With these words, the mother was relieved of her agony. Thereafter, she followed the Buddha's path and eventually achieved liberation.

This is how the Buddha relieves sentient beings from suffering.

The armor of patience is like a protective suit.
It cannot be pierced by anger, and it will increase all one's virtuous qualities.
Through patience, one will attain a body adorned by the major and minor marks.
This is my heart's advice.

THE THIRD PERFECTION is patience. If a warrior is well protected by armor, he will have more confidence and less fear. Others' weapons will not be able to harm him, so his enemies' strength and confidence will diminish and eventually disappear completely. This same principle works for us in the battle of samsara. We need armor that will protect us from harm. That protection is patience. When we are well protected, our enemies, the negative emotions, cannot pierce our peace of mind.

What is meant here by patience? It is a mind free from rage, resentment, and harmful thoughts, a mind that is not disturbed by others' criticism, that does not blame others in anger. Perhaps in English the word *patience* gives an impression of weakness and of wasted time. But here, patience means that anger is not allowed to penetrate our mental peace. This kind of patience requires great strength and courage. At present, it is very easy for anger and negative thoughts to penetrate our mind, and we are weakened by these thoughts. But when anger is not allowed to arise in the mind, there is such mental strength and clarity. So make an effort to cultivate this practice of patience. Deeply rooted afflicting emotions are not easy to purify and uproot. We need strong dedication and enduring patience in order to eliminate them thoroughly.

Practicing patience is actually the best use of our time. With patience, we gain strength and courage, as Milarepa did. Milarepa had great patience, enduring hardships in the mountains. However, he was very impatient if someone wasted his time and energy. "I have no time for this," he would say. "I will go my way, and you go yours. We will both do what needs to be done." That kind of courage and strength, built on wisdom and compassion, is called "patience." The following story demonstrates this:

Many kalpas ago, there lived a king named Tso Jung. In his country, a great practitioner of patience lived in the forest with five hundred disciples. One day the king, together with his queens and ministers, went to the countryside for refreshment. The king became tired after they reached the top of a high mountain, so they rested there, and he fell asleep. The queens, exploring the surrounding area, chanced upon that great practitioner, who was sitting up very straight in a state of peace and calm. On seeing him, the queens experienced strong devotion. They made offerings of flowers and then sat next to him in order to receive blessings and teachings.

On awakening, the king noticed that his queens were missing, so he sent his four ministers to look for them. They found the queens together with the saint. The king quickly arrived before the saint and asked, "Have you achieved the four states of samadhi?" The sage said that he had not. "Have you achieved the four 'miraculous feet'?" Again, the sage replied that he had not. The king became angry: "Without this knowledge, what do you think you are doing? You are just an ordinary man who is deceiving women." The great saint said, "I am here to practice patience." "We'll see whether you're practicing patience or not, " the king replied. And with that, he took out a razor-sharp blade and cut off the sage's hands. "Who are you now?" The great saint only said, "I practice patience." Then the king cut off the sage's feet and asked, "Who are you now?" and the great saint just said, "I practice patience."

At this point, the earth shook six times and five hundred gods proclaimed from the sky, "Even though this great teacher has been dreadfully injured and is suffering terribly, his mind has not withdrawn from the practice of patience." "Are they talking about you?" asked the king. The saint said, "Yes. My practice of patience has not declined at all." The king asked, "How do I know that you are practicing patience?" And the saint replied, "If my mind has not wavered from the practice of patience, may this blood turn into milk and may my body fully recover." As soon as he said this, his spilled blood turned into milk and his four limbs were rejoined. The king became very frightened and lamented, "Why did I harm this great saint? Please give me your blessing! I sincerely apologize. I very much regret my actions." The sage replied, "You still hold in your hand the sword with which you cut off my limbs. But my patience is as firm as this ground, and through this practice I have purified obscurations, negative thoughts, and karma. There is no doubt that I will achieve buddhahood in the future. At that time, may I cut through your three poisons with the wisdom sword of mind."

The gods and nagas were furious with that king and prepared to kill him. Clouds gathered in the sky, causing ominous thunderclaps and hailstorms. But the great saint stopped them, saying, "Don't do this for my sake. Please don't harm this unfortunate king." The gods and nagas were moved by this and gave rise to strong devotion for the saint. They took refuge in that saint and prostrated to him. Thereafter, the king followed the saint, sincerely practiced Dharma, and attained the nonreturning state.

This practitioner of patience was highly accomplished. We may not be able to compare with him, but we can at least see the importance of the practice of patience. Encouraged by this story, let us also take advantage of this great opportunity to practice Dharma and purify our negative thoughts. That will bring peace to our own hearts and minds and, through that, blessings will pervade our surroundings. May everyone obtain peace and happiness!

When you endure mental or physical suffering or when you face obstacles, instead of blaming someone else, reflect that this situation is the result of your own previous negative actions. Accept these conditions and develop great compassion for those who face the same, or even more difficult, obstacles. Look at the confusion of those who abuse and criticize you, or who use unpleasant words against the Buddha and Dharma. See how deluded they are and develop compassion rather than anger and resentment. Look for skillful methods to free them from their confusion. This is the way to bring about peace and harmony.

Even if you are physically beautiful, as soon as anger arises in your heart you become ugly and people do not want to associate with you. But a patient person is always beautiful. People admire and like to be around such a person. Because of this, virtue will increase.

When we are angry, we have no peace. And if we hold on to that resentment, this destroys our clarity of mind and our health as well. If, in the middle of a delicious lunch, someone brings up a topic that angers you, your food loses its taste; your face changes. From that moment, you can no longer enjoy your lunch.

Sometimes we may feel that we have a good reason to be angry. That may be true, but that anger will still just bring us suffering. Whether you have a right to be angry or not, never allow anger to arise in your mind. It can only destroy peace—peace in your mind, your family, and society. It never brings a good result. Unruly beings fill the whole universe. We cannot conquer or control them all. If we manage to subdue one, another takes his place. If we manage to subdue five, ten appear. It is better to control our own mind, to thoroughly pacify and tame the mind by establishing a practice of patience. This has the same result as controlling all the other sentient beings in the universe. Suppose the land were covered with thorns and you were barefoot. It would not be possible to cover all the thorns with leather. But if you put the leather on your feet instead, this would be the same as covering all the thorny land. In the same way, when your mind is fully tamed and trained in wisdom and compassion, everyone you encounter will present you with an opportunity to train in bodhicitta, regardless of whether you encounter them in positive or negative conditions.

We need especially strong patience to practice the precious Dharma. It takes powerful patience to study and practice step by step, to take full responsibility to purify oneself with the various methods of Dharma. Sometimes it is difficult to understand the meaning of Dharma, especially without direct experience. This is like sitting down to eat a delicious meal—the food will not jump into our mouth. We must put it there, chew, and experience its taste. If we want to wear beautiful clothes, they will not simply jump onto our bodies. We have to put them on and see for ourselves whether they fit.

Sometimes we practice with high expectations, thinking that all our problems and suffering will be solved by one session of meditation or by chanting a few mantras. When that doesn't happen, we become impatient and think that meditation doesn't "work" or that mantras are not helpful, and we give up our practice. This reflects a complete misunderstanding of Dharma practice. You may feel that the teachings are not helping you, or you may even resent them. At other times it may be difficult to please Dharma masters, or you may resent them because of their behavior. At such times, refrain from negative thoughts. Maintain your patience in order to calm your mind. When hearing about the infinite qualities of the Buddha, you might ask, "How could I possibly achieve such qualities?" Or you may be frightened when you learn about the profound nature of emptiness or find such teachings difficult to believe. At these times, immediately remind yourself how precious, profound and vast the Dharma is. Practice patience and inspire yourself. Recall that your mind, too, is infinite and most profound. Remember that without studying, understanding, and practicing, it is not possible to attain buddhahood.

Adorned with the major and minor marks refers to the Buddha's perfect body, which is free from all faults in every part. There are 112 such attributes that indicate the Buddha is unequaled among all beings. These kinds of excellent qualities are achieved through the practice of patience. Generally, when a person is compassionate and patient they seem very beautiful to us. Patience supports others whether they are old or young, beautiful or not—*all* people.

The following story illustrates how the Buddha exhibited his skill and patience.

> Once there was a bandit who hid in an isolated place waiting for victims. He showed no mercy to anyone who passed through that area. He either robbed them or killed them. It happened that the Buddha passed by one day. The robber stopped the Buddha and said, "Give me all your possessions or I will kill you." The Buddha said, "I have no possessions to give you," so the bandit replied, "Then I will have to kill you."

With skillful compassion, the Buddha said to the bandit, "Before you kill me, I have some questions to ask. There is a large tree over there. Can you cut down all its leaves?" The bandit did this very easily, showing both his strength and the sharpness of his sword.

The Buddha praised him and said, "Well done! I'm impressed!" And the bandit asked, "What is your next question?"

The Buddha asked, "Now can you put all those leaves back on the tree?" The bandit became confused and embarrassed and asked, "How could anyone do such a thing?" The Buddha replied, "Since you cut them all down, you should be able to put them back up."

The bandit began to think about what he had been asked and forgot about killing the Buddha. The Buddha blessed him and said, "You could kill me just as easily as you cut down those leaves. But you cannot give me life, just as you cannot put the leaves back on the tree. Recollect how many people you have harmed during your life. How many were helped or given life? If someone took your own life, how would you feel? If someone gave you back your life, how would you feel? Everyone feels these things, too. Just think about that."

The bandit then felt great remorse for having killed so many people in the past. He recalled them all, and despaired over the lives he had destroyed until his mind was completely changed. "You must possess powerful compassion and wisdom to have changed my mind like this. I understand that I made mistakes in the past. Now I want to follow in your footsteps. Please accept me," he cried. The Buddha replied, "Just follow me." The Buddha then gave the man instructions on the practice of compassion, calm abiding, tolerance, and especially incisive insight meditation. The new student sincerely practiced these teachings and attained a high level of realization.

We need this kind of great skill and patience to benefit others. It is very easy to destroy others' peace and happiness. A single harsh word can wound another's heart as easily as if you had used a knife. It is difficult to comfort others, yet this is exactly what they need. Therefore, use the sword of patience to cut down the tree of ignorance and arrogance. Be vigilant and recall the good qualities of your mind that adorn your beauty.

It is very important to be mindful of our behavior when dealing with bodhisattvas. If we become angry or abusive toward bodhisattvas, this creates a condition that destroys a vast amount of virtue. This is because a bodhisattva's mind extends itself to all sentient beings. Therefore, if we harm one bodhisattva, this is like harming all beings. We should respect and admire all bodhisattvas for their courageous mind bent on benefiting sentient beings.

When you do this practice, fully dedicate it to the attainment of enlightenment for the benefit of all. You can say, "By this practice of patience, may all sentient beings experience joy and happiness and be free from suffering." Saying this prayer from your heart will refresh you like a cool breeze in hot weather. When very strong anger arises, say, "May my anger serve as a substitute for the anger of all sentient beings, and may they be free from anger. May all sentient beings, boundless as the sky, achieve happiness and the causes of happiness." Repeating this prayer many times, like a mantra, will loosen the grip of anger.

A buddha sees the afflictions, kleshas, as enemies, but regards with compassion any person suffering from the kleshas. Thus, it is very important to distinguish between these two. We seek to eliminate the afflictions, but we want those suffering from the afflictions to achieve peace and happiness and to attain buddhahood. We should understand that whatever comes in our lives is a result of our karma—whether good or bad. By recognizing our experiences as results of the causes we have created, in the future we will be sure to develop positive karma and perform good actions.

When you are sick or face obstacles, think about sentient beings, have compassion for those who experience the same kinds of suffering, and say prayers like this: "May all the sickness and obstacles of sentient beings be fully exhausted by my own. May all beings experience good health and be free from obstacles." This is the way to successfully practice patience.

The three kinds of perseverance are like the whips that
   encourage a steed.
They are the supreme method to perfect the holy Dharma
And to quickly free oneself from samsara.
This is my heart's advice.

PERSEVERANCE, the fourth perfection, means studying and practicing Dharma joyfully despite hardships. Dharma's only function is to free us from all suffering and to bring relative and absolute joy. We should rejoice at this magnificent opportunity. Some individuals risk their lives for the pleasure of skiing, sky diving, or car racing. They are convinced that this is the path to happiness and pursue these activities single-mindedly. They eagerly face dangers because of the joy that they experience. This is the kind of motivation we need when we study and practice the Dharma. This is not just a hobby. We must direct our entire being and all our efforts toward buddhahood.

A *steed* is alert and strong even without being prompted. When *encouraged by the whip*, though, it will run even faster and won't stop until its destination is reached. In the same way, we should study and practice the precious Dharma with the encouragement of seeing the sufferings of samsara and with the understanding that all phenomena are impermanent. These are crucial, foundational contemplations. No matter what we do, there is no end of suffering in samsara. Driven by this understanding, we should follow the path to buddhahood.

There are *three kinds of perseverance*:

- armor-like perseverance
- perseverance in accumulating virtue
- perseverance without limitation

With the first, you make a commitment to put the Dharma teachings into practice until you attain buddhahood for the sake of all sentient beings. You firmly resolve to purify all mental obscurations and to unveil the true nature of the mind. You then "wear" that determination or resolve as armor so that nothing can deter you from reaching your goal. This is known as wearing the armor of joyous effort.

You put this commitment into action by accumulating virtue through the practices of generosity, moral ethics, patience, meditation and wisdom awareness. Perseverance is the remedy for all types of laziness, including procrastination and indolence. Laziness will bring no benefit to oneself or anyone else. From limitless lifetimes up until now we have been spiritually lazy and have cared only about protecting ourselves and our attachment to samsaric activities. We have not been able to accomplish anything, and if we continue in this way the result will be the same. Without Dharma practice, even if we remained alive and enjoyed every possible luxury for a thousand years, in the end we would still be left with nothing. It would have been like a wonderful dream, and we would go on to the next life empty-handed.

Our perseverance should have no limit. Until we have become free from samsara and attained enlightenment, we should never be satisfied with small achievements. Instead, we should make effort joyfully until we have purified all obscurations and gained the qualities of a buddha. Even shravakas and pratyekabuddhas fully dedicate their mind-streams to their own enlightenment. Even if their body were to fall apart, they would pursue their path without yielding. Understanding the nature of samsara, they see that no matter where they go in samsara they can find no genuine happiness or joy. Bodhisattvas, on the other hand, not only pursue their own liberation but do so for the benefit of sentient beings throughout the whole universe. Especially in this case, it is essential to maintain single-minded joyous effort.

Our perseverance must be insatiable. If you do a session of meditation practice in the morning, don't be satisfied with that. Instead, carry that awareness with you throughout the day regardless of your activities. This way, your whole day becomes a practice. In any case, we must practice until we attain enlightenment. Each day, perform virtuous deeds with the motivation of bodhicitta and then dedicate the merit. Avoid nonvirtuous thoughts and actions.

Joyous effort in gathering virtue directed toward the attainment of enlightenment for the benefit of all beings is highly praised by buddhas and bodhisattvas. It is like the force of a great river that rushes down from the mountain and reaches the ocean without stopping. If we practice in this way, our practice will be not just to gain some title or authority, but it will, instead, be a service for all sentient beings. So joyfully practice perseverance in these three ways.

Without receiving clear instructions in Dharma, we may work hard in many ways to bring peace, happiness, and joy into our lives. Sometimes our efforts bring happiness and sometimes they bring suffering. We never know for sure what we are doing. We know that we are making effort, but we cannot always be sure what the result will be. On the other hand, if we have a clear understanding and practice according to the Dharma, we can clear away our obstacles and experience peace and happiness. We should consistently apply perseverance without becoming tired in our body or mind. This way of practicing Dharma is like an elephant's walk—a gentle, smooth, and even pace without stopping. It is also like the well-known story of the turtle and the hare:

> One day a turtle and a hare met and became friends. They agreed to hold a race to see who could cross a mountain the fastest. The turtle walked as smoothly and gently as he could, keeping up a steady pace. The hare raced ahead at top speed. But when he reached the midway point, he thought, "I am much farther ahead than my friend the turtle. I can afford to rest here for a while." The hare went off to the side to rest, and soon fell fast asleep. The turtle, with his slow but steady steps, continued walking without pause until he arrived at the goal. After a long while, the sleeping hare woke up and again raced for the finish, only to find that the turtle had already won.

This story tells us that we need to make effort every day to progress in our practice.

When we are following a joyous path and approaching a joyous result, how could we possibly be depressed? Why would we stop? We practice the Dharma joyfully; this is called "perseverance."

There were many times when the Buddha sacrificed his life so that he could receive teachings. He did this joyfully, feeling that he was fortunate. He thought, "This life is impermanent anyway. If I can sacrifice it for the teachings—for complete enlightenment for the benefit of sentient beings—it will be worthwhile. My life will have been useful." It doesn't matter whether we are monks, nuns, or laypeople, we all desire happiness and wish to be free from suffering. So each of us individually has to take responsibility for our practice.

Take a moment and reflect on this. In hot weather, it is joyful to go to the beach or to visit a breezy mountain. In the same way, it is joyful to be free from all suffering, and especially from the suffering of the mental afflictions. Aspire to this, and dedicate yourself to making a joyous effort to reach that joyful state.

Meditative equipoise is like a glorious palace.
One can abide there in peace and joy and can rest there
   from samsara.
Practice samadhi without a wandering mind.
This is my heart's advice.

MEDITATIVE EQUIPOISE or concentration is the fifth perfection. *A glorious palace* is a place suitable for a universal monarch to live. Such a palace is perfectly and beautifully decorated with jewels, brocades, silks, and all the finest ornaments. It contains every imaginable luxury, like gardens, pools, and performances, all arranged to please the monarch. All the most enjoyable things in the world are gathered there. No better place exists, and the universal monarch enjoys his life there in complete comfort. Similarly, no greater joy exists in the world than a virtuous, one-pointed mind. When our mind is enslaved by thoughts of anger, hatred, attachment, pride, and jealousy, we fall entirely under the control of these afflictions. On the other hand, when our mind is peaceful, adorned by the ten virtues, and imbued with loving-kindness, compassion, and bodhicitta, this itself is the glorious palace of genuine peace and joy. No matter how rich or famous one may be, there is no happiness for someone who is flooded with afflictions, suffering, and fear.

When we achieve meditative equipoise, a one-pointed mind focused on virtue, we can *abide there in peace and joy.* When our mind is tranquil and relaxed, that itself is joy. There is no need to search for joy elsewhere. This joy cannot be matched by any experience in samsara. This doesn't mean that in such a "palace" we are entirely free from samsara, but we can rest there in stability and clarity.

An intellectual understanding of meditation is not sufficient. We must repeatedly *practice samadhi without a wandering mind.* There is a saying that one's body should be where the meditation cushion is, and one's mind should be where the body is. Mind should be relaxed and free from grasping and fixation. This helps one to achieve samadhi, or meditative concentration.

Under ordinary circumstances, the conditions are not present for the mind to calmly abide. And without having established calm-abiding, critical insight cannot penetrate into our experience. Therefore, the first step is to at least reduce the power of our coarse mind. To accomplish this, contemplate impermanence, the sufferings of samsara, loving-kindness, and compassion. These contemplations are critically important, and this is why the teachings present so many descriptions of suffering and its causes. With mental stability and insight into the nature of samsara, we can develop the motivation to be free. Our mind can then find ease, and we can build genuine self-esteem out of wisdom instead of arrogance.

Through the actual practice of meditation we can gain three qualities of samadhi:

1. As soon as we experience calm-abiding, a feeling of ease and joy will arise.
2. This then becomes a basis on which to accomplish the infinite and inexhaustible qualities of buddhas and bodhisattvas.
3. Because we possess these infinite qualities, we can then effortlessly benefit sentient beings.

Various methods to align our mind with Dharma are fully described in *The Jewel Ornament of Liberation* and other texts. For example:

- To counter anger and aversion, contemplate loving-kindness and compassion and say this prayer: "May my anger exhaust the anger and resentment of all sentient beings, and may they achieve the total clarity of samadhi."
- To counter desire and attachment, contemplate impermanence and the empty nature of all phenomena and say this prayer: "Through my attachment, may all sentient beings be freed from all desires and attachments of their own, and may they enjoy the unafflicted peace of samadhi."
- To counter pride and jealousy, practice equalizing and exchanging yourself and others. To do this, take a deep breath and expel

all your tension. Bring your mind into your heart, and reflect: "Just as we ourselves wish for peace and happiness, so do all sentient beings. May everyone be freed from pride and jealousy, and may all enjoy unafflicted peace." With this thought, we can heal our arrogance and pride.

► To maintain equipoise when facing obstacles or suffering, pray: "May my own small suffering fully exhaust the suffering of all sentient beings."

► Instead of becoming attached to any peace, happiness, or success we might experience, think: "May I bring peace to all sentient beings. May peace prevail throughout the universe." Focus these thoughts specifically on those of whom you are jealous.

If your mind perceives phenomena as concrete and tangible, and you grasp at yourself and others as real, it is crucial to generate a sense of interdependence. If, for example, you see a nice shirt and experience attachment for it, consider that the shirt is not really an independent entity. First, its designer used mental activity to create its design. Someone else then made the fabric, and yet other people then operated the machinery that made the shirt, transported it, and sold it. Only after all these steps were successfully completed did the shirt manifest for you. This is only one example of how things are interdependently created. By seeing that all phenomena are similarly interconnected, one can purify the misconception that any object independently exists. With that understanding, attachment or aversion for the object naturally subsides.

Similarly, when we have mental suffering, we may feel completely consumed by it. When a situation is difficult to handle, we may see that difficulty as being very powerful and concrete. Without insight into how suffering arises, we could perceive the cause of our pain as something independent and become so traumatized that we feel life itself is meaningless. However, if we were to investigate and carefully contemplate, we would see that mental pain depends on many causes and conditions. First, our delusion perceives some object as "real." Then we become involved either by becoming attached to the object or by feeling aversion. It is through these causes and conditions alone that one experiences suffering. By means of a thorough analysis, we can come to understand that nothing exists independently, and we can then gain skill in handling our activities and circumstances wisely and will no longer create the causes of suffering.

In order to transform the mind, we must let go of our old habitual tendencies and open our heart. If we do this, we will realize that all afflicting emotions—including ignorance itself—are nonexistent, like a mirage. This insight into interdependence is called the "awakened mind." In brief, when these different methods are utilized, gross thoughts have less space in which to operate, and this supports the practice of calm-abiding meditation where we can experience bliss, clarity, and nonconceptual thought.

Without the stability of calm-abiding, the special insight and other excellent qualities of a bodhisattva will not arise within. But having only the good foundation of equipoise and mental clarity is not enough. Without special insight, these two will not bring the result of enlightenment. There are stories from the past of great practitioners who achieved very high degrees of meditative concentration but who were not freed from samsara because they lacked critical insight. Instead, they attained one of the four states of samadhi in the form realm or in the formless realm.

These two qualities, calm-abiding and special insight, must be combined. Then, just as water from many rivers flows into a single ocean, the qualities of all the buddhas and bodhisattvas will flow together into the ocean of enlightenment, and one will experience true joy and happiness.

There are so many benefits that arise from the practice of calm-abiding. At present, our mind is agitated and unstable, like a candle in a strong wind, so we forget many things. In such a state, it is difficult to achieve good qualities. But when our mind is peaceful, calm, and clear, much can be perceived in the endless depths of mind, including past and future lives.

Now, take a few moments to practice. With upright but relaxed body posture, take a deep breath and exhale all your tension. Gaze with the eyes directed downward and relax. Breathe naturally, and watch as your breath flows in and out. Do this practice for five to ten minutes or longer. Let go of all hope and fear. Allow your mind to be calm and peaceful. Dedicate your merit at the end.

Discriminating awareness is like a clear-seeing eye.
It can distinguish all dharmas without mistake.
It is the lamp on the path to liberation.
This is my heart's advice.

DISCRIMINATING AWARENESS is the sixth perfection, and is like *a clear-seeing eye*. When someone's eye is free from cataracts, glaucoma, and so forth, that person has clear sight. Such a person can read books, walk along a road without danger, drive a car, pilot an airplane, and distinguish people when he meets them. In the same way, one who possesses the eye of incisive insight can perceive all phenomena distinctly and understand how they function. That mind can fully "see" reality and know without mistake what causes suffering and what causes happiness. Because of this, one will abstain from nonvirtuous action and follow the virtuous path.

Pristine wisdom is like a lamplight that illuminates the way to freedom from samsara. Without such awareness, that path remains dark and hidden from view. Timeless truth is the nature of all phenomena—samsara and nirvana. To penetrate that meaning, we need this unfabricated lamplight. Without the wisdom that penetrates the nature of phenomena, there would be no way to free ourselves from samsara. Even though the timeless truth of all phenomena in samsara and nirvana is of a single mode of abiding, only one who has powerful wisdom can see it perfectly.

There are two truths—relative truth and ultimate truth, and there are two types of wisdom that perceive them. Relative truth consists of the "reality" that everyone apprehends in their own way through their own experience or through others' explanations. From beings in the hell realms to great bodhisattvas, each individual experiences reality according to their karma. These projections change according to causes and conditions, and because of this, they are said to be like a mirage, rainbow, magician's trick, dream, or bubble. These analogies help us to realize that all the phenomena are illusory, though they may seem quite real and tangible. All causality is perceived by the wisdom that knows all aspects that are knowable.

In the ultimate reality, there is no impediment to truth. Mind is completely perfected, and all mental obscurations have been purified so that one sees through delusion. Since all phenomena are like a mirage, illusion, or dream—unfabricated in their basic nature—the wisdom that perceives this is called the wisdom of "knowing as-it-is." To better understand how phenomena are like an illusion or dream, consider this example: Suppose you have a good friend with whom you are close, and some small incident completely changes the relationship so that you now see each other as enemies. Observe the power of your mental state and see how it changes perception. That perception is called "illusory" because the experience we once had does not exist now. It has vanished like a dream. Those who lack critical insight become fully involved in their world. They are gripped by delusion, and their suffering continues without end. On the other hand, those who perceive all experiences as being like a dream or magic show are not even slightly perturbed. One must fully understand the nature of conventional reality in order to follow the path to freedom from suffering.

In connection with this, it is critically important to investigate whether a "self" exists. Over time, we have built up a cocoon of "self" through ignorance and self-aggrandizement. Because of this, we perceive whatever we experience to be real and self-existent. This is called "confusion." The nature of existence and our perception of it are two entirely different things. Phenomena are mirage-like, interdependent, and illusory. But we perceive them as tangible and as really existing. On that mistaken basis, attachment, aversion, and a predisposition for neuroses arise. Thus, suffering and its causes will be endless until we can free ourselves from that cocoon. Lord Jigten Sumgön said:

> The talented son of a barren woman
> climbs a ladder made of rabbit horn and
> swallows the sky's sun and moon—
> thus [with such delusions], the six realms wander in an ocean
>   of darkness.
> This is how ego-clinging functions.

Two types of "self-existence" are taught—that of the person and that of phenomena. When investigating the existence of the person, we analyze whether this exists within one's body, in one's name, or in the mind. The body is not one unit; it is a composite of many parts. Pursuing this investigation, we can therefore conclude that the body is not the self. It is more like a scarecrow, appearing to be a man but actually just straw-stuffed clothing.

A name is also not the self because one's name is merely a temporary label. If someone disparages our name or praises our reputation, we have a corresponding reaction of like or dislike as if our self existed in that name. But we can change our name many times. Thus, we can see that no self exists there, either.

Given that this is the case, one may think that the self must exist within the mind. But we cannot perceive the mind either inside or outside our body, so how can we say that the self exists in the mind? By means of this analysis as well, we cannot find a self. Logically "proving" that the self does not exist is not enough, however. We must use analysis to understand the true nature of all phenomena in order to uproot our habit of grasping at a self. We need to practice this again and again. Once we are theoretically convinced and have experienced that the self does not exist, we can be freed from that grasping. Only by dispelling our delusions about reality can we be freed from suffering.

The mistaken notion of a self is like a turtle's hair. Someone may tell you that turtle hair is smooth, soft, warm, and of very light weight and that, because of these qualities, cloth made from turtle hair is very expensive. People who don't know that a turtle actually has no hair may believe these tales and want to buy some. They will then waste their time looking here and there for turtle hair and asking people where to get it. But if someone knows that a turtle has no hair, they will neither yearn to own a sweater made of turtle hair, nor hate turtle hair because they can't find it. Attachment and aversion will have no basis at all on which to arise. In the same way, when we possess the wisdom to understand that the "self" is a fiction, attachments and aversions naturally drop away just as the trunk, branches, and leaves of a giant tree will dry up by themselves if we cut the tree at its root.

Compared to a table, a stick is short. But that same stick may be long when compared to a pen. You may say that the table is long, but when compared to the length of a room it is short. And that formerly short pen is no longer short when compared to a toothpick. The pen does not inherently exist as "long" or "short." All these things are relative. This is the meaning of emptiness, and this is why phenomena are described as being like a mirage or rainbow— very precise and vivid but nonexistent in the way that we perceive them. All objects are empty in this way. If we can deeply apply this understanding, all delusions and defilements will subside and vanish within emptiness.

The most important function of these meditations is to release our attachment to a self. But this does not mean that labels or concepts have no purpose. Everything has a label according to relative truth. Even the Buddha, who fully realized and explained selflessness, communicated with us by using labels such as "samsara" and "nirvana." But merely having a name and being able to perform a function do not mean that an object exists independently or substantially. It is important not to fall into either extreme of being an eternalist or a nihilist.

The first five perfections are collectively called the "method" by which we can bring about happiness and create positive karma. A precious human life allows us to study and practice the vast and profound Dharma. In order to obtain a precious human life, the practice of moral ethics is indispensable. Generosity then creates the conditions to support our study and practice, including food and shelter. Patience results in good health, a long life, and good friends. Without perseverance, nothing at all can be achieved. And calm-abiding prepares the ground for the achievement of further good qualities. However, these five by themselves are insufficient to free us from samsara. Wisdom, the sixth perfection, is essential. Wisdom and method work hand in hand; they cannot be separated. The five perfections comprising method bring us strength of mind, courage, stability, and clarity, and these allow the critical insight of wisdom to fully penetrate the confusion of samsara. Then, confusion can no longer obstruct our view of reality. When method and wisdom are realized as nondual, the three trainings are naturally and inseparably present in one state of mind.

No matter what success we may feel we have achieved in samsara, there will be no end to our suffering. Therefore, it is critically important to understand how these teachings are practiced and take them into our heart. In order to free ourselves from samsara through the support of method and wisdom, it is crucial to realize the inseparable nature of relative truth and absolute truth. We should fully dedicate the rest of our lives to this pursuit. Gampopa's text *The Jewel Ornament of Liberation* contains further teachings and explanations of this practice, so please study that book in detail.

Up to this point, Bhande Dharmaradza's text has presented the study and practice according to the sutra system, which is the foundation for all further practices. Once we have established our mind in bodhicitta and an understanding of emptiness, we will have a solid basis for the study and practice of Vajrayana.

Advice for Vajrayana Practitioners

51 *The supreme vajra vehicle is like the lord of elephants.*
   In an instant, without difficulty, it brings complete enlighten-
      ment.
   It is the essence of the teachings.
   This is my heart's advice.

WITH THIS verse, the author begins his comments on the
Vajrayana teachings. Vajrayana practice is likened here to *the
lord* or leader *of elephants*. Carefully and without mistake, such an
elephant gathers his herd together and leads it to the best grass and
water. The elephants in the herd are a metaphor for the Dharma that
we have already studied and practiced according to the sutra system.
When these teachings are used together with Vajrayana methods,
one can quickly achieve enlightenment. The practices of Vajrayana,
or tantra, are entered by receiving an empowerment, or *abhisheka*.
If a meditation practice requires an empowerment, it is classified as
a tantric practice. If an empowerment ceremony is not required, the
practice is classified as sutra.

The ultimate goal, enlightenment, is the same in both sutra and
tantra. In both systems, considerable obstacles and adverse conditions must be met with indefatigable courage. However, the
Vajrayana offers many advanced methods and skills with which
to attain buddhahood more easily and quickly. There are accounts
of bodhisattvas such as Sadaprarudita, who attained the eighth or
tenth bhumi in one lifetime by practicing according to sutra. But
most masters say that it takes a long time—three limitless kalpas
or more—to attain buddhahood through the sutra system. In the

Vajrayana, one can attain enlightenment in one lifetime, or at most in seven or sixteen lifetimes.

Traditionally, one must endure many hardships on the bodhisattva path, such as nonattachment to one's own body while still immersed in ordinary perceptions. Using the methods of Vajrayana, our ordinary body transforms into the "body" of an enlightened deity whose nature is inseparable appearance and emptiness. This allows us to perfect the practice of freeing ourselves from attachment to the ordinary body without having to actually give parts of it to others.

The sutra system includes practices of fasting and arduous physical hardship. In the Vajrayana system, food and drink are used as a *ganachakra,* or an offering to the deities. Here, we are not attached to food and drink for our own enjoyment alone; rather, we use it as an offering. When one perceives all others as enlightened deities, one develops a mind free from attachment and hatred. In this practice of transformation, self-grasping and fixation become fully purified. Vajrayana, therefore, is called the "fruition" vehicle, because in Vajrayana one repeatedly practices manifesting in the form of an enlightened deity, which itself is the ultimate goal, or fruit, to be achieved. In contrast, the sutra system is called the "causal" vehicle, because in that system one practices in the ordinary state to create the causes to attain buddhahood.

All buddhas of the past, present, and future have attained and will attain buddhahood through the Vajrayana path. For one with indomitable courage, great skill, and supreme capacity to comprehend the Vajrayana methods, the result can be achieved completely in a short period of time. Thus, the Vajrayana is called the supreme vehicle.

In tantra, the term "vajra" is often used—as in Vajrayana, vajra master, vajra disciple, vajra hell, vajra samaya, vajra seed, and vajra vase, for example. In all cases, "vajra" refers to emptiness, which pervades beginningless time and cannot be destroyed. Even if one is completely bewildered by delusion, still, that nature is present. As soon as one glimpses this timeless truth, all confusion is demolished. Therefore, Vajrayana is said to be the supreme method that captures primordial awareness.

Tantra is most commonly classified into four types:

- *kriya tantra*, which emphasizes physical cleanliness and purification while internally maintaining a deity yoga practice in which the yidam is viewed as being far superior to oneself
- *carya tantra*, which emphasizes verbal discipline and chanting while mentally maintaining a deity yoga practice in which the yidam is viewed as being like a close friend
- *yoga tantra*, which emphasizes mental discipline and uniting oneself with the deity
- *anuttara yoga tantra*, or highest yoga tantra, in which everything is transformed into the enlightened state through the practices of *chakras*, *prana*, and so forth using the arising and completion stages

Each method can be said to mature its practitioners according to their own needs and capabilities. For example, kriya tantra is useful for those who are more concerned with external appearances and ritual. Carya tantra shares characteristics with kriya and yoga tantras and is most effective for practitioners with an interest in both external and internal processes. Some who are unconcerned with external appearances are intent on internal yogic development, and for them the yoga tantras are taught. Highest yoga tantra is taught for those who are capable of meditating in a state where method and wisdom are indistinguishable.

Earlier, in the commentary to verse 33, there was a description of the general, or outer, nature of refuge—the Buddha, Dharma and Sangha. Here, it is good to have some understanding of Vajrayana, or inner, refuge. Root and lineage teachers, or lamas, are perceived as buddhas. Yidam deities are seen as Dharma. Dakinis and Dharma protectors are known as sangha. When we say the refuge prayers according to the Vajrayana system, we visualize the refuge field in this way:

> I and all sentient beings take refuge in the root and lineage lamas.
> We take refuge in the mandala of the yidams.
> We take refuge in all the exalted buddhas.
> We take refuge in the sublime Dharma.

We take refuge in the assembly of the supreme sangha.
We take refuge in all the dakas, dakinis, and Dharma
protectors who possess the wisdom eye.

Repeat this prayer as many times as you like. When you dissolve
the visualized images into yourself, you receive all their blessings.

The root lama is like a wish-fulfilling jewel
He is the source of all good qualities.
Therefore, attend him with flawless respect.
This is my heart's advice.

THE QUALITIES of a spiritual master have already been described on page 70 and in verse 27. It is important to have a good understanding of this subject. It is explained again here because we must have an authentic spiritual master in order to gain success in study and meditation practice. Although the help of a spiritual master is important at all levels of Dharma practice, it becomes essential in Vajrayana.

The root lama is like a wish-fulfilling jewel, one of the most prized possessions in all the world. Such a jewel is the pinnacle of wealth, very rare and precious. In legends, merchants traveled the oceans for months in search of this great jewel, and when they found one, they used it to obtain whatever they wished for. In the same way, the root lama, or Vajrayana teacher, is our source for the precious teachings, the good qualities of a buddha, and enlightenment itself. The root master represents the Buddha and holds the knowledge and experience of the lineage.

Thus, in order to study and practice Vajrayana, it is crucial to find a proper master. One who has received the proper empowerments, who understands the different systems of tantra and has experienced the meaning of Dharma through meditation practice, who is skilled in the practice of a deity's mandala, who possesses the realization of the arising and completion stages and can introduce this wisdom to others during an empowerment, who is well trained and trustworthy, who possesses discriminating wisdom, and who is indefatigable and sincere—this is a qualified root lama. His or her activities are done solely for others' benefit and never out of concern for honor or wealth. He or she shows the path of fearlessness to trainees and always follows the supreme vehicle, the Mahayana. Among the qualified masters, a fully ordained lama is supreme, a novice monk or nun lama is second best, and third is a lay-practitioner lama.

It is imperative to have a vajra master because this matter of freeing ourselves from samsara is very serious. For example, in order to learn when one attends school, the teacher must be educated, articulate, patient, and skilled in the relevant subject matter. At the same time, the student must be disciplined, attentive, and interested in study. When these things come together, a student gets a good education. Likewise, in order to free ourselves from samsara, we need even greater dedication and application. Attaining freedom from samsara is not an easy task, especially for ordinary people like us who see things from a dualistic point of view and cannot perceive the sublime qualities of enlightened beings. We must apply great effort to purify our negative habits. Unless both the teacher and disciple have good qualities, good results will not manifest no matter how much effort is made. It would be like trying to squeeze cooking oil from sand.

If we perceive the lama as the dharmakaya, this becomes a cause to attain the dharmakaya. If we perceive him or her as the sambhogakaya, one will accomplish the meaning of Dharma. If we perceived the lama as the nirmanakaya, the relationship will be a cause to benefit many sentient beings. But if we perceive the lama only as an ordinary person, we will not achieve any good qualities. Therefore, we must meditate on the lama as the dharmakaya, the nature of primordial wisdom. This is the embodiment of the body, speech, and mind of the buddhas of the three times, and is coemergent, self-arising, and beyond conceptual thought or verbal expression. Perceiving the lama in this way, make offerings of everything that exists, including your own body, speech, and mind, with no expectation of return. Gather the two great accumulations of merit and wisdom in order to accomplish the perfection of buddhahood.

Attending spiritual masters in this way brings limitless benefits. One will not be affected by worldly defilements or by obstacles created by humans and non-human beings. The three types of obscuration will be purified. Meditation and realization will steadily increase. After death, one will not be reborn in the three lower realms, and one will meet authentic spiritual masters in the future. Finally, one will accomplish the ordinary and supreme attainments.

Faultless devotion is like a well-plowed field.
It is the basis of all virtuous Dharma and prosperity.
Supplicate respectfully.
This is my heart's advice.

IN ORDER to have a good harvest, a farmer must prepare a *well-plowed field* by removing all its rocks, plowing it, and fertilizing it well. Then, when he plants the seed, it will grow without hindrance. Similarly, when the rocks of ego are removed, arrogance will no longer harden the soil of our mind. *Faultless devotion* is the fertile ground in which the qualities of buddhahood can grow. When we have devotion for the Dharma and our teacher, we cultivate our mind all the more in order to free ourselves from samsara, and thus we achieve excellent qualities. This is a skillful method to link our unenlightened mind with the enlightened mind of the Buddha and to gradually attain buddhahood.

Devotion is not just a tradition tied to a particular culture, nor is it blind faith or emotional attachment. Rather, it is a method to open our mind to the precious Dharma and to allow wisdom and bodhicitta to fully establish themselves in our mind-stream. Some may feel that practicing devotion means surrendering their autonomy and freedom to a master, leaving them with nothing. But if the master has the good qualities described earlier, and is guided by bodhicitta, one can only benefit. On the other hand, if the disciple is selfish and arrogant, or swaggers with self-importance, he or she will lose all opportunity to be free. No matter how much a master tries to help such students, those attempts will come to no result.

There is a saying: "Do not treat the master as a deer or an oyster, or the teachings as deer-musk or a pearl." In such a case, you would simply hunt the deer or oyster and appropriate their valuables without any regard for their welfare. Instead, treat the master like a medicine tree or a light bulb. Protect and care for the tree in order for it to grow good fruit for a long time. Handle the fragile light bulb carefully in order to keep its light shining.

In order to receive Dharma fully and, especially, to integrate the meaning of the teachings into one's heart, it is very important to have faultless devotion for those teachings and for the master who teaches them. The purpose of all our study and practice, as was described before, is to free ourselves from samsara and attain complete enlightenment. Upon reflection, we can see that samsara is like a prison, and even if a prison is comfortable the prisoner still has no freedom and his status is uncertain. Because of this, a prisoner will always think of escape. It is the same with samsara—suffering is always near and the future is always uncertain. No matter how "successful" we may be in our lives, when we see the real nature of samsara, we will be inspired to follow the Dharma. It is the only door leading out of the prison of samsara.

To *supplicate respectfully* means to ask for teachings and to meditate on the lama. The more we practice, the more we appreciate the teachings we have received. They become like a nectar that transforms all our negative thoughts and suffering. Acting respectfully toward one's teacher is not just a cultural tradition but rather is something that comes from the heart. If the teachings are important to us, we cherish and care for both them and the teacher. When a person is hungry, he will desperately look for food and will eat with full attention when he finally finds it. In the same way, if you see samsara as suffering and know that Dharma is the only method to free yourself from it, then you will pursue Dharma unremittingly.

In the Vajrayana, one's experience and realization of the teachings depend entirely on devotion. We can see this clearly in Milarepa's life story. Lord Jigten Sumgön also demonstrated the importance of devotion when he said:

> I, a yogin, realized the unity
> of the lama, my own mind, and the Buddha.
> I have no need of contrived devotion.
> In non-effort I, the yogin, am happy.
> This happy yogin experiences joy.
> This experience of joy is the lama's kindness.

Now, take a moment to sit in the proper posture and generate bodhicitta. Visualize the master as the primordial buddha, Vajradhara: the complete form of perfection who embodies the dharmakaya, sambhogakaya, nirmanakaya, and svabhavikakaya of all buddhas. With deep, yearning devotion, supplicate from the bottom of your heart with tears in your eyes and recite the following mantra:

OM AH VAJRA DRIK MULA GURU MAHAMUDRA
SIDDHI PHALA HUNG

Then receive the blessings and enlightened qualities through the power of this devotion. From Vajradhara's forehead, the nature of the wisdom body enters your forehead as white light and purifies your physical obscurations. From his throat, the nature of wisdom speech emerges as red light and enters through your throat, purifying your verbal obscurations. From his heart, the nature of enlightened mind emerges as blue and enters your heart to purify your mental obscurations. From his navel, the unified nature of Vajradhara's body, speech, and mind emerges as yellow light. This is received at your navel, and pervades your own body, speech, and mind, purifying the subtle obscurations to omniscience. Because of your one-pointed devotion, Vajradhara dissolves into blue light. That light dissolves into you through the top of your head and pervades your whole body and being. Thus, you are transformed into the nature of Vajradhara, inseparable appearance and emptiness, insubstantial and unfabricated. Set your mind in equipoise and rest in that natural state for some time.

One can do this meditation again and again. This is one of the most powerful and effective methods to unify your own mind with the enlightened mind of the Buddha. At the end, say prayers of dedication.

The lama's teachings are like a healing medicine.
His beneficial words are spoken for your sake.
Therefore, practice according to his instructions.
This is my heart's advice.

OUR BODY is composed of the five elements: earth, water, fire, air, and space. When these five are balanced, our body is healthy. If there is an imbalance or disorder among the elements, we get sick. Then, we consult a doctor who is familiar with the various kinds of medicine, and take the medicine that is best suited to our illness. We do this freely, with an open mind and with high expectations of recovery. Here, in samsara, we are sick with the endless suffering caused by delusion and confusion. *The lama's teachings* "cure" those mental afflictions just as a *healing medicine* cures an ordinary sickness.

In samsara, one's mind is characterized by ignorance, attachment, and aversion. Many confused and deluded thoughts manifest endlessly as a result. We then make mistakes and create various types of karma, from which different types of suffering arise. Only the lama's teachings are effective in healing these mental wounds. At the level of sutra, the lama teaches the four common foundations, the three trainings, the two types of bodhicitta, and the practice of the six perfections. In the Vajrayana, he or she teaches the two practices of arising and completion. All the teachings of Dharma concern how to abandon nonvirtue, which is the cause of suffering, and how to increase virtue, which is the cause of temporary and definite peace and happiness. All that is spoken by a lama is therefore spoken solely to heal the confused mind of trainees. Therefore, fully accept those lessons and apply them in your life. Let them heal and transform your mind.

The lama represents the Buddha as his regent. We don't have the good fortune to see the face of the Buddha or to receive his teachings directly, but we are fortunate enough to follow the unbroken lineage of the Buddha carried by a qualified lama. The words of an authentic lama are precious because they are the words of the Buddha himself, come down to us through the blessings of the lineage. A lama who possesses bodhicitta gives teachings to his or her disciples sincerely, and not out of any selfish concern. These teachings are taught only for our sake and for the sake of all sentient beings. If we receive these teachings with an open heart and mind, we will have every opportunity to become like those who have already attained enlightenment. Therefore, with courage and determination, and the understanding that the teachings are for your own benefit, receive that teaching fully and practice it without compromise.

When we receive these precious teachings, we should be free from the three faults. First, if we try to pour tea into a cup that is upside down, not one drop will enter the cup. Second, if there is a hole in the bottom of the cup, all the tea will leak through. Third, if the cup contains poison, the tea will be spoiled. In the same way, if our body is physically present at teachings, but our mind wanders or sinks into sleep, we won't receive a word of Dharma. If we cannot keep the teachings in our heart, all the Dharma we have heard will be easily forgotten. Finally, if we receive Dharma teachings with an improper motivation, such as to become famous or rich or to compete with others out of jealousy or pride, Dharma's purpose is not fulfilled and may even be misused.

Therefore, we should have the proper motivation and receive Dharma teachings with our full attention. We should perceive the spiritual teacher as a kind physician, ourselves as patients, and the Dharma as medicine. When we receive teachings, it is like taking the medicine that heals the chronic disease of mental affliction. In this way, we will have every opportunity to attain enlightenment. Therefore, we should make every effort to purify all obscurations without exception and to actualize every excellent quality of the buddhas and bodhisattvas.

Take a moment to breathe deeply. Visualize Lord Kyobpa Jigten Sumgön as an embodiment of all the buddhas' wisdom, compassion, and excellent qualities and chant his mantra:

OM RATNA SHRI HUNG

Repeat the mantra as many times as you like. While reciting, light radiates from him and pervades all sentient beings, including yourself. This light dispels all mental confusion and obscuration. When you are finished, visualize that you receive the four empowerments (see verse 57). Finally, Lord Kyobpa Jigten Sumgön melts into light, which dissolves into you. Rest in the state of Mahamudra. At the end, say dedication prayers.

Making offerings of the three ways of pleasing is like polishing
   a jewel.
   It brings the rainfall of the supreme and common attainments.
   The lama is the embodiment of all objects of refuge.
   This is my heart's advice.

As THE VERSE above states, we should please an authentic, qualified spiritual master in three ways. *The three ways of pleasing* consist of the following:

1. Offering material things as part of our training in generosity. This helps us to accumulate great merit and allows us to build confidence in that master by relating to him over time. This should be done with pure motivation and sincerity free from deceit. Only make offerings that have been obtained through right livelihood, and offer whatever is needed without hesitation. This purifies our stinginess and clinging.

2. Engaging in the practice of service to further develop our devotion and faith. Without devotion, we cannot receive or experience the Dharma in our being, just as the moon cannot be reflected when there is no pool of water and as crops cannot grow without fertilized ground. With full confidence in the lama, attend him and provide various services. Always be mindful of your physical and verbal behavior in the presence of the lama. This is one of the most effective and important ways to release our tenacious habitual tendencies. Continually think, "May I be of good service to the lama with my body, speech, and mind." This purifies arrogance and pride.

3. Perceiving the lama as a buddha and wholeheartedly studying and practicing the Dharma to develop our own mind. A qualified lama always thinks of what is best for sentient beings and wishes them to experience every peace and happiness, be free from all types of suffering and undesirable conditions,

and attain the complete enlightenment of a buddha. Practicing Dharma fulfills the lama's deepest wish for us, so this is what will please him or her the most. Sincere practice will please the lama more than if you offered enough wish-granting jewels to fill the whole universe.

Pleasing the lama in these ways has great benefits. It is a critical method we can use to purify obscurations, be free from downfalls, and increase our experience with meditation practice. By practicing this way, we will not be reborn in the lower realms. Additionally, these practices will create the connection that allows us to meet great spiritual masters again in our next life. Finally, we will attain the common and uncommon attainments and will please all the buddhas.

Polishing a jewel has the same meaning that was explained in verse 34. Though a jewel has the power to grant wishes, it cannot do this if stained. Thus, when we find a wish-granting jewel, we have to polish it carefully. Then it can grant the wishes of all the people in the region. In the same way, pleasing a qualified master in the three ways polishes one's stained mind-jewel. This should be the motivation of those individuals who want to attain buddhahood without facing obstacles.

When we find a well-qualified spiritual master, we need to discard the habits of attachment and display courage and determination. We should view that master as the actual Buddha and attend him or her regardless of hardship. Without regard for our own suffering, food, clothes, or shelter, we should practice patience. We should take complete responsibility onto ourselves to understand the Dharma and to gain realization.

It is also important not to be satisfied with just a small understanding of the Dharma. One must attend the spiritual master for a long time. One must train repeatedly through study, meditation practice, purification, and the gathering of the two great accumulations. If we should perceive faults in the spiritual master's behavior, we should immediately think, "This is the fault of my own impure mind and perception. This great teacher is performing actions according to the needs of sentient beings." In this way, we should see the lama as being equal to the Buddha. We are not making the lama *into* a buddha, but this is how to receive the blessings of the Buddha *through* the lama. We can use all these methods to reveal our own enlightenment and to allow our own compassion, wisdom, power, and activities to manifest.

There are two types of *siddhis,* or *attainments.* The common types of siddhis are supernatural powers such as clairvoyance, levitation, telepathy, and so forth. These can be achieved by both enlightened and unenlightened beings through samadhi meditation. Although these powers can be impressive, they do not solve our underlying problems. Uncommon siddhis consist of special insight, the dispelling of obscurations, and revelation of the pristine nature of mind. Supported by these realizations and by bodhicitta practice, we follow the path and finally achieve buddhahood, the highest attainment or siddhi of all.

Embodiment of all the refuges refers to the authentic spiritual master who possesses all the great qualities and completely embodies and represents the objects of refuge:

- ▸ The lama's enlightened mind is the buddha; the lama's speech, which transmits the teachings, is the Dharma; the lama's body is the sangha. These are the outer refuges.
- ▸ The lama's mind is the buddha Vajradhara; the lama's speech is the yidam; the lama's body is the dakini or the Dharma protector, inseparable appearance and emptiness. These three are the inner refuges.
- ▸ The lama's mind is dharmakaya, his speech is sambhogakaya, and his body is nirmanakaya. The inseparability of these three is svabhavikakaya. This is the refuge of the four kayas.

Thus, the lama is the embodiment of all refuges. When we have this understanding, experience, and pure view, we will receive all the blessings without exception.

The samaya of the lama is like one's consciousness and life.
Abandoning it creates a corpse that cannot be revived.
One cannot do without it.
This is my heart's advice.

SAMAYA is a Sanskrit word meaning "pledge." In Tibetan, the term is *damtsig*, a combination of the words *dampa* and *tsig*. *Dampa* literally means holy, pure, or noble, and figuratively refers to the Buddha—the most holy, pure, and noble being—and his representative, the authentic spiritual master who holds the Buddha's lineage. *Tsig* means "word," the speech of the Buddha, and encompasses all the Dharma teachings that the Buddha taught and that are clearly explained by the spiritual master.

Keeping the samaya requires maintaining a pure view of the spiritual master; applying all of our activity, study, and practice without reservation toward whatever he or she teaches; and, especially, purely maintaining an enlightened state of mind. It means to thoroughly tame our mind by avoiding all nonvirtue whatsoever; to engage in every possible virtuous action; and generally to give up our samsaric habits. No matter what Vajrayana empowerment or teaching may be given, this is the essential point. More specifically, though, samaya is the commitment we make when receiving an empowerment. At that time, we pledge to recite a deity's mantra and to practice the related meditation. And since we receive these teachings and empowerments from a lama, that commitment is called the *samaya of the lama.*

Without *consciousness and life,* we would be dead, a corpse without life, energy, or the ability to accomplish anything. Now, because our life and consciousness are connected, we can distinguish feelings of happiness, peace, suffering, and sadness. We can therefore act to abandon the causes of suffering and create the causes of happiness. In the same way, the samaya of an authentic lama is essential to our spiritual life. So long as our connection with the lama is intact, our mind is fully linked with the Dharma. Samaya is the bridge between the darkness of samsara and the brilliance of enlightenment.

Properly keeping samaya means that we unwaveringly maintain our connection with the lineage and the teachings of the Buddha no matter what obstacles or impediments we may encounter. If we abandon samaya because our afflicting emotions are too powerful, our connection with the spiritual master and the precious Dharma will be severed. Only a spiritual corpse then remains, and for as long as we remain in that state, there is no hope of restoring our spiritual qualities. There would be no way at all to free ourselves from samsara. How would it be possible for us to experience the meaning of the holy Dharma?

Since we now have some insight into the pure teachings, we must make every effort not to give up Dharma even at the risk of our lives. No matter what happens, we should always maintain our connection with the Buddha, Dharma, and Sangha and with a qualified, authentic lama. One cannot practice Dharma without them. Understanding how important samaya and the lama are, be very careful about investigating the qualities of the lama, as described in verse 27. Don't rely on first impressions.

Some people misunderstand this point, and think that by accepting and keeping samaya they become trapped. They worry that their commitment will not allow them to freely roam about and do anything they like. On the contrary: accepting and fully keeping samaya means that our heart is more widely opened so that we can see the true nature of samsara and nirvana.

Samsara is like a pit of fire. As long as we remain in that pit, we cannot hope for peace or joy; we can only experience the fire. Dharma is the only tool we can use to free ourselves. Therefore, keeping samaya means holding our body, speech, and mind in the sphere of Dharma. Why? Because nonvirtue is the cause of the suffering that we seek to avoid. Keeping samaya, therefore, means expanding our virtues, because these are the source of all peace and harmony. Whether we are in a palace or a fire pit, we must continually watch our mind and thereby keep our samaya at all times. On the other hand, if we disregard samaya, thinking of it as a trap, our mind will be left open to nonvirtue. Confusion and suffering are the real traps. Because of this, always think of the kindness of the spiritual master and the purity of the Dharma and recall that they are indispensable to freedom from suffering.

By purely observing samaya, one experiences both temporary and ultimate joy and happiness. Dakinis will dispel obstacles and support us in whatever we want to do, and all the prosperity of this life will arise. Conventional and absolute results will manifest just as we have wished. Conditions in our future lives will progressively improve. But if we cannot keep samaya purely, we will be reborn in lower realms and will not accomplish what we had hoped to achieve in this life. Moreover, we will encounter one or all of the eight fears. Whatever merit we may have accumulated will decrease. And even if we try to accomplish the attainments, we will not succeed. Therefore, make every effort to keep samaya.

The ripening four empowerments are like a stream of nectar.
They purify the four obscurations and plant the seeds of the
*   four kayas.*
They are the root of the path of mantra.
This is my heart's advice.

THE RITUAL of empowerment, or *abhisheka*, is an effective method
to purify obscurations. In this ritual, one has the opportunity to
experience wisdom awareness. Even though the view of emptiness
is the same in both sutra and tantra, tantra has many techniques
that enable one to realize that view without great hardship. But
practitioners still need courage, precision of mind, and skill to comprehend these teachings. The empowerment ceremony itself distinguishes a Vajrayana or tantric practice from sutra-style practice. If
an empowerment is required, the practice is Vajrayana; if not, it is
a sutra-style practice. It is said that through the practice of alchemy
hundreds of base metals can be transformed into gold. In the same
way, through abhisheka, one's base and confused mind can be transformed into the golden, pure, transcendent mind of enlightenment.

In the Vajrayana, the deluded mind is said to be raw or unripened.
We can't eat unripe fruit. Similarly, our unruly, unripened mind is
not amenable to gathering the causes of virtue and the enlightened
qualities. But, when the mind is ripened by bodhicitta and the Buddha's wisdom, it becomes fully workable. The empowerment ceremony is the process by which one is *ripened*, meaning that one's
inherent enlightened qualities are revealed. In order to perfect those
qualities, one is introduced to the arising, or generation, stage and
the completion stage of meditation. This method of ripening and
liberating is the pinnacle of all the sublime methods of Dharma. If
one is sufficiently fortunate, the empowerment ceremony washes
away the dirt of obscurations and reveals the full, pristine luminosity of mind.

Each of the four classes of tantra has its own type of empowerment ceremony. The *four empowerments* referred to in this verse belong to the class of anuttara tantra. They purify the *four obscurations*, and help us to eventually actualize the *four kayas* and the five wisdoms. These steps are the basic elements of the tantric path, *the root of the path of mantra.* Without these skillful methods, we would have no authority to practice Vajrayana, so we should cherish them and practice as instructed. The four empowerments are the vase, secret, wisdom, and precious word, or "fourth," empowerment. The four obscurations to be purified are the physical, verbal, mental, and subtle obscurations. The four kayas to be achieved are the nirmanakaya, sambhogakaya, dharmakaya, and svabhavikakaya. The five wisdoms to be actualized are the all-pervading elemental wisdom, mirror-like wisdom, equanimity wisdom, discriminating wisdom, and all-accomplishing activity wisdom.

The vase empowerment. There are four types of mandala: sand, drawing on cloth or paper, aggregated, and mentally visualized. Depending on the mandala that has been created, one receives the vase empowerment by means of nectar, crown, vajra and bell, name, or vajra master. Through this ceremony, all obscurations of impure vision, the five aggregates (*skandha*), eighteen elements (*dhatu*), and twelve sense-sources (*ayatana*) are purified, and we are presented with the opportunity to see inseparable appearance and emptiness in a deity's form. Here is where the five wisdoms are introduced as the true nature of the five afflicting emotions. Our conventional conception of ourselves as substantial forms of flesh and bone is a source of suffering. If, as a result of the empowerment ceremony, we can clearly perceive ourselves in an insubstantial form, like a rainbow, we can transform our physical body into an enlightened form. In other words, we transform ourselves into an enlightened deity or buddha, and by attaining the state of a deity, we plant the seed to achieve the nirmanakaya.

The secret empowerment. By means of the nectar received on our tongues during this empowerment, we are established in the nature of the *ali* and *kali.* Our impure speech is fully purified, and we purify the obscurations caused by speech. All the chakras and channels are actualized as nothing other than the enlightened state. In meditation, we are introduced to the nonduality of bliss and emptiness, and our ceaseless chatter and negative words are transformed into a buddha's speech. By thus purifying our verbal obscurations, we plant the seed to achieve the sambhogakaya.

The wisdom empowerment. Receiving this ceremonial nectar introduces us to the nature of our mind as primordial awareness and purifies our mental obscurations. All our delusions are transformed into pristine wisdom, and our mind is experienced as limitless. By thus purifying our mental obscurations, we plant the seed to achieve the dharmakaya.

The precious word, or fourth, empowerment. The ultimate, primordial citadel of pristine awareness is introduced by the word empowerment. Here, we receive instructions on the nature of ultimate peace, the unborn nature of selfless phenomena. We see that all existence is beyond the concepts of existence and nonexistence and thus release our fixation on the aggregates, elements, and sense-sources. During this empowerment ceremony, we are introduced to the nature of mind, and we gain every opportunity to realize Mahamudra. By receiving this empowerment, we purify the subtle obscurations to enlightenment and plant the seed to achieve the svabhavikakaya.

Through these four empowerments, we can realize that all the phenomena of samsara and nirvana are of the same nature, the nature free from all boundaries. When this experience is fully stabilized, one is fully liberated.

The reference in this verse to *a stream of nectar* recalls the quality of transformation mentioned earlier. Nectar, *amrita* in Sanskrit and *dütsi* in Tibetan, is that which transforms poison into nectar or medicine. In alchemy, base metals are transformed into gold, and in tantra our mind is transformed into the gold of enlightenment through the empowerment ceremony. When this stream of nectar is poured into us during the ceremony, we should meditate that we are transformed into a deity, thereby purifying all our defilements and obscurations. In this way, our whole being—body, speech, and mind—is transformed into the mandala of the deity. The poison of the obscurations is not literally transformed, however. Instead, this method allows us to realize that the poison itself does not inherently exist. When we fully understand that poison's nonexistence, that itself is real nectar. The empowerment must be reinforced by subsequent meditation practice in order to habituate oneself to the deity state to which one was introduced.

What does it mean to have received an empowerment? If it means just participating in the program, you and a dog sitting next to you could receive the same thing. So merely participating in the ritual is not enough. To have truly received an empowerment means that all details of the ceremony were explained and that we paid attention to everything. At least, we need to have glimpsed or achieved some understanding of each step. Thus, disciples will receive an empowerment at many different levels depending on their capacity to comprehend or experience the quality of enlightenment.

Those who are fully ready can achieve liberation at the time of the ceremony itself. Milarepa is an example of one who gained full realization of the meaning of an empowerment. During the major Chakrasamvara empowerment ceremony, Milarepa's teacher Marpa pointed to the sand mandala as being only a symbol, and instructed his disciples to look at the actual deity mandala which was present there in front of them. Milarepa looked and saw all the details of the mandala's deity and retinue. At that very moment, the yidam Chakrasamvara gave Milarepa the secret name *Mila Shepa Dorje* (Mila Vajra Laughter).

After having received an empowerment from a vajra master, one needs to practice and then to receive the empowerment again and again until realization is perfected. This is called the "path" empowerment. When this path is perfected—that is, when one is inseparable from the deity—this is called the "fruition" empowerment.

Take a moment and relax, following the instructions in the commentary to verse 53. Receive the four empowerments yourself and absorb the experience.

The generation stage is like the enthronement of a king.
Through that, one becomes lord of all samsara and nirvana.
Therefore, abandon ordinary view.
This is my heart's advice.

AFTER RECEIVING an empowerment, we should receive instructions about the *generation stage* from the lama who bestowed it, learn how to follow the steps of the meditation practice, and then practice as instructed in order to accomplish realization. The purpose of practicing this generation stage is to purify our impure vision, our samsaric delusion, and to reveal the form of complete enlightenment.

When the obscurations are seen as nonexistent, we experience primordial luminosity and pristine awareness in a vivid, clear way. The nature of samsara is then purified and the enlightened nature is embraced. We accomplish this by visualizing ourselves as a deity. This is also called "arising as the deity," "manifesting in the deity's form," and "generating oneself as the deity."

The process of generating oneself as a deity is likened here to the *enthronement of a king*. Without an enthronement or investiture, one cannot perform as the leader of a country, regardless of one's qualifications. When one is installed in office, though, one immediately has all the attributes of a king, president, or prime minister. As such, one has the power to rule; the ability to protect the citizens; the responsibility to maintain peace, harmony, and prosperity; and generally the ability to bring benefit to the entire country. In the same way, after receiving an empowerment, one has the authority to practice the generation stage. When we are "enthroned" as Chenrezig or Tara, for example, and we take on their attributes, we can manifest all the qualities and activities of that enlightened being. When we manifest in the unlimited state of enlightenment we purify all our limitations.

However, this will not come merely by receiving the blessings of an empowerment ceremony. We must practice the generation stage;

otherwise, we will not receive the benefit we hope for. We need to sustain this practice until it becomes effortless. It is just like computer training. When you are first trained, you understand how to open files and so forth, but without enough practice you forget it very easily. It takes time to get used to these skills, but if we practice long enough, they become effortless.

When we have accomplished manifesting ourselves as an enlightened deity, the principal figure of a mandala, then all the excellent qualities of the Buddha—loving-kindness, compassion, bodhicitta, enlightened form, all-pervading wisdom, limitless ability, spontaneous activities, and so forth—will be perfectly achieved. All delusions are replaced by insight. In this way, one becomes *lord of all samsara and nirvana. Lord* means leader, one who can bring benefit and help to all sentient beings without exception.

In our *ordinary view*, confused by duality, we perceive things as "good" or "bad" and as a result develop like and dislike. This confusion is the root cause of suffering. We become attached to what we like and feel aversion for what we don't like. With practice of the generation stage, we transcend all this discrimination and establish pure view. But we should understand that we are not making purity out of something naturally impure; rather, we are recognizing our own ultimate nature and that of all sentient beings. In the Vajrayana, *abandoning ordinary view* is crucial to achieving buddhahood. With the support of this kind of meditation, we can transform the darkness of our delusions into the sunshine of the enlightened state and rest the mind in the state of inseparable appearance and emptiness that transcends ignorance. There is no need for arduous hardship— just the ability to understand and maintain this practice. This is such a skillful method!

Not only do we manifest ourselves as an enlightened deity, but we also practice seeing all other sentient beings in the same way. This is possible because every sentient being has buddha nature. There is no difference between the essential nature of a dog, a cat, or an ant. Each has the same buddha nature that we all have. So first practice loving-kindness and compassion in order to abandon hatred, resentment, and negative thoughts. On that basis, practice seeing all beings as enlightened instead of as ordinary. Remain absorbed in that view. This is called tantric practice.

The clarity of appearances is like Indra's bow.
They are unmixed, vivid, complete, and insubstantial.
Abandon grasping at them.
This is my heart's advice.

INDRA'S BOW is a synonym for a rainbow. When a spectacular rainbow appears, its colors are precise, unmixed, vivid, and complete. It seems so real that you might try to touch it or hold on to it. Yet we all know it is insubstantial and can't be grasped. In the same way, when we practice the generation stage of an enlightened deity, all the details of the visualization appear clearly and precisely in the mind. The deity's form is free from bone, flesh, and blood and is like a hologram or a reflection. The deity's throne—including lotus, sun and moon discs—and the ornaments and robes all clearly appear but do not substantially exist.

Call the picture of the deity to your mind in this manner, whether above your crown, in front of you, or as your own form. For example, if you visualize Chenrezig in sambhogakaya form, there are thirteen different attributes, five related to robes and eight related to ornaments. Chenrezig's silk garments consist of a ribbon knotting the hair above his head, a scarf, an upper garment, a belt, and a lower garment. The ornaments include the five-pointed crown on his head, earrings, necklaces, arm bracelets, wrist bracelets, ankle bracelets, and finger rings. Visualize these attributes in detail. In addition, clearly and completely picture his face, body position, and hand gestures.

Recalling that the visualized deity is insubstantial like a rainbow or a reflection is a special antidote to attachment and grasping. In this insubstantial nature, there is nothing to grasp and nothing to hold on to. There is only an appearance. When a rainbow appears, we enjoy looking at it, but we make no effort to hold on to it. Similarly, in deity yoga we use the visualization as an antidote to our attachment to our own body. By visualizing ourselves in this insubstantial state or by meditating on the deity this way, attachment and hatred naturally decline. Repeatedly sustaining this meditation practice provides a great opportunity to calm our mind and to manifest or achieve the enlightened form. This is a special method to actualize the sambhogakaya.

In becoming accustomed to this practice, the mind becomes more subtle and precise. When you arise as the deity, contemplate where that deity form came from. Where has your ordinary form gone? The deity form did not come from anywhere, and your own form has not gone anywhere. You must seriously meditate on these two questions. This practice will free you from the illusion of coming and going, and will cause you to realize the nondual, inseparable nature of appearance and emptiness.

Pure mindfulness is like a rosary of jewels.
It displays its various qualities one by one.
Each of them is needed.
This is my heart's advice.

WHEN WE USE a *rosary of jewels*, each bead is a precious support for our mindfulness. We must count them one by one to make a complete round. If we miss a bead, our practice is incomplete. The meditation of the arising stage is similar to this. Each attribute or quality of the visualized deity is precious, like a jewel. They are all connected to each other like the elements of a rosary, or *mala*. Each should be seen as a reflection in a mirror, or like a reflection of the moon in water.

Each attribute of an enlightened deity contributes an important meaning that helps us understand and actualize the richness of the qualities of a buddha. For example, the lotus seat symbolizes the unafflicted, pure mind unstained by the mud of samsara. The sun disc symbolizes the pristine luminosity of mind that dispels the darkness of confusion. The moon disc symbolizes the completely impartial compassion that cools the heat of suffering. Sitting on such a seat demonstrates that an enlightened being embodies these qualities. A sambhogakaya buddha's knotted hair piled at the crown of the head signifies that he is free from attachment to samsara. Wearing the five-pointed crown signifies the accomplishment of the five wisdoms or the five buddhas. The three necklaces symbolize the actualization of all three forms, or *kayas*, of the Buddha. The two earrings symbolize perfection of the two truths. The jewel ornaments—the bracelets and rings and so forth—symbolize perfection of the six paramitas.

The color of the different deities is also rich in meaning. White signifies that all aversion has entirely dissolved into unafflicted peace. Blue indicates that ignorance has dissolved into all-pervading emptiness. Red symbolizes that desire and attachment have been transcended in the nature of clear wisdom. Yellow symbolizes the perfection of all the qualities of wealth. Dark blue-black symbolizes that hatred has been transcended. Green symbolizes that jealousy has been transformed into activity wisdom.

In this way, each and every attribute and ornament has a necessary and symbolic meaning. We must practice these qualities and eventually actualize them. We are not trying to experience mere emptiness but rather emptiness inseparable from these perfect qualities of a buddha. This is very important: to become a buddha—an enlightened one—we must perfect every quality. So when we arise as a particular deity through meditation, we should focus on achieving these qualities rather than conceptualizing the attributes as being substantial. Reflect on these qualities as you visualize the deity, and practice accordingly with pure mindfulness.

Firm pride is like a hero's jewel.
There is no need to search outside, as it is fully established
*   from the beginning.*
Understand your own true nature.
This is my heart's advice.

A *HERO* is brave and powerful, is free from all fears, and has the ability to protect others while gaining victory on their behalf. Because of his wisdom and compassion, a bodhisattva-hero is victorious in his battle with the afflicting emotions. He can protect himself by abstaining from nonvirtuous actions and at the same time bring benefit to others by showing them the right path. A hero's *jewel* refers to wealth that unquestionably belongs to its owner, the hero—something that no one can take away. The hero has full confidence that he can use this wealth, and his mind is uplifted by the knowledge that he is free from poverty. *Firm pride* refers to vajra pride, based in confidence. Recognizing and sustaining your own true, primordial, unfabricated nature is called vajra pride. When you "become" a deity in meditation, this pride does not arise out of arrogance or attachment. It arises from the wisdom and confidence of being in that state. It is the ultimate mode of abiding.

Through Vajrayana methods and instructions, we can confidently manifest in the form of a yidam deity. We are not merely imagining ourselves to be the yidam. Rather, without ignorance or delusion, we meditate on assuming the deity's form. There is no need to *search outside* ourselves for the deity; we *are* the deity. The outer deities are examples of what we aspire to become, of how we can manifest by dispelling the adventitious defilements. At first, we study their history to learn how they attained buddhahood and how they manifest their activities. This provides us with a clear picture of how we can do the same.

Assuming a deity form is not an artificial invention, but rather is something inherent within us *from the beginning*. Each and every sentient being has buddha nature. It is only a question of whether that nature is revealed. Revealed, one is called a buddha. If we have not revealed it, we remain miserable in samsara. As verse 34 states, "The stain of bad deeds and obscurations is like mud covering a jewel. Even though the alaya is pure, it cannot manifest the qualities." In other words, we already possess all the pure qualities of a buddha; we just need to reveal them through these meditation practices. There is infinite potential within us for growth. For example, we learn the alphabet in kindergarten and then gradually progress up to a Ph.D. But still there is more to know.

Since each sentient being possesses buddha nature, anyone who takes the responsibility to follow this path can reveal the buddha within. For example, the small seed of a great redwood tree contains a complete tree. In the same way, we can "grow" a complete buddha from the seed of buddha nature within us.

Once, when Lord Jigten Sumgön was in retreat, a man became possessed by a spirit that caused him excruciating pain. Inspired merely by hearing Lord Jigten Sumgön's name, the man undertook an arduous trip to see that lord. Because Lord Jigten Sumgön was in retreat, they couldn't meet face to face, so the man sent his request for instructions on how to rid himself of this spirit through an attendant. He was advised to firmly visualize himself in the form of Chenrezig for at least a week. As soon as the man meditated on Chenrezig, the spirit perceived only Chenrezig in his place. The spirit felt that he had lost his prey and searched everywhere, asking, "Where is my man?" Finally the spirit departed and the man was freed from his pain and suffering. Take these instructions to heart and maintain your own mindfulness.

The three qualities required for yidam practice are purity, clarity, and stability, inseparable from bodhicitta. When we practice this method, the body, speech, and mind are all engaged. All our activities become buddha activity. For example, when we arise as the yidam deity, everything we eat and drink becomes an offering. We recognize our body as the body of a buddha, a form free from all nonvirtuous action. Since our body is just a collection of many parts and is of an insubstantial nature, we can become the pure illusory body. Our speech, as enlightened speech, is free from all negative or nonvirtuous qualities and is the expression of wisdom and compassion. Our mind, as the deity's mind, is free from delusion and is clear, luminous, and joyful. That mind is like space—free from boundaries, grasping and fixation. Understand your own true nature as the Buddha's mind, and rest your mind. This will help you to purify your impure vision and realize Mahamudra.

In order to get results from this arising stage, it is essential to follow these instructions. Therefore, rest your mind in the pure state of the deity rather than allowing it to wander in an impure state of delusion. This is also an important method to establish calm abiding meditation. This completes the instruction on the Vajrayana meditation practice of generating yourself as a deity.

Vajra recitation is like a forest fire.
In an instant, it burns the two obscurations and all sickness,
  propensities, and döns.
By means of it, one will quickly accomplish power.
This is my heart's advice.

THIS VERSE BEGINS the section on tantric completion stage practices. There are two types: those with signs and those without signs. Practice "with signs" consists of reciting mantras and performing channel and chakra practices while visualizing yidam deities. Practice "without signs" is the practice of Mahamudra, which follows later in this book.

Vajra recitation is the chanting of a mantra with full mindfulness of being in the deity state. Chanting consists of the sound, breath, and the mantra itself. Since this is a purification practice, if we use the four powers described in the commentary to verse 34, this method will be unrivaled for purification and for establishing ourselves in the enlightened state. This is an especially effective practice that quickly burns the forest of obscurations, negative propensities, and sickness in the same way that a *forest fire* completely consumes all trees, grasses, and brush in its path. It is so effective because we maintain our body, speech, and mind in a pure state: physically manifesting in a deity's form purifies samsaric appearances, reciting the mantra is the Buddha's speech, and the mind is held in the enlightened state.

Reciting a mantra invokes the enlightened energy that transforms all negativity. The deity that we visualize previously cultivated bodhicitta and practiced on the path. Having generated the altruistic thought by saying, "May whoever merely hears my name or sees my form be free from samsara and attain enlightenment," that deity purified all obscurations and attained complete enlightenment; therefore, their mantra bears magnificent and manifold blessings.

Because of this, we too are able to cultivate bodhicitta and manifest as yidam deities.

The *two obscurations* are the afflicting emotions that obscure liberation, and the subtle obscurations to enlightenment. Both can be purified by the recitation of mantras. How? Abiding in the state of a deity itself transforms all our suffering and obscurations. Through the power of remaining in the enlightened state, sicknesses, negative propensities, and demons, or *döns,* are naturally dispelled. Döns are evil spirits, entities that create obstacles and mischief. In particular, they bring negative energies that influence an already confused and deluded mind. When one abides in the deity state and chants mantras with the motivation of bodhicitta, these beings can become Dharma protectors and create a good environment for us.

When the results of practice are described in this way, people sometimes develop high expectations that all their problems will be easily solved. However, when we practice these powerful meditations, it is possible that, as a sign of purification, negative karma may occasionally arise and one will face obstacles of sickness and misfortune. For example, when Lord Jigten Sumgön was nearing the end of a seven-year retreat, negative karma ripened and he contracted leprosy. He thought of all sentient beings and reflected, "I have received such profound and vast teachings. Because of this, even if I now die I will be free from samsara. But then all the sentient beings in samsara will have no protection from their endless suffering." This thought caused him to give rise to unbearable, great compassion. He continued meditating in that state, and this dispelled the remainder of his obscurations. Within a few days, he achieved complete enlightenment.

When such ripenings occur, we need the courage to carry them onto the path as a sign of purification instead of thinking of them as obstacles to our meditation. When we read the life stories of great masters, we see that they went through similar experiences. Instead of viewing their problems as obstacles, they used them as causes for enlightenment. Generally speaking, without suffering one will not be inspired to practice Dharma. When you encounter difficulty in life while practicing Dharma, try to endure it joyfully as a magnificent opportunity for purification. At least, do not use it as an excuse to give up Dharma practice. This would be an absolute obstacle to your practice. There is no greater obstacle than abandoning Dharma.

Since everything is linked through interdependence, we know that a complete set of causes and conditions will easily manifest a result. But if one cause is missing or only partial conditions are present, the result cannot manifest. Therefore, knowing how to visualize is very important when reciting mantras. First, we need to establish bodhicitta as the foundation for our practice. Then, with complete mindfulness, we assume a deity's form and chant the mantra according to the instructions for that deity's practice. But if our mind is unstable, wandering in different directions and not able to sustain purity, clarity and stability, then our chanting becomes like the chattering of a parrot.

With proper practice, the *power* of wisdom, compassion, and purity develop quickly. When the mind becomes clear, pure, and stable, all the excellent qualities of the Buddha will manifest, and we can then perform activities to benefit all sentient beings. Suchness, or the intrinsic nature, of body is the deity's form. Suchness of speech is the chanting of mantras free from the distraction of idle talk and the like. Suchness of mind is samadhi free from mental scattering. If we practice with a scattered mind, we will not achieve the result that we expect. Buddhahood will not arise if we practice in an ordinary state, even if we practiced the six paramitas for many eons. But practicing tantra with pure vision of the enlightened state supported by bodhicitta will cause buddhahood swiftly.

The following is a simple vajra recitation practice for all practitioners. This meditation practice is based on chanting the mantra OM AH HUNG. These three syllables are the essence and the root of all other mantras The white OM has the nature of the wisdom body of the Buddha, the red AH is the wisdom speech of the Buddha, and the blue HUNG is the wisdom mind of the Buddha. There are, in fact, countless buddhas, but to make comprehension easier they are often described as being gathered into five families based on the purification of the five primary mental afflictions:

- ▸ When purified, aversion or hatred is realized in its primordial nature as Buddha Akshobya. Its wisdom is the mirror-like primordial awareness, the perfection of the pure alaya.

- When purified, pride or arrogance is realized in its primordial nature as Buddha Ratnasambhava. Its wisdom is equanimity primordial awareness, the perfection of afflicted consciousness.
- When purified, desire or attachment is realized in its primordial nature as Buddha Amitabha. Its wisdom is discerning primordial awareness, the perfection of the sixth consciousness.
- When purified, jealousy or envy is realized in its primordial nature as Buddha Amoghasiddhi. Its wisdom is all-accomplishing activity primordial awareness, the perfection of the five doors of sense-organ consciousness.
- When purified, ignorance is realized in its primordial nature as Buddha Vairochana. Its wisdom is Dharma-expanse primordial awareness, the perfection of the alaya consciousness.

Each buddha has the same wisdom body, speech, and mind. Therefore, if we practice one, we can accomplish all five. Limitless buddhas can appear as one, and each buddha can manifest into infinite forms. This is like saying that the universe can be contained in a single atom and that one small atom can manifest as the entire universe.

To practice this meditation, relax your mind and manifest the form of a buddha with which you are familiar—Vajrasattva, Chenrezig, or Vajradhara, for example. Visualize yourself precisely in the deity form: inseparable appearance and emptiness. Then visualize a white OM, representing the wisdom body, inside the crown chakra above the level of your eyebrows. Chant the mantra OM AH HUNG for one mala round or more, while white light radiates from the white OM and completely fills your body, purifying all the obscurations and negative karma related to the body, especially ignorance.

OM   AH   HUNG

Next visualize a red AH, representing wisdom speech, at the throat chakra. Chant the mantra as before, while red light radiates and completely fills your body, purifying all the obscurations and negative karma related to speech, especially desire and attachment.

Then visualize a blue HUNG, representing the wisdom mind, at the heart chakra inside your chest. Chant the mantra as before, while blue light radiates and completely pervades your body, purifying all the obscurations and negative karma related to thought, especially hatred and aversion.

Chant the mantra for a fourth round. From all three syllables simultaneously, the three colors of light radiate and fill the universe with compassion and wisdom. First, the lights purify the outer universe and transform it into a pure land. Then the lights touch each and every sentient being, purifying all their defilements and negative karma related to body, speech, and mind and establishing them all in the state of buddhahood. The lights return and dissolve into you.

To end the session, dissolve your visualized buddha-body into the three syllables. The white OM then dissolves into the red AH, and the AH into the blue HUNG. The HUNG then dissolves from the bottom upwards and disappears into all-pervading emptiness. Relax the mind and meditate in that unfabricated state. Finally, dedicate the merit.

This practice, especially the dissolution section, provides very profound preparation for realization at the time of death. As we described in the commentary to verse 18, one experiences many different sensations during the dying process. After the four elements dissolve, the three subtle experiences of white appearance, red increase, and darkness near-attainment occur. Ordinary people without meditation experience go through these three briefly without any awareness—completely unconscious, as in a deep sleep.

On the other hand, meditators who can maintain stable equipoise can recognize each stage as they pass through it. The stage following darkness near-attainment is the experience of luminosity, the original face of the mind, the direct nature of mind free from all boundary. Those with no meditation experience or with no instructions concerning these practices pass through this stage and go on to the bardo state according to their karma and habitual propensities. Those who are highly accomplished in meditation practice can recognize the experience of luminosity as an opportunity to become instantly free from samsara and achieve enlightenment. If practiced repeatedly with mindfulness, this practice of dissolving the white, red, and blue syllables helps enable the practitioner to utilize the dying process as an opportunity to attain realization.

The samaya of secret mantra is like a snake in a length
   of bamboo.
   If one keeps it, it brings complete enlightenment; if one doesn't,
      it is a cause of the hells.
   Therefore, protect it as you would your eyes.
   This is my heart's advice.

KEEPING *the samaya of secret mantra* means avoiding all nonvirtuous thoughts and activities and engaging in virtuous activities, especially those that accomplish good qualities. There are physical, verbal, and mental samayas. Physically, you should maintain your own appearance as the pure form of a deity and the appearance of the outer universe as a pure mandala. Verbally, regard all sounds as mantra, the speech of the Buddha. Regard every sound that is produced without attachment or hatred, as if it were an echo. Mentally, abide in the wisdom and compassion of the Buddha. Liberate into luminosity whatever mental factors arise.

A *length of bamboo* has openings only at the top and bottom; there is no middle door. So a snake held inside the bamboo can only go up or down. It is the same with the samaya of secret mantra. If we keep them, we can go upward and attain enlightenment. But if we break the samayas, we will slide downward to the lower realms.

This much is very clear: if we don't practice these teachings and instead engage in deluded, negative thoughts and activities, the result of those mental formations will lead us to rebirth in a lower realm. Even this very life can become like a hell realm because of our negative thoughts. It is important to always have positive thoughts regardless of the situations we find ourselves in. If we stay in the enlightened state mentally, enlightenment is right there. You don't have to "go" anywhere. That state *is* the enlightenment state. This is very much like the snake caught in a piece of bamboo; there is no in-between place to go. Keep this in mind and take full responsibility to remain in the enlightened state, or at least to familiarize yourself with enlightened qualities. This is the way to use mindfulness to maintain our samaya.

If we correctly practice Dharma—especially these methods of the Vajrayana—we will be close to the enlightened state. But if we display our arrogance and look down on others because we lack pure vision of them, that impure vision itself will create the lower realms for us.

The Vajrayana may be the highest teaching of the Buddha, but it has its foundation in all the other levels of Buddhist teachings. As Vajrayana practitioners, we cannot ignore or look down on the basic meditation practices. First, we must pay attention to the four common foundations, for without them there is no basis for renunciation or transformation. Without the practice of refuge, there would be nothing we could even call "Buddha's teaching" or "Buddhist meditation practice." Avoiding the ten nonvirtues and engaging in the ten virtues support our understanding of karma. Without this, we cannot know what to take up and what to avoid. The pratimoksha vows comprise one of the main causes of a precious human life and are the foundation of all Buddhist practice—the three trainings and so forth. Without a precious human life, one loses all opportunity to study and practice the precious Vajrayana. Bodhicitta is the heart of Mahayana practice. Without our practice of bodhicitta, the Vajrayana methods do not become a cause for enlightenment. The samayas of the five Buddha families help us to recall this important point:

- ▸ Tathagata family: Keep the three vows of abstaining from all nonvirtues, accumulating the excellent qualities of the Buddha, and benefiting sentient beings. Make offerings to the unsurpassable refuge—the Buddha, Dharma and Sangha.
- ▸ Vajra family: Do not abandon the vajra and bell or forsake your spiritual master. Practice wisdom and compassion, and keep the samaya of the five Buddha families.
- ▸ Ratna family: Practice the four types of generosity: giving wealth, fearlessness, Dharma, and loving-kindness.
- ▸ Lotus family: Do not abandon any of the three vehicles. Thoroughly study and always practice the outer vehicle of the Vinaya's moral ethics, the inner vehicle of bodhicitta, and the secret vehicle of Vajrayana.

> ► Karma family: Keep all the vows and engage in the offering and torma practices.

There are 14 root downfalls:

- ► to disparage the vajra master
- ► to transgress the three levels of vows
- ► to be hostile to vajra brothers and sisters
- ► to forsake loving-kindness on behalf of sentient beings
- ► to abandon bodhicitta
- ► to disparage one's own doctrine or that of others
- ► to divulge secrets to the immature
- ► to abuse the five skandhas or aggregates, which are primordially pure
- ► to be prejudiced about phenomena that are, in any case, intrinsically pure
- ► to have love for (i.e., befriend or support) evil beings who harm sentient beings and the Doctrine
- ► to apply conceptualization to the ineffable
- ► to belittle those who have faith
- ► to violate the commitments that have been undertaken
- ► to disparage women, the nature of wisdom

We should carefully study and keep these vows and become vividly aware of them, for what will we do when we fall to the hell realms? Now, before that happens, we have the opportunity to handle samaya wisely. This is a very important instruction. If we are mindful and careful, these teachings are not difficult to follow. Sometimes people think, "I had better not take these vows." That thinking is not the way to become free from suffering. Without taking vows, receiving teachings, and applying them, there is no way to be free from suffering. Sometimes the process is difficult. But if you consistently apply it year after year, you will experience the result— a clear and joyful mind free from afflictions. You will appreciate the path and be inspired to continue to follow it.

The beneficial effects of magnificent blessings are like
a supreme and all-victorious medicine.
Because of them, the afflicting emotions are self-liberated, and it
is not difficult to gain complete enlightenment.
Secret mantra is the supreme, quick path.
This is my heart's advice.

THIS VERSE introduces the beneficial effects of practicing the Vajrayana. When we use a *supreme medicine*, such as the *arura nam-gyel* (Skt.: Haritaki), it heals all types of sickness. With an extremely powerful medicine, though, there is no need to ingest it. Just touching, smelling, or being near to it will effect healing. There was that kind of medicine in Drigung, Tibet.

Lord Jigten Sumgön once asked his closest disciples to display their special miracle powers. One of those disciples instantaneously went to India and brought back some arura. After Lord Jigten Sumgön passed away, that medicine was placed in a stupa with other relics. People who could not be cured by other medicines were advised to circumambulate this stupa because of the medicine it contained. There are many accounts of people who were cured or healed in this way. In the same way, the *magnificent blessings* of Vajrayana practice have extraordinary powers to purify all mental obscurations. If these practices are correctly applied, they can heal our negative thoughts and actions, especially with the practice of the fivefold path of Mahamudra.

Through these magnificent blessings, the afflicting emotions are *self-liberated*. When we know how to look at negative thoughts, they disappear without a trace by themselves. This is the meaning of self-liberation. Sometimes, we are taught to apply an antidote to purify negative thoughts, and other times we are instructed to transform our negative thoughts. With self-liberation, though, we do not suppress afflictions or chase them away. Rather, we look directly at their wisdom nature. When you completely abide in the state of deity meditation and look directly at the face of the deity's thoughts, you find that there is nothing to see, nothing to grasp. This is what is meant by "self-liberated." Like a drawing made on water, thoughts cannot remain. Even while you are drawing, the picture disappears.

For example, when anger arises, look at that anger. Where is it located? It has no special location and it comes from nowhere. It is a negative pattern that arises because of the habits of many lifetimes. In the same way, desire and attachment arise from our negative propensities but have no real source. To purify these habits we need these practices. Instead of being swept away by our negative habits and allowing them to steal our virtue, we need to apply mindfulness to see their true nature. When we have the wisdom to see anger's face, it is self-liberated. Shantideva's text, the *Bodhicaryavatara*, says:

> Afflicting defilements, dispelled by the eye of wisdom:
> where will you go?
> Now where can you dwell and work to destroy me?

Consider a tornado or a tsunami. These are so powerful they can destroy whole villages—but they are just wind, just water. In the same way, negative emotions are so powerful that they can wipe out our peace and harmony in a moment. We can feel completely helpless, as though we were in a hell realm. But when we purge these emotions with mental clarity, stability, and unshakable confidence, they have no place in our mind. They are merely a reflection of the mind. So, *mindfulness* is the key.

These practices contain magnificent blessings, but we must be able to comprehend and appreciate them. To do this, we must construct a good foundation by building experience, confidence, and mental strength by practicing the preliminaries. We must have strong mindfulness, confidence in meditation, a sense of renunciation toward the cause of suffering, and admiration for the Dharma. Then, attainment of complete enlightenment is not difficult. What we need to do is habituate ourselves to practice and become rooted in practice. We have to diligently cultivate the habit of meditation in order to change our samsaric habits. Tantra then becomes a supreme, quick path.

At the beginning, we must establish the four foundations. This is the method to build strength step by step, like a child going through kindergarten and school. The Buddha was so skillful! Many of us would like to receive instructions in Mahamudra or Dzogchen immediately. But our gross minds are so powerful that these instructions would just remain intellectual ideas for us. You might even be able to say, "I know these teachings." But they won't do you any good because the influence of your negative thoughts is so powerful, so real.

When we have gained some experience of the foundations, other teachings become effective and we can become successful practitioners. In this way, it is not difficult to gain enlightenment even in one lifetime. But we have to pave the road in order to progress and we must take all the steps without falling back. Even if we take only one or two steps—we still did that much. It is better than taking one step forward and two steps back or doing nothing.

When we assume the enlightened state in tantric meditation, our physical form is an enlightened one but our emotions are still present. We can look directly at their face and see that they have no substance and that their nature is the wisdom of emptiness. We cannot find wisdom apart from our mental activities. We cannot find wisdom apart from our own mind. The nature of this very mind that we have is wisdom and compassion.

View, action, and meditation are like the king of beasts.
Fearlessly, they overpower anything.
They form the pinnacle of the path.
This is my heart's advice.

THESE THREE—*view, meditation, and action*—are very important.
When we practice meditation, we need a view of our goal. What
are we trying to realize? What is the nature of phenomena? What
is enlightenment? Having answered these questions, we then need
meditation to achieve that goal. The awakened conduct we engage
in is the action. Possessing these three together is the most powerful
means to attain enlightenment. Without them, there is no way to
free ourselves from suffering or attain enlightenment.

In the Mahayana, and particularly in the Vajrayana, view is very
important because it is the ultimate goal to be achieved. It is the
ultimate mode of abiding of all phenomena, free from extremes, the
unfabricated state. Without a correct introduction to view by an
experienced vajra master, we labor under a false vision.

The *view* is that of all-pervading emptiness, total freedom from
all boundaries, grasping, and attachment. Without space, this earth
could not manifest, function, or dissolve. In the same way, all our
mental activities function in emptiness and dissolve into emptiness.
Our *meditation* should be free from excitement and lethargy. We
can meditate on all-pervading emptiness without contradicting view
or action. *Action* is free from contrivance or falsity. In Mahamudra
practice, this includes avoiding nonvirtue and developing all the virtues of body, speech, and mind. For example, upholding the Vinaya
system of moral ethics is an "action," and bodhicitta practice is a
"meditation" through which one realizes the "view" of Mahamudra.

The *king of beasts* is the snow lion, which overcomes all other
animals and fearlessly rules over them. When we possess the view
of Mahamudra, the meditation practice of the Six Yogas of Naropa,
and conduct according to the Vinaya and bodhisattva vow, there

can be nothing to fear. Through these methods, the "beasts" of negative thought and delusion are fully overpowered, subjugated, and uprooted. Milarepa expressed this in a vajra song:

> The view is to look at reality beyond intellect.
> The meditation is to rest in a state of nondistraction.
> The conduct is to unceasingly sustain whatever naturally
> occurs.
> The result is to abandon hope, fear, and conventionality.

These three form the *pinnacle of the path*—the highest, most powerful means to free ourselves from all delusions and attain enlightenment. When we accomplish realization of mind, there is nothing higher to achieve. The mind is the center of everything. When we realize mind, this is called buddhahood. When we are confused by mind, this is called samsara. Neither state exists outside the mind.

Whether the mind is resting without conceptual thoughts in the nature of the view, and we feel harmonious, relaxed, peaceful, clear, pristinely pure, and joyful; or whether the mind is disturbed by negative thoughts, fear, agitation, and loneliness—all this is the play of the mind. When we don't understand this, we seek protection outside ourselves. But when the great teachers perfected this practice, no matter where they went they had no fear at all, anywhere, with anyone. That is the power of the mind. We can see it, reveal it, and manifest its nature through this teaching and practice.

Sometimes, confusion arises about the view. We hear that the view is free from boundaries and confusion, and that in that state, there is nothing to give up and nothing to accept. Because we think there is nothing to give up, we may keep our negative thoughts. Because we think there is nothing to accept, we may give up our virtues. This creates a conflict between our view and action, and between our view and meditation. Some may say, "There is nothing on which to meditate." And, in reality, this is true. But in order to really understand this, we must meditate. We should not create conflict between our view, action, and meditation. If we do, this method won't be a king of beasts. Maybe it will become a small insect! It is extremely important to have a correct understanding of how to practice the precious Dharma.

66 *Untimely yogic behavior is like a butterfly matched against*
a garuda.
Through this, one destroys oneself and falls to the vajra hell.
Therefore, avoid heedless, mad activity.
This is my heart's advice.

UNTIMELY YOGIC BEHAVIOR is the behavior of a practitioner who has
not completely actualized the meaning of the view, meditation, and
action but acts as if he had. It is necessary to become familiar with
their inseparability. Lord Jigten Sumgön said:

> I, a yogin, realized the unity
> of view, meditation, and action.
> There are no sessions to practice.
> In non-effort I, a yogin, am happy.
> This happy yogin experiences joy.
> This experience of joy is the guru's kindness.

Sometimes, sexual activity, the consumption of alcohol, and other
activities are mentioned in the context of tantra. Merely receiving
practice instructions, some practitioners mistakenly think that they
are qualified to engage in these activities. Without any experience or
realization, they say, "I received all these empowerments and instructions. Now I can perform this tantric practice." This is untimely
behavior because they remain without any experience or realization
of the enlightened qualities. Until we have realized the meaning of
Dharma ourselves, it can create great confusion to attempt to lead
others.

Just because we have practiced some tantra, this does not mean
that we have achieved higher realization and have the ability to perform great yogic deeds. One who acts as if he is highly accomplished
before he is ready is like a *butterfly matched against a garuda*. There
is no question who will win.

Avoid these unnecessary dangers. Protect yourself as if you were a small medicinal plant. We put a small plant in the ground and let it grow into a giant tree by protecting it with fences and so on. Then, when it is fully grown, it can produce fruits, flowers, and leaves that can help many people. But if we harvest the tree while it's small, not much benefit will come from it.

There is no special place called *vajra hell*. This hell is no different from the hell realms described earlier. This is simply a term used in Vajrayana for the sake of emphasis.

So always be a simple, sincere, modest practitioner. Practice one day at a time, step by step. Start from where you are instead of trying to change the big things all at once. When you are confused, you may create negative karma and become a victim of abuse from others. Instead, it is better to become a victor by gradually clarifying confusion, clearing the mind, and developing wisdom and compassion. These are the important things.

Sometimes, within the sangha community, high titles are prematurely given to individual practitioners. They then misuse these titles and create great confusion for other people. This is extremely unfortunate. As I mentioned earlier, our Dharma studies and practices are for the purpose of freeing ourselves from samsara, not enriching samsara. We can recall this famous episode from the life story of Milarepa:

> One day Milarepa traveled to a place where the villagers suggested, "Since your teacher Marpa has a wife, we will arrange a special place for you to stay here with a wife." Milarepa responded, "I cannot match my teacher. He is like a tiger and I am like a fox. If a fox tries to jump where the tiger has jumped, the fox will only break his back."

In this example, Milarepa is showing future practitioners how to behave. Instead of receiving a high title, it's much better to gain the "title" of wisdom, compassion, and skill, and only *then* perform the activities of a bodhisattva.

67 *The all-creating mind is like a magician.*
All the suffering and joy of samsara and nirvana arise from it.
Hold well the real meaning of the mind.
This is my heart's advice.

MIND CREATES EVERYTHING. It is like an artist who can draw beautiful pictures of the world depicting different countries, cities, mountains, valleys, rivers, oceans, plants, and people. In the same way, the mind can create the different kinds of karma, both positive and negative. Science, technology, communications, and transportation are all creations of the mind. Look at a computer, for example. It is very complex and sophisticated. Each and every detail was created by the mind. But at the same time, people don't really know the mind and cannot find it. Where does the mind exist? We can say that the brain plays an important role in the functioning of mind, but every human being has a brain and each is different, even among children of the same parents. The children have the same genes, but their ways of thinking may be very different.

The brain and heart are where the mind performs its activities, but the mind itself is infinite and insubstantial, like space. It is consciousness, which is a very abstract subject; it is not material; it neither exists nor doesn't exist. Because mind is infinite, there can be no end to invention and discovery. The Buddha fully revealed the nature of mind, his own and all others'. For him, no subject or object is hidden. Everything is obvious, clear, and precise, including the causes and results of all the phenomena of samsara and nirvana. He fully revealed both the enlightened mind and the unenlightened mind of sentient beings. Therefore, he was able to teach and demonstrate the path perfectly.

Neither samsara nor nirvana exists apart from the mind. When mind is deluded, when it fails to recognize the nature of phenomena or the nature of mind, we create all sorts of karma and then suffer in the six realms according to the karma we created. But when this delusion is dispelled and the pure mind is recognized, that realization is the source of all joy and happiness.

All the sufferings that occur in samsara are creations of our mind. Enlightenment also is a manifestation of our mind. Knowing this, we should make effort to practice every day, to hold the real meaning of wisdom. The purpose of Dharma practice is to truly see your mind. Whether we recite mantras, chant prayers, sit quietly, or do prostrations, all these are means to hold the mind in its true place. This is very, very important. It is the main point of our practice.

The mind is like a magician who can create whatever he wants—animals, palaces, beautiful things and frightening things—and when he's done they dissolve. If you go to Disneyland you can see so many different shows. All these are creations of the mind. Samsara and nirvana are also like a dream. The different experiences of the dream state may seem very real, but at the moment you awake, the dream disappears. Where has the dream-world gone? Nowhere. Where did it come from? Nowhere. And as soon as we go to sleep again, this waking world dissolves. This is all just a state of mind.

This can be seen clearly in our daily life. When our mind is peaceful, calm, and relaxed, everything seems fine, and we are full of confidence. Anyone who comes along can greet us, and we feel very comfortable talking to them. At other times our mind is agitated and confused, so that when we see people we feel uncomfortable. If someone approaches us, we feel annoyed. This is called the *all-creating mind*. Everything is created by the mind because of different habits. When these habits arise, we are captured by them.

Dharma is not too difficult to understand, but it is difficult to practice. Our minds are very difficult to train. People say, "I cannot practice this. It is too much for me." Then they go back to their old ways of thinking, remain confused, and create further suffering. You must know your own mind and how difficult it is to work with. When you are relaxed and peaceful, practice seems simple. Then you are happy and you say that your practice is going well. But at other times things turn completely upside down. You forget about your practices and sink deeply into samsara. Then you wonder what happened, what went wrong. These are all just mental states.

Sometimes we may think that Dharma has no effect. "I have been practicing for many years," we say, "and I have not progressed at all. I've recited hundreds and thousands of mantras but nothing has changed. What went wrong?" We don't realize that we have not practiced properly, so we blame the meditation and say it does no good. Then we are in danger of giving up. This is very unfortunate. It is not the fault of Dharma but rather is a case of our not being able to handle our own minds in the right way. Instead of saying Dharma must do something for us, we should use the Dharma as a tool; we have to take on the responsibility to purify ourselves. These are very important points. Mind can be a wish-fulfilling jewel when we can handle it well.

This is called studying the "inner meaning" or the "inner mind." The inner mind is difficult to understand because it is a profound and complex subject. Our mind is always with us, yet we still don't know much about it—that's how profound it is. If we look for our mind, we cannot find it. We cannot find it, and yet it rules our life. Mind is a very hidden subject. We cannot comprehend its profundity, even with very sophisticated technologies. Dharma is the only tool that can reveal it.

Because the Buddha is omniscient, the teachings that he gave show us how to restructure our mind in the right way. This is why we repeat what the Buddha said and believe that we should follow him. If we could practice according to the real meaning of the Buddha's instruction, we would be free from suffering and delusion. We would be able to bring happiness to our day-to-day lives and eventually achieve the ultimate happiness. This is the precious nature of the Buddha's teachings. For example, historical figures like Milarepa and Lord Jigten Sumgön followed the Buddha's path and revealed the ultimate state, the total nature of mind. Through this, they helped countless beings to also free themselves from confused suffering.

If we can practice in this way, our confidence in the Buddha's teaching will be very firm and stable. No matter what happens, no matter what other people may think, nothing will shake our faith and devotion. If on this basis we can be of service to the Dharma, this will be very effective. We should try to be of good service and be helpful to everyone. No matter who that person may be, try to show them the right path. This is the way to bring about happiness and to stop suffering—not according to one's belief, but according to the law of causality, the "law" of samsara and nirvana. This is why the teachings emphasize motivation, and why we should always cultivate the mind of enlightenment, bodhicitta.

This subject is profound and vast. Once we understand this, we will hold all the methods to free ourselves from samsara and to achieve complete enlightenment. We will know how to cultivate and practice bodhicitta, and with the practices of the arising and completion stages of the yidam deity, we possess the ability to give rise to great devotion for our lama and to practice the four kayas of Guru Yoga. Because of this, we will be able to practice calm abiding, critical special insight, and Mahamudra successfully. And we will know how to dedicate virtues to achieve the absolute result.

Because this verse emphasizes the importance of mind, some may think it promotes the Mind-Only (Skt.: *Cittamatra*) school of thought. Such individuals have little knowledge of the Buddhadharma. First, we must understand through the reasoning of the Madhyamaka system how to deconstruct our incorrect concepts about outer phenomena and those about the mind that projects them. If we can do this, buddhahood is possible.

The mind is the factory of samsara and nirvana. Our confused and deluded mind manufactures the six realms of samsara and the many levels within each of them. An unconfused and enlightened mind manufactures the various states of enlightenment and frees us from all suffering.

The completion stage is like a reflection in a mirror.
   It is inexpressible and is free from the elaborations of existence
      and nonexistence.
   It is a matter of self-awareness.
   This is my heart's advice.

IN YIDAM PRACTICE there are two stages, the generation stage and completion stage. This verse pertains to the completion stage, of which there are two types. The first is called "completion with signs," referring to meditation using the different chakras, channels, and so forth. The second, which we are discussing here, is called "completion without signs" or "dissolution into all-pervading emptiness." In either case, the completion stage is *inexpressible* and *free from elaboration.*

Appearances are like a reflection in which objects appear clearly and vividly even though there is nothing to hold on to. The color, size, and shape of your reflection may be present in a small mirror although neither the mirror nor your face changes size. Still the mirror holds the complete image. But that reflection has no substance; it is just an illusion. There is nothing to become attached to or to reject. This demonstrates the inseparable nature of appearance and emptiness. Again, it is your mind both when it dissolves into emptiness and when it manifests in form as a yidam deity. In the same way, all phenomena are simply a reflection of mind, neither existing nor not existing. This is inexpressible nonduality, free from all extremes.

Words are inadequate to describe this. We can only experience it. Take the example of sugar cane. Even if we remember its quality very clearly and describe it precisely, we cannot make anyone else experience it. But if they put some on their tongue, they can say, "Ah, this is sugar cane." We could say "sweet," but that is just a label. What would you say if someone asked what "sweet" is? You can only explain so much; you cannot express the taste itself. This is what we mean when we say the completion stage is *inexpressible.*

To achieve enlightenment, we must purify the unenlightened mind by ourselves. A teacher cannot give enlightenment to us, but a teacher can show us the path. We have to travel it ourselves. We must meditate and experience it. Enlightenment is inexpressible and is free from elaboration, beyond words, beyond all limits. That is the quality of radiant mind.

We cannot say of something, "This exists." If it really existed, then someone could explain how it exists. But after analyzing all the details of how something exists, we still cannot find any existence. But if something doesn't exist, how can we perceive it? In fact, it is beyond "existence" and "nonexistence." This is a matter of self-awareness. When we look at mind and think that it does not exist, something then seems to arise. When we have self-awareness, we can achieve self-liberation. How? We don't have to "liberate" mind. Mind is already liberated; we only have to realize this. We just have to relax and be aware of it.

Keeping to one's practice is like enjoying one's own wealth.
It doesn't come from anyone else and is spontaneously estab-
lished by oneself.
Guard your mind.
This is my heart's advice.

WHEN YOU POSSESS your *own wealth*, you don't have to depend
on anyone else. You don't have to consult or thank anyone. In the
same way, when you practice meditation and achieve a good result,
this is revealed within your own experience. Occurrences of heat or
visions and so forth do not come from outside oneself; they cannot
be given to you by anyone else. They are reflections of the *spontaneously established* quality of your own mind. When you wholeheartedly practice loving-kindness, compassion, bodhicitta, calm abiding,
special insight, clairvoyance, and other infinite qualities, these are
your own primordial wealth from which you have never been separated. This wealth can give you all possible comfort and benefits in
life after life until you attain buddhahood. We just need to purify the
temporary obscurations and reveal our innate good qualities.

If we plant a seed, it blossoms as a flower above the ground. If the
seed's own nature had not contained the potential for this flower, no
flower would have manifested no matter what we did. If we plant
an orange seed, an orange tree will grow. That small orange seed
contains the potential to produce hundreds of perfect oranges. In
the same way, we all have the potential to become a buddha. Joyous effort is all it takes to manifest such perfect qualities. While this
potential is still unrealized, we call it "buddha nature." When it is
actualized, we call it "buddhahood." Therefore, *guard your mind* as
carefully as you can; it is your greatest wealth.

We must always guard our mind against delusion and hold it
in the right place. This is the proper way to sustain such wealth.
Wealth of the mind is like a vajra that destroys all delusion. It is like
a lion, free from all fears. It is as endless as space. All possible joy

and confidence are there. We may search for peace, happiness, and joy, only to discover that that very wealth is within our own mind. In one way, this is very simple since nothing is closer to us than our own minds. But that wealth can also seem so far from us! We cannot grasp it with our confused mind. All this is truly inexpressible.

Advice on Preparing for Mahamudra Practice

70 *Giving up concern for this life is like a merchant whose*
work is done.
There is no better method to perfect the holy Dharma.
It is the king of actions.
This is my heart's advice.

AT THIS POINT in the text, the Mahamudra teachings are presented. Here, the author again reminds us of renunciation and
the four foundations since before we begin any higher practice, we
first need to be fully established and grounded in the preliminaries
to successful Mahamudra practice. Depending on our ability, we
can then gradually engage in the higher practices like Mahamudra.

Giving up concern for this life refers to giving up attachment.
This doesn't mean that we don't eat or wear clothes. We must eat,
we must wear clothes, but we should do these things without attachment. No matter how attached we may be to this life, we will have
to die some day and leave everything behind. Even Rechungpa Dorje
Drakpa (Milarepa's great disciple) who stayed with his teacher for
many years, suffered from pride and arrogance after he had successfully studied various aspects of knowledge, especially the dialectic
system. Once when he returned from a trip to India, Milarepa perceived this and taught him many ways to eliminate his attachment.
Milarepa would say, "We don't need this knowledge that gives rise
to pride. Dharma should tame the mind, not make it worse!" In the
end, Milarepa was able to help Rechungpa purify his confusion. We
should read such stories and learn from them how to handle our
own attachment to this life.

Renunciation is a crucial support for successful practice. This is why we learn about the various sufferings of samsara. This gives us the wisdom to see that this life is like a dream. Even if we could live for one hundred or two hundred years, eventually we would die. What benefit could an ordinary person get by living for so long? It would only create the causes for more suffering.

Already, we often sacrifice today's happiness and joy for some benefit tomorrow or next year. We don't need to work that hard just for today's needs. Therefore, expand your perspective and take a longer view that includes your next life and future lives. Expand this all the way to the end of samsara and you will see how this life is akin to only a short day that we could easily sacrifice for some future good. This contemplation could change your entire view of things.

A successful *merchant* is one who made careful plans and was successful in all his endeavors. His business did well, and he made enough profit so that he can now relax and enjoy life. Once we have purified attachment to this life, we, too, will relax. But for now, our mind goes in all directions because of concerns for this life.

Some may say that by giving up attachment we are only avoiding responsibility. But we are actually taking on more responsibility than anyone else. Achieving complete enlightenment is the way to truly take on responsibility, since we do this not just for ourselves but for all sentient beings. How could there be any greater responsibility than this?

There is no better way to perfect our Dharma practice than to cultivate nonattachment to this life and settle our mind fully in the Dharma. It may not be easy at first to give up concern for this life. This cannot be done all at once—we have to work at it every day. This is a process of slowly progressing step by step, with full determination. This is the *king of actions*. There is no better way to practice Dharma.

Calm abiding is like a lamp unmoved by the wind.
Although the six objects are clearly present, they are free from
  grasping by the mind.
Don't allow awareness to sink.
This is my heart's advice.

IN ORDER to actualize Mahamudra and accomplish special insight, we must have experience in the practice of calm abiding meditation (also called *shamatha* and *samadhi*). The general description of and instructions for *calm abiding* were given at verse 49, so please review them. When a *lamp's* flame is well protected and is *not moved by the wind*, it is calm and clear. It is the same with meditative equipoise. Mind is in a state of incisive awareness—profound and immovable like a great mountain. That mind can perceive *the six objects* like reflections in a mirror without being moved by thoughts of attraction or aversion. These six objects are

- visible form—color and shape;
- sounds made by animate and inanimate sources;
- pleasant and unpleasant odors;
- tastes of sweet, sour, bitter, salty, and so forth;
- textures that are soft, rough, light, heavy and so forth;
- mental phenomena.

When the mind is well established in shamatha meditation, we may see forms but the mind isn't disturbed. We may hear sounds, but the mind doesn't follow them. We may smell something delightful or rotten, but the mind has no reaction. Taste also doesn't matter. The mind isn't moved by any of this. Mind has become very clear and precise. Where there is attachment, there is also aversion; the two are interdependent. First we need to let go of concern for this life and then receive proper instruction on how to calm the mind. When the six sense objects no longer disturb us, the mind can be stable as a mountain. No matter how strong the wind may blow, a mountain cannot be moved. Meditate in this way.

Though you may be free from mental grasping, *don't allow your awareness to sink*. Some people think that in a "good" meditation you will not be aware of anything, but there is no clarity in that state of mind. A dull mind cannot penetrate the nature of reality. Supported by skillful means, establish a one-pointed mind.

Take a moment to relax in the proper body posture. Breathe in and out through the nostrils. Focus on the breath and rest there.

Advice for Mahamudra Practitioners

72 *Panoramic awareness is like a calm, clear ocean.*
In clarity and joy, sustain the recognition of movement
and abiding.
Cut to the root of mind-as-such.
This is my heart's advice.

P ANORAMIC AWARENESS is awareness that is very clear, vast, and
unobstructed like a calm ocean. When we look at a calm ocean,
we can see through to its depths, but when that ocean is disturbed
by strong waves or mud, we can see only the surface. To attain deep
realization, we must learn to sustain the mind in the clear, stable,
calm, and joyful state of awareness. When we are naturally calm
and peaceful, we can be aware of all that is happening; we can see
the mind clearly. When the mind is moving, we should be aware that
it is moving. When the mind is still, we should notice that, too. The
more calmly the mind stays, the more it supports the attainment of
special insight. Thus, calm abiding, or shamatha, is indispensable
for the achievement of special insight.

Calm abiding is not enough to free us from samsara; we must
continue meditating until we cut through to the very nature of mind.
Cutting to the root of mind-as-such means directly and completely
penetrating the nature of mind with critical insight. When we do
this successfully, nothing remains hidden. This is called *lhagtong* in
Tibetan or *vipashyana* in Sanskrit.

Cut means to penetrate through delusion to the root of mind so
that not even a trace of obscuration by the adventitious defilements
is left. Having done this, we can directly recognize the nature of the
mind itself. This is like cutting the root of a tree. When we cut the

root, the branches dry up by themselves. We don't have to cut each branch individually. In the same way, if we cut delusion or ignorance at the root, all other afflictions and neuroses naturally dissolve on their own. We don't have to destroy each and every negative thought one by one.

During this practice, anger, attachment, or pride will manifest. To counteract them, first sustain the mind in the calm abiding state. Supported by this shamatha, look at the nature of the mind. Ask yourself what anger looks like. Where does it come from? Where does it abide? Where does it go when it disappears? Look at these things without pushing thoughts away or chasing after them. Simply look directly at their face. If you can't find them, this doesn't mean that you failed to find something that exists. You can't find them because they don't exist. Once you realize that the afflictions don't independently exist, sustain that meditation. Allow your mind to rest in the unfabricated state. This is an important instruction on how to release tension and practice with full mindfulness. This is the only antidote we need.

73 *Establishing the appearance of the mind is like a thief*
  in an empty house.
  It is beyond color, form, shape, and characteristics.
  There is no searcher and no object of a search.
  This is my heart's advice.

HERE, the author explains the different types of thought processes as they appear in Mahamudra meditation. *Appearance of the mind* refers to the mind's manifestations, the different types of thought, whatever arises in the mind. This includes any thought, whether positive or negative. Since thoughts are the display of mind, they both manifest from the mind and dissolve into the mind. We have to realize this.

Establishing the appearance of the mind means that we cut to the root of mind-as-such. Suppose a *thief* goes to an *empty house* looking for something to steal. He thoroughly searches the house but ends up empty-handed because the place is empty. Though he tries to find something, he is completely disappointed. Similarly, once we establish the appearance of the mind, we see that the various thoughts, attachments, jealousies, hatred, and so forth that we imagine to be important actually have no substance. They are not tangible, substantial things at all. When we look at their nature, it's like looking into an empty house. We can search and search, but nothing is there, neither inside our body nor outside nor in between. One-pointed shamatha meditation is a crucial support for this kind of investigation.

Thoughts of hatred, pride, jealousy, and so forth can crowd our mind. But when they are gone, the mind is empty. These thoughts have no color that we can see, no forms that we can feel, and no characteristics that we can explain. They are inexpressible. Some say, "Search for your mind." When we look closer, though, we come up with the question, who is the searcher and what exactly is he searching for? After we have established our mind in *lhagtong*, or the state of special insight, there is nothing to see or to achieve, nothing to keep or to lose. Once they are gone, disturbing thoughts leave no trace. Freed from attachment and fear, the mind experiences inexpressible calm, clarity, and joy. This state of mind is our natural home, and all our wealth is contained within it. There is nothing to be attached to, yet one must sustain it with the support of mindfulness. Unless we post the guard of mindfulness by continuing our meditation practice, it will be lost.

This is what is called "self-liberation." No other antidote is needed. Just look at mind's own nature. Waves arise from the ocean and dissolve back into the ocean. There is no need to apply an antidote to dissolve the waves. Similarly, clouds appear in the sky and dissolve without a trace. We need to meditate in this same way. Practicing is very important. Without practice, these teachings are just more accumulated knowledge. But if we practice, then they become a supreme method for awakening.

Mind and conceptual thought are like water and ice.
They have always been inseparable,
yet cannot be said to be one thing or two.
This is my heart's advice.

THIS VERSE continues with profound, step-by-step instructions for Mahamudra practice.

Are *water and ice* two different things? If they were, then when the ice melted we would be able to distinguish the ice-water from the non-ice water. But we find that we cannot do this. Can we say instead that they are one thing? No, for if they were, we could not differentiate ice and water. In the same way, mind and conceptual thought appear to be two separate things when we don't recognize their true nature. But as soon as we recognize the nature of conceptual thought, we find that it is not separate from mind. Mind and thought are of one nature.

There can be no ice without water, but water can exist without ice. Ice is not separate from water, however. Ice appears to be separate from water but, in reality, it is not, as ice could not have been produced without it. Similarly, without mind, there is no conceptual thought. Can there be conceptual thought without mind? Conceptual thoughts create the negative and positive karma that keep us wandering in samsara. Recognizing their true nature is, itself, enlightenment.

Just as water and ice have always been inseparable, conceptual thoughts and mind have always been inseparable. We cannot say, "This is mind and that is conceptual thought," since they cannot be said to be one thing or two. This is what is meant by "nonduality." Intellectual investigation and analysis will not lead us to the taste of meditation. For this, devotion to the lineage and to the root master is of the utmost importance. Masters are like the sun and our conceptual thoughts are ice. The blessing of the lama's sunshine is needed to melt the ice of conceptual thought into the water of unfabricated mind.

Mind and conceptual thought can also be said to be like waves and the ocean. Without the ocean, there can be no waves, and waves cannot be separated from the ocean. Yet if we say they are one thing, how could we speak of them as two? And if we say they are two separate things, how can we show that the waves exist without the ocean? If we closely meditate on these examples, we can understand why these things are said to be "inexpressible." Attachment, or desire, and aversion, or anger, are not separate from one's mind. Meditating this way with a combination of shamatha and special insight is crucial in order to resolve all mental conflicts.

Look at the mind itself in this way. Without mind, no thoughts can be produced. But thought itself is just a manifestation of mind. It is not separate from mind. It is neither one thing nor two. Meditate on this. We cannot chase all the thoughts away from mind. We can only resolve them by comprehending mind's nature itself as wisdom. The following verse clearly expresses this:

> Whatever is visualized vanishes into emptiness.
> Mind has no form, color, or substance.
> It is not to be found outside or within the body, nor in
>   between.
> It is not found to be a concrete thing.
>
> Even if one were to search throughout the ten directions,
> it does not arise anywhere, nor does it abide or disappear
>   at any place.
> Yet, it is not nonexistent, since mind is vividly awake.
> It is not a singularity, because it manifests in manifold ways.
> Nor is it a plurality, because all these are of one essence.
> There is no one who can describe its nature.
> But in expressing its resemblance, there is no end to what
>   can be said.
> It is the very basis of all samsara and nirvana.
> It is nirvana when one has realized its nature, and
> samsara when one is confused.

We must know how to protect the mind, how to relate to our mind in a positive way. This is how we develop compassion and loving-kindness for ourselves and how to protect ourselves from all that is negative. It is also one of the most effective methods we can use to purify mental obscurations.

Here, take a moment. Relax the mind and visualize Vajradhara as the embodiment of wisdom and compassion, the inseparability of appearance and emptiness. Supplicate with one-pointed devotion and receive his blessings in the form of rays of light. Vajradhara then dissolves into you and you become inseparable from emptiness-clarity. Rest your mind in that state, which is the nature of space.

The inseparability of appearance and mind is like last night's dream.

It possesses the four characteristics and is the union of appearance and emptiness.

It cannot be said to be one thing or two.

This is my heart's advice.

THIS VERSE EXPLAINS the nature of mind in a different way. In the last verse, mind and conceptual thought were taught as being inseparable. Here, *inseparability* is related to physical objects and to the mind that projects their appearance. Usually we perceive and believe in all these things that surround us. Because mind and objects appear to be "real," we live in a state of duality. But when we understand mind's true nature, we see that the all-creating mind is like a magician. Samsara is simply a state of mind and nirvana is also a state of mind. When we understand this, it is easy to see that all appearance is just a projection of mind.

When you see something, look closely at the mind and at what you see in the mind. What is the difference between them? If you see a beautiful flower reflected in your mind, examine the image of the flower in your mind, and the mind itself. Appearances do not arise or abide outside the mind.

Last night's dream is the example given in this verse. Suppose that in a dream you go to a beautiful place, a country with lakes, flowers, and green grass. You are so peaceful and relaxed in that place. You meet your friends and family there, and everyone is happy. When you wake up, though, they may remain vivid in the mind, yet all this is just a memory. Where do those things exist? Are they in the mind or outside? How could that big lake fit into your room? Everything we see "outside" is just our mind's projection. Without realizing this, we project objects and perceive the projections as things that exist independently. Then we helplessly try to grasp at them. Look at how much suffering this causes! When we know that everything is a projection of mind, we can relax and be free from attachment and aversion.

Sometimes it is difficult for us to understand how something like a hard table is really just one's mind. A story from Milarepa's life may help us understand:

> Once, two logicians came to debate with Milarepa. Milarepa said, "I have resolved all my questions. I have nothing left unresolved to debate with you." But the logicians insisted, "Who knows who has genuinely finished with debate? Either you must ask questions and we will answer, or we will ask questions and you must answer." Milarepa then relented, saying, "If you really won't listen to me, I will now ask you a question whose answer should be obvious for anyone: Does space have substance or not?"
>
> This very simple question puzzled the logicians. They did not expect him to ask such a thing. "How can you ask such question?" they replied. "It is obvious that space is insubstantial." Because Milarepa was realized and accomplished in the practice of Mahamudra, he entered into the vajra-like samadhi and walked back and forth in the air. Then he sat down in space and meditated. Milarepa asked the logicians to move, but they could not move at all. It was as though they were held between large rocks. Milarepa released his meditation and asked them, "Now what do you think?" The logicians declared that this was just a trick of black magic. Milarepa exclaimed, "But you yourselves saw that you could not move!"
>
> Milarepa then asked a second question: "Are the rock walls of this cave substantial?" The logicians discussed this point and concluded that the rock was indeed substantial. Milarepa then entered into the space-like meditation and walked back and forth through the cave walls. He lifted a huge rock and threw it onto his visitors, but they felt nothing.

For us, who are not yet accomplished in meditation, these stories can be helpful. Otherwise it may be hard to see how a table could simply be a mental projection.

Dharma Lord Gampopa's small house could hold only about five people. The meditator Loten once came to make an offering, and Gampopa's attendant allowed him to go in and make the offering in person. When Loten emerged from the house, he asked, "Who built that huge thousand-armed Chenrezig statue? It is so beautiful and inspiring! But where does the lama live?" The attendant took him back inside, and this time no statue could be seen, only the lama. That statue had been as big as the mountain Takla Gampo, but it fit into the lama's small house! This also illustrates what can be demonstrated by one whose mind is perfected.

There is a simple example that may clarify this point for you. When you make a friend, you see that person as beautiful and perfect and you like each other very much. No matter what that person does, you regard it as pleasing. Even if that person makes a mistake, you unconditionally accept it and are very protective of that person. After a few years pass, however, conditions may change because of a disagreement. Then you no longer accept each other, and the situation deteriorates. Your mental projection of the person completely changes. Even if that person does good things, you say they are stupid, and perceive whatever he or she does as negative or hostile. This demonstrates how everything is a mental projection.

The *four characteristics* of phenomena mentioned here are

1. conventional phenomena do not inherently exist;
2. they are potent, or capable of performing a function;
3. they are similarly apprehendable by the senses of people in the community;
4. they exist by means of the interdependence of many causes and conditions.

If we investigate carefully, phenomena do not independently exist. Even if we make a cup of tea, that cup of tea arises through many causes and conditions. There is no "real" cup of tea. Here, *potent* means that something is capable of performing a function. The cup of tea can quench thirst. Also, everyone around can perceive that cup of tea. However, without the interdependence of the water, stove, teapot, tea leaves, the farmers who grew the tea, cups, and so forth there would have been no tea. All relative phenomena possess these four characteristics.

This story may help us to understand the four characteristics of phenomena:

> A hundred monkeys came upon a well. They looked in, saw the moon's reflection, and became alarmed: "The moon has fallen into this well!" they screamed. "We must get the moon out and put it back where it belongs." Based on their shared delusion that the moon had fallen into the well, they determined to rescue it.
>
> One monkey held on to the branch of a tree, and all the other monkeys held the leg or tail of the monkey above him, thus making a long chain of monkeys. But the tree branch broke and they all fell into the well. They then looked up and saw the moon was back in the sky. "We did it!" they exclaimed. "Even though we will die here, we fixed the world and put everything back in its right place."

Because all those monkeys saw the same thing, we can say that the phenomenon was apprehended by all of them together. But the reflection in the well was interdependent—the moon in the sky and the water in the well were both needed for the reflection to appear. If there were no moon, the water alone could not have reflected anything. And if there were no water, the moon could not have been reflected.

The *union of appearance and emptiness* refers to the nonduality of appearance and emptiness.

Although phenomena appear, their nature is emptiness, and that emptiness itself appears as form. They cannot be said to be one thing or two. This union of appearance and emptiness can be directly experienced only by a bodhisattva who has attained at least the eighth bhumi. In the Vajrayana, this concept is symbolized by male and female figures shown in union.

All the phenomena of samsara and nirvana are included within Mahamudra. For example, just as a sesame seed is pervaded by oil, sugar cane by sweet, a flower by fragrance, and milk by butterfat, Mahamudra pervades all sentient beings. Mahamudra is like space, primordially unborn. We may think these phenomena—various forms and so forth—are not Mahamudra. But in reality all outer appearances such as earth, rocks, mountains, trees, forests, jungles, men, women, and so forth—the entire outer and inner world that we see—are nothing more than the effects of our deeply rooted propensities. Recall that in the vajra song *Meaningful to Behold*, Nagarjuna is quoted as saying:

> When propensities arise, the seeds of further propensities
>   are sown.
> Out of these accumulated propensities, samsara-sprouts
>   are grown.

Also, the precious lord Jigten Sumgön said, "Although different traditions conclude that it is either the mind or the body that wanders in samsara, I don't take a particular position on this. But I would say that causes and conditions give rise to conceptual thought. Because of that, embodied propensities wander [in samsara]."

An illusion, a magic show, a dream, a city of gandharvas, a mirage: all of these are perfect examples of phenomena that can be seen but that we know do not exist. In the same way, when we have fully purified our samsaric propensities, all our mistaken perceptions dissolve into the space of Mahamudra. The true nature of affliction is primordial wisdom, but if we have not realized this, we cannot say that affliction is wisdom. The moment that we realize the afflictions do not exist, though, that itself is primordial wisdom. We cannot find wisdom apart from the afflictions. Because of this, samsara and nirvana are said to be nondual. These are very profound teachings. We will have to make a great deal of effort to realize them for ourselves.

The following quotations from the *Heart Essence of the Mahayana Teachings* are so beautiful and make it easy to understand the nature of reality, the inseparability of appearance and emptiness. Read them carefully and put them into practice.

> All the awareness, clarity, and experience one gains about
> the phenomena of samsara and nirvana are due to real-
> ization of them as unborn, empty, and selfless. The *Moon
> Lamp Sutra* states:

Whatever arises from conditions does not arise;
such things have no reality-nature of arising.
Whatever depends on conditions is emptiness.
To know emptiness is to be conscientious.

And from the *Tantra of the Completely Victorious, Non-dual Secret Essence*:

The secret of all perfect buddhas is that these
amazing, magnificent, wonderful phenomena
all arose from nonarising.
Their nonarising is in the very fact that they arose.

Why is this so? It is because, when realized as mind/
non-mind, body/non-body, appearance/nonappearance,
all phenomena of samsara and nirvana are seen to arise
as nondual entwined pairs, cease as nondual entwined
pairs, and abide as nondual entwined pairs, and thus there
is nondual entwined pair conduct. The *King of Samadhi
Sutra* states:

There come occasions for the material universe to
    arise,
and occasions for all its worlds to return to space.
Such has it always been, and such it shall always be—
know that all phenomena are just like this.

Just as mandalas of clouds can instantly
appear in a cloud-free sky,
whatever has arisen from the beginning will always
    come again—
know that all phenomena are just like this.

Just as the many bubbles popping up
seen by a person floating in a river
have no essence whatsoever upon investigation—
know that all phenomena are just like this.

Just as the moon, rising in a clear sky
appears reflected in a clear lake

but without movement of moon into water—
know that all phenomena are just like this.

Just as people living in mountainous areas
hear singing, talking, laughter, and crying
echoing from the rocks, but see no one—
know that all phenomena are just like this.

Just as only someone very immature
remains beholden to their desire after they wake up
to find the lover in their dream has disappeared—
know that all phenomena are just like this.

Just as magicians know that there is
nothing real about the various illusionary forms
the horses, elephants, and chariots they create—
know that all phenomena are just like this.

Just as a person stricken with thirst
sees pools of water in mirages
when walking at mid-day in summer—
know that all phenomena are just like this.

Just as a young woman who sees herself in a dream
give birth to a child who then dies
is happy when it is born and sad when it dies—
know that all phenomena are just like this.

Like the imaginary city of gandharvas,
like an illusion, like a dream,
conceptual things are devoid of entity-ness—
know that all phenomena are just like this.

Coemergent mind-as-such is like an ocean wave.
Although discursive thought is settled, the six objects
  are clearly present.
Clarity and emptiness are inseparable.
This is my heart's advice.

THIS VERSE CONTINUES the instructions on Mahamudra. Until we have practiced these, it will be difficult to understand the subtle differences between these verses. But when we practice step by step using the methods as described earlier, we will see the differences clearly and more precisely.

Whatever emerges in the mind, whatever thought arises in the mind, is *coemergent* with the mind. That very thought—whether positive or negative—is not separate from mind. Mind and thought may seem to be two, just as the ocean and a wave may seem to be two different things. But in actuality that wave is not separate from the ocean. The ocean itself manifests as the wave. When that wave dissolves into the ocean, no independent entity identifiable as "wave" remains. In the same way, when the waves of our discursive thoughts are settled by calm abiding meditation, only the ocean-like mind remains.

Lord Jigten Sumgön says in the *Wish-granting Jewel*:

Do not seek buddhahood elsewhere.
The mind is the cause of the arising of primordial
  wisdom.

Cherish seeing the nature of mind
more than seeing however many buddhas
abide throughout the three times
and all the yidam deities there are.
This is what is actually meant by "buddha."

As the Sugata Physician [Gampopa] said,
Unborn mind is the dharmakaya,
unceasing mind abides as the sambhogakaya,
unidentifiable mind is the nirmanakaya, and
svabhavikakaya is these three, inseparable.

Therefore, mind-as-it-is is greatly magnificent.
When mind radiates, it is unceasing primordial wisdom.
When mind fabricates, it becomes many.
And so the Master would say [to us]:

Unfabricated, ordinary awareness
is not an object of holder or held.
Disappearance of adventitious discursive thought
is the finality mode of abiding.

In general, when one thinks of the nature of mind
    as singular,
it is unidentifiable;
as dual, it is inseparable;
as many, it is unclassifiable.

The primordial wisdom of the buddhas of the three times,
the mindset of the sublime lamas, and
the minds of the sentient beings of samsara's three realms
are inseparable because they have the same nature.

This is why the *Samaya, Clear and Beautiful* states:

The victorious Mahamudra is one's own body,
and the sentient being constituent element should likewise
    be known.
What it is is not other than oneself and
is the very essence of sugatahood.

When the mind-as-it-is is realized, it is just this:
emptiness possesses no ultimate reality.

It is just as the *Heart Sutra* states,
"There is no primordial wisdom."

In general, all the teachings on the stages of the vehicles
are for particular people's intellects.
There are too many teaching traditions
to express them all here,
[but] this is the concise meaning of the earlier-expressed
    tenets:

Because the three realms have no root-basis,
there is no need to make a point of abandoning samsara.
Because the three kayas have been spontaneously established
    from beginningless time,
there is no need to seek an outside result.
Because mind-as-it-is has been unborn from beginningless
    time,
do not refer to samsara and nirvana as two.

The author mentions this here because some think that when you
have a "good" meditation, you won't see or hear anything at all,
that your mind is completely blank. But it is not like that. Instead,
the six objects (see verse 71) are clearly perceived in panoramic
awareness. We see things very clearly, yet our mind is not disturbed.
For those who possess that quality of mind, clarity and emptiness
can easily be realized as inseparable.

Whatever arises in the mind has the nature of wisdom, whether
we recognize it or not. This point is reiterated as *The Four Dharmas
of Gampopa:*

Grant your blessings so that my mind may follow the
    Dharma.
Grant your blessings so that Dharma may follow along
    the path.
Grant your blessings so that obstacles may be dispelled
    from the path.
Grant your blessings so that confusion may dawn
    as wisdom.

Whatever arises in the mind is mind-as-such and possesses the nature of wisdom. Waves arise from the ocean, yet both possess the nature of water. Just as waves and ocean possess the nature of water, the mind and wisdom are coemergent and inseparable. Whether mind is settled or not, whatever arises is coemergent wisdom. Mental activities and mind's own nature of emptiness are inseparable. This is the Mahamudra.

Ordinary mind is like the center of the sky.
It is untouched by thoughts of the three times
And its mode of being is uncreated awareness.
This is my heart's advice.

THIS VERSE COMPLETES the author's instruction on the different stages of Mahamudra. We can experience these things only when our practices are well developed and our meditation has become so strong that all mental activities are realized as mind-as-such. Conceptual thought is then subsumed within the nature of wisdom, emptiness. This is direct realization of the naked and fresh nature of mind.

Ordinary mind here refers to basic mind, original mind, unfabricated mind, and not to our customary confused and afflicted mind. Ordinary mind is uncreated and is untouched by ignorance or conceptual thought; it is the Buddha's mind. Usually, when we say that something is "ordinary," this means it is nothing special. We say that a person who is educated and has a high title is not an ordinary person, while an ordinary person is free from such distinctions. But here, ordinary mind is original mind, the uncreated buddha nature. When we have experienced realization of this, there is nothing to distinguish meditation from non-meditation. No matter what kind of thought arises in the mind, we will not be separated from ordinary mind, the union of effulgence and emptiness.

What is the difference between the *center of the sky* and the edge of the sky? Can the sky be said to have a center? No, because the sky is free from "center" and "boundaries." In the same way, any thought that arises is unbounded mind. There is no difference at all between the mind of the past, that of the present, and that of the future. This does not mean that a buddha is unaware of past, present, and future—only that his mind is not afflicted by these thoughts. Thus, the unfabricated mind of a buddha is not different in the past, present, or future. *Its mode of being is uncreated awareness*, just as it is.

If we look at the nature of strong anger and attachment, we see that they, too, are uncreated. But we must come to actually realize the way in which this is so. If we follow these thoughts and grasp at them, we become caught up by them, enslaved, and helplessly suffer. But this does not happen if we can see their nature as uncreated. We just need mindfulness and strength to sustain that practice. When we meditate, negative thoughts will naturally diminish until they leave no trace, just like ripples on a lake.

We can relate to the mind directly only when our mind is free from elaborations. Then, we can realize mind's sky-nature, free from concerns of "boundaries" and "center," and with no division into past, future, or present. Mind's mode of being is uncreated awareness and that ordinary mind itself is Mahamudra. Mind is unchanging like space. Even though there may be stages of partial realization, full realization, and perfect realization, still there is no increase or decrease in the nature of the luminous mind itself. This nature of the mind is beyond expression and can be comprehended only through experience. And this experience is only possible when we have truly renounced samsara, have attained full meditative stability, and possess one-pointed devotion to the lama, Vajradhara.

Here is a beautiful quotation concerning Mahamudra from Lord Jigten Sumgön (in the *Wish-granting Jewel*):

> To have an unfabricated mind, leave it alone.
>
> Habituate yourself to the total absence of these cognitions:
> existence and nonexistence, empty and nonempty,
> self and nonself, pacified and nonpacified,
> equipoise and moving about.
>
> When samsara—mental afflictions, discursive thought—
> is liberated in its own places by the yogi,
> samsara becomes the dharmakaya.
>
> The precious lama, protector of the three worlds, taught that
> all confusion is primordial wisdom.

When a person frightened by a scarecrow
realizes that there is no person, all fear and anxiety vanish.
All discursive thoughts of self and self-grasping are like that.

For the yogi who understands without acceptance or rejection
the fundamental misunderstanding about discursive
    thought—
that the basic character of discursive thought is spontaneously
    established nonthought—
which of the dharmas has not been internalized?
What is left to abandon in the ocean of samsara?
Who else attains nirvana?

Never be separated from this blissful equivalence!

Furthermore, the *Magic Staircase* states:

The sky has always had no center or edge.
Space has always been clear.
Any type of obscuring cloud
will be destroyed by a strong windstorm.

The natural state of the ocean is to be free of change.
Water has no [ice] within it.
Heat will melt any ice-layer that naturally forms
back into the very same water.

Sentient beings have always been buddhas.
Mind itself, luminosity from beginningless time—
when this has not been realized, confusion causes suffering.
Know it from your own side and you are liberated in your
    own place.

The *Wish-granting Jewel* also says:

The fourth [of the five paths] is the self-arising Mahamudra,
the principal nature of everything in samsara and nirvana.

This great and inconceivable ultimate state
transcends the empty–nonempty [dichotomy],
annihilates hordes of maras and mental afflictions, is
    sugatahood,
is unsullied by mentally fabricated emptiness,
and is free of the stains of experiences and experiencing.

The coemergent wisdom
is realized by noble beings
through the kindness of the World Protector.

When the white-silver mirror of one's own mind is
free of tarnish—the elaborations of the karmic, afflicting,
and cognitive obscurations having been polished away—
all good qualities and the like of everything in
samsara and nirvana, without remainder, arise from this.

Unbroken practice is like a watchful guard.
It is simply unscattered and is free from acceptance or rejection.
There is no duality of things to be abandoned and their anti-
    dotes.
This is my heart's advice.

THIS VERSE and the following instructions concern how to continue with Mahamudra practice. Once we have received instructions, we have to accomplish them and perfect the practice. Continuity of practice is essential for the perfection of enlightenment.

Unbroken practice means that one is mindful all the time, *like a watchful guard*. Thieves and robbers may come at any time, so the guard of a mansion containing great treasure must be alert twenty-four hours a day. In the same way, it is important to watch our mind since the thieves of attachment, desire, anger, and forgetfulness can come at any time and steal the wealth of our compassion and wisdom, along with our realization of Mahamudra.

Once mindfulness is continuously established, an *unscattered* mind is "just there," on the spot, whether we are walking, eating, driving, or performing other activities. We can watch the mind and see how our mental state shapes our world. But when we watch it, we should just relax. Milarepa advises us in a vajra song:

> Rest naturally, like a small child.
> Rest like an ocean without waves.
> Rest with clarity, like a candle flame.
> Rest without self-concern, like a corpse.
> Rest unmoving like a mountain.

In the state of Mahamudra, there is nothing to accept and nothing to reject. As long as we are mindful, we simply need to watch the nature of mind. When we can do this, we won't be overpowered by negative thoughts. Instead, we will simply watch them dissolve and vanish. As mentioned before, when waves arise from the ocean, they are still just part of the water. "The wave is a manifestation of the ocean," Milarepa said. "It arises from the ocean and dissolves into the ocean." Thus, there is nothing to accept, nothing to reject.

Samsara's antidotes, compassion and wisdom, are not different from this. Therefore, *there is no duality of things to be abandoned and their antidotes.* The nature of that which is to be abandoned is emptiness; thus, there is nothing to abandon. The antidote also dissolves into emptiness. It is only our deluded perception of duality that creates samsara. This is what we need to work on by meditating with an intense focus. With full vigilance and mindfulness, we should sustain meditation of Mahamudra until this is perfected. All apparent elaborations, all experiences of grasping and fixation, are of one taste in Mahamudra.

The "born" and "unborn" are also of one taste. The Buddha said, "That which is born from conditions is unborn because it has no inherent birth. That which depends on conditions is emptiness. One who realizes emptiness possesses full awareness." Possessing full awareness means being aware and vigilant regarding cause and result. Emptiness does not contradict the causality of phenomena. Therefore, one who has realized emptiness becomes even more disciplined and possesses purer conduct. This is how we progress on the path to enlightenment.

Lord Jigten Sumgön expressed the eight Mahamudra samayas this way in the *Wish-granting Jewel*:

1. Do not abandon the vajra master lama, even after realizing him to be your own unborn mind.
2. Do not discuss the faults of friends or others, or the relative profundity of any of the teachings, from the sublime Dharma, Vinaya, up through the secret mantra vajra vehicle.
3. Do not interrupt your Dharmic conduct, even after you no longer hope for exalted buddhahood.
4. Continue to avoid all gross and subtle misdeeds, even after you no longer fear "debased samsara."
5. Do not self-aggrandize, even if you have mastered the samadhis of not sinking in water and the like.
6. Be open to others' views and conduct, even after you know

samsara and nirvana to be nondual.

7. Realize that buddhas and sentient beings share a continuum and let compassion effortlessly arise.

8. Remain in solitude, even after your meditation becomes free of the equipoise/post-meditation dichotomy.

Bringing everything to the path is like the medicine of
    Youthful Healer.
  Even harmful beings do not exist apart from one's mind.
  Release, without grasping, whatever arises.
  This is my heart's advice.

THIS VERSE instructs the Mahamudra practitioner in to how to utilize all conditions, whether positive or negative, on the path. *Youthful Healer* was a famous physician at the time of the Buddha. He could recognize the medicinal qualities of all types of plants and rocks and knew how to use anything, even poison, to produce medicine. In the same way, we can use all of our experiences in our practice. Especially in the study and practice of Mahamudra, we learn that the nature of everything is emptiness, so that there is nothing to give up. If attachment arises, for instance, resist following those thoughts and practice looking at its nature as emptiness. Good thoughts, bad thoughts, and obstacles: carry them all onto the path. They can all become part of meditation. An enemy who destroys us does not exist apart from our mind. Consider the way that a flood sweeps away both valuables and garbage alike. Similarly, all our experiences of happiness and suffering are washed away into the sphere of emptiness.

When negative thoughts like anger and attachment arise, we usually feel bad and think, "These thoughts shouldn't arise in my mind." Instead of pushing them away, look directly at them. Meditate on the nature of mind itself. When you meet harmful people or those who make you angry, look at your mind and think: "That person is illusory and this anger is my mind's reaction." The nature of mind is that very anger or resentment, which is empty. Then, without anger, you can communicate with that person and resolve the problem. Regard the encounter as a reminder of your practice. Used mindfully, all positive and negative conditions can become powerful meditation practices.

In the mind training of bodhicitta, we can even use negative thoughts as an object of meditation. If we feel bad or uncomfortable or are physically unwell, instead of rejecting these feelings or becoming overwhelmed by them or viewing them as obstacles, we can use them as our path: "May these feelings purify all the negativity and unfavorable conditions of all sentient beings. These feelings will also purify my own negative karma, so I welcome them." If we have a disagreement with a friend, instead of directing resentment or rage toward that person, we can look at our mind and use these feelings to purify the resentments of all sentient beings. In this way, the anger does not become our enemy, destroying our peace and mental harmony. Instead, it can open our hearts in a limitless way. This is how we can bring everything onto the path through bodhicitta practice.

When we encounter unfavorable conditions, we should look at how attached we are to feeling good. Such circumstances are actually good teachers because we don't realize how much attachment we have until something opposes it. Once we find them, we can purify our attachments, resentments, and other negative thoughts. Relatively, we can utilize them as a special means to develop compassion and loving-kindness for sentient beings. In absolute terms, their nature is illusory and mirage-like emptiness.

Sometimes we may believe that we perceive a monster, but this is just a mental projection. The monster, the perception of a monster, and the one who perceives it are interdependent. Without the one, the others cannot arise. Though they appear to exist, they are illusions and do not inherently exist. According to the bardo teachings, even the wrathful deities are a manifestation of our own minds. There is no difference at all between the manifestations of the bardo and the things we see now. All are projections of mind. Since this is the case, we should watch our minds and meditate free from all boundaries.

Having little renunciation and remaining involved with attachment and hatred is not the way to realize Mahamudra. Realization comes gradually. Expectations and wishes will not bring us realization. We must practice with conviction, based on confidence in the teachings.

Realization of the inseparable nature of appearance and emptiness, and of the conventional and ultimate meaning: this is what is called "pure view." Maintaining that view in the inseparability of calm-abiding and the post-meditation experience is what is called "pure meditation." Manifesting activity within the sphere of interdependence, pure view, and meditation is what is called "pure conduct."

Dharmakaya, whose nature is the two types of purity, unceasingly manifests the two form bodies in order to benefit trainees and other sentient beings. For the yogin who has actualized the meaning of nonduality, everything manifests within the sphere of Mahamudra. And since all Dharma is contained in Mahamudra, there is nothing further to accomplish or avoid. Sustaining meditation within the unity of nonduality purifies all the subtle obscurations. Just as a bird that flies over the ocean away from a ship has nowhere to land except on that same ship, all the appearances of phenomena and mental activity are contained within Mahamudra. For a fire that rages in the forest, everything nearby becomes fuel. In the same way, every positive and negative action feeds the realization of Mahamudra. The realized yogin is untouched by samsara. Freed from the eight worldly concerns, he is like a lotus born in the mud but not stained by it.

Advice on How to Dispel Obstacles
When They Are Encountered

80   *Attachment to calm abiding is like the frozen surface of a lake.*
It is dull and undiscriminating mind.
It leads to the error of the formless realm.
This is my heart's advice.

T HE NEXT FEW verses tell us how to recognize obstacles in meditation and clarifies how to dispel them. We need a one-pointed
meditative stability in order to develop vipashyana, or special
insight. But if we develop *attachment to calm abiding*, this is coun-
terproductive. Instead of becoming a means to free ourselves from
samsara, it becomes a cause of continuing to wander in samsara.
Sometimes, while practicing calm abiding meditation, we may be
very peaceful and free from thoughts. But if we become attached to
this experience, our mind will become like a frozen lake—unclear,
dull, and undiscriminating, and with no awareness of direct valid
cognition or critical insight. This will cause rebirth in a form or
formless realm.

We might have a wonderful meditation one day but not the next.
Then we may worry that we might not experience that peace again.
Our mind becomes agitated, and we become irritable. We should
understand that these experiences of peace are not the final result
and just continue on with our practice without expectation. Different appearances may arise during meditation, but these are not
always the same. Whether they arise or not, we must continue with
our meditation practice.

If we become attached to the peace of calm abiding and try to hold on to that experience, this may cause us to be reborn in a formless realm or in one of the four stages of samadhi in the form realm. The most important thing, once having calmed our mind, is to join that calm with insight. Calm alone is not the goal. Rather, it is a tool we use to reach enlightenment. Recollection of the four foundations is especially necessary for successful meditation.

In order to realize Mahamudra, it is not sufficient merely to study and engage in intellectual investigation. One needs strong devotion to the teacher and the teachings, as well as a great accumulation of merit and full dedication to the path. Here is a beautiful quotation from *Engaging the Intellect* (as quoted in the *Wish-granting Jewel*) that can help us gain this realization:

> [You may] understand a sky-like [amount of] Dharma
>   through study and contemplation,
> but clouds of thought will obscure [that sky].
> You will have no clarity.
>
> [You may] meditate on conceptual emptiness for a kalpa,
> but, bound by golden chains, [you will] have no opportunity
>   for liberation.
> How could [you] realize the dharmadhatu, free of elaboration
>   and appearance,
> meditating on any conceptual-elaboration referent?
>
> Desiring the union of recollection and non-recollection
> is a view constructed from a study-and-contemplation
>   understanding.
> Not comprehending the sky-realm, the frog splashes itself
>   with water
> repeating, "Try to remember! Try!"
>
> If [you] seek the ultimate with study and contemplation
> while saying, "That which has not been found is the
>   ultimate,"
> this [error] is subsumed under "seeking through artificial
>   mental fabrication."
> How could this become equal to the nondual sky?

If [you] meditate on the inexpressible, contemplation-free
    Mahamudra
with any stain of discursive thought,
how could [you] attain buddhahood, free of elaboration?

With what else besides abiding in the natural, ordinary state
with the stainless nectar, respect and devotion, [and] all the
    [other] conditions,
could [you] expand the full moon of the enlightenment sky?

[You] people may be serious and committed, but you need a
    qualified lama!

*Grasping at the duality of things to be abandoned and their
     antidotes is like a man with faulty vision.
Not understanding the mode of being, one holds one's own pro-
     jections as the enemy.
Cherish nonscattering and nongrasping mind.
This is my heart's advice.*

SOMETIMES, when thoughts arise during shamatha practice, we may think that our meditation is not going well. Especially in the case of negative thoughts, we may regard these as disturbances or as obstacles to our meditation. We may even come to hate all thoughts that arise in the mind, but this only strengthens our conception of duality. If something catches our eye, we don't want to see it. If we hear a noise, we hate it. We struggle with one thing after another. What this means is that we don't know how to bring everything onto the path. Like *a man with faulty vision*, we do not see reality clearly. Constantly fighting conceptual thought means that we still don't realize that both positive and negative thoughts are empty by their own nature.

Just as Youthful Healer utilized all plants, rocks, and poisons as medicine, so too do we have to use everything that arises in the mind, both positive and negative. Otherwise, when thoughts arise and we perceive them as obstacles, our conceptual thoughts become "enemies" of our meditation. This is dangerous. We must practice so that no matter what thoughts arise, we include them in our meditation.

A *non-scattered mind* does not judge, nor does a *non-grasping mind* cling to calm abiding or reject thoughts and sounds. Therefore, *cherish* the mind that is free from attachment and aversion, because it is not easy to obtain.

Generally, one who possesses one-pointed renunciation and devotion to the vajra master and the Dharma can experience Mahamudra easily. However, some practitioners may face obstacles when they practice Mahamudra. The most frequently encountered obstacles are taught as the four sidetracks and the three errors.

The four sidetracks, or four ways of losing the experience of Mahamudra, are the following:

- loss on the basis of the mode of abiding, which consists of intellectually fabricating the thought, "All phenomena lack inherent existence," instead of having the actual experience of Mahamudra
- loss on the basis of remedy, which happens when one uses emptiness as an antidote to the afflicting emotions instead of realizing that the nature of those very afflictions is emptiness itself
- loss through the path, which occurs when one is meditating on Mahamudra as path and hopes to achieve dharmakaya as something separate from one's impure state instead of realizing that the path itself is dharmakaya
- loss through fabrication, which happens during deity yoga practice when one relies on the three mantras to purify phenomena instead of realizing emptiness directly

This is just a brief introduction to this subject. There are many more details to be found in the Mahamudra texts.

The three errors that we may encounter as we progress in our Mahamudra meditation are the following:

- We may experience a blissful state. Attachment to this state or abiding there will cause rebirth in the desire realm.
- We may experience a state of clarity in which we possess clairvoyance, can see through solid objects, know past and future lives, and so forth. Attachment to this state or abiding there will cause rebirth in the form realm.
- We may experience a nonconceptual state where nothing affects our meditation. Attachment to this state or abiding there will cause rebirth in the formless realm.

The Mahamudra practitioner who experiences these errors and obstacles must transcend them with direct valid cognition in order to make further progress on the path.

An artificial view of emptiness is like medicine becoming poison.
Disavowing cause and result and saying there are no deities and no ghosts:
this is incurable.
This is my heart's advice.

THIS VERSE warns against having only a crude understanding of emptiness. We may hear special instructions on Mahamudra that say "nothing exists" according to some higher view. We may also be told to just "be where we are," and that there is no virtue to accept and no nonvirtue to abandon. Before one has fully realized the meaning of Mahamudra, however, holding to this kind of belief is dangerous, as it can cause us to disavow cause and result. Thinking that no deities, no buddhas, or no ghosts exist, we could become nihilists and create the causes to be reborn in lower realms. It is as Nagarjuna says: "Emptiness is like a snake." If we don't know how to grab hold of a snake properly, it will be dangerous for us to handle one. In the same way, if we don't know how to grab the practice of emptiness properly, we put ourselves in great peril of falling into nihilism.

Meditation on emptiness is intended as a method to counter our negative thoughts. But with only a crude understanding of emptiness, our mind can become more gross. If, through misunderstanding emptiness, we forget about karma, we will backslide into the lower realms and be left with no antidote. This kind of mistake is called *incurable*. In such a case, it would be better to remain trapped for a while in duality. At least then we will make efforts to purify our negative actions and develop positive thoughts.

Until dualistic conceptions have been overcome, do not waste your breath saying, "I don't exist." One who is confused and deceived by his arrogance in the Dharma will become fuel for the fires of the hells because, as was mentioned earlier, emptiness doesn't negate the role of causality. It is important to be honest with oneself and others, and take Nagarjuna's advice:

> If you desire higher rebirth or liberation,
> make correct view your habit.
> For persons holding a distorted view,
> even virtue will have unbearable results.

The discipline of highly developed Mahamudra practitioners is very pure. Just like the Buddha and his disciples, they watch their conduct very carefully. They understand the true mode of abiding— that form is emptiness and emptiness is also form. Believing that appearances exist on one side and emptiness exists on the other is called an artificial view of emptiness and is not the unfabricated emptiness that we seek. If we really understand the instructions on Mahamudra, we will be very careful about the causes we create. Everything that manifests from emptiness is dissolved back into emptiness; emptiness and appearance are indivisible.

This is why the *Prajñaparamita, the Mother of the Buddhas*, says:

> Buddha Shakyamuni proclaimed,
> "Bodhisattva, do not seek!
> There is no ultimate [state] apart from
> realizing one's own mind."
> Apart from mind-as-it-is, there is nothing;
> there is no realization or non-realization whatsoever.
> As Arya Manjushri said,
> "Great king, mind has no shape or color;
> So-called mind is nothing."
> Therefore, everything is nothing.

This means that there is no entity that exists independently. Investigation discloses that everything, including the mind, neither exists nor doesn't exist, yet it manifests unceasingly.

Attachment to cessation is like a raven's walk.
It cannot arrive at complete enlightenment.
It will fall to the vehicle of the shravakas.
This is my heart's advice.

How DOES A *raven walk* and why is this used here as an analogy?
When a raven walks, its tail swings back and forth, causing the bird
to sway from side to side so that it can't easily reach its destination.
If we, too, proceed like this, it will take a long time for us to reach
buddhahood.

There are two types of nirvana: the nirvana that is partial and that
which is nonabiding. Partial nirvana is the state achieved by arhats.
In the shravaka system, one's focus is primarily on attaining the
arhat state of individual liberation and freedom from one's own suffering. This state is called partial *cessation*, or *nirodha* in Sanskrit,
and is the state where all conceptual thoughts have ceased and no
personal self remains. Arhats remain in that state for thousands of
kalpas. But since it is not the final enlightenment, they again have
to strive for buddhahood for many more kalpas. Since that path
takes a very long time to attain buddhahood, it is better to cultivate
bodhicitta from the beginning.

Nonabiding nirvana is achieved by bodhisattvas, who focus on
the practices of wisdom and skillful means which comprise bodhicitta. Wisdom transcends samsara and is free from all suffering.
Skillful means manifests as great compassion that benefits all sentient beings without rest or lingering in partial nirvana. The result
of bodhisattvas' practice is buddhahood, called nonabiding nirvana
since it abides neither in samsara nor in nirvana.

Partial nirvana is achieved by purifying the obscurations of the
afflicting emotions, while bodhisattvas attain nonabiding nirvana
by purifying both the gross obscurations of the afflicting emotions
and the subtle obscurations to omniscience.

Being strongly motivated to attain cessation only for one's own benefit and being without concern for others are obstacles to attaining complete enlightenment. These attitudes will cause one to achieve the arhat state of the shravakas, where one can remain sidetracked for a long time. But since it is not the final attainment, it is just a resting place. The Buddha will eventually awaken those caught there and urge them forward toward enlightenment, as explained in the first chapter of *The Jewel Ornament of Liberation*.

Diverse experiences are like a summer meadow.
There is nothing that will not arise, such as clairvoyance
*   and so forth.*
Avoid pride and arrogance.
This is my heart's advice.

IN A *summer meadow*, many attractive and varied grasses, plants, and flowers grow spontaneously. When one meditates well, the mind becomes disciplined; clarity and stability become firmly established. Eventually, a good meditator can achieve samadhi, the state of equipoise corresponding to the experiences in the four stages of the form world and the four stages of the formless world. One gains a sense of profundity and strength and of being capable. Within that state, attractive and varied experiences such as *clairvoyance*, levitation, visions, great bliss, nonconceptual thoughts, and so forth, can arise, but one must not become attached to these things. They are only the play of mind that appears and disappears. On the path, various experiences can occur, but one should go forward to complete enlightenment without attachment to them.

In Gampopa's life story, we can read about the many experiences he had during the time he spent with his teacher, Milarepa. Gampopa had visions of the thousand buddhas, the seven Medicine Buddhas, and the sambhogakaya yidam deities. Sometimes he experienced complete darkness during the day, and sometimes he directly perceived all six realms of samsara. He recounted each of these experiences to Milarepa, but Milarepa only replied, "This is neither good nor bad. Continue with your meditation. None of these experiences is the final realization." Milarepa then gave Gampopa instructions on how to dispel obstacles and how to enhance his practice. In this way, Gampopa did not become satisfied with or attached to these different experiences of attainment and was able to grow in his practice until he achieved complete buddhahood.

We, too, should have no *pride or arrogance* about such things and should keep in mind that our final goal is enlightenment. Meditation should simplify our mind, not complicate it. Instead of becoming distracted by meditative experiences, we should continue practicing until we actualize the dharmakaya.

Self-grasping and wrong desire are like crops destroyed by frost.
If the Dharma, which is meant to tame the mind, becomes
*   a cause of arrogance,*
the root of virtue is cut.
This is my heart's advice.

A FARMER CLEARS and fertilizes his field, plants seeds, carefully weeds the plants, and finally harvests the result. In the same way, we carefully tend the mind by reflecting on the impermanence of phenomena, the sufferings of samsara, the interdependence of causality, and the precious ability and opportunity that we possess. Thus, we clear away the rocks and pebbles of confusion, attachment, aversion, and so forth. We should then plant the seed of bodhicitta in the softened soil of our mind. By carefully weeding out arrogance and pride, we can grow the plants of relative and absolute bodhicitta. Finally, we can harvest the crop of enlightenment. On the other hand, if one gives rise to arrogance and pride due to some meditation experience, then all the positive qualities that we have gained are destroyed. This is like a mature crop being *destroyed by frost* just before it can be harvested. Without a proper foundation and pure motivation, our effort is wasted and there is no good result. If the Dharma that is *meant to tame the mind* is used to further delusion, then *the root of virtue is cut* and we are left with no way to tame the mind.

When he was first enlightened, the Buddha said, "In samsara, there is cause enough for suffering. If there is a chance people will misuse the Dharma, it would be better if I didn't teach." Clearly, there is a danger of this, so we must be especially careful to avoid it. For example, those who go into a long retreat may think, "Now I am somebody special because I have done something that others can't do." The practice and retreat experience that were supposed to reduce ego thus end up supporting it instead. Gampopa also warned of this danger, saying, "If you don't practice Dharma according to Dharma, then practicing Dharma may cause you to be reborn in lower realms." It is critically important that we not make this mistake.

We should practice Dharma to make ourselves better people who are more sincere and less confused. Dharma is not a method to detect others' mistakes; rather, it is a way to look into our own mind and see what mistakes are there. It is a way to uncover our own shortcomings. This is most important. As long as our own mind is not perfected, we will perceive flaws even in those who are highly accomplished. We must constantly remind ourselves of this. Ego is tricky—it will look for any opening and then take over. On the other hand, Dharma is like a mirror. We can't see our own face with our eyes, but we can easily do so with the support of a mirror. Without Dharma, it is difficult to see our own mistakes. Thus, Dharma study and practice provide the support we need to recognize our faults and weaknesses.

We should be especially careful about this in our Dharma centers and groups. The more we practice, the more the mind should become gentle and peaceful. We should be supportive of newcomers instead of being bossy. If new people come, we should welcome them, give them support, and show them what things are to be done. Then Dharma becomes a good service to society. We have already had enough suffering in our groups. Sometimes, sangha members fight with each other in the name of the Dharma, but this is not practicing Dharma. Instead, we should sincerely practice in order to uproot the weeds of our neuroses. Say prayers like this: "May I benefit others through my body, speech, and mind. Like the elements of earth, water, fire, and air, may I be of service to all beings."

86 *The premature benefit of beings is like a leader with no sight.*
It does not help others and is a cause of suffering for oneself.
Make effort in loving-kindness, aspiration, and dedication.
This is my heart's advice.

THIS VERSE CONTAINS especially helpful advice. If, for example, someone prematurely becomes the leader of a group, he is certain to make many mistakes because of his lack of knowledge and experience in the position. Then, people will become confused and conflicts will arise. Everyone will suffer and will create more negative karma.

It is the same with a spiritual leader who possesses little wisdom or experience. We may have studied some Dharma and gained a small amount of knowledge, but we may not be ready to be a leader in the Dharma if we haven't fully benefited from our practice. This would be like the blind leading the blind. When we have really established ourselves in practice, then we can benefit others. The Buddha himself practiced for three limitless kalpas. There is no need for us to rush to become a leader before we are fully matured. There are countless sentient beings to be helped, and we can help them through many lifetimes after we have built up the strength and wisdom to do so.

Most serious practitioners stay in retreat and practice. When they have properly digested what they have learned, their wisdom, compassion, and bodhicitta will no longer be artificial, intellectual concepts; they will be a way of life. They can then more effectively help sentient beings.

When we act too soon, we act with arrogance, ego, pride, jealousy, and false expectations. We then only create more suffering for ourselves and others. Instead, we should put all our effort into cultivating loving-kindness, into bringing patience into our heart. We should repeatedly aspire and train ourselves to attain enlightenment and dedicate all the virtue and merit that we create toward the enlightenment of all sentient beings. We must keep these things in mind in order to practice Dharma sincerely. We must make constant effort, not just in one session but for twenty-four hours a day.

Lord Jigten Sumgön said:

> Son, for as long as your nonobjectified compassion is still unstable, diligently practice aspiration and do not be overly ambitious about benefiting others. You would be at risk of running after results for which there were no causes.

Untimely signs and marks are like sky-flowers.
Results without causes are deceptive.
These are obstacles of maras.
This is my heart's advice.

SIGNS AND MARKS are indications of meditative accomplishment. They arise as things like special dreams or magnificent visions, especially when one's mind is softened and well tamed. *Untimely signs* are those that arise when we haven't done enough practice to genuinely experience such things and when we don't actually possess the qualities that those signs and marks signify. They are like sky-flowers—an attractive fantasy with no basis in reality. But sometimes they appear in what seem to be significant dreams or visions. We may then mistakenly believe that we have achieved an advanced stage of meditation. These signs are called inner obstacles, and the author is warning us to not become involved with them and to continue with our practice.

Maras do not always appear as monsters displaying fangs and drinking blood. They can also seem to be gentle, peaceful, and beautiful. These are more dangerous for us, because when maras approach in a threatening way, they are easy to recognize and we are automatically on our guard. Thus, untimely signs and marks are *obstacles of maras*, created especially to deter Dharma practice. Be cautious and do not be fooled by them.

Advice on the Six Yogas of Naropa

88 *The wisdom blaze of tummo is like the cosmic fire.*
Through tummo, even this ordinary body can gain
enlightenment in this life.
It is the center-beam of the path.
This is my heart's advice.

WITH THIS verse, Bhande Dharmaradza begins his introduction to the Six Yogas of Naropa. The details of these profound methods of meditation are not described or included here. If you want to practice them, you will need to find an authentic master and meditate according to his instructions.

Of these six yogas, the first is inner heat, or *tummo*. Great dedication and indomitable courage are needed to support tummo practice. Bodhicitta and a well-established deity yoga practice, especially of the generation stage, are prerequisites. To bring up the tummo fire, your mind must be well established in samadhi, the equipoise meditative state. Otherwise, this will not be possible.

Generally speaking, our body is composed of six elements: earth, water, fire, air, space, and consciousness. When we are under the influence of an afflicted mind, our body is the basis of samsara and wanders in the six realms according to the degree of our afflictions and karma. On the other hand, through the mechanism of wisdom and compassion, this body transforms into the enlightened state when it is infused with the practices of the yidam deity, chakra, prana, and bindu by means of inner psychic heat.

There are two types of tummo practice: the common and uncommon. The common tummo practice generates inner heat with the support of chakra, prana, and bindu. In uncommon tummo practice, one actualizes the dharmakaya through the power of inner heat that completely consumes the fuel of psychic imprints. This practice is highly recommended for those who are dedicated and capable.

Cosmic fire refers to the fire that consumes this planet at the end of a kalpa. In the same way, the wisdom fire of tummo, if practiced properly, can completely burn the obscurations of the ordinary body and mind, and transform them into the enlightened state. This will not happen through casual practice over a week or month; steady practice, month after month, in complete seclusion is required.

The reference to *center beam of the path* means that when one has fully accomplished tummo practices, the other five yogas of Naropa can be accomplished easily. In fact, one can attain buddhahood through tummo practice alone. Milarepa was very successful in tummo practice and so he could display miracle powers to an extent unequaled by other great teachers. Not content with miracle powers, though, he achieved complete buddhahood in a single lifetime.

Luminosity, which dispels the darkness of ignorance, is like
    a brilliant light.
    It dispels the obstructions of the afflicting emotions and brings
        realization of the freshness of self-awareness.
    It is the essence of the path.
    This is my heart's advice.

THIS VERSE CONCERNS luminosity, sometimes called *clear light*—a brilliance that dispels the darkness of ignorance just as sunrise or a lamp dispels ordinary darkness. Where does darkness go when a light comes on? Is it driven somewhere else? Is it absorbed into the light? Conventionally, we say that the darkness is dispelled, but in fact there is nowhere for it to go. There are no words to express this, just as the dispelling of mental obscurations is beyond expression. This process brings realization, a *freshness* of mind untouched by fabrication. We see the essence of the path directly.

A meditator who is well established in the practice of the Fivefold Path of Mahamudra has a mind as stable as a mountain, a mind that cannot be moved by the tornadoes of thoughts and activities. Generally, ignorance consists of not knowing right from wrong, virtue from nonvirtue, or the different aspects of knowledge. Sleep is one of the forms ignorance takes. When we go to sleep, everything dissolves into darkness as at death and we lose all awareness and mindfulness. But if we can sustain a stable meditative state, even sleep will not produce a gap in our awareness. When a practitioner receives instructions from a vajra master, especially the instructions on how to recognize this state, that practitioner will come to maintain full awareness even during deep sleep. For such a meditator, there is no difference between "awake" and "asleep," or "samsara" and "nirvana." This is called the realization of luminosity or clear light.

Essence of the path means that clear light practice results in an unobstructed mind. All the adventitious mental defilements, both gross and subtle, are fully dispelled. Through direct, valid cognition, the freshness of mind is revealed. This is dharmakaya, the basis luminosity, the unity of compassion and emptiness.

The manifestations and transformations of dream practice are like a steed being trained in its skill.
Through this, one masters manifestation and transformation, blending the appearance of day and night.
It is the measure of the path.
This is my heart's advice.

IF A HORSE is wild, it is difficult to ride and it might even throw its rider to the ground. But if a horse is well trained, it can be used in many ways. Similarly, an untrained, wild mind is also difficult to control and may throw us onto the ground of the lower realms. But a mind well trained in dream practice is powerful. It can display many manifestations and can purposefully shift from one form to another while in the dream state.

Dream yoga practice *blends day and night*. At first, we practice it while asleep and use acutely sharp awareness to recognize dream as illusion while we are dreaming. We can then use this realization of insubstantiality to manipulate the dream-world and create various manifestations. This is what is sometimes called lucid dreaming. Later, that realization can be brought into the waking state, which is then also seen as insubstantial and as being no different from the dream state.

The purpose of dream yoga is to free ourselves from attachment and aversion. By seeing everything as a dream, we can actualize the mental ability to free ourselves from grasping and fixation, and to achieve fearlessness. At present, we perceive a duality: our dream is not "real," but our waking experiences are "real." Through this practice, we come to realize that daytime and dream-time are not different. Everything is as an illusion; everything is a dream. This is an important method to enhance Mahamudra practice, and to freely display manifestations of activities to benefit countless sentient beings.

Measure of the path means that, by means of dream practice, the practitioner gains a view of the entire path. Everything is seen as a dream, like a mirage or illusion—the transitory nature. With this method, one has the opportunity to realize Mahamudra, inseparable phenomena and emptiness.

The illusory body is like a reflection of the moon in water.
This instruction destroys attachment to ordinary appearance,
   the eight worldly concerns, and self-grasping.
It is the foundation of the path.
This is my heart's advice.

THIS VERSE CONCERNS the practice of the illusory body. Generally, we use "illusory" to mean deceptive, unreal, or without essence. But we have a paradoxical conception of reality. In our confusion, we perceive everything as real and tangible, so that our perception and the actual nature of reality are quite different. This is an important distinction. We can prove phenomena to be illusions through analogies and examples, but we cannot prove that they are real, concrete, or substantial in the way that we perceive them. By contemplating this, we can realize that all phenomena are illusions and without essence by their nature.

Illusory body practice allows us to regard all phenomena in the same way that we see a *reflection of the moon*. A reflection of the moon can be clear and precise and it can look quite real. But everyone knows the reflection is not the real moon. Using this analogy, we can view everything as a reflection and see that all appearances are temporary and subject to momentary change. When we realize these appearances are like reflections, we lose our attachment to them because there is nothing to which we can become attached. Our mind is thereby freed from hope and fear. And as all appearances are transcended and purified, we experience great bliss and inexpressible joy. This practice destroys attachment to ordinary appearances and self-grasping, so it is said to be the *foundation of the path*.

We can use other metaphors to examine ourselves in similar ways. Consider these:

▸ Our body is like a mirage. It comes and goes; it is merely insubstantial.

► Our mind is like the sky. Clouds appears in the sky and disappear into the sky. In the same way, our thoughts arise from mind and dissolve into the sky-mind.

► Waves arise from the ocean and dissolve into the ocean. In the same way, thoughts arise from the ocean-mind and dissolve into the ocean-mind. When you go to the ocean, carefully watch the ocean waves as they wash up and disappear. Then look at your mind and see how thoughts arise from mind and then dissolve.

When we investigate in this way, involvement with the *eight worldly concerns* also falls away. Whether we are Buddhist, non-Buddhist, educated, or uneducated—everyone, from the leader of a country to a person living in the street, tries to avoid pain and to gain pleasure, to be free from blame and disgrace and to gain fame and praise. But what lasting benefit do we get from this endless struggle? Despite all we do, we still just suffer.

Investigate this carefully and determine for yourself whether it is true. The Buddha said, "Investigate my teaching as a goldsmith examines gold." By melting, rubbing, and cutting, a goldsmith understands whether the gold is pure. So for us to understand the meaning of Dharma, it is not enough just to have faith or devotion. If, after examining them, we find these teachings to be true, we should follow and practice them.

We should remember here that there are two different types of "self." One is the noble self that we seek to cultivate by studying Dharma teachings; understanding the nature of samsara; working to be free from samsara; developing love, compassion, and bodhicitta; and attaining enlightenment in order to help all sentient beings. This kind of "self" is a useful notion: "I will attain complete enlightenment and bring benefit to all sentient beings." The other kind of self is bound to ignorance, attachment, hatred, resentment, greed, pride, arrogance, jealousy, and so forth. It brings no benefit and has no use. The purpose of our practice is to release our grasping to this ego-related self, because it is the root cause of samsara and suffering.

Since everything is interdependent, both "selves" are just a notion and do not actually exist in their own nature. The bodhisattva who realizes this can use that which has been labeled "self" to exercise bodhicitta. Samsaric beings who don't have this wisdom grasp the self as real and attach to it. That attachment becomes a habit, and then aversion and attachment operate uncontrollably. This is how the cyclic existence of samsara continues.

Phowa is like a giant garuda flying in the sky.
In an instant, it arrives at the pure land.
It is the messenger of the path.
This is my heart's advice.

THE FIFTH YOGA is *phowa*, the practice by which one can eject one's consciousness through the crown of the head and send it to a pure land. A *garuda* is a mythical bird that is thought to be very powerful and to fly very fast. In pictures, it is often shown landing with a snake in its mouth. Thus, the garuda represents the wisdom that consumes the snake of ego and ignorance. Here in this verse, phowa is likened to a garuda: At the time of death, it flies you to a pure land surely and quickly like an efficient *messenger*.

As mentioned in the earlier verses that described the mind and consciousness in more detail, mind is something that cannot be directly seen by ordinary people, yet it produces thoughts ceaselessly. This abstract subject is vast and profound; mind cannot be measured by technology yet it continues for life after life. Unenlightened beings don't remember this continuity at all, but this doesn't mean that there is no mind. Buddhas and great bodhisattvas have directly perceived mind and precisely described it. They have shown many methods to free sentient beings from suffering. Phowa is a special practice used at the time of death, or before, to transfer the consciousness to a pure land or to realize Mahamudra. In either case, the result is that one's mind-stream can be separated from samsara.

There are many different types of phowa, but the supreme phowa is the practice of Mahamudra. If one realizes dharmakaya through this practice, this is the ultimate path. There are also phowas of sambhogakaya and nirmanakaya, and then ordinary phowa. In ordinary phowa, which is practiced at the time of death, the practitioner transforms into the yidam deity, and then visualizes his or her consciousness as a syllable or drop (*bindu*) at the level of the navel or heart. Using the techniques of phowa, the practitioner then transfers his or her consciousness to the Buddha's mind. Through this path, one can become free from samsara and attain buddhahood.

The practice of bardo is like traveling a familiar road.
Free from fear, one recognizes confusion as one's own projection.
It is the receptionist of the path.
This is my heart's advice.

THIS VERSE INTRODUCES the last of the Six Yogas of Naropa. *Bardo* refers to something "in-between." There are six types of bardo:

- the bardo of birth and death
- the bardo of dreams, between day and night
- the bardo of meditation, between the beginning and end of a meditation session
- the bardo at the time of death
- the bardo of dharmata, or the experience of the essential nature of reality
- the bardo of existence

We are especially concerned here with the bardos at the time of death, dharmata, and existence.

At the time of death, the dying person experiences the sensation of being overwhelmed by four fearsome events:

- a falling mountain
- a maelstrom
- a raging fire
- hurricanes

We practice the bardo of death while still alive by imagining these four experiences arising in our mind and recognizing them as mere mental projections. If we practice this repeatedly and become familiar with the experience, the actual experience of bardo will not frighten or confuse us. Instead, it will be like visiting a familiar place. If we don't have this practice of bardo, though, we will be overpowered by fear at the time of our death and become totally confused. To free ourselves from this fear, there are specific instructions we can follow on how to relate to and transform the perceived events.

In the bardo of dharmata, the experiences of original mind-as-such are like the practices of luminosity, and the peaceful and wrathful deities arise. Our practice of the generation and completion stages of yidam deities will be especially useful in familiarizing ourselves with this bardo experience.

The practice of the bardo of existence will help us to choose a good rebirth, especially rebirth in a pure land. Without this practice and understanding, we could be reborn in any of samsara's six realms, depending on our karma.

When we arrive at a hotel or guest house, a *receptionist* will greet us, tell us where our room is, give us advice on places to visit, and so forth, so that we have no confusion or uncertainty about our surroundings. Similarly, if we are experienced in bardo practice, we will go through the dying process without confusion. The dream yoga and illusory body practices and their realization are also indispensable for understanding the bardo experience. Thus, all Six Yogas of Naropa are methods that free us from the confusion of samsara and help us to realize Mahamudra.

The profound path of the Six Dharmas is like a treasury of jewels.
It contains all essentials of the classes of tantra.
It is the supreme instruction.
This is my heart's advice.

A *TREASURY OF JEWELS* contains all the jewels and wealth that could possibly exist in the world. Tummo, luminosity, dream, illusory body, phowa, and the bardo—these Six Yogas of Naropa are just such a treasury, for they are a collection of the heart-essence of all the ocean-like teachings of Buddhist tantra. Serious practitioners should seek out a vajra master who has spent his life practicing Mahamudra and the Six Yogas in mountains and caves. Because of the interdependence between student and teacher, the student practitioner can then also spend an entire lifetime studying and practicing. These teachings contain the essence of the practices of all the *classes of tantra*—kriya tantra, carya tantra, yoga tantra, and anuttara yoga tantra. There are no greater, higher, or more profound practices than these. With these practices, one can fully realize Mahamudra and attain buddhahood perfectly.

Once you obtain these powerful, complete instructions, there is no need to look for anything else. Just sit and practice. There is a saying in Tibet: "When you have found your elephant, there is no need to keep looking for its tracks." Some people find their elephant, don't recognize it, and keep looking for something more that they never find.

Advice about the Final Result of Dharma Practice

 The three vows are like a carpenter's tools.
Without all three together, one cannot achieve perfect
  enlightenment.
Therefore, one should know how to keep them without
  contradiction.
This is my heart's advice.

HERE AGAIN, the author emphasizes the importance of the *three vows* and how to keep them all without contradiction. We should not think that one type of vow is better than another. Respect them equally and practice accordingly because the attainment of buddhahood depends on them.

Everything functions through interdependence. Even enlightenment itself depends on many causes and conditions. Thus, the author points out how we can practice successfully by making use of causes and conditions. A carpenter has to have all his tools in order to build a cupboard or a house. If even one tool is missing, the project cannot be finished. In the same way, the three types of vows—Vinaya, bodhisattva, and tantra—are a practitioner's essential tools to "build" enlightenment. We cannot neglect any of them. If we do, we cannot achieve the complete goal, for the three vows support each other. If we maintain good Vinaya discipline and abstain from nonvirtuous action, we can then practice bodhicitta successfully and benefit others. And once our mind is fully established in bodhicitta, we will have the foundation for successful Vajrayana practice. The vows build up in this way, one after another.

Vinaya is like the ground, the foundation from which we may

study and practice all the Buddha's teachings. By discerning the basic virtues and nonvirtues, we can create a soft, gentle, and workable soil. We can moisten that ground with compassion, plant the seed of bodhicitta, and then let the seedling sprout. This much is not enough, though. We must let the tree of bodhicitta grow until it bears the flowers and fruit of the Vajrayana. In this way, we can follow the path systematically, gaining experience with Dharma step by step. In reality, Vajrayana is more difficult than Vinaya to practice correctly. Atisha said, "I did not have a single problem keeping the Vinaya vows. Sometimes I had experiences that contradicted the bodhisattva vow, but I immediately renewed it. But in the Vajrayana, I stumbled." Thus, we should practice all three vows *without contradiction* in order to attain buddhahood.

The Buddha taught all aspects of the path without exception. Gradually, he trained himself from being an ordinary person until he attained the perfection of complete enlightenment and became omniscient. Guided by this example, we should practice Dharma outwardly with Vinaya, inwardly with bodhicitta, and secretly with the two stages of generation and completion. In this way, we can purify all obscurations and attain buddhahood.

Literal interpretation is like a physician with little knowledge.
Without agreement, one meaning may help, another may harm.
Therefore, one should understand the intention of the Kagyus.
This is my heart's advice.

A PHYSICIAN WITH LITTLE KNOWLEDGE of medicine lacks the experience to know how different medicines work. This can be dangerous, as he may harm his patient by giving the wrong prescription. For our part, we should know how to relate to all Dharma as medicine. We cannot regard some teachings as inferior and others as superior. There are 84,000 types of afflicting emotions for which the Buddha gave 84,000 teachings. Each antidote exactly matches a disease. One must be able to practice all Dharma teachings, as each is an antidote for our afflictions and delusions. Thus, all Dharma is equally needed for the purification of both gross and subtle obstacles.

Right from the beginning, the great Kagyu lamas taught their disciples to practice Dharma without conflict or contradiction. For example, the moral ethics of Vinaya are indispensable to the practices of bodhicitta and secret mantra. Desire is a hindrance not only in the Vinaya but also in the practices of bodhicitta and tantra. Aversion is a hindrance to bodhicitta and also in the practices of Vinaya and Vajrayana. A nonvirtue as defined by the Vinaya cannot become a virtue in tantra. In the same way, wrathful activities that harm another's life are not permitted under any of the vows.

In particular, it was Lord Gampopa who established the complete form of Buddhism in Tibet. He thoroughly studied the sutra system according to the Kadampa tradition and became a well-known master. Later he studied and practiced under Milarepa, from whom he received the complete Vajrayana teachings, including the Six Yogas of Naropa. Practicing them in their entirety, he established himself in the enlightened state. From within that state, he taught *all* the stages of the Dharma without contradiction. By showing how each supports the others, he produced thousands of great disciples and masters. All the different Kagyu lineages came from Gampopa's teachings. Even in modern times, many great teachers revere Gampopa's teachings. This is what the author advises us to understand about the *intention of the Kagyus*.

Lord Jigten Sumgön briefly and concisely summarized the intention of the great Kagyu masters in his *Nectar of Heart Advice:*

> One should not have scattered mindfulness even if there is nothing to meditate [on] in the uncontrived, clear state. Do not fabricate emptiness for outer appearances and do not make an effort to meditate on the inner mind. In order to set the mind in the uncontrived, the state of emptiness, or mind itself, untie the knot of grasping at meditation. Let the fundamental awareness be set as it is.

> That which is called Mahamudra is self-awareness itself.
> Maintaining non-distraction is innate dharmakaya meditation.
> Mahamudra enhancement is respect and devotion for the sublime lama.
> Understanding that experiences are dharmakaya is realization of Mahamudra.
> The arising of the happiness and joy of samsara and nirvana is the good quality of Mahamudra.

The essential point of the three vows is like a chariot's wheel.
  Behaving like a shravaka, practicing secret mantra, and holding
    to bodhicitta
  accomplish the goal.
  This is my heart's advice.

IN ORDER TO operate a *chariot*, all its parts are needed, including the wheels. When all parts are functioning, one can ride in the chariot and reach one's destination. In modern terms, we can think of a car—all the engine parts and all four tires are needed in order to drive anywhere. If any part is missing, the vehicle will not function properly. It is the same with the path to buddhahood. Complete practices are essential so that one can purify the gross and subtle obscurations. This is clearly explained in Lord Jigten Sumgön's *One Thought*.

Behaving like a shravaka refers to outward physical and verbal action: being gentle, disciplined, peaceful, harmonious, and calm according to the Vinaya. Inwardly, we should maintain the practices of loving-kindness, compassion, and bodhicitta, the thought of enlightenment. We should thoroughly tame the mind so it can extend to all sentient beings and achieve enlightenment for their benefit. In order to achieve that perfection swiftly, we should secretly practice the generation and completion stages of tantra. Through these methods, we can purify all the adventitious obscurations and accomplish the stages of the path to buddhahood. However, we will progress only when complete causes and conditions have come together. This is why we pray, "May I not experience an untimely death." This precious human life brings with it every opportunity to accomplish the excellent qualities of a buddha. Please do not waste this precious occasion.

The ten bhumis and five paths are like a climbing staircase.
Because of complete causes and conditions, one can gradually progress.
One should maintain the activity of a bodhisattva.
This is my heart's advice.

ONCE WE BEGIN to understand the precious Dharma, we can follow it step by step just as earlier bodhisattvas did. The bodhisattva's practice consists of *five paths* and *ten bhumis.* The five paths are called

- the path of accumulation
- the path of preparation, or linking, that connects samsara and nirvana
- the path of seeing
- the path of meditation, during which we practice and enhance our realizations
- the path of perfection, or enlightenment itself.

Fully renouncing samsara and properly attending a spiritual master comprise the path of accumulation. One begins on the path of accumulation by reflecting on the four mindfulnesses:

- mindfulness of the body as impermanent, being of the nature of decay, and so forth
- mindfulness of feelings—joy, suffering, and neutral feelings—as transitory
- mindfulness of mind as being like a cloud
- mindfulness of phenomena as being interdependent

The path of accumulation then continues with the practice of the four abandonments:

- abandoning nonvirtuous actions that have previously been taken up

- not developing new nonvirtues
- adopting virtues that have not previously arisen
- perfecting all virtues that have arisen

One completes the progressive path of accumulation by training in the four feet of, or supports for, miracle powers:

- absorption of aspiration
- absorption of perseverance
- absorption of meditation
- absorption of investigation, which develops precision of mind in the meditative state

The path of preparation consists of successfully applying the lama's instructions regarding both wisdom and compassion. One first develops five powers:

- faith
- perseverance
- mindfulness
- absorption
- wisdom awareness

When the five powers have become even more powerful, they develop into five strengths:

- faith
- perseverance
- mindfulness
- absorption
- wisdom awareness

These ten are the tools used in meditation practice. By training in the first five, the practitioner experiences meditative states called the "heat of emptiness" and the "maximum heat of emptiness." By being patient with these experiences of emptiness, one realizes the highest worldly dharma, which signals completion of the path of preparation.

The path of seeing consists of applying the seven branches of enlightenment in order to directly and validly comprehend the meaning of the ultimate truth. These seven branches are

- perfect mindfulness
- perfect discrimination
- perfect perseverance
- perfect joy
- perfect relaxation
- perfect absorption
- perfect equanimity.

On the path of meditation, that which has been "seen" is repeatedly made familiar through meditation practice. After the practitioner develops experience with incisive special insight, he or she trains in the Eightfold Path:

- perfect view
- perfect conception
- perfect speech
- perfect action
- perfect livelihood
- perfect effort
- perfect mindfulness
- perfect absorption

When one has fully perfected these trainings, the unsurpassed state of buddhahood is fully attained on the final (fifth) path, the path of perfection.

The *ten bhumis*, or levels, begin on the third path, the path of special insight. The first bhumi, called Great Joy, is achieved through special insight. The second bhumi starts when the path of meditation begins. As the bodhisattva progresses toward enlightenment, ten perfections are accomplished on the ten bhumis:

- At the level called Great Joy, generosity is perfected.
- At the level called Stainless, moral ethics is perfected.
- At the level called Radiant, patience is perfected.
- At the level called Luminous, joyous effort is perfected.
- At the level called Very Difficult to Train, meditative concentration is perfected.
- At the level called Obviously Transcendent, wisdom awareness is perfected.

- ▸ At the level called Gone Afar, skillful means is perfected.
- ▸ At the level called Immovable, aspiration is perfected.
- ▸ At the level called Good Discriminating Wisdom, strength is perfected.
- ▸ At the level called Cloud of Dharma, primordial wisdom awareness is perfected.

After the tenth bhumi, one achieves the level called All-pervading Radiance, which is buddhahood. So this process is like climbing *a staircase* step by step. A full description of these five paths and ten bhumis is contained in *The Jewel Ornament of Liberation*, in chapters eighteen and nineteen.

What is the *activity of a bodhisattva*? Bodhisattvas purify their obscurations and develop all the qualities of a buddha without exception until they, too, attain buddhahood. They are then able to benefit countless sentient beings. When we help others by giving them food, clothing, or shelter, these are noble acts. But because bodhisattvas maintain a stable state of mind with peace, calm, and ease, those around them also feel peaceful and calm. This, in turn, inspires them to follow the path, and that is the greatest benefit because it will eventually free them from all their sufferings.

To complete this journey, we need determination, devotion, and perseverance. Enlightenment is not something bestowed from outside. It doesn't come from reading books or debating, nor can we attain it by asking questions. This journey is an inward one, so we must cultivate awakening within our own mind and reveal our buddha nature completely.

99 *The fruit of perfection is like a universal king.*
It is without equal and fulfills all wishes.
It is completely free from hope and fear.
This is my heart's advice.

AFTER PERFECTING the five paths and ten bhumis, one attains *the fruit of perfection* and becomes a buddha. Of course, even a *universal king* cannot compare to an enlightened one, but such a king is mentioned here because he is unequaled in his own world. Just as a universal king skillfully rules over his kingdom and brings happiness to his subjects, a buddha can fulfill the wishes of all sentient beings. A universal king may rule a whole continent and bring benefit to his subjects, but he is still hampered by uncertainty about the results of his actions. Because a buddha acts spontaneously out of perfect compassion and wisdom, there is no doubt that his efforts to benefit others will be successful, so he is said to be *free from hope and fear.*

Buddhahood is the nonabiding nirvana that is achieved by perfecting wisdom awareness and compassion. It is called "enlightenment" because it is the perfection of the two types of bodhicitta, relative and absolute. Buddhas are called "omniscient" because their own, innate mental qualities are fully realized. They understand all that is knowable; nothing is hidden from them. They are called "Sugata," the Well-gone Ones, because they have gone through life perfectly. They are called "Buddha," the Fully Awakened Ones, because they have awakened from the sleep of the two obscurations.

Buddhahood is the realization of the sameness of all phenomena in samsara and nirvana. The perfection of the practices of morality, bodhicitta, and tantra fully reveal the profound nature of interdependence of the outer, inner, and secret, the distinctive result. It is the completely unfabricated equipoise state of the nondual nature of objects and subjects. Lord Jigten Sumgön described it this way in the *Wish-granting Jewel*:

The Mahamudra of one's own mind
is the king of both samsara and nirvana.
The various insubstantial discursive thoughts
are the ministers of that king.
The nonduality of the king and ministers
are the accouterments of that king.
Establishing all sentient beings throughout space in supreme
    bliss
is the law of that king.

The state of enlightenment is described in Chen-nga Sherab Jungne's vajra song *Manifesting the Mystic Body*, an account of the life
and liberation of Lord Jigten Sumgön:

You are the spontaneously established dharmadhatu, free
    from elaboration.
You do not waver from the completely pure luminosity.
You have fully perfected the faultless qualities of the Buddha.
You are the lama, the Dharma lord, the incomparable
    protector of beings.

You are the universal monarch of the unsurpassed Dharma.
You are the fire that consumes the fuel of the obscurations
    of the two kinds of grasping.
You are the shade tree that gives rest for those wearied by
    the burden of the lesser vehicle.
You are the lion that grants fearlessness to those who are
    timid.

The dharmakaya, which has seven characteristics, is like space.
It is free from grasping and fixation and from the elaborations
of face, hands, and attributes.
It is beyond being an object of seeing or hearing.
This is my heart's advice.

DHARMAKAYA is the all-pervading nature of original mind, the ultimate identity of the Buddha. It is total peace, the state of perfection. But its form is not a form that we can identify as existent. It is like space. Does space have any form or color? Is there something there to touch or smell? Does space have an end or a beginning? If we try to describe space, there are no words to do so; it is inexpressible. It is free from elaboration, so there is nothing to grasp. It is the same with the dharmakaya. *Face, hands, and attributes, seeing,* and *hearing* are all relative descriptions, and the dharmakaya is beyond such expression. Yet it is the basis of the infinite qualities of a buddha.

Dharmakaya is the result of complete purification of the obscurations of karma, afflicting emotions, and the subtle obscurations. It is the perfection of the two purities; it is permanent; it is the perfection of the three trainings; and it contains all the qualities of the three vows. Absolute buddhahood should be considered to be the dharmakaya, not the rupakayas or form bodies.

The qualities of dharmakaya cannot be differentiated, though they can be described from different angles. Consider a lamp, for example. The lamp's light, color, and heat can be described separately but cannot actually be separated. Nonetheless, to enable us to have some idea of what dharmakaya is, it is described as having *seven characteristics*:

▸ Dharmakaya pervades all phenomena. The all-pervading emptiness of dharmakaya pervades all phenomena in the same way that space pervades the whole universe.

- Dharmakaya is the unification of all-pervading emptiness and nonobjectified great compassion.
- Dharmakaya is unafflicted bliss, completely free from all suffering.
- Dharmakaya is inherently nonexistent and is free from elaboration in its mode of abiding. It is uncreated, total perfection.
- Dharmakaya is the embodiment of great compassion, unchanging from coemergent wisdom.
- Dharmakaya never varies from the qualities described above and is free from coming, going, increasing, or decreasing.
- Dharmakaya is unceasing and is not "just nothing." Instead, it is the embodiment of the ultimate bliss and the enlightened activities that will not cease until the end of samsara.

Buddhahood is also described as the perfection of ten strengths or powers:

- knowing right from wrong
- knowing the consequences of actions
- knowing the various mental inclinations
- knowing the various mental faculties
- knowing the various degrees of intelligence
- knowing the paths to all goals
- knowing both afflicted and purified phenomena
- knowing past lives
- knowing deaths and births
- knowing the exhaustion of all afflictions

A buddha possesses four fearlessnesses. The first and second of these were displayed when the Buddha proclaimed, "I purified all obscurations without exception and actualized the complete and perfect qualities." No one in the world could dispute this. The third and fourth were revealed when the Buddha said to his disciples, "These are the obscurations to be dispelled and purified and these are the methods of meditation practice that will cause that result." No one could contradict these teachings.

A buddha also possesses eighteen unmatched qualities. There are six regarding behavior:

- ▸ possessing unmistaken bodily qualities
- ▸ possessing skillful speech
- ▸ possessing unimpaired memory
- ▸ constantly abiding in meditative equipoise
- ▸ realizing that cultivation and elimination are not inherently different
- ▸ possessing equanimity

There are six regarding insight:

- ▸ possessing unimpaired aspiration
- ▸ possessing unimpaired effort
- ▸ possessing unimpaired mindfulness as a means for taming sentient beings
- ▸ possessing single-pointed concentration
- ▸ possessing unimpaired wisdom
- ▸ possessing irreversibility from liberated paths

There are three regarding virtuous activity:

- ▸ virtuous activity of body
- ▸ virtuous activity of speech
- ▸ virtuous activity of mind

There are three regarding time:

- ▸ unobstructed wisdom concerning the past
- ▸ unobstructed wisdom concerning the future
- ▸ unobstructed wisdom concerning the present

Dharmakaya is the uncompounded state in which all excellent qualities are primordially and spontaneously established. This state can be realized only by oneself. Enlightenment is dharmakaya because it is the perfection of innate nature. It is sambhogakaya because it is the perfection of all wisdoms. It is nirmanakaya because it is the perfection of all types of meditative concentration. These are all inseparable.

The qualities of an enlightened one are expressed eloquently in *Manifesting the Mystic Body:*

You are the precious body of supreme bodhicitta.
You are the ground of glory, the marks of the ocean of merit.
You are the guide of all beings without exception, equal to the
   infinity of space.
You abide in the ten directions of the world.

. . .

You are free from birth, aging, sickness, and death.
You have perfected the qualities of purity, self, bliss, and
   permanence.
You are the vajra king, who does not abide in nirvana.
I bow down to you who are unchanging in the three times.

. . .

Your manifestations are limitless but do not exist.
Nor do they not exist, nor both of these, nor neither.
They are beyond limitation
and beyond utterance, thought, and expression.

Your dharmakaya cannot be seen by any means.
Yet apart from this, nothing can be found.
When discriminating wisdom perceives this mind,
they are inseparable, equal, and the source of great bliss.

The two kinds of form body are like the mandala of the sun
    and moon.
Even though they are without conceptual thought, they appear
    according to the needs of beings.
They are the manifestation of compassion.
This is my heart's advice.

OUT OF PERFECT compassion, a buddha manifests the *two kinds
of form body*—the sambhogakaya and nirmanakaya. Just as clouds
arise from empty space, and rain and lightning manifest from clouds,
the sambhogakaya appears from within the space of dharmakaya,
and from this the lightning of nirmanakaya unceasingly manifests
until the end of samsara. A buddha appears in sambhogakaya form
to those bodhisattvas who have attained the higher bhumis. For
ordinary beings, the Buddha appears in nirmanakaya form.

Mandala here refers to a sphere—a metaphor for completeness
or essence. The sambhogakaya is like the sun, which brings heat
and causes crops and trees to grow, mature, and produce fruit. The
nirmanakaya is like the moon, which brings cool freshness when it
rises. Both effortlessly manifest their activities, both dispel darkness,
and both abide in space. The sambhogakaya and nirmanakaya arise
from the space of dharmakaya and are inseparable from it. Thus,
they are *without conceptual thought*. Their compassionate activities are unceasing and impartially given. We can think about it like
this: though there may be millions of pools of water on the ground,
a reflection can appear in all of them simultaneously without any
effort. This is beautifully expressed in *Manifesting the Mystic Body*:

> Limitless realms appear in your body
> and your body manifests in limitless realms.
> In the same way, your mind, speech, qualities, and activities
>   without exception
> appear throughout the infinity of space.

. . .

> Your manifestations are as many as particles of dust, moving
>   and still,
> limitless as space, and arranged like jewels.
> They do not obstruct or crowd each other.
> Nothing need be added or taken away.

There are many different nirmanakaya manifestations. An example of a nirmanakaya of supreme manifestation is the historical Buddha who performed the twelve deeds, through which countless sentient beings were established in buddhahood. From *Twenty Verses of Praise:*

> Sometimes you dwell in Tushita and, from there,
> enter a womb, take birth, and so forth.
> From within the dharmakaya, you perform limitless activities.
> I prostrate to you who have the power of various miracles.

A nirmanakaya of inferior manifestation can appear as a craftsman, a lion, or an elephant, for example. There are no limits to the manifestations that a buddha can emanate to benefit the countless sentient beings. From *Twenty Verses of Praise:*

> Sometimes, for the benefit of others,
> you manifest as a shravaka, a pratyekabuddha,
> a lion, an elephant, and so forth.
> Sometimes you appear as a craftsman.
> Your limitless manifestations benefit beings.
> I prostrate to you who have the power of various
>   emanations.

Buddhas likewise give teachings in different languages according to the needs and dispositions of sentient beings without limit. From *Manifesting the Mystic Body:*

> A word of your speech is as limitless as space
> and instructs all beings according to their needs.

Your teaching pervades the dharmadhatu.
In this way, you proclaim your limitless, melodious speech.

Even though a buddha's activities are unceasing, limitless, and all-pervasive, whether an individual is benefited by them depends on the level of that being's fortune. Because all phenomena are interdependent, the activity of a buddha alone is not enough. In order to encounter a buddha's blessings, wisdom, and teachings, an individual must possess good karma, inspiration, devotion, and perseverance. Those who have purified the subtle obscurations can meet a sambhogakaya. Those who have purified only the obscurations of karma can meet a nirmanakaya.

Uninterrupted compassion is like a river.
It doesn't tire or become discouraged.
It is equal to the limits of samsara.
This is my heart's advice.

COMPASSION IS the source of the Buddha's limitless, uninterrupted, and unconditional great activities. Just as a river flows unceasingly without effort, the Buddha's activities unceasingly flow to all sentient beings until they are free from suffering. Even this book is a manifestation of the Buddha's activity. It can bring many benefits to its readers, particularly if they put its instructions into practice. Because he has perfected compassion, the Buddha is never tired or discouraged; his activities continue without end.

If the Buddha's activities alone were sufficient to end samsara, all beings would have attained enlightenment by now. Since this is not the case, we must understand that we ourselves must make the connection through study and practice. Nor is enlightenment something that sentient beings can accomplish on their own. The Buddha shows the path; it is our responsibility to follow that path step by step. Therefore, we should build confidence in the Three Jewels: the Buddha, Dharma, and Sangha.

Buddhas arise from bodhisattvas, and bodhisattvas arise from the cultivation of bodhicitta. Compassion is the ground from which we cultivate bodhicitta, then enhance its practice, attain buddhahood, and finally display the activities of a buddha. Just as water is needed for seeds to sprout and then for a plant to grow until its fruits are fully ripened, the water of compassion supports the blossoming of buddhahood and all its attendant activities. Compassion establishes the connection between buddhas and sentient beings.

All buddhas have infinite and perfect compassion, wisdom, activities, and abilities. However, whether a sentient being is able to benefit from them depends on three interdependent connections: the impartial blessings of the dharmakaya, the motivation of the being, and the Buddha's aspiration. One or even two of these is not enough; all three must come together in order for someone to become free of samsara and achieve enlightenment. This is explained in more detail in texts such as *The Jewel Ornament of Liberation* and the *One Thought*.

Buddhas and bodhisattvas sometimes manifest as physicians and use medicine as the basis for healing and support. To benefit beings, they also manifest as the sun to dispel darkness or the moon to cool unbearable heat. Sometimes they manifest as a child or an old person, a sick person, or a corpse. The buddhas and bodhisattvas do not actually turn into any of those things, though. They are just the appearances of enlightened activity, effortlessly displayed until all sentient beings are freed. From *Manifesting the Mystic Body:*

> In an instant, you manifest in an ocean of kalpas.
> You can fit limitless realms into a single atom.
> Though you enact these countless contradictions,
> they take place, free from error, in the mode of abiding.

The Buddha skillfully gives teachings for the sake of trainees. These authentic teachings are marked by four seals, that

- all composite phenomena are impermanent
- samsara is suffering
- phenomena are without a "self"
- nirvana is peace

Once trainees develop their understanding of these points through practice, the master gradually teaches greater skillful means and wisdom. This causes them to follow the Mahayana path and eventually become established in buddhahood.

When the moon rises in the sky, it is simultaneously reflected in thousands of pools of water on earth. Thousands of television sets can display the same program in an instant without effort or thought. Thousands of radios play the same song at the same moment. In analogous ways, the Buddha's activities instantaneously reach all sentient beings. From *Manifesting the Mystic Body:*

You have perfected the taking of responsibility for beings
without becoming worn out, discouraged, or exhausted
    in samsara.
You fully accomplish whatever supreme purpose arises
    in your mind.
For you, these things become causes for delight.

Although, for the benefit of each and every sentient being,
you send out emanations equal to the infinity of space
and manifest in the ten directions and in many kalpas,
this all arises free from error in the dharmata.

103 *This advice is like a treasury of jewels.*
It lacks nothing for those who take the holy Dharma
to their heart.
Practice it accordingly.
This is my heart's advice.

THESE HUNDRED VERSES of advice contain all the jewels of Dharma we could ever need. The early verses explain how to relate to others in society and how to maintain a proper motivation. Then, teachings for practitioners are given step by step without missing a single point. So we are left with no excuses. If we sincerely follow these instructions, we can be of use to the world and of good service to many other people in these difficult times. Eventually, we can attain buddhahood.

We should memorize these verses or at least read a few stanzas every morning and evening until we attain enlightenment. This will remind us of our practice, of the nature of samsara, and of the preciousness of the teachings. In fact, Buddha's teachings in their complete form are contained within this small book.

Here, I've presented a limited commentary to accompany these root verses in the sincere hope that it will help practitioners deepen their understanding of the precious Dharma. You may find that some points have been made repeatedly. I did this in order to coincide with the root text, but also with the understanding that different readers and practitioners will understand the meaning from different angles.

Conclusion with Concise Advice

Thus, this heart advice is given as a series of analogies. Because they are analogies, they are not ultimately real, but if there were no similarity, they could not be used as examples. In particular, the profound path, the completion stage, the three kayas, and so forth cannot be defined by analogy. Yet, to further partial understanding, these analogies are given.

B HANDE DHARMARADZA shows great skill in presenting these teachings in a very clear way. He not only gives us the philosophy but supplies practical instructions on how to apply it in practice. He gives this from his heart for those who are interested in freeing themselves from all the different types of suffering and their causes.

The analogies he uses are beautiful and have profound meaning. They give readers and practitioners a vivid and precise understanding of the intention of the Dharma. Like Milarepa's songs, which also use metaphors and examples, these analogies are easy to understand. However, the meaning and realization of Mahamudra and the three kayas are beyond the conceptual thought of ordinary people. Their profundity and vastness of meaning are beyond boundary and are infinite. They transcend the samsaric state, so these analogies cannot completely show their true measure. Yet poetry helps us to glimpse their meaning. In order to fully understand and experience this, we have to practice and realize the meaning in our own mind. Then, we won't have to depend on analogies.

Alas! These days, some who pretend to be practitioners achieve a few of the experiences of calm abiding and so forth, and have some experience of the practice of inner channels. Possessing clairvoyance and so forth, they are deceived by maras. Because of this, they arrogantly believe they have achieved the dharmakaya.

Some think that the purpose of tummo is warmth. If this were true, even fire, clothing and the sun could fulfill tummo's purpose. But through the practice of tummo, one can obtain the seven characteristics in this life. Some are confused by the words "clear light." They think it is like the radiance of the sun. When they gain some experience of shallow clear light, they think they have achieved the supreme clear light of deep sleep.

Without even understanding the recitation of the three syllables, some think they are tantrikas and disparage the Vinaya. Some proclaim themselves as realized, but their five poisons are coarser than others'. In solitude, some behave improperly. They excuse whatever they do as the display of dharmata. They misbehave and disavow cause and result. All this is only a cause of great sorrow.

Therefore, if you wish to practice the holy Dharma from the depths of your heart, receive the nectar of the teachings from an authentic lama. Then go to a solitary place, far from the activities of this life. Further, do not engage in heedless behavior. Outwardly, do not transgress the Vinaya. Give up expectations of clairvoyance and miracle power.

This prose is clear and straightforward. The *seven characteristics* mentioned here belong to the dharmakaya and were explained in the commentary to verse 100. The sole purpose of Dharma study and practice is to free ourselves and others from all causes of suffering. But because of delusions, the mara of arrogance can arise and cause practitioners to create confusion and suffering in the name of spirituality. This is deeply unfortunate. With compassion, the author here sincerely gives advice from his heart and points out the kinds of delusional thoughts that may arise. Practitioners should carefully take this advice to heart and continuously practice. In this way, our minds can be as firm as mountains. That stability will allow the trees of Dharma to grow steadily, and then many trainees can benefit from the fruit. This is the only way to transcend samsara. Otherwise, we will be like a blind person wandering about at an intersection looking for the right road to take.

Revulsion is the foot and protector of meditation. Hold in your mind an awareness of impermanence and the sufferings of samsara. Contemplate the essenceless nature and join your life span with accomplishment.

Developing an awareness of impermanence and suffering brings us quickly to our goal. If we had no *revulsion* for the causes of suffering in samsara, we would not be moved to achieve nirvana. So revulsion and renunciation are vehicles that, together with loving-kindness, compassion, and bodhicitta, enable us to reach enlightenment. Without these supports, no matter how much we may have studied and meditated, we will not progress, because the afflictions of attachment and aversion will still be active. The following is an account of the beneficial effects of renunciation:

> Once there was a king of Magadha whose name was Shinga Shupa. He had a son called Kundukye who possessed great devotion and a clear mind. After he was grown, Kundukye could no longer bear the sufferings of birth, aging, sickness, and death, so he decided to go to a forested mountain to practice the Dharma. The kingdom's citizens begged the prince to abandon his plan and stay with them in the kingdom but could not persuade him. King Shinga Shupa became very depressed and asked King Daway Ö of Varanasi to advise him on how to convince the prince to remain in the kingdom and not go into retreat.
>
> King Daway Ö went to Prince Kundukye and said, "Alas! What a pity! You are giving up a glorious palace for a tree. Perhaps you have been deceived by demons or have gone mad. Please listen carefully to what I say: You can rule the country and practice Dharma at the same time." The prince replied, "Alas, Great King, you yourself must listen to me. I appreciate your kind words and compassion, but I am determined. When you have seen the true

palace of forest solitude, the palace of a king appears as a nest of ants."

King Daway Ö persisted, "If you don't want to rule the kingdom, at least remain in the palace and practice Dharma there." The prince replied, "Alas, the palace is full of afflictions and confusion. The past is complicated, and continuing to face problems in the future is exhausting. That house is like a nest of snakes. I don't want to remain in the kingdom."

Then King Daway Ö countered, "If you don't want to live in the palace, at least go to a monastery and study Dharma there." And the prince replied, "When you have realized the nature of emptiness, merely studying texts is like the chattering of parrots. That kind of attachment is just busyness and a fit object for compassion. I long ago gave up such chattering."

Then King Daway Ö said, "If you don't want to live in the monks' community, at least keep some wealth for yourself and practice generosity." The prince replied, "Even a mountain of gold adorned with turquoise could not attract me to wealth. Instead, with a focused mind, I will retain the wealth of contentment."

King Daway Ö then reasoned, "If you don't want wealth, you should at least have some trustworthy friends." The prince countered, "Even a hundred trustworthy subjects are not as dependable as enlightenment."

Then King Daway Ö said, "If you don't want servants, you should at least have some good clothes." The prince replied, "When you have the clothing of contentment, all other silks and brocades become objects for compassion."

"If you don't want clothes, at least have good food to eat and then practice the Dharma," the king said. And the prince replied, "Being fed by stainless and virtuous non-conceptual thought is the best nutrition."

There was nothing King Daway Ö could do, and he lost all hope for the prince. But the prince said to him, "This samsara is illusory and impermanent. Those who are ignorant are attracted to it, but the wise flee from it. Therefore, I too want to abide in solitude. O King, you should do the same. The sufferings of birth, aging, sickness, and death are unbearable. Samsara is tortured and endless. Your palace is only a dream." In this way, he gave advice to the king and invited him to accompany him in his mountain retreat. As a result, King Daway Ö also renounced his kingdom, followed the path of practice, and became accomplished.

Understanding the moral of this story, we should renounce the causes of suffering. Instead of building a big mansion with a "great view" of samsara, we should look beyond that to the palace of nirvana, which is eternal, the source of all peace and happiness, and the source of genuine benefit for all sentient beings.

Devotion is the head and catalyst of meditation. Therefore, with devotion, see the lama as the Buddha in person and supplicate continuously with respect.

Devotion to the root and lineage teachers, including all the buddhas and yidam deities, is of crucial importance. If we have an excruciating pain, we become one-pointedly focused on seeing a doctor. When we find a good doctor and receive his prescription, we will happily accept his advice without negotiation or compromise because we want to be free from pain. In the same way, when we finally perceive the nature of samsara and desperately wish to be free from that state, we will develop strong devotion for the spiritual master and confidence in his or her instructions. There is then no doubt that we will gain the blessings of enlightenment, just as Milarepa did.

Mindfulness is a sentry and the actual practice. Therefore, never be apart from recollection of the mode of being.

Mindfulness, here, is *recollection* of our meditation practices. This recollection transforms our samsaric habits into a buddha's habits, the perfection of wisdom and compassion. There are two types of mindfulness: with effort and effortless. As beginners, we have to remind ourselves of our meditation repeatedly. Once we become accustomed to meditation, effortless mindfulness will arise. This is like the working of an engine. Once an engine is turned on, it continues to run without effort. With effortless mindfulness, meditation becomes a natural part of our life. As if we were driving on a highway, we maintain a steady pace of meditation until we reach the "destination" of buddhahood. Thus, mindfulness itself is inseparable from the dharmakaya.

Compassion is the activity of meditation. For the benefit of beings contemplate bodhicitta, say prayers, and dedicate the merit. If you have no realization of your own, superficially guiding others and performing ceremonies of protection and so forth are obstacles of maras. Therefore, give these up.

The infinite and effortless activities of buddhas and bodhisattvas that impartially benefit sentient beings depend on loving-kindness and *compassion*, which are based in turn on transcendent wisdom awareness. Those who are on the path must constantly remind themselves to perfect bodhicitta and to dedicate all their virtues, merits, and good qualities to the enlightenment of others. We must practice continuously until we gain realization. Without a personal realization of these qualities, *superficially guiding others* will not be helpful. Sometimes, it may even bring confusion and disappointment and may give rise to resentment. Here, the author advises us not to be hasty about performing activities before our compassion is well established and we have realized the nonexistence of self.

The armor of meditation is regard for oneself and others. Be your own judge and do not arouse the concern of the lama, the Three Jewels, or your spiritual friends.

There are two *judges*. The first one consists of the lamas, Three Jewels, and spiritual friends who sincerely practice Dharma. We should be careful not to dismay them by our actions. The second and more important judge is our own mind. We should always consider that if we create negative karma, this harms only ourselves. We alone will experience the consequences. On the other hand, if we sincerely practice Dharma by purifying delusions and afflictions, we ourselves will receive the benefits. Guided by these two judges, we should wear the *armor of meditation*. Use this precious human life to the fullest by practicing Dharma.

Fully cut the rope of attachment to this life. Although the practice of winds and channels with consort is proclaimed, if there arises even one moment of ordinary view, one will fall to the howling or vajra hell. This is therefore the activity of those on pure bhumis, the eighth through the tenth. If performed by ordinary beings, the result of this practice of Dharma will be a rock to sink one to the depths of samsara. Camphor is a supreme medicine, but if it is used for treating chills, there can be no hope. It is important to practice according to one's own ability. Faultless practice brings the vision of one's own primordial face.

Again, this instruction is very clear and precise. In this short text, Bhande Dharmaradza presents the complete path of the Buddha's teachings, both sutra and tantra, including instructions on Mahamudra. This is like a clear light that dispels the darkness of ignorance.

Thus, I have presented—as a garland of words and verses—this common advice, the series of a hundred heart-teachings with analogies, and again the essential points of the practice of holy Dharma.

Because I, the Drigung Bhande Dharmaradza—a follower of the Victorious Lord Ratna Shri—opened a little the lotus of my wisdom because of the radiant sun of the holy Dharma speech of the glorious lama Karma Bhadra, and because of my deep sorrow at the sufferings of samsara and my desire to practice one-pointedly the essential meaning of the path, and in order to remind myself of the Dharma, and at the request of my attendant Könchok Drakden, and also in order to benefit those who take the Dharma to their heart, this was written.

The author, *Bhande Dharmaradza*, was highly accomplished in scholarship and in his mastery of all the different types of knowledge, and especially in the profound and vast wisdom of enlightenment. He received this wisdom from the teachings of the victorious Lord Jigten Sumgön through his root guru Ratna Karma Bhadra. He then put this wisdom into words for the benefit of future Dharma practitioners. It is now our responsibility to study and practice these teachings carefully, both for our own benefit and in order to pass them on to future followers. Only we can help future generations appreciate and admire the past masters just as we do. This is how the teachings continue, especially in the practice lineage of the Kagyus.

By this virtue, may all sentient beings attain the level of buddhahood. May I, also, abandon the confusion of distracting activities. In this way, may I perfect and achieve the fruit of the three kayas in this life.

Here we can see the strength of the author's renunciation. Because he clearly perceived the suffering of samsara, he dedicated his entire life to the service of all sentient beings, demonstrating his pervading compassion.

Dedication

As the author dedicates his virtue, likewise we should dedicate our merit and virtue. There are numerous dedication prayers, but this one, written by Lord Jigten Sumgön, is complete and concise. To begin we assemble witnesses to hear our prayer by visualizing them in the space just in front of and above ourselves. We invoke the root and lineage lamas, those who kept the teachings alive by receiving the holy instructions and passing them on to us along with their own experience. Yidams are special manifestations of the pure enlightenment state, free from confusion, attachments, and delusions. Buddhas are historical beings in the past, present, and future of the world who abide in the dharmakaya form. Bodhisattvas are beings on the way to enlightenment. Yogins, yoginis, and dakinis are those beings who are successful in their practice. We establish all of them as witnesses for our dedication prayer.

It is not just our own merit that we dedicate but that of all the buddhas, bodhisattvas, and yidams, as well as that of all sentient beings. We add to this the buddha nature that all sentient beings, ourselves included, have within their own minds. This powerful collection of virtue is what is needed to uproot delusion and purify obscuration. We commit ourselves to use this merit in order to be of service to others. Then we pray to eliminate negative influences and establish the true causes for peace and happiness. So, once we have established a solid foundation by dispelling our confusion and gathering infinite good qualities, we pray for the supreme attainment, Mahamudra, the dharmakaya.

This dedication prayer can be recited three or more times:

> Glorious, holy, venerable, precious, kind root and
>   lineage lamas,

divine assembly of yidam deities and assemblies of buddhas,
    bodhisattvas, yogins, yoginis, and dakinis dwelling in the
    ten directions,
please hear my prayer!

May the virtues collected in the three times
by myself and all sentient beings in samsara and nirvana
and the innate root of virtue
not result in the eight worldly concerns, the four causes of
    samsara,
or rebirth as a shravaka or pratyekabuddha.

May all mother sentient beings,
especially those enemies who hate me and mine,
obstructers who harm, misleading maras, and the hordes
    of demons
experience happiness, be separated from suffering,
and swiftly attain unsurpassed, perfect, complete, and
    precious buddhahood.
By the power of this vast root of virtue,
may I benefit all beings through my body, speech, and
    mind.
May the afflictions of desire, hatred, ignorance, arrogance,
    and jealousy not arise in my mind.
May attachment to fame, reputation, wealth, honor, and
    concern for this life not arise for even a moment.
May my mind-stream be moistened by loving-kindness,
    compassion, and bodhicitta
and, through that, may I become a spiritual master
with good qualities equal to the infinity of space.
May I gain the supreme attainment of Mahamudra in this
    very life.

May the torment of suffering not arise even at the time
    of my death.
May I not die with negative thoughts.
May I not die confused by wrong view.
May I not experience an untimely death.

May I die joyfully and happily in the great luminosity
    of mind-as-such
and the pervading clarity of dharmata.
May I, in any case, gain the supreme attainment
    of Mahamudra
at the time of death or in the bardo.

This prayer can be repeated many times:

By the virtues collected in the three times
by myself and all beings in samsara and nirvana
and by the innate root of virtue,
may I and all sentient beings quickly attain
unsurpassed, perfect, complete, precious Enlightenment.

Prayer for the continuation and increase of the teachings:

May the teachings of the Great Drigungpa, Ratnashri,
who is omniscient, Lord of the Dharma, Master of
    Interdependence,
continue and increase through study, practice, contemplation,
    and meditation
until the end of samsara.

⠇ Appendix: The Life of Drigung Bhande Dharmaradza

You are the embodiment of the vajra dance,
the three secrets of the Three Jewels,
the inconceivable activity of holding
the Victor's teachings and liberating all beings.
Döndrub Chökyi Gyalpo, I supplicate you.

TRINLEY DÖNDRUB CHÖGYAL (Dharmaradza), the reincarnation of the great Drigung Dharmakirti, was born on the morning of the twenty-fifth day of the Moon Month of the Wood Monkey year (1704) in Jang. His father's name was Dresay Ngödrup Tashi, and his mother's name was Namjom. His birth was accompanied by many auspicious signs, and, on that same day, rainbows appeared and flowers fell from the sky in the area of Drigung.

The omniscient Könchok Trinley Sangpo, the second Drigung Kyabgon Chetsang, whose fame pervades the three worlds, had meanwhile received a clear and unobstructed vision of this event and had written down its details. Giving directions and advice to the *chöppön* Chöjor, the *tsorpön* Bukge, and two other monks, he sent them to find the tulku. These four traveled south to Jang and searched in many places. Then they came to Laphir, a place whose qualities and features matched those found in the description given by Könchok Trinley Sangpo. When the search party heard that a special child had been born to Ngödrup Tashi, they immediately went to investigate.

The child, who was still only a few months old, became delighted when he saw them, and the party realized that he was without a doubt the reincarnation they were seeking. They then returned to make their report, and on the way they discussed the situation with

Taksham Tertön, who confirmed the child's identity. Then they arrived in Drigung and recounted all that had happened to Könchok Trinley Sangpo. Könchok Trinley Sangpo confirmed that they had indeed found the tulku, and he gave them a statue of Amitayus— together with many offerings and blessing pills—and sent them back to Jang. Eventually, they arrived again in Laphir. On an auspicious day, they named the child Könchok Trinley Döndrub and presented him with the statue and other gifts and offered prayers for his long life.

Könchok Trinley Sangpo then sent a party of seven, including the lama Trinley Wangchuk and the *drönyer* Rinchen Urgyen, with a complete set of the Kangyur and vast riches to obtain the child. When they arrived in Laphir, they offered all this to the child's father, but the father refused to part with his son, and this delayed matters for a time. During this period, the entire group visited the Five Deities Temple in Gyaltang, Döndrup Ling monastery, and Kongtse Rawa.

After finally receiving the father's permission to take the child, they began, on the first day of the first month, the return journey to Central Tibet. Although the boy was only six years old, he had already mastered Tibetan perfectly and was able to give Dharma teachings. Marvelous visions of Guru Padmasambhava and other enlightened beings appeared to him on the way. He visited Chamdo and many places in Nangchen. As his predecessor, Dharmakirti, had predicted, he opened the secret place of Lawa Gangchik. He then traveled through Jang, Pangchik, Wanak Gön, and other places. Large parties were sent out from Drigung Thil and Yangrigar to receive him, and in their company he went to the palace of Trolung. Rainbows appeared and flowers rained down from the sky.

On the third day of the ninth month, Hlotrul Chökyi Gyatso, the chief disciple of Könchok Trinley Sangpo, and the general secretary Namgyal Horpön Sönam Wangchuk, along with other senior lamas and leading figures, received the young incarnation at the Supreme Vajra Place of Saten, greeting him with banners, parasols, and music that seemed to rival the wealth of the gods. The two lamas [Könchok Trinley Sangpo and Drigung Dharmaradza] then met like father and son, and soon afterward they proceeded to Jangchub Ling at Drigung Thil to perform the hair-cutting ceremony before the statue of the peerless Lord Jigten Sumgön, Ratna Shri, which is like a wish-fulfilling jewel. And to the young lama's name was now added the title Chökyi Gyalpo. Visiting the shrine of Serkhang Dzamling Gyen, the chapel of the protectors, and other temples, Chökyi Gyalpo made great offerings, and he also made vast offerings to the assembly of monks.

Chökyi Gyalpo then began his studies and quickly mastered all known systems of reading and writing Tibetan. To his attendants, he spontaneously recounted the story of how the Buddha in one of his previous lives as a bodhisattva had offered his body to a tigress, how he himself had stayed in his wisdom-body form on the Copper-colored Mountain, and how he had then come to be born to his mother, and all who heard him were amazed.

At the age of seven, Chökyi Gyalpo received pre-novice vows from Könchok Trinley Sangpo. Then, over time, he attended Hlotrul Chökyi Gyatso, Taklung Wojo Tulku, Pelri Tulku, and many other great beings and studied the profound teachings of Lord Jigten Sumgön, the Fivefold Profound Path of Mahamudra, and all the teachings of the earlier great masters. He received numerous teachings and empowerments: the Vajra Mala; the Seven Mandalas of Ngok; the three traditions of Chakrasamvara (those of Luipa, Nakpopa, and Drilbupa); and various empowerments of the Four-armed Mahakala. He also studied the teachings of the great treasure-revealers: Nyang, Sangye Lingpa, Karma Lingpa, Ratna Lingpa, Jatsönpa, and others. In this way, he received countless teachings and empowerments from the ancient and new traditions. In addition, he memorized the ritual systems and styles of dance, drawing, and chanting of the Drigung Kagyu monasteries. He also studied poetry and the astrological systems of India and China. He mastered all common knowledge to perfection.

In the month of Saga Dawa in the Water Snake year, the father and son went to Lhasa to see the Jowo Shakya and to offer gold leaf to that statue and others. Together, they made great offerings of butter lamps, scarves, and so forth and made prayers of vast aspiration. At that time, Chökyi Gyalpo made a second offering of hair to the regent of the sixth Dalai Lama and received the name Könchok Döndrub Rinchen. From Lhasa, he traveled to Drigung Thil and Terdrom Tsokhang, where Yeshe Tsogyal had stayed for many years practicing Dharma. A five-colored rainbow, witnessed by everyone, greeted him on his arrival. He then went to Tsewa Saten, where he settled for a time. In the Horse year, many people gathered at the monastery of Trolung to mark a change in the administration, and both father and son went there and gave many vast and profound teachings.

In the Wood Sheep year, when he was twelve, Chökyi Gyalpo entered into retreat to perform the practices of various yidam deities. In the first month of the Fire Monkey year, he undertook a retreat on Yamantaka and experienced all the traditional signs of accomplishment. On this occasion Könchok Trinley Sangpo carved, from red and white sandalwood, images of the Sixteen Arhats, the Buddha, the eight manifestations of Mahakala, and so forth. Chökyi Gyalpo carved images of Yamantaka with his consort and retinue and of the peaceful and wrathful Manjushri. All these were done in precise detail and were magnificently beautiful.

In the sixth month of that same year, Chökyi Gyalpo went on pilgrimage to Terdrom. If interdependence and auspiciousness had come together, his life span would have increased to seventy-six years and he would have revealed terma. But his attendant, Gelong Do Dorje, created obstacles to his activities. It thus became inauspicious for him to visit the holy places of the ancient and new traditions, and he could not open new ones. He undertook a strict retreat of one week, and on the tenth day he conferred an empowerment of the peaceful Guru Rinpoche on a large gathering of people. He then returned to Tsewa.

In the Fire Bird year, when he was fourteen, he took the vows of a novice monk with Könchok Trinley Sangpo acting as *khenpo*, and Hlotrul Chökyi Gyatso acting as *loppön*. He then received, in their entirety, the empowerments and teachings of the Eight Herukas of the Nyang tradition in the midst of a large gathering. He also received the teachings and empowerments of Lama Gongdu, together with instructions on Dharma medicine practice. Soon after this, the Dzungar Mongols invaded Tibet, and Chökyi Gyalpo went to Lhasa. The Dzungars destroyed the monasteries of Dorje Drak, Mindröling, and Dranang, killing many lamas and causing much turmoil. But through the blessings and skill of the father and son, no harm came to the Drigung Kagyu.

In the Earth Dog year, Chökyi Gyalpo returned to his monastery. Könchok Trinley Sangpo's health then began to fail, and Chökyi Gyalpo remained in his presence to guard him and pray for his long life. After Könchok Trinley Sangpo passed away, Chökyi Gyalpo took charge of his cremation and invited many great lamas to gather and perform ceremonies, all of which were successfully completed. In particular, Shabdrung Chödrak of Lungkar came to offer condolences and to help in whatever way he could. As an offering to Chökyi Gyalpo, Shabdrung Chödrak presented him with an image of a youthful Manjushri made of *dzikyim*, which had been the special practice support of Loppön Prabahasti. He also gave him a cup made from the skull of one who had been born a Brahmin for seven consecutive lives. Both of these objects had been revealed as terma by Chöje Lingpa.

During this time, in the dream state, Chökyi Gyalpo had a vision of Könchok Trinley Sangpo, who transmitted to him a full empowerment of the Eight Herukas. This was a sign that he would later establish a tradition of the great accomplishment ceremony of this practice. In that same year, on the twenty-third day of the tenth month, at Layel Thang at Jangchub Ling, Chökyi Gyalpo ascended the golden throne as the regent of Lord Jigten Sumgön. In the Earth Pig year, he completed work on the silver stupa of Könchok Trinley Sangpo, and an assembly of monks consecrated this with the performance of a Chakrasamvara sadhana. He also raised a statue at Trolung which was consecrated in the same way. Then, in a dream, Könchok Trinley Sangpo appeared again in his wisdom body, and Chökyi Gyalpo asked if he had made any mistake in the consecration of these supports. To Chökyi Gyalpo's relief, Könchok Trinley Sangpo assured him that all had been properly fulfilled.

With the Chödze of Depa Lumpa, Chökyi Gyalpo then studied the two systems of Sanskrit—Kalapa and Tsandrapa—and, just on hearing them presented, quickly understood them. To further fulfill the intentions of Könchok Trinley Sangpo, he established, in the Iron Bird year at Yangrigar, the tradition of the great accomplishment ceremony of the deity Tsogu, which had been composed by Dharmakirti.

Then, to protect Tibet from the ravages of the Dzumgars, the K'ang-hsi emperor came. Chökyi Gyalpo went to meet him at Tsar

Gungthang, where the two honored each other with an exchange of gifts. Soon after, the reincarnation of the sixth Dalai Lama arrived from Lithang, and Chökyi Gyalpo went to receive him at Radreng valley by way of Lungsho. Chökyi Gyalpo and his entourage welcomed him with great ceremony, and they then traveled together through Phenyul to Lhasa, where Chökyi Gyalpo made great offerings during the Dalai Lama's enthronement. He then returned to Drigung.

In the Iron Ox year, Chökyi Gyalpo traveled through Lhasa to Drepung to see the Dalai Lama, make long-life offerings, and hold intimate and open discussions. While in Lhasa, he met many Chinese, Mongolians, and Tibetans whom he satisfied with teachings according to their individual wishes. He then returned again to Drigung.

During the time of the Dzungar occupation, there had been a break in the continuity of the reversal ceremonies of Shinje and Sotor, and these had gradually been lost. In the Water Tiger year, Chökyi Gyalpo restored these ceremonies to their former strength. At Yangrigar, monastic discipline had declined. Because of his conviction that the root of the Buddha's teachings is the Vinaya—and especially because Lord Jigten Sumgön had praised moral ethics— Chökyi Gyalpo tightened the discipline at Yangrigar, using both peaceful and wrathful means, and he encouraged the monks in their study, contemplation, and meditation and in the path of the ten virtuous activities. For the use of the monasteries, he gathered images, different types of cymbals from Hor, brocades, silks, and other precious materials. Each year, he made offerings of these in quantities and of a quality beyond the imagination of ordinary people. In the Wood Dragon year, he commissioned thirty-nine thangkas depicting the holders of the Golden Linage of the Drigung Kagyu, and he completed the construction of Dzongsar Tashi Tsuk, which had been begun by Dharmakirti. Then he conducted elaborate consecrations.

Although inauspicious circumstances had manifested before when he had visited Terdrom, a chance remained that he could open secret places, in particular the Urgyen Cave. But when he sent some monks to find a road to these sites, Gelong Dode said that there was no way to go, and this became an obstacle to their discovery. In the later part of that year, Chökyi Gyalpo went to Terdrom and visited most of the old and new holy places nearby of pure aspiration. When he arrived at the top of one of the new holy places, a mountain, a rainbow appeared, and all who were present heard the sound of a drum being beaten in the Mahakala Cave. Chökyi Gyalpo himself received visions of Milarepa, Tara, Dzambhala, and other awakened beings, and he pointed out the many self-arisen images that had appeared in that holy place.

By stages, he traveled around the mountain and came to the glorious retreat place, Tsa-Uk. In the Dorje Lokar Cave, Lord Jigten Sumgön's footprints had, over time, become hidden by dirt, and people could not easily find them. Chökyi Gyalpo found them all and showed them to his companions. At Terdrom and at Tsa-Uk, Chökyi Gyalpo's party performed a longevity practice in retreat.

In the Wood Snake year, on the fourth day of the sixth month— the day when Lord Buddha taught the Four Noble Truths—Chökyi Gyalpo traveled north with a large entourage to Taklung, Yangpachen, and other holy places. At Dechen Chökyi Phodrang in Shang Takna, on the auspicious eighth day of the month of Saga Dawa, he received the vows of full ordination from Trewo Rinpoche, Jangchub Nyingpo. The two lamas then exchanged empowerments. Chökyi Gyalpo then toured the great holy place of Saphu Lung and the retreat place of Tashak.

Even though the principal meditation practice of Lord Jigten Sumgön had been Chakrasamvara, the numbers of people performing this meditation had decreased since his time. Chökyi Gyalpo therefore composed an abbreviated text for this sadhana and reestablished its practice. During this period, Chökyi Gyalpo received limitless offerings, gave many teachings, and distributed wealth to satisfy the needy. In the autumn, he returned to Yangrigar in Drigung. There, he strengthened the three streams of practice and established the *sojong* of the fourteenth and fifteenth days.

In the Earth Monkey year, when problems arose in U-Tsang, he quickly went to Kongpo but returned soon after. Könchok Trinley Sangpo's reincarnation was then born to the Orong family of Kongpo. Chökyi Gyalpo clearly perceived this, and he sent Gelong Chöjor to find the tulku. The child was recognized without error, but Önpo Hla Sithar and Sölpön Leksang disputed the recognition, and many people became confused by maras. The matter was taken to court.

Because of misinterpretation of a prophecy of the oracle of a Dharma protector, the son of Hlasi was mistakenly recognized as the tulku, and this resulted in great controversy. Because of this, Chökyi Gyalpo went to Lhasa to see the ruler to present his case, and he received permission to conduct an urn ceremony in front of the precious Jowo. The first name to emerge from the urn was that of the son of Orong, who was the unmistaken incarnation. The second name was that of a candidate in a distant place. The third name, that of the son of Hlasi, did not come out at all. Thus, all ended well.

Then, in order to revive and increase the tradition of secret mantra of the Ancient Translation School, and also—as a root cause for the happiness of the Tibetan people—to reverse the causes of war, Chökyi Gyalpo established the great accomplishment ceremony of Nyang's Kagye Deshek Dupa at Yangrigar. He assigned the responsibilities for mandala construction, mask-making, and the gathering of materials and compiled the necessary texts. In this way, he benefited the teachings of the Nyingma school.

Soon after this, the former abbot of Yangrigar, Gyalse Trinley Tsedak—along with many others—went to bring back the tulku of Könchok Trinley Sangpo, and in the ninth month of the Earth Bird year they arrived without obstacle in Drigung. With great joy, the father and son met at Tsewa. Then, in front of the statue of Lord Jigten Sumgön at Drigung Thil, they performed the first hair-cutting ceremony. It was a common practice at that time for people to eat meat during religious ceremonies. Chökyi Gyalpo felt that this was improper, especially during the recitation of longevity prayers, and asked everyone to reduce their attachment to this custom. He then gave all the teachings and empowerments—common and uncommon—of the Drigung Kagyu to the young tulku. In addition, both father and son received many teachings and empowerments from Hlotrul Chökyi Gyatso.

Before the Dzungar occupation, Trolung monastery had successfully maintained the torma-throwing traditions of Kagye, Mahakala, Trochu, and Guru Drakpo. In the Wood Tiger year, Chökyi Gyalpo appointed teachers to restore these traditions. In the same way that he had tightened discipline at Yangrigar, Chökyi Gyalpo then began to speak against the consumption of alcohol by monks, even though they argued that by boiling liquor they removed its bad effects. Even in the preparation of the nectar used for blessing tormas, no one performed this system properly because of a general decline of realization due to obscurations of conceptual thought. Because Lord Jigten Sumgön had said that for those with realization there is no difference between water, beer, and milk, Chökyi Gyalpo established the use of milk, tea, or clean water for this purpose and taught that alcohol should not be used at all.

Chökyi Gyalpo performed many retreats on Yamantaka, Chakrasamvara, Kalachakra, Yangsab, and the Dharma protector Achi and accomplished all the signs and realizations described in those texts. Once, while doing a longevity practice in retreat, he had a vision of Guru Rinpoche and the Dharma King Trisong Detsen surrounded by a rainbow.

Every six years, there was a rotation of the administrators of Yangrigar and Drigung Thil. On these occasions, Chökyi Gyalpo would present to retreatants the profound teachings of Lord Jigten Sumgön, the Fivefold Profound Path of Mahamudra, the Six Yogas of Naropa, Dzogchen according to the Yangsab, and other instructions. As a result of his teachings, many practitioners were produced who gave up all attachment to this life—in particular, Gampo Tulku, Kunzang Ngedön Wangpo, the omniscient Drukpa Kagyu Trinley Shingta, Katok Rigdzin Tsewang Norbu, Pawo Dorje Tsuklak, and others. These great beings received empowerments and teachings of both the old and new schools from Chökyi Gyalpo on many occasions. In Do-Me Tongkhor, Sara Chöje made offerings of wealth to Chökyi Gyalpo that rivaled the riches of Vaishravana.

Chökyi Gyalpo once painted a thangka of the Kagye Dedu, including depictions of his own future lives as Peljung Atima and so forth. He also commissioned statues, made from red and white sandalwood, depicting the twelve deeds of the Buddha. The artisan, Lujin, began work on these but then passed away, and the work was discontinued.

At Laphir in Jang, Chökyi Gyalpo established a new monastery, Thubten Dargye Ling, which was still flourishing at the time that this account was written [in the eighteenth or nineteenth century].

Then—in order to maintain the continuity of the Buddha's teachings and to provide a support for the gathering of the two accumulations—he decided to build a temple, complete with images and furnishings, at Trolung. On an auspicious day of an auspicious month in the Earth Horse year, he conducted elaborate groundbreaking ceremonies, and he then quickly built a temple of two stories and twelve pillars. This was completed in the first month of the Earth Sheep year, and in the Iron Monkey year he finished work on the interior—including paintings and shrine-shelves—and brought many images that had previously had no home. In the Iron Bird year, he invited many Tibetan and Nepalese artisans to build an Enlightenment Stupa and a Miracle Stupa to subjugate evil forces, along with a Harmonizing Stupa for the blessings of life. Each of these was one and a half stories tall, made from gold and silver, ornamented with precious jewels, and of beautiful form. They were placed in the Hlundrub Dorje chapel, where Chökyi Gyalpo consecrated them many times.

In the Water Dog year, Chökyi Gyalpo invited more artisans—along with their leader, Dorshing, and including those who had previously built the stupas—to construct an image called Great Sage, Ornament of the Three Worlds, Shower of Blessings. Together with its golden parasol and throne, this stood two stories tall. To build this amazing statue—the mere sight of which inspires pure devotion—Chökyi Gyalpo used more than three thousand gold pieces and six hundred horse-loads of copper. It was located in the chapel called Mingyur Dorje Den and was consecrated many times through elaborate ceremony with the practices of Chakrasamvara, Yamantaka, and the peaceful and wrathful deities.

In the Water Pig year, many of those same artisans made images of the Sixteen Arhats from gold and copper. Using more than seven hundred *sang* of silver, Chökyi Gyalpo then built a statue of Könchok Trinley Sangpo, of greater than life size, called Meaningful to Behold. Chökyi Gyalpo's monks, led by Epa Norbu Chöphel, fashioned representations of the Buddha's fifteen miracles at Shravasti out of ground gems and powdered silk and built rock caves to shelter the images of the arhats. The miracle representations were placed in the chapel called Ogmin, and the arhats were placed in the chapel called Deden. They were repeatedly consecrated with the practice of an ocean of tantras.

In the thirteenth *rabjung*, in the Fire Horse year, the unfinished work of Jujin was begun again by some wealthy monks led by Epa Gyaltsen. Then, accompanied by the scattering of auspicious flowers, the tulku of Könchok Trinley Sangpo was enthroned on the lion throne at the great seat, Jangchub Ling.

At Trolung, Chökyi Gyalpo established a tradition of the dances of the Dharma protectors, adding those of Beng Mahakala, Tsering Chen-nga, Vaishravana, and so forth. By the end of that year, the carvings of the twelve deeds were completed.

When Könchok Trinley Sangpo was alive, he had repeatedly said that it would be good to build a model of the Chakrasamvara mandala of sixty-two deities. In order to fulfill this intention, and to provide a crucial support for the practice of that meditation, Chökyi Gyalpo constructed that mandala—both its outer form and inner contents—in astonishing detail. The artisans he employed were the same as before. The mandala was completed in the Dragon year and was placed in the Ngönga chapel and consecrated.

In the Earth Snake year, the mahapandita Situ Chökyi Jungne came to visit Chökyi Gyalpo, and they exchanged many teachings and empowerments. In the Horse year, Chökyi Gyalpo became seriously ill but soon recovered.

At Trolung monastery, the great accomplishment ceremony of Tsogu was performed on the twenty-ninth day of the sixth month of each year to fulfill the intention of Könchok Trinley Sangpo. On these occasions, Chökyi Gyalpo made vast offerings to the assembly of monks. In the second month of the Water Monkey year, many Tibetan and Nepalese artisans, joined later by Dhanoshing, began to gather to construct images of the lineage lamas of Drigung, beginning with Vajradhara and including yidams and Dharma protectors. All were life size and made from gold and copper. These were completed in the Water Bird year and were placed in the Chökor Dorje Nyingpo chapel. Then, using gold and silver, Chökyi Gyalpo built a Descending from the God Realm Stupa and a Lotus Heap Stupa. He also built an Auspicious Stupa of Many Doors, a little higher than the others, which contained the sixty-two deities of Chakrasamvara.

For reasons of auspiciousness, he then built a Completely Victorious Stupa instead of a Parinirvana Stupa. To the right and left of the temple's main statue were placed images of Amitabha and the All-seeing Lord. The main statue stood two stories high, and the flanking images stood at a height of a little more than a story each. Their thrones and back supports were also made of gold and silver.

In the third month of the Wood Dog year, all of this was completed without obstacle. From Lhasa, Chökyi Gyalpo then brought a complete set of the Kangyur and the Tengyur, and from Derge he brought two sets of the Kangyur printed in a special red ink. He then quickly fashioned images of the Thirty-five Buddhas out of red and white sandalwood, along with a representation of the buddha field of Dewachen. One by one, he opened the mandalas—from both the old and new traditions—of the Three Roots, the wrathful and peaceful deities, Yamantaka, Chakrasamvara, and so forth, and these were consecrated many times with auspicious prayers in gatherings led by the father and son. When the artisans had finished their work, Chökyi Gyalpo pleased them with many gifts. Each of the six chapels was adorned with canopies and wall-hangings, all as colorful and bright as if they had come from the treasury of the emperor of China. The images were dressed in excellent clothes and scarves. Marvelous butterlamps were brought in countless numbers from China, Hor, Kashmir, and other places. In brief, many inconceivably wonderful varieties of offering materials were made and taken there.

Thus, Chökyi Gyalpo accomplished all that he had intended. When he had completed his benefit of beings in that life, many inauspicious signs were observed. He gave extensive advice to all his followers, including the tulku of Könchok Trinley Sangpo, saying especially that if it were not possible for them to build his stupa in gold and silver, they should build many stupas of various sizes in the upper and lower parts of Drigung valley and divide his relics among them. This, he said, would provide many causes for the spread of the Dharma. Then, pointing to a lotus in a representation of Dewachen, he said: "I will be sitting here. Because I have prayed with one-pointed mind, there is no doubt that I will be born in Dewachen."

Then, although no particular disease had been diagnosed, Chökyi

Gyalpo's health began to fail. On the twenty-first day of the month of Saga Dawa in his fifty-first year, as the first warmth of the morning sun struck the ground, his profound mind dissolved into the dharmadhatu, and the area was filled with rainbows and the sounds of music. Many other marvelous signs occurred. On the twenty-ninth day, Chökyi Gyalpo's holy remains were cremated in the midst of a large gathering accompanied by a Yamantaka ceremony led by the supreme emanation of Tendzin Drodul, the tulku of Könchok Trinley Sangpo.

On the forth-ninth day following the parinirvana, a stupa called One Hundred Thousand Relics was built during a special ceremony at Trolung. At the end of that year, ceremonies were also held in Tsewa, and following that, in the Wood Pig year, a large image of Chökyi Gyalpo made of gold and silver was placed in the hall at Trolung. A large silver stupa, more than two stories high, was built at the great seat, Drigung Thil. A golden stupa was also built at Kailash. All this was done in accordance with custom.

Chökyi Gyalpo's successor was the peerless precious Dharma Lord Tendzin Drodul and his chief disciple was Gartrul Könchok Tendzin Chökyi Nyima, who held the vast and profound teachings of the Drigung Kagyu that ripen and free. When Lord Jigten Sumgön appeared as the tathagata Lurik Drön, Gartrul was born as the youngest prince. At the time of Lord Jigten Sumgön himself, he appeared as Gar Chödingpa Shakya Pel, a principal disciple. At the time of the Victorious Ratna, he appeared as Ngawang Döndrub, a lama of Tsang. At the time of the peerless Chögyal Phuntsok he appeared as Tendzin Phuntsok. At the time of Dharmakirti, he was called Tendzin Drakpa. Thus, he has been recognized as the reincarnation of many great beings.

Gartrul Rinpoche was born in Nangchen. From Chökyi Gyalpo he received, in succession, the vows of an upasaka, of a novice monk, and of full ordination. He received the complete teachings of the Drigung Kagyu and all knowledge contained in the sutras and tantras. He attended the lords Tendzin Drodul and Hlotrul Chökyi Gyatso, mastered all their teachings, and gained direct realization. In each moment, he was unstained by the eight worldly concerns. Later, he became the vajra master of Chökyi Nyima, the incarnation of Chökyi Gyalpo, and gave him all the teachings of the Drigung Kagyu, including instructions on the Eight Herukas. Thus, he showed inconceivable great kindness to this Dharma lineage. There were also many others who perfected the two stages.

⦂ Guideline for Dharma Practitioners

THESE KEY POINTS were assembled so that practitioners may be reminded of their Dharma practice and reflect on them repeatedly.

FOUR FOUNDATIONS:
- ▸ recollecting the blessedness and possibilities of a precious human life
- ▸ contemplating ever-changing impermanence
- ▸ contemplating the nature of samsara, the wheel of transmigration
- ▸ action and its result

FOUR SEALS OF DHARMA:
- ▸ All composite phenomena are impermanent.
- ▸ All the afflicted states are suffering.
- ▸ All phenomena are devoid of self.
- ▸ The unconditional, ultimate peace is nirvana.

FOUR NOBLE TRUTHS:
- ▸ the truth of suffering
- ▸ the truth of the cause of suffering
- ▸ the truth of the cessation of suffering
- ▸ the path to cessation of suffering

FOUR IMMEASURABLES:
- ▸ friendliness of loving-kindness
- ▸ compassion
- ▸ joy of rejoicing

▸ equanimity

Practitioners should contemplate these four by directing them sincerely toward all sentient beings.

THREE REFUGES:
- ▸ Buddha, the fully awakened and enlightened one
- ▸ Dharma, the teachings of scripture and experience
- ▸ Sangha, those highly accomplished in the experience of meditation

These three are the goal to be achieved, as well as the path toward the goal—the gateway to be entered in order to be free from samsara.

TWO ACCUMULATIONS:

To actualize bodhicitta and experience emptiness, the two accumulations of virtue and wisdom are the indispensable method.

FOURFOLD STATEMENT OF EMPTINESS:
- ▸ Dependent origination—
- ▸ that nature is declared to be emptiness.
- ▸ Dependent designation—
- ▸ that itself is the middle way.

FOUR PRACTICES OF THE BODHISATTVA:
- ▸ contemplating these topics
- ▸ having the wisdom which has insight into the meaning of these topics
- ▸ following the path joyfully
- ▸ purifying the mind for the welfare of all sentient beings

SIX PERFECTIONS:
- ▸ generosity
- ▸ moral ethics
- ▸ enduring patience
- ▸ joyous effort
- ▸ meditative concentration
- ▸ wisdom

These six constitute the perfection of the mind and achievement of enlightenment.

PURITY OF DEITY YOGA:

- ▸ having the mind of enlightenment for all sentient beings
- ▸ emptiness of all phenomena
- ▸ perceiving all sentient beings in the enlightened state
- ▸ dedication of the virtues of the practices

: Glossary of Enumerations

TWO

two accumulations: merit and wisdom

two form bodies: sambhogakaya and nirmanakaya

two obscurations: afflicting emotions that obscure liberation and the subtle obscurations to enlightenment

two siddhis: common and uncommon. Common types of siddhis are supernatural powers such as clairvoyance, levitation, telepathy, and so forth. Uncommon siddhis consist of special insight, the dispelling of obscurations, and revelation of the pristine nature of mind.

two stages of yidam practice: arising, or generation, and completion

two truths: relative and ultimate

two types of relative bodhicitta: aspiration and action

two types of completion stage meditation: with signs and without signs

two ways of life: religious life and secular life

THREE

three bodies or kayas (of a buddha):

1. *nirmanakaya,* the emanation body
2. *sambhogakaya,* the complete enjoyment body
3. *dharmakaya,* the perfect wisdom body

three excellences:

1. pure bodhicitta motivation
2. actual meditation practice
3. dedication of all virtues for the benefit of sentient beings

three faults to avoid while listening to teachings:
1. not listening to the teachings
2. forgetting the teachings
3. mixing the teachings with impure thoughts

three higher realms:
1. human
2. demi-god
3. god

Three Jewels:
1. Buddha
2. Dharma
3. Sangha

three kayas: see three bodies

three kinds of perseverance:
1. armor of perseverance
2. action of perseverance
3. perseverance beyond limitation

three lower realms:
1. animal realm
2. hungry ghost realm
3. hell realms

three mental virtues:
1. avoiding covetousness, and practicing contentment instead
2. avoiding malicious thought, and practicing love and compassion instead
3. avoiding wrong view, especially with relation to cause and result

three moralities of a bodhisattva:
1. abstaining from nonvirtuous actions
2. discipline of studying and practicing all the Dharma teachings
3. benefiting all sentient beings

three obscurations:
1. karmic obscurations
2. afflictive obscurations
3. subtle obscurations to omniscience

three physical virtues:
1. avoiding killing, and protecting and respecting others' lives instead, especially those of human beings
2. avoiding stealing and cheating, and practicing generosity instead
3. abstaining from sexual misconduct (for householders) and abstaining from sexual activity altogether (for the ordained)

three poisons:
1. ignorance
2. attachment
3. aversion or hatred

three purifying mantras:
1. OM SWABHAWA SHUDDHO SARWA DHARMA SWABHAWA SHUDDHO HANG
2. OM BAZRA SHUDDHA SARVA DHARMA BAZRA SHUDDHO HANG
3. OM YOGA SHUDDHA SARVA DHARMA YOGA SHUDDHO HANG

three qualities of a good Dharma student:
1. being honest and stable
2. having the mental power of discernment that understands the teachings
3. having sincere inspiration to follow the path

three qualities of samadhi:
1. a feeling of ease and joy
2. a basis for actualizing of the qualities of the buddhas and bodhisattvas
3. allows one to benefit sentient beings effortlessly

three refuges: see Three Jewels

three times:
1. past
2. present
3. future

three trainings:
1. moral ethics, or *shila*
2. meditative concentration, or *samadhi*
3. incisive wisdom, or *prajña*

three types of laziness:
1. attachment to pleasure
2. attachment to worldly activities
3. listlessness

three types of suffering:
1. the suffering of suffering
2. the suffering of change
3. the all-pervasive suffering or suffering of condition

three vows:
1. Vinaya vows
2. Bodhisattva vows
3. Vajrayana vows

three ways of pleasing the spiritual master:
1. providing necessities
2. being of service
3. especially, practicing Dharma

FOUR
four abandonments:
1. abandoning nonvirtuous actions that had been taken up
2. not developing new nonvirtues
3. adopting new virtues that had not previously arisen
4. perfecting virtues that have arisen

four bodies or kayas:
1. *nirmanakaya,* the emanation body
2. *sambhogakaya,* the complete enjoyment body
3. *dharmakaya,* the perfect wisdom body
4. *svabhavikakaya,* the basis for the manifestation of the other three forms

four causes of samsara:
1. failing to accumulate virtue and wisdom
2. creating massive nonvirtue
3. creating obstacles for others' virtuous activities
4. failing to dedicate virtue to complete enlightenment

four characteristics of phenomena:
1. All conventional phenomena are not inherently existent
2. but they are potent, or capable of performing a function.
3. They are similarly apprehendable by the senses of people in the community.
4. They exist by means of the interdependence of many causes and conditions.

four classes of tantra:
1. *kriya tantra,* which involves physical cleanliness and purification while mentally maintaining a deity yoga practice
2. *carya tantra,* which involves verbal discipline and chanting while mentally maintaining a deity yoga practice
3. *yoga tantra,* which involves further mental discipline, uniting oneself with the deity
4. *anuttara yoga tantra,* or highest yoga tantra, in which one transforms everything into the enlightened state

Four Dharmas of Gampopa:
1. Grant your blessings so that my mind may follow the Dharma.
2. Grant your blessings so that Dharma may follow along the path.
3. Grant your blessings so that obstacles may be dispelled from the path.

4. Grant your blessings so that confusion may dawn as wisdom.

four elements:
1. earth
2. water
3. fire
4. wind

four empowerments:
1. vase
2. secret
3. wisdom
4. precious word, or fourth empowerment

four fearlessnesses:
1. certainty that all obscurations without exception have been purified and all defilements exhausted
2. certainty that all complete and perfect qualities have been actualized
3. certainty that all obstacles have been identified as such and purified
4. certainty of having taught the methods that will produce enlightenment

four feet of miracle powers:
1. absorption of aspiration
2. absorption of perseverance
3. absorption of meditation
4. absorption of investigation that develops precision of mind in the meditative state

four groups of practitioners:
1. *bhikshu* (monk)
2. *bhikshuni* (nun)
3. *upasaka* (layman)
4. *upasika* (laywoman)

four immeasurable thoughts:
1. loving-kindness
2. compassion
3. joy
4. equanimity

four kayas: see four bodies

four mindfulnesses:
1. mindfulness of the body as impermanent and subject to decay
2. mindfulness of feelings—joy, suffering, and neutral feelings—as being transitory
3. mindfulness of mind as being like a cloud
4. mindfulness of phenomena as being interdependent

Four Noble Truths:
1. the truth of suffering
2. the truth of the origin of suffering
3. the truth of the cessation of suffering
4. the truth of the path to achieve cessation

four obscurations:
1. physical
2. verbal
3. mental
4. subtle

four powers:
1. remorse
2. antidote
3. resolution
4. refuge or reliance

four preliminary contemplations:
1. precious human life, the basis of working toward buddha-hood
2. the impermanence of all phenomena

3. the sufferings of samsara
4. the cause and result of all the actions that we do or have done

four root downfalls (of bodhicitta):
1. telling lies that deceive your root master, any other bodhisattvas, or those who are worthy of respect
2. abusing other bodhisattvas, especially if it causes them to lose their vow
3. creating regret in others for the virtuous deeds they have accomplished for the Dharma
4. deceiving others through insincere motivation

four seals (of an authentic teaching):
1. All composite phenomena are impermanent.
2. Samsara is suffering.
3. Phenomena are without a self.
4. Nirvana is peace.

four verbal virtues:
1. avoiding telling lies, especially spiritual lies, and speaking the truth instead
2. not dividing a community, especially the sangha, and harmonizing others instead
3. avoiding the use of harsh words, and speaking gently instead
4. avoiding idle talk, and speaking meaningfully and to the subject instead.

four wholesome deeds:
1. respecting the root master and never telling a lie to him or anyone worthy of respect, even at the risk of your life
2. perceiving all bodhisattvas as buddhas and praising them
3. rejoicing in others' virtuous deeds and inspiring them to further Dharma activities, especially Mahayana practice
4. perceiving all sentient beings as your best friend, and treating them with sincerity

FIVE

five afflicting emotions:
1. ignorance
2. attachment
3. hatred
4. pride or arrogance
5. jealousy

five aggregates:
1. form
2. feeling or sensation
3. perception or recognition
4. formation
5. consciousness

five Buddha families:
1. Tathagata family
2. Vajra family
3. Ratna family
4. Lotus family
5. Karma family

five elements:
1. earth
2. water
3. fire
4. air
5. space

five heinous acts:
1. killing one's father
2. killing one's mother
3. killing an arhat
4. dividing the sangha
5. injuring a buddha

Fivefold Path of Mahamudra:
1. bodhicitta development
2. yidam practice
3. guru yoga
4. Mahamudra
5. dedication of merit

five lay precepts:
1. not taking life, especially that of human beings
2. not stealing from others
3. not telling lies, particularly spiritual lies
4. not engaging in sexual misconduct
5. not using intoxicants, such as alcohol or drugs

five major classes of knowledge:
1. creative arts
2. healing arts
3. linguistic arts
4. logic or reasoning
5. metaphysics or inner meaning

five minor classes of knowledge:
1. performance
2. astrology
3. poetry
4. synonyms
5. composition

five nearly heinous acts:
1. disrobing an ordained female arhat
2. knowingly killing a bodhisattva
3. killing a trainee
4. misappropriating the sangha's property
5. destroying a stupa

five paths:
1. the path of accumulation
2. the path of preparation or linking

3. the path of seeing
4. the path of meditation
5. the path of perfection or enlightenment

five poisons: see five afflicting emotions

five powers:
 1. faith
 2. perseverance
 3. mindfulness
 4. absorption
 5. wisdom awareness

five precepts: see five lay precepts

five strengths:
 1. faith
 2. perseverance
 3. mindfulness
 4. absorption
 5. wisdom awareness

five wisdoms:
 1. the all-pervading elemental wisdom
 2. mirror-like wisdom
 3. equanimity wisdom
 4. discriminating wisdom
 5. all-accomplishing activity wisdom

SIX
six bardos:
 1. between birth and death
 2. between day and night (called dream bardo)
 3. between the beginning and end of a meditation session
 4. at the time of death
 5. bardo of dharmata
 6. bardo of existence

six paramitas or perfections:
1. generosity
2. moral ethics
3. patience
4. perseverance
5. meditative concentration
6. wisdom awareness

six realms:
1. hell realms
2. hungry ghost realm
3. animal realm
4. human realm
5. demi-god realm
6. god realms

six sense objects:
1. visible form—colors and shapes
2. sounds made by animate and inanimate sources
3. pleasant and unpleasant odors
4. tastes of sweet, sour, bitter, salty and so forth
5. textures of soft, rough, light, heavy and so forth
6. mental phenomena

six yogas of Naropa: the practices of
1. tummo
2. illusory body
3. dream yoga
4. clear light
5. phowa
6. bardo

SEVEN
seven articles of a universal monarch:
1. thousand-spoked golden wheel
2. wish-fulfilling jewel
3. precious queen
4. precious minister

5. precious elephant
6. precious horse
7. precious military commander

seven branches of enlightenment:
1. perfect mindfulness
2. perfect discrimination
3. perfect perseverance
4. perfect joy
5. perfect relaxation
6. perfect absorption
7. perfect equanimity

seven characteristics of dharmakaya:
1. pervades all phenomena
2. is the unification of supreme all-pervading emptiness and nonobjectified great compassion
3. is great unafflicted bliss, completely free from all suffering
4. is inherently nonexistent and free from elaboration in its mode of abiding
5. is the great embodiment of full compassion, unchanging from coemergent wisdom
6. never varies from all the qualities described above and is free from coming, going, increasing, or decreasing
7. is unceasing and not "just nothing"

seven limb offering practice:
1. prostration and praise
2. offering
3. confession
4. rejoicing
5. beseeching
6. praying
7. dedication

seven qualities of a spiritual master:
1. has mastered the three trainings
2. has strong renunciation of samsara with little concern for

his or her own life and is able to dispel the confusion of
others

3. is well versed in the sutra teachings
4. has actualized critical insight
5. possesses skill in articulating the teachings
6. has a compassionate nature
7. is free from discouragement

EIGHT

eight fears:
   1. fire
   2. water
   3. earth
   4. air
   5. elephants
   6. snakes
   7. thieves
   8. kings

Eightfold Path:
   1. perfect view
   2. perfect conception
   3. perfect speech
   4. perfect action
   5. perfect livelihood
   6. perfect effort
   7. perfect mindfulness
   8. perfect absorption

eight unfavorable conditions: being born
   1. in the hell realms
   2. as a hungry ghost
   3. as an animal
   4. as a barbarian with no sense of virtue and nonvirtue
   5. as a long-life god
   6. without full faculties
   7. holding wrong views of causality
   8. at a time when no buddha has appeared

eight worldly concerns:

    1–2. gain and loss

    3–4. pleasure and pain

    5–6. praise and blame

    7–8. fame and disgrace

TEN

ten bhumis:

    1. Great Joy

    2. Stainless

    3. Radiant

    4. Luminous

    5. Very Difficult to Train

    6. Obviously Transcendent

    7. Gone Afar

    8. Immovable

    9. Good Discriminating Wisdom

    10. Cloud of Dharma

ten directions:

    1–4. four cardinal directions (north, south, east, west)

    5–8. four intermediate directions (southeast, southwest, northwest, northeast)

    9. zenith

    10. nadir

ten endowments:

These five have to be achieved within oneself:

    1. being a human being

    2. living in a place where there are Dharma teachings

    3. having all the faculties

    4. being free of heavy negative karma

    5. having devotion or understanding of the Three Jewels and acknowledging the Vinaya as the foundation for all spiritual practice.

Five excellent conditions have to be encountered:

    6. a buddha must have appeared in the world

    7. a buddha must have taught the Dharma

8. the Dharma that he taught continues
9. sangha members exist who practice Dharma and follow masters
10. compassionate support exists

ten perfections:
1. generosity
2. moral ethics
3. patience
4. joyous effort
5. meditative concentration
6. wisdom awareness
7. skillful means
8. aspiration
9. strength
10. primordial wisdom awareness

ten strengths of a buddha:
1. knowing right from wrong
2. knowing consequences of actions
3. knowing various mental inclinations
4. knowing various mental faculties
5. knowing various degrees of intelligence
6. knowing the path to all goals
7. knowing ever-afflicted and purified phenomena
8. knowing past lives
9. knowing deaths and births
10. knowing the exhaustion of continuations

THIRTEEN
thirteen sambhogakaya ornaments:
Five related to silk garments:
1. a ribbon knotting the hair
2. a scarf
3. an upper garment
4. a belt
5. a lower garment

Eight related to ornaments:
6. five-pointed crown
7. earrings
8. short necklace
9. long necklaces
10. arm bracelets
11. wrist bracelets
12. ankle bracelets
13. finger rings

FOURTEEN
fourteen root downfalls of samaya:
1. to disparage or harm the master
2. to transgress the three levels of vows
3. to be hostile to vajra brothers and sisters
4. to forsake loving-kindness on behalf of sentient beings
5. to abandon bodhicitta
6. to disparage one's own doctrine or that of others
7. to divulge secrets to the immature
8. to abuse the five components that are primordially pure (i.e., one's own body)
9. to be prejudiced about phenomena that are, in any case, intrinsically pure
10. to have love for (i.e., befriend or support) evil beings who harm sentient beings and the Doctrine
11. to apply conceptualization to ineffable nature
12. to belittle those who have faith
13. to violate the commitments that have been undertaken
14. to disparage women, the source of discriminating wisdom

EIGHTEEN
eighteen downfalls of the bodhisattva's vow:
Downfalls 1, 2, 3, and 4 are held by both kings and ministers and, so, are counted twice to total eighteen.
1, 5. stealing the wealth of the Three Jewels
2, 6. forbidding the precious Dharma

3, 7. seizing the robes of a monk, beating or imprisoning a monk who has renounced his vows, or causing a monk to renounce his vows

4, 8. committing any of the five heinous crimes

9. holding a wrong view

10. destroying cities and towns

11. expressing emptiness to beings who are not fully trained

12. causing those who have entered the path toward buddhahood to renounce complete enlightenment

13. causing someone to give up a pratimoksha vow by connecting to the Mahayana vehicle

14. holding the belief oneself that the training path will not dispel the afflicting emotions of desire and so forth and influencing others to go this way

15. expressing one's good qualities in order to get wealth, honor, and praise and to abuse others

16. falsely expressing that "I have the patience of the profound teaching."

17. causing a practitioner to be punished, falsely taking an offering intended for the Three Jewels, or accepting bribery

18. disrupting someone in calm abiding meditation, or taking the provisions of a retreat practitioner and giving them to someone who merely recites prayers

eighteen unmatched qualities of a buddha:
Six of behavior:

1. possessing unmistaken bodily qualities

2. not possessing unskillful speech

3. possessing unimpaired memory

4. constant abidance in meditative equipoise

5. realizing that cultivation and elimination are not inherently different

6. possessing indiscriminate equanimity.

Six of insight:

7. possessing unimpaired aspiration

8. possessing unimpaired effort

9. possessing unimpaired mindfulness as a means for taming sentient beings
10. possessing single-pointed concentration
11. possessing unimpaired wisdom
12. possessing irreversibility from liberated paths

Three of virtuous activity:

13. virtuous activity of body
14. virtuous activity of speech
15. virtuous activity of mind

Three of time:

16. unobstructed wisdom concerning the past
17. unobstructed wisdom concerning the future
18. unobstructed wisdom concerning the present

THIRTY-TWO

thirty-two major marks of a buddha:

1. The palms of his hands and soles of his feet bear signs of a wheel
2. His feet are well set upon the ground like a tortoise
3. His fingers and toes are webbed.
4. The palms of his hands and soles of his feet are smooth and tender
5. His body has seven prominent features: broad heels, broad hands, broad shoulder blades and broad neck
6. His fingers are long
7. His heels are soft
8. He is tall and straight
9. His ankle-bones do not protrude
10. The hairs on his body point upward
11. His ankles are like an antelope's
12. His hands are long and beautiful
13. His male organ is withdrawn
14. His body is the color of gold
15. His skin is thin and smooth
16. Each hair curls to the right
17. His face is adorned by a coiled hair between his eyebrows

18. The upper part of his body is like that of a lion
19. His head and shoulders are perfectly round
20. His shoulders are broad
21. He has an excellent sense of taste, even of the worst tastes
22. His body has the proportions of a banyan tree
23. He has a protrusion on the crown of his head
24. His tongue is long and thin
25. His voice is mellifluent
26. His cheeks are like those of a lion
27. His teeth are white
28. There are no gaps between his teeth
29. His teeth are evenly set
30. He has a total of forty teeth
31. His eyes are the color of sapphire
32. His eyelashes are like those of a magnificent heifer

THIRTY-SEVEN
thirty-seven branches of enlightenment:
   1–4. the four mindfulnesses
   5–8. the four abandonments
   9–12. the four feet of miracle powers
   13–17. the five powers
   18–22. the five strengths
   23–29. the seven branches of enlightenment
   30–37. the Eightfold Path

FORTY-SIX
forty-six subsidiary downfalls of the bodhisattva's vow:
1. not making offerings to the Three Jewels once a day
2. following attachment with the mind
3. not venerating senior practitioners out of laziness
4. not responding to others' questions
5. not accepting others' invitations out of negligence
6. not accepting gold and so forth offered for the sangha community
7. not giving Dharma to those who desire it

8. looking down on and ignoring those who renounce moral ethics
9. avoiding study that could inspire other's confidence
10. making less effort for others' benefit like a hearer
11. through a lack of compassion, not acting nonvirtuously when it is necessary to do so.
12. accepting wrong livelihood (i.e., flattery, excitement, entertainment, deception)
13. taking pleasure in frivolous activities such as sports
14. thinking that one will stay in samsara because nirvana cannot be attained
15. not dispelling the defects of others
16. not purifying others' afflicting emotions when they are afflicted
17. not practicing the four trainings of practitioners:
    a. not scolding others, although they scold you
    b. not becoming angry when incited to anger
    c. not revealing another's faults, even if another reveals yours
    d. not hitting another in return for being hit
18. neglecting or abandoning those who are angry with you by not helping them
19. not accepting the apology of one who apologizes according to Dharma
20. following thoughts of anger
21. gathering a retinue for fame and wealth
22. not avoiding the laziness of sleep and pleasure
23. scattering your interest in frivolous gossip and idle talk
24. not making effort to stabilize your mind
25. not giving up the five obscurations to meditative concentration:
    a. excitement and regret
    b. harmful thoughts
    c. sleep and lethargy
    d. desire
    e. hesitation
26. becoming attached to the bliss, clarity, and other experiences of meditative concentrations

27. forsaking respect for the hearer vehicle
28. making effort for the hearer pitaka by avoiding the bodhi-
    sattva's training
29. making effort in the tirthika writings without making effort
    in the study of the Buddhadharma
30 making more effort in the tirthika writings than in the
    Buddhadharma
31. abusing the Mahayana vehicle
32. praising oneself and abusing others
33. out of arrogance, laziness, and so forth, not searching for
    precious Dharma teachings
34. looking down on the teacher and relying on mere words
    instead of meaning
35. not helping those who need it
36. avoiding caring for the sick
37. not making effort to dispel others' suffering
38. not correcting well those who are heedless
39. not repaying those who are kind to you
40. not dispelling the suffering of those who are depressed
41. not giving necessities to others who need them while you are
    able to do so
42. not taking care of your surroundings with teachings and
    material necessities when you have the means to do so
43. not harmonizing and agreeing with others' virtuous actions
44. not praising others' good qualities
45. not preventing those who are committing nonvirtuous
    actions
46. not taming others with spiritual powers when necessary

EIGHTY
eighty minor marks of a buddha:
   1. His nails are copper-colored.
   2. His nails are moderately shiny.
   3. His nails are raised.
   4. His nails are round.
   5. His nails are broad.
   6. His nails are tapered.
   7. His veins do not protrude.

8. His veins are free of knots.
9. His ankles do not protrude.
10. His feet are not uneven.
11. He walks with a lion's gait.
12. He walks with an elephant's gait.
13. He walks with a goose's gait.
14. He walks with a bull's gait.
15. His gait tends to the right.
16. His gait is elegant.
17. His gait is steady.
18. His body is well covered.
19. His body looks as if it were polished.
20. His body is well proportioned.
21. His body is clean and pure.
22. His body is smooth.
23. His body is perfect.
24. His sex organs are fully developed.
25. His physical bearing is excellent and dignified.
26. His steps are even.
27. His eyes are perfect.
28. He is youthful.
29. His body is not sunken.
30. His body is broad.
31. His body is not loose.
32. His limbs are well proportioned.
33. His vision is clear and unblurred.
34. His belly is round.
35. His belly is perfectly moderate.
36. His belly is not long.
37. His belly does not bulge.
38. His navel is deep.
39. His navel winds to the right.
40. He is perfectly handsome.
41. His habits are clean.
42. His body is free of moles and discoloration.
43. His hands are soft as cotton wool.
44. The lines of his palms are clear.
45. The lines of his palms are deep.

46. The lines of his palms are long.
47. His face is not too long.
48. His lips are red like copper.
49. His tongue is pliant.
50. His tongue is thin.
51. His tongue is red.
52. His voice is like thunder.
53. His voice is sweet and gentle.
54. His teeth are round.
55. His teeth are sharp.
56. His teeth are white.
57. His teeth are even.
58. His teeth are tapered.
59. His nose is prominent.
60. His nose is clean.
61. His eyes are clear.
62. His eyelashes are thick.
63. The black and white parts of his eyes are well defined and are like lotus petals.
64. His eyebrows are long.
65. His eyebrows are smooth.
66. His eyebrows are soft.
67. His eyebrows are evenly haired.
68. His hands are long and extended.
69. His ears are of equal size.
70. He has perfect hearing.
71. His forehead is well formed and well defined.
72. His forehead is broad.
73. His head is very large.
74. His hair is black as a bumble bee.
75. His hair is thick.
76. His hair is soft.
77. His hair is untangled.
78. His hair is not unruly.
79. His hair is fragrant.
80. His hands and feet are marked with auspicious emblems such as the srivasta and swastika.

⦂ Glossary of Terms and Names

Acharya: Literally, "master," generally construed as an academic title.

Afflicting emotions: In general, any defilement or poison which obscures the clarity of mind. These are often summarized as three: ignorance, attachment, and aversion. All other negative predispositions are produced on the basis of these three poisons.

Aggregates (Skt.: *skandha*): The collection of characteristics that constitutes a sentient being. Like a heap of grain, a being appears to be a single entity until, upon closer examination, it is understood to be composed of many pieces.

Alaya: A foundational aspect of mind that can hold the seeds of dualistic thought or blossom into wisdom. It can also mean emptiness.

Ananda: Cousin and personal attendant of Buddha Shakyamuni. He is noted for having memorized all the Buddha's teachings verbatim and having recited them at the First Council.

Arhat: Literally, a "foe destroyer." The culmination of the Hinayana path, it refers to one who has overcome the outward manifestation of the afflicting emotions but who has not completely uprooted their psychic imprint. Although free of samsara, an arhat is not fully enlightened.

Arising stage (of tantric meditation): A meditation characterized by identifying all physical, mental, and verbal phenomena with a yidam deity through highly developed visualization techniques. It is performed in order to directly reveal the practitioner's buddha nature.

Asanga (fourth century C.E.): An Indian master who is most remembered for having received five celebrated texts from Arya Maitreya (*Abhisamayalankara*, *Uttaratantra*, *Mahayanasutralankara*, *Madhyantavibhaga*, and *Dharma-dharmatavibhaga*) and for founding the Vast Action lineage. One of the Six Ornaments of this world.

Atisha (982–1055): An Indian master invited by the king of Tibet to revive Buddhism there. He was the founder of the Kadampa lineage in which Dharma Lord Gampopa and Phagmo Drupa trained for many years.

Ayatana: The base on which mental processes depend, the sphere or field in which they operate, or simply their point of reference.

Bhumi: Literally, "ground" or "foundation." Refers to the progressive levels of a bodhisattva's training, each one of which successively provides the foundation for the next.

Bodhicitta: Literally, "mind of enlightenment." The intention to accomplish perfect, complete enlightenment for the benefit of all beings. Buddhahood is the perfection of the practice of bodhicitta.

Bodhisattva: Literally, "enlightenment being." One who has generated bodhicitta and who works tirelessly for the benefit of all beings.

Buddha: One who has attained unsurpassable, complete, perfect enlightenment; i.e., one who has fully awakened all wisdom and fully purified all obscurations.

Buddha fields: Existences created by buddhas wherein conditions are perfect for the attainment of enlightenment by its inhabitants. Many practitioners aspire to rebirth in this state because reversion to lower states is impossible. Also called pure lands.

Buddha Maitreya: One of the eight great bodhisattva disciples of Buddha Shakyamuni. He will be the next (i.e., fifth) buddha in this fortunate kalpa in which one thousand buddhas will appear, and currently manifests in the Tushita heaven.

Buddha nature: The pure essence potential to attain enlightenment that is inherent in every sentient being. It is obscured to varying degrees by afflicting emotions and subtle obscurations, but it can be actualized through the practices of moral ethics, meditation, and wisdom.

Chandrakirti (ca. 600–ca. 650): An Indian master who was a scholar at Nalanda University, a student of Nagarjuna's school, and a major commentator on Nagarjuna's works. He is prominently associated with the Prasangika school of Madhyamaka.

Chenrezig: The great bodhisattva who is associated most with the quality of compassion. He is frequently depicted with two arms, four arms, or a thousand arms, holding a mala, jewel, and lotus. His is the most famous of all mantras: OM MANI PADME HUNG.

Completion stage (of tantric meditation): A meditation performed once one has identified oneself as a yidam deity. There are two types of completion stage practice: with signs and without. Practice with signs consists of reciting mantras as well as channel and chakra practices. Practice without signs is the practice of Mahamudra.

Deity yoga: The characteristic type of Vajrayana meditation practice, in which mundane phenomena are identified with those of a yidam. The term encompasses both the generation or arising stage and the completion stage of meditation.

Devadatta: Cousin of Buddha Shakyamuni. Once a monk under Lord Buddha, he created a schism in the sangha by attracting five hundred monks to a more ascetic lifestyle. He plotted to physically injure the Buddha but was unsuccessful.

Dharma: The holy teachings of Lord Buddha, categorized in two parts: the Dharma that is studied and the Dharma that has been realized.

Dharmakaya: One of the three bodies of a buddha. It denotes the ultimate nature of a buddha's wisdom form, which is nonconceptual and undefinable.

Dharmata: The essential nature of reality.

Drigung Kagyu: The branch of the Kagyu tradition founded by Lord Jigten Sumgön.

Dzogchen: Literally, "Great Completion." An absolute view, like Mahamudra, and an advanced meditation practice.

Empowerment: The tantric ritual by which one is empowered to perform a specific meditation practice.

Emptiness: The lack of inherent reality of a phenomenon or person.

Enlightenment: The ultimate achievement of buddhahood.

Gampopa (1074–1153): Renowned as one of Tibet's greatest teachers, he is one of the foremost figures in the Kagyu lineage. His writings include *The Jewel Ornament of Liberation* and *The Precious Garland of the Excellent Path*.

Garuda: A large and powerful mythological eagle often used as a symbol of primordial wisdom.

Hinayana: Of the two major branches of Buddhist philosophy and practice, the Buddhist school which emphasizes individual liberation and practice of the Four Noble Truths.

Hundred-syllable mantra: The purifying mantra of Vajrasattva: OM BAZRA SATTWA SAMAYA MANU PALAYA BAZRA SATTWA TENOPA TISHTHA DRIDO ME BHAWA SUTO KHYOME BHAWA SUPO KHYOME BHAWA ANU RAKTO ME BHAWA SARWA SIDDHIM-ME PRA-YATSHA SARWA KARMA SUTSA-ME TSIT-TAN SHRIYA KURU HUNG HAHA HAHA HO BHAGAWAN SARWA TATHAGATA BAZRA-MAME MUNTSA BAZRI BHAWA MAHA SAMAYA SATTWA AH.

Jigten Sumgön (1143–1217): Founder of the Drigung Kagyu tradition. He was the heart-son of Phagmo Drupa, and widely recognized as an incarnation of Nagarjuna. His most famous writings include *One Thought* (Tib.: *Gong Chig*) and *Heart Essence of the Mahayana Teachings* (Tib.: *Ten Nying*).

Kagyu: Literally, "oral transmission" lineage. One of the four principal traditions within Tibetan Buddhism, it originated with Buddha Vajradhara and was primarily transmitted by Tilopa and Naropa in

India, and Marpa, Milarepa, and Gampopa in Tibet. It holds Mahamudra and the Six Yogas of Naropa as its central teachings.

Kalpa: Generically, an eon or other nearly limitless length of time. In Buddhist cosmology, it has the specific meaning of a complete cycle of a universe consisting of four stages: emptiness, formation, maintenance, and destruction.

Karma: Literally, "action." Physical, verbal or mental acts which imprint habitual tendencies in the mind. Upon meeting with suitable conditions, these habits ripen and become manifest in future events.

Katyayana: One of Buddha Shakyamuni's principal disciples. He was best known as a master of discussion and explanation of the Dharma.

Kaya: Literally, "body," "form," "heap," or "collection." The various forms in which a Buddha manifests. Generally classified as three— nirmanakaya, sambhogakaya, and dharmakaya—but occasionally a fourth classification is added, namely the svabhavikakaya or nature body, to express the inseparable nature of these three. The term *rupakaya* (form body) is also used to refer to the second and third classifications together.

Lama: An authentic teacher authorized to transmit Buddhist teachings to suitable students. Depending on tradition, a lama may or may not be a monk.

Madhyamaka: Literally, "Middle Way." The school of Mahayana Buddhism founded by Nagarjuna. The name describes their position taken with regard to the emptiness of phenomena, a mid-point between nihilism and eternalism.

Maha-arya: One who directly experiences and abides in the wisdom of emptiness; a highly accomplished practitioner who has attained the eighth bhumi or above.

Mahakashyapa: One of Buddha Shakyamuni's principal disciples. He was particularly skilled in asceticism and moral discipline, and became the leader of the sangha upon the Buddha's parinirvana.

Mahamudra: Literally, the "Great Seal." The highest, most conclusive view that unites bliss and emptiness into one, the primordial effulgent nature of mind, and is the ultimate realization of all phenomena of samsara and nirvana as they actually are. Its practice reveals the practitioner's basic, pure nature and leads to the experience of highest enlightenment.

Mahasiddha: A tantric yogin who has accomplished very high levels of spiritual realization.

Mahayana: Literally, the "Great Vehicle." The Buddhist school that holds the bodhisattva ideal as the highest practice and teaches the aspiration to attainment of enlightenment for the benefit of all sentient beings.

Mandala: Literally, "wheel, "circle," or "essence." The connotation in Tibetan is of a container and its contents. In deity yoga, it often refers to the "palace" of a deity, arranged as a circular diagram or three-dimensional structure with symbolic components surrounding a central figure.

Manjushri: The great bodhisattva who is associated most with the quality of wisdom. He is usually represented holding a sword in one hand and a lotus flower on which rests a Prajnaparamita text in the other.

Mantra: Literally, "mind-protection." Sacred speech which, in the context of Vajrayana practices, serves to purify one's ordinary speech and identify it with a yidam deity's wisdom speech in order to attain enlightenment.

Mara: Any negative influences on ordinary people that obstruct spiritual development, frequently personified as demon-like beings named Mara.

Marpa (1012–1097): A Tibetan layman who is especially renowned for bringing many teachings to Tibet from India and translating them. These include Mahamudra texts and the Six Yogas of Naropa. As Naropa's disciple and Milarepa's primary teacher, he is a major figure in the Kagyu lineage.

Merit: Any virtuous thought or activity which has the result of imprinting positive habitual tendencies in one's mind-stream.

Milarepa (1052–1135): One of the great masters of the Kagyu lineage, he is often referred to as an example of someone who attained enlightenment in a single lifetime. His vajra songs possess great healing qualities. He was Dharma Lord Gampopa's primary teacher.

Nagarjuna (second century C.E.): An Indian master of such critical importance to the propagation of the Mahayana and Vajrayana that he is often called the "second Buddha." He founded the Madhyamaka philosophical school which systematized the Prajnaparamita (Perfection of Wisdom) teachings and composed many texts which remain authoritative to the present day. One of the Six Ornaments of this world.

Naropa (1016–1100): One of the founding masters of the Kagyu tradition. He was a leading scholar at Nalanda University in India, which he renounced to become a yogi-practitioner under Tilopa. He is most remembered for being Marpa's teacher and for being the propagator of the teachings known as the Six Yogas of Naropa.

Nirmanakaya: Literally, "emanation body." The physical form of a buddha or other great being, purposefully manifested for the benefit of common sentient beings. This is not necessarily a human form; buddhas can appear as whatever is necessary.

Nirvana: The unconfused state without suffering; the transcendence of samsara.

Paramitas: *see* Perfections.

Parinirvana: The death of one who has attained enlightenment.

Perfections: The training to be completed by bodhisattvas, consisting of the perfection of generosity, moral ethics, patience, perseverance, meditative concentration, and wisdom awareness.

Pratimoksha: Literally, "individual liberation." Rules of moral ethics which protect one from commission of nonvirtuous deeds; the method for liberation.

Pratyekabuddhas: Self-liberated buddhas, whose attainment is less than the ultimate buddhahood. While they may receive Dharma teachings during the time of a buddha or any time they are still taught, they do not attain realization until after the Buddha's teachings have disappeared. Being without bodhicitta, they do not teach how to reach enlightenment, but they do display miracle powers to inspire devotion.

Rechungpa Dorje Drakpa (1083–1161): One of Milarepa's two foremost students. Rechungpa traveled to India three times and obtained teachings and transmissions that Marpa had not received during his time in India.

Rupakaya: Literally, "form body." A collective term referring to the nirmanakaya and sambhogakaya forms of a buddha.

Samadhi: Meditative absorption.

Samaya: A sacred pledge between a disciple and teacher or the teachings regarding Vajrayana practice.

Sambhogakaya: Literally, "enjoyment body." A nonsubstantial yet visible body of a buddha or other great being, manifested to directly benefit bodhisattvas at high stages of realization and to serve as an object of devotion for practitioners.

Samsara: The beginningless and endless cycle of rebirths throughout the six realms; the confused state of suffering from which Buddhists seek liberation.

Sangha: Generally, the entire community of practitioners. In different contexts, it can refer specifically to the monastic community or to the assembly of highly realized beings (arhats and bodhisattvas at the first bhumi and above).

Sense source: *see* Ayatana.

Sentient beings: All conscious creatures reborn within the six realms.

Shamatha: A meditation in which the mind is stabilized in a state of pacification or control. Also called calm abiding or mental quiescence.

Shantideva (seventh to eighth century C.E.): An Indian master from Nalanda University most remembered as the author of *Bodhicaryavatara* and the *Collection of Transcendent Instructions*. To this day, the *Bodhicaryavatara* is one of the most revered and widely read texts in the Mahayana literature.

Shariputra: One of Buddha Shakyamuni's two closest disciples, he is generally depicted as standing to the Buddha's right. He was particularly distinguished by his wisdom.

Shravaka: A Hinayana disciple who hears the words of the Buddha's teachings, shares them with others, and aspires to become an arhat for his/her own benefit.

Siddhi: Mastery over physical forms and forces that can be ordinary or extraordinary. The ordinary siddhis are accomplishments such as being able to fly, becoming invisible, seeing at long distances, and so forth. The only extraordinary siddhi is enlightenment itself.

Six-syllable mantra: Chenrezig's mantra of compassion: OM MANI PADME HUNG.

Skandha: *see* Aggregates.

Stupa: Sacred structures generally categorized as reliquaries, which are universally used by Buddhists as objects of veneration and devotion.

Svabhavikakaya: The underlying indivisible essence of all enlightened forms.

Tilopa (988–1069): A renowned Indian mahasiddha and the first human teacher of Mahamudra. Naropa received the complete teachings from him.

Vajra: When used as an adjective, the term implies the attribute of indestructibility or an adamantine quality. As a noun used in conjunction with a bell that symbolizes wisdom, a vajra is a ritual object symbolizing compassion or skillful means.

Vajradhara: The primordial, dharmakaya buddha. He is often depicted as being a deep blue color to symbolizes his limitless qualities

—infinite as the blue sky, fresh and clear after a rainfall when there are no clouds or dust to obscure its profundity.

Vajrayana: The diamond path or "vehicle" of Buddhist tantra.

Vinaya: The code of discipline for Buddhist practitioners, especially for monks and nuns.

Yidam deity: A deity whose form and attributes embody a particular aspect of enlightenment and with whom a practitioner identifies in meditation.

⠸ Annotated Bibliography of Works Mentioned in *A Complete Guide to the Buddhist Path*

Bodhicaryavatara
A beautiful presentation of the bodhisattva's training, in verse form, by the Indian master Shantideva. It is one of the most widely read and quoted of all Mahayana texts.

Batchelor, Stephen. *A Guide to the Bodhisattva's Way of Life.* Dharamsala: Library of Tibetan Works and Archives, 1979.

Crosby, Kate and Andrew Skilton. *The Bodhicaryavatara.* Oxford, New York: Oxford University Press, 1996.

Matics, Marion L. *Entering the Path of Enlightenment.* New York: MacMillan, 1970.

Padmakara Translation Group. *The Way of the Bodhisattva.* Boston: Shambhala Publications, 1997.

Sharma, Parmananda. *Shantideva's Bodhicharyavatara.* New Delhi: Aditya Prakashan, 1990.

Wallace, Vesna and B. Alan Wallace. *A Guide to the Bodhisattva Way of Life.* Ithaca: Snow Lion Publications, 1997.

Buddha Avatamsaka Sutra
A large collection of teachings illustrating the Buddhist path to enlightenment primarily through stories of various bodhisattvas' experiences.

Buddhist Text Translation Society of the Sino-American Buddhist Association. *The Great Means Expansive Buddha Flower Adornment Sutra.* 23 volumes. San Francisco, 1979-1982.

Cleary, Thomas. *The Flower Ornament Scripture.* Boston: Shambhala Publications, 1993.

Calling to the Lama from Afar
A collection of prayers and devotions concerning Kyobpa Jigten Sumgön, the founder of the Drigung Kagyu lineage of Tibetan Buddhism. The prayers translated in this text express the depth of genuine devotion in a manner that is characteristic of this genre of Tibetan literature.
Gyaltshen, Khenchen Konchog. *Calling to the Lama from Afar*. Gainesville, FL: Vajra Publications, 2002.

Engaging the Intellect
A poem written by Phagmo Drupa that covers many topics, including Mahamudra. No known English translation.

Four Dharmas of Gampopa
A famous restatement of the entire Buddhist path in four lines that was taught by Lord Gampopa. They are sometimes formulated as a supplication prayer, as in this book, and sometimes as philosophical assertions. Many masters have composed extensive commentaries based on these four sentences.

The Great Kagyu Masters
Translation of a thirteenth-century text that gathers the life stories of the founders of the Kagyu lineage together in one volume. It is very helpful to practitioners to have these accounts available for inspiration and guidance.
Gyaltsen, Khenpo Konchog. *The Great Kagyu Masters*. Ithaca: Snow Lion Publications, 1990.

Heart Essence of the Mahayana Teachings (Tib.: Ten Nying)
A comprehensive lamrim text covering both the sutra and tantra systems, written by Ngorje Repa, a prominent disciple of Jigten Sumgön. No known English translation.

Heart Sutra (Prajnaparamita Hrdaya)
A very popular condensation of the wisdom teachings of the Buddha.
Hanh, Thich Nhat. *The Heart of Understanding*. Berkeley: Parallax Press, 1988.

Lopez, Donald S. *Elaborations on Emptiness*. Princeton: Princeton University Press, 1998.
Lopez, Donald S. *The Heart Sutra Explained*. Albany: SUNY Press, 1987.

In Search of the Stainless Ambrosia

An introduction for beginners and a reminder for more advanced practitioners. First, it summarizes the fundamental teachings of refuge, love and compassion, and the six paramitas. Then, there are short sections on Mahamudra and Yidam practices, the experience of dying, an explanation of Chöd practice, and some Phowa teachings.

Gyaltsen, Khenpo Konchog. *In Search of the Stainless Ambrosia*. Ithaca: Snow Lion Publications, 1988.

Inner Teachings

A collection of profound teachings of Jigten Sumgön related to Mahamudra, the Six Yogas of Naropa, and meditation practices. No known English translation.

The Jewel Ornament of Liberation

Translation of Lord Gampopa's essential philosophy text, which is said to act as Gampopa's regent in these times. This book contains a complete form of Buddhism—right from the starting point, the ground where you enter into the path, until you achieve Buddhahood and manifest activities for the benefit of infinite sentient beings.

Guenther, H. V. *The Jewel Ornament of Liberation*. Boston: Shambhala Publications: 1971.
Gyaltsen, Khenpo Konchog. *The Jewel Ornament of Liberation*. Ithaca: Snow Lion Publications, 1998.
Holmes, Ken and Katia Holmes. *Gems of Dharma, Jewels of Freedom*. Forres, Scotland: Altea Publishing: 1995.

King of Samadhi Sutra (Samadhirajasutra)

A discourse between the bodhisattva Dawo Shonnu, who was an earlier incarnation of Dharma Lord Gampopa, and Buddha Shakyamuni, in 41 or 42 chapters. It deals with the practice of various states of meditative concentration (*samadhi*) based on patience, discipline, renunciation and yearning for realization.

Cuppers, Christoph. *The IXth Chapter of the Samadhirajasutra.* Alt- und Neu-Indische Studien 41. Stuttgart: Franz Steiner Verlag, 1990. Partial translation: chapter 9.

Gómez, Luis O. and Jonathan A. Silk, eds. *Studies in the Literature of the Great Vehicle.* Ann Arbor: University of Michigan, 1989. Partial translation: chapters 1–4.

Régamey, Konstanty. *Philosophy in the Samadhirajasutra.* Warsaw: The Warsaw Society of Sciences and Letters, 1938. Reprint Delhi: Motilal Banarsidass, 1990; Talent, OR: Canon Publications, 1984. Partial translation: chapters 8, 19 and 22.

Rockwell, John, Jr. *Samadhi and Patient Acceptance: Four Chapters of the Samadhiraja-sutra.* M.A. thesis, The Naropa Institute, Boulder, Colorado, 1980. Partial translation: chapters 1–4.

Tatz, Mark. *Revelation in Madhyamika Buddhism.* M.A.thesis, University of Washington, 1972. Partial translation: Chapter 11.

Thrangu Rinpoche. *King of Samadhi.* Trans. Erik Pema Kunsang. Hong Kong, Boudhanath and Arhus: Rangjung Yeshe Publications, 1994. Partial translation: fragments.

Lankavatara Sutra

A text dealing with the elimination of dualistic conceptuality, largely associated with the Cittamatra school.

Suzuki, D.T. *The Lankavatara Sutra, a Mahayana Text.* London: Routledge and Kegan Paul, 1932. Reprint Taipei: SMC Publishing, 1991, 1994.

Letter to a Friend (*Suhrllekha*)

Instructions written by Nagarjuna and addressed to his friend, a king, on how to practice Dharma while engaged in worldly life.

Dharmamitra, Bhikshu. *Letter from a Friend.* Seattle: Kalavinka Press, 2009.

Jamspal, Lozang, Ngawang Samten Chophel, and Peter Della Santina. *Nagarjuna's Letter to King Gautamaiputra.* Delhi: Motilal Banarsidass, 1978.

Kawamura, Leslie. *Golden Zephyr.* Emeryville: Dharma Publishing, 1975.

Karma Thinley Rinpoche. *The Telescope of Wisdom: A Condensed Interlinear Commentary on the Great Master Nagarjuna's The Letter to a Friend*. Trans. Adrian O'Sullivan. London: Ganesha Press, 2009.
Padmakara Translation Group. *Nagarjuna's Letter to a Friend*. Ithaca: Snow Lion Publications, 2005.
Tharchin, Geshe Lobsang and Artemus B. Engle. *Nagarjuna's Letter*. Howell, NJ: Rashi Gempil Ling, First Kalmuk Buddhist Temple, 1977.

Madhyamakavatara
A commentary on Nagarjuna's teachings on wisdom (i.e., emptiness) by Chandrakirti.
Hopkins, Jeffrey. *Compassion in Tibetan Buddhism*. Ithaca: Snow Lion Publications, 1980. Partial translation.
Fenner, Peter. *The Ontology of the Middle Way*. Dordrecht, Boston: Khewar Academic Publishers, 1990.
Padmakara Translation Group. *Introduction to the Middle Way: Chandrakirti's Madhyamakavatara with Commentary by Jamgön Mipham*. Boston: Shambhala Publications, 2005.

Magic Staircase
An unidentified work quoted in the *Wish-granting Jewel*. No known English translation.

Manifesting the Mystic Body
A song in praise of Jigten Sumgön that describes the manner of qualities arising from dharmakaya written by Che-nga Sherab Jungne, one of his principal disciples. Published in *Calling to the Lama from Afar*.

Meaningful to Behold
A poetic account of Jigten Sumgön's life and liberation during countless eons of enlightenment written by Che-nga Sherab Jungne, one of his principal disciples. Published in *Calling to the Lama from Afar*.

Nectar of Heart Advice
An unidentified work quoted in the *Wish-granting Jewel*. No known English translation.

One Thought
A concise presentation of the oral instructions of the Drigung Kagyu lineage that explains the unified, enlightened intention that is a common thread in all the teachings of the Buddha. Usually divided into seven chapters, it consists of vajra statements that were spoken by Jigten Sumgön and recorded by his disciple Che-nga Sherab Jungne.
Viehbeck, Markus. *Gongchig, The Single Intent, the Sacred Dharma*. Munich: Otter Verlag, 2009.

Ornament of the Mahayana Sutra (Mahayanasutralamkara)
One of the five treatises by Maitreya that were transmitted through Asanga. It covers a broad range of topics within the Mahayana teachings.
Limaye, Surekha Vijay. *Mahayanasutralamkara*. Delhi: Indian Books Centre, 1992.
Thurman, Robert. *The Universal Vehicle Discourse Literature*. New York: American Institute of Buddhist Studies, 2004.

Prajñaparamita
This term can refer to a class of literature dealing with the perfection of wisdom or to particular works within that category. There are many works ranging from the very concise to very extensive. In this book, the reference is to the most extensive one, containing 100,000 verses.
Conze, Edward. *The Large Sutra on Perfect Wisdom*. Berkeley: University of California Press, 1975.

Prayer Flags
A small book that contains brief life stories of Gampopa, Phagmo Drupa, and Lord Jigten Sumgön, as well as some songs of realization by lineage masters. There are some short teachings on the stages of Mahamudra practice, and condensed instructions on how to carry the experiences of sickness and death into one's practice.

Gyaltsen, Khenpo Konchog. *Prayer Flags: The Life and Spiritual Teachings of Jigten Sumgön.* Ithaca: Snow Lion Publications, 1984, 1986.

Samaya, Clear and Beautiful
An unidentified work quoted in the *Wish-granting Jewel.* No known English translation.

The Song That Clarifies Recollection
A song of instruction by Jigten Sumgön to his disciple Rinchen Drak. Published in *Prayer Flags.*

Sutra Requested by Householder Drakshulchen
An unidentified work quoted in *The Jewel Ornament of Liberation.* No known English translation.

Tantra of the Completely Victorious, Nondual Secret Essence
An unidentified work quoted in the *Wish-granting Jewel.* No known English translation.

Tibetan Book of the Dead
Translation of Padmasambhava's important description of the period between dead and rebirth.
Coleman, Graham, Thupten Jinpa, and Gyurme Dorje. *The Tibetan Book of the Dead: First Complete Translation.* New York: Penguin Classics, 2007.
Evans-Wentz, W.Y. *The Tibetan Book of the Dead.* 1927. Reprint London: Arcturus Publishing, 2009.
Fremantle, Franscesca and Chogyam Trungpa. *The Tibetan Book of the Dead: The Great Liberation through Hearing in the Bardo.* Boston: Shambhala Publications, 2003.
Thurman, Robert. *The Tibetan Book of the Dead (The Great Book of Natural Liberation Through Understanding in the Between).* New York: Bantam Books, 1993.

Transformation of Suffering
Containing all the foundational teachings of Buddhism, this book was designed for study by individuals or groups without ready

access to a lama.

Gyaltshen, Khenchen Konchog. *Transformation of Suffering.* Gainesville, FL: Vajra Publications, 1997, 2006.

Twenty Verses of Praise

A devotional poem in praise of Jigten Sumgön written by Lingje Repa. The poem, as well as an account of the circumstances of its composition, are published in *Calling to the Lama from Afar.*

Vast as the Heavens, Deep as the Sea

Translation of a set of 365 verses, revered for their inspirational treatment of bodhicitta, written by Khunu Rinpoche in the twentieth century.

Khunu Rinpoche. *Vast as the Heavens, Deep as the Sea: Verses in Praise of Bodhicitta.* Gareth Sparham, trans. Somerville, MA: Wisdom Publications, 1999.

Wish-granting Jewel (Tsin-dha Mani)

The title of both a root text written by Jigten Sumgön and a commentary on the text by his disciple Drakpa Rinchen. The subject is the Fivefold path of Mahamudra. No known English translation.

Index of First Lines of the *Hundred Verses of Advice*

ADVICE FOR MAHAYANA PRACTITIONERS

ADVICE ABOUT THE SIX PERFECTIONS

ADVICE FOR VAJRAYANA PRACTITIONERS

Advice on Preparing for Mahamudra Practice

Advice for Mahamudra Practitioners

ADVICE ON HOW TO DISPEL OBSTACLES WHEN THEY ARE ENCOUNTERED

ADVICE ON THE SIX YOGAS OF NAROPA

Advice about the Final Result of Dharma Practice

: Index

Hinayana 128, 186, 190, 212, 451,
454, 459
hungry ghost realm 84, 125–127,
142, 177, 198, 428, 438, 440
idle talk 22, 36, 37, 100, 196, 198,
292, 434, 447
ignorance 13, 24, 42, 73, 89, 93,
101, 102, 106, 110, 131, 141,
145, 149, 156, 175, 190, 200,
202, 205, 214, 215, 218, 228,
232, 253, 255, 268, 282, 285,
287, 293, 319, 336, 364, 369,
371, 404, 407, 429, 435, 451
illusory body 288, 368, 374, 375,
438
impermanence 49, 58, 74, 81,
85–87, 112, 121, 124,138, 140,
155–158, 237, 251, 357, 400,
423, 433, 486
impure vision 278, 281, 289, 297
In Search of the Stainless Ambrosia
54, 462, 486
incisive insight 163, 167, 168, 190,
244, 254. *See also* critical insight
Indra 171, 283
Inner Teachings 13, 463
jealousy 52, 58, 101, 139, 141, 153,
177, 222, 232, 250–252, 269,
286, 293, 320, 359, 369, 407,
435
Jewel Ornament of Liberation 11,
21, 70, 86, 108, 124, 127, 216,
222, 251, 258, 354, 384, 395,
454, 466, 467, 483, 486
Jigten Sumgon 3, 11, 13, 14, 17, 29,
71, 106, 113, 119, 134, 138, 161,
162, 164, 189, 255, 266, 269,
270, 288, 291, 299, 304, 308,
329, 332, 337, 341, 360, 379,
380, 385, 386, 404, 406, 411,
413–417, 421, 453, 454, 462,
463, 465, 466, 467, 468, 484
joy 19, 27, 29, 32, 39, 41, 42, 49,
69, 80, 86, 90, 110, 113, 124,
129, 131, 132, 134, 138, 145,
163, 165, 181, 202, 204, 207,
209, 210, 215, 223, 224, 228,
231, 232, 235, 236, 238, 245–

248, 250, 251, 253, 266, 275,
304, 306, 307, 312, 313, 315,
318, 321, 368, 379, 381, 383,
416, 423, 429, 433, 439, 441
Kagyu 2, 3, 378, 379, 405, 454,
456, 457, 466. *See also* Drigung
Kagyu
karma 39, 54–56, 100, 103, 105,
113, 122–126, 135, 137, 148,
158, 171, 173–175, 177, 194,
195, 200, 241, 245, 254, 268,
297, 298, 306, 351, 362, 374,
387, 455, 484, 486. *See also*
negative karma; positive karma
King of Samadhi Sutra 330, 463
Konchog Drakden 18, 404
kriya 162, 261, 375, 431
lama 13–15, 70, 71, 117, 162, 164,
169, 261, 263, 264, 266, 268,
269, 271–275, 281, 309, 322,
327, 333, 337, 341, 348, 378,
379, 382, 386, 399, 402, 403,
406, 419, 455, 462, 465, 467,
468, 485, 486
Lankavatara Sutra 14, 464
laziness 85, 139, 140, 150, 247, 430,
446, 447, 448
leisure 19, 21, 142
Letter to a Friend 138, 187, 464
liberation 101, 125, 127, 128, 131,
142, 147, 162, 170, 182, 183,
186, 203, 212, 223, 233, 238,
247, 254, 280, 291, 347, 353,
386, 427, 454, 457, 458, 465
lineage 2, 3, 8, 13, 23, 161, 162,
164, 261, 263, 269, 274, 275,
322, 379, 402, 405, 406, 419,
422, 452, 454, 456, 462, 465,
466, 484
liquor 31, 417
listlessness 139, 430
Lord of Death 82, 83, 118, 122
loving-kindness 32, 50, 52, 75, 77,
93, 100, 124, 138, 152, 162, 169,
174, 176, 181, 204, 205–208,
212, 213, 250, 251, 282, 297,
298, 312, 324, 344, 359, 380,
403, 407, 423, 433, 443

: About the Author

THE VILLAGE of Tsari and the surrounding areas are among the most sacred places in Tibet. It was there that Khenchen Rinpoche, Konchog Gyaltshen was born in the spring of 1946, and it was there that he spent his early years. In 1960, because of the political situation in Tibet, Khenchen Rinpoche fled to India with his family. The family then settled in Darjeeling, where he began his education. Even at a young age, he was an excellent and dedicated student, and he was able to complete his middle school studies in less than the average time.

At about the time that he completed middle school, a new university, the Central Institute of Higher Tibetan Studies, opened in Varanasi, India. Determined to be among its first students, Khenchen Rinpoche traveled to Varanasi in October 1967 to seek admission. He then began a nine-year course of study that included Madhyamaka, Abhidharma, Vinaya, the *Abhisamayalankara*, and the *Uttaratantra*, as well as history, logic, and Tibetan grammar. In early 1968, he had the good fortune to take full monastic ordination from the great Kalu Rinpoche and, shortly after graduating from the Institute, he received teachings from the sixteenth Gyalwa Karmapa on *The Eight Treasures of Mahamudra Songs* by the Indian mahasiddhas.

Even after completing this long and arduous course of study, Khenchen Rinpoche wanted only to deepen his knowledge and practice of the Dharma. With the same intensity that he brought to his earlier studies, Rinpoche sought out and received teachings and instructions from great Buddhist masters. One was the Venerable Khunu Lama Rinpoche, with whom Khenchen Rinpoche studied two works of Gampopa—*The Jewel Ornament of Liberation* and *The Precious Garland of the Excellent Path*. His studies with the

Venerable Khunu Lama also included Mahamudra and many of the songs of Milarepa.

Maintaining a balance between theoretical understanding and the practice of meditation, Khenchen Rinpoche began a three-year retreat in 1978 under the guidance of the enlightened master Khyunga Rinpoche. During this time, he was able to deepen and enhance his understanding of *The Fivefold Path of Mahamudra* and the profound *One Thought* of Lord Jigten Sumgön. He also received many other transmissions.

In 1985, Khenchen Rinpoche traveled to the main seat of the Drigung Kagyu lineage, Drigung Thil, in Tibet. There, he was able to receive personal blessings, as well as instructions and transmissions of Mahamudra and the Six Yogas of Naropa, from the enlightened master Venerable Pachung Rinpoche.

In 1982, the force of karma and the requests of many practitioners combined to bring Khenchen Rinpoche to the United States. By late 1983, the Tibetan Meditation Center was well established in Washington, D.C. Their original location was the site of innumerable teachings, practices, retreats, and ceremonies. In September 1984, and again in 1987, the young center was blessed with personal visits and teachings by His Holiness the Dalai Lama. Through Khenchen Rinpoche's and the center's efforts, Drigung Kyabgon Chetsang Rinpoche visited in 1987, 1994, and 1999, and people in several states were able to receive benefit from his teachings and presence.

With the Tibetan Meditation Center as his base, Khenchen Rinpoche went on to establish practice centers in Big Sur, CA; Boston, MA; Boulder, CO; Chicago, IL (currently under the direction of Drupon Rinchen Dorjee); Gainesville, FL; Los Angeles, CA; Madison, WI; Pittsburgh, PA; San Francisco, CA; Tampa Bay, FL (currently under the direction of Drupon Thinley Nyingpo); Virginia Beach, VA; as well as Dharmakirti College in Tucson, AZ and Vajra Publications. He also established centers in Lidingö, Sweden and Santiago, Chile (currently under the direction of Khenpo Phuntzok Tenzin).

Wanting the teachings of Dharma to reach as many people as possible, Khenchen Rinpoche has quickly adapted himself to Western forms of communication. He has made appearances on television, been a guest on many radio programs, lectured extensively at colleges and universities, and spoken to the public through countless newspaper articles. Between 1983 and 1990, Khenchen Rinpoche single-handedly translated critical Drigung Kagyu practices, prayers, and histories into English. Among the practice texts he translated were Achi Chökyi Drolma, Amitabha, Amitayus, Bodhicitta, Long Chakrasamvara, Shorter Chakrasamvara, Chenrezig, Chöd, Dharma Protectors, Four-session Guru Yoga, Green Tara, Guru Yoga, Lama Chöpa, Mandala Offering, Manjushri, Medicine Buddha, Ngondro practices, Nyung Ne, Peaceful Guru Rinpoche, Phowa, Refuge, Torma Offering, Tsog, Vajrapani, Vajrasattva, Vajrayogini, and White Tara. Before Tibetan fonts were available for computers, he wrote all these texts out by hand. Later, when automation became available, the translations were polished and republished. This priceless work formed the essential base from which the holy Dharma could be taught and practiced.

Khenchen Rinpoche and the Tibetan Meditation Center moved to Frederick, Maryland in November 1991. Nestled inside a state park, the Center is now situated on four wooded acres. A small temple was built there and was consecrated by Drigung Kyabgon Chetsang Rinpoche in 1994. With this larger facility and in surroundings more conducive to contemplation, Khenchen Rinpoche has been able to benefit even more people with his teachings. Now that Western students are becoming interested in long-term retreat practice, plans are being made to establish a residential retreat center nearby.

Recently, Khenchen Rinpoche has been spending more of this time teaching in India and Tibet. He often teaches *One Thought* to the monks and nuns at the Drigung Kagyu Institute in Dehra Dun, India as well as monasteries in Tibet as conditions allow. With the financial assistance of the Tibetan Meditation Center's Text Project, he arranged for 1,200 copies of the text to be printed, and then distributed them to monks, nuns, and monasteries in India, Nepal, and Tibet.

Khenchen Rinpoche consistently strives to make important texts available to the public and to provide his students with thorough and systematic training in the Dharma. A skilled and dedicated author, he has published nine books prior to this one:

Prayer Flags, which is described in the Annotated Bibliography (see page 466).

The Garland of Mahamudra Practices is very helpful for those who already have a little understanding of the Dharma. It contains a description of all the Ngondro practices: the four foundation thoughts (precious human life, awareness of impermanence, karma, and the suffering of samsara), the four extraordinary preliminary practices (refuge, Vajrasattva, mandala offering, and Guru Yoga), Yidam practice, special guru yoga, and a Mahamudra session.

In Search of the Stainless Ambrosia (see the Annotated Bibliography, page 463).

The Great Kagyu Masters (see the Annotated Bibliography, page 462).

The Jewel Treasury of Advice is a translation of a profound teaching in verse, written by Drigung Dharmaradza.

The Jewel Ornament of Liberation (see the Annotated Bibliography, page 463).

Calling to the Lama from Afar (see the Annotated Bibliography, page 462).

Transformation of Suffering: A Handbook for Practitioners (see the Annotated Bibliography, page 467).

Pearl Rosary is another work that Khenchen Rinpoche himself wrote. It contains detailed instructions on twelve common deity yoga practices, such as Chenrezig, Tara, and Manjushri, as well as the translated sadhanas or practice texts. This book is also especially valuable for those who do not have the good fortune to see a qualified lama often, and for serious practitioners to use as a reminder.

Remembering the struggles of his early years, Khenchen Rinpoche inspires and supports monks, nuns and lay people in their practice of the Dharma and is always ready to assist them in whatever way he can. To all, he gives of himself freely. With his heart and mind turned firmly toward the Dharma, he compassionately and patiently shows the way.